MEMOIRS
OF A
VICTORIAN
GENTLEMAN

WILLIAM MAKEPEACE
THACKERAY

MEMOIRS OF A VICTORIAN GENTLEMAN

WILLIAM MAKEPEACE
THACKERAY

by
MARGARET FORSTER

ILLUSTRATIONS BY
WILLIAM MAKEPEACE THACKERAY

WILLIAM MORROW AND COMPANY, INC.
NEW YORK   1979

THIS BOOK IS
AFFECTIONATELY DEDICATED TO
GORDON FORSTER Esq.

NOTES ON THE ILLUSTRATIONS

All the drawings in this book are by Thackeray himself collected from many published sources by Margaret Forster, and arranged to illustrate this text as aptly as possible.

The endpaper illustrations are reproduced by kind permission of the Master and Fellows of Trinity College, Cambridge. The left-hand illustration shows page 1 of the original manuscript of Esmond *(published in 1852) and headed* The History of Henry Esmond. *Page 73a of the same manuscript appears on the right, being a sample of Thackeray's upright and his italic scripts together.*

The illustration of the front cover of the first issue of the Cornhill Magazine *which appears on page 345 is reproduced by kind permission of the Bodleian Library.*

CONTENTS

Chapter I

AN ACCOUNT OF THE BIRTH AND
UPBRINGING OF YOUR HERO

NCE upon a time in the city of London there lived a very tall man who had written a good many books. Some people thought well of these volumes but the man himself remained dissatisfied with them though they had made him a great deal of money. One day he was sitting in the study of his fine house in Palace Green, Kensington, feeling tired and ill and dispirited and not at all inclined to work when he suddenly thought how much he would like those who came after him, and perhaps read his books, to know what kind of fellow he was and what he had been trying to do when he wrote them. He sat and stared out at the great elm trees in front of him and wondered what he could do about this feeling. He could, he supposed, ask someone to write his life – after all, he was quite a literary lion and there would be many pleased to try – but that was not at all the kind of thing he had in mind. He fidgeted in his chair and frowned at the sunshine outside which mocked the gloom inside himself, and took a turn or two round the room and rapped on his desk with a pencil and said " No " out loud, and then " Yes " even more fiercely, and all this ended in him dipping his pen in ink and writing something on a piece of paper in front of him. I am not going to tell you what that something was for no sooner had the man written it in his slanting hand than he crumpled it up and threw it into a bin, only it missed the bin and lay looking untidy on the beautiful carpet. (I may add everything in the room was beautiful – it was the most beautiful room you ever saw.)

There followed many more sighs and exclamations – even, I am afraid, a d. .n or two – before the man folded his arms and sat still, thinking. He was troubled about something – that much you will have gathered – and seemed unable to come to a decision. On the one hand he had an urge to address himself to posterity that I have told you about – only don't shout it to everyone for he was shy about putting this into vulgar words – but on the other hand such an idea seemed a little too much, if you know what I mean. After all, who was he ? Not a king or a great statesman or a famous explorer or a brilliant doctor or a worthy divine but simply a writer, and a writer mostly of fiction furthermore, and why the devil should such a low sort of chap think about writing his memoirs ? He could hear people sneering before he began and asking what the world was coming to if every Tompkins started writing about his life – it would be dustmen next boring us with accounts of good dust heaps they have known, not to mention kitchen maids droning on about potatoes they have peeled and footmen – well, we have had a line or two recently from footmen so I had better say no more. There was, then, a problem which divided neatly into one, two and three.

Number one may surprise you, for number one in the man's opinion was would anyone want to read what he had to say about his own life ? Do you despise him straight away for caring about this ? Well, he was an honest man and he knew that if he was to write for himself, so to speak, there was very little point for he already knew it all, therefore he preferred not to labour at something if he thought nobody would read it. He asked himself would I like to read Fielding's life written by himself, and you can be sure he almost jumped out of his chair with joy at the thought. But then he asked himself would he like to read Bloggs' account of his dreary life, and he knew he would not. Now, as he had no means of knowing whether those who came after him would regard him as a Fielding or a Bloggs what was he to do ? The most sensible way was to regard himself as halfway between Fielding and Bloggs and ask the same question again, which he did, and back came the answer that were there only a little of the Fielding in him posterity would be interested and would read his own account. The man was relieved and pleased at his own answer and proceeded at once to Number two, which was whether he was a fit person to deal with his own life ? There is a degree of presumption in autobiography that worried him, especially since he knew well enough there were no great events of historic interest to describe. For a while he was despondent at this truth, but then he thought of what he liked to read himself in men's memoirs and he knew it was not the detailed accounts of the last charge at Waterloo that engaged his interest so much as what each soldier was thinking and feeling and hoping as he ran with his bayonet fixed. He told himself that men are fascinated by the detail of other men's lives, not by the grand designs. History is not happenings but those to whom things happened – or something of the kind. We ought not to be ashamed of our curiosity about other people but rather see it as healthy and right and to be indulged. The man smiled when he reached this stage of reflection and nodded and looked rather pleased with himself, though there was nobody to see except you and I. He now had it clear in his mind on his own authority that he both had justification for attempting his memoirs and every right to do them himself since he alone knew how he had felt at any given time. But then immediately the thought of Number three wiped

the smile from his face, for Number three was an ogre, a monster, a hideous spectacle that he preferred not to look in the face – Number three, in short, was a matter of content. What, when all was said and done, did he want to write and how did he want to write it ?

There were in this man's study – patience, I shall soon reveal his illustrious name – several large volumes of memoirs that he now took down and began to leaf through. The man had read them all before, you may be sure, for he was a prodigious reader, but nevertheless he thought he ought to remind himself of what he had read so he turned the pages and said "Ah yes," and " I remember " to himself and went on flicking and dipping until he began to groan and slammed the books shut and put his head in his hands, and a very large shaggy grey head it was. A great depression overwhelmed him. He knew he did not want in the least to write one of those books of memoirs nor to have one written about him. What did he want ? What was all this fuss about ? A life is a life, is it not ? We begin with the birth and the schooldays and we work our way through to the wedding and the patter of tiny feet and the first wage and the successes and failures till we end up sitting white-haired by the fire moralising for all we are worth. It was all quite straightforward as laid out in those volumes, but the man did not like it – it was not at all what he had in mind. Just because a man has made a stir in some kind of way seemed to be an excuse to drag in all kinds of wearisome facts that held no attractions for him at all. He sat and pondered upon this problem for a long time, asking why anyone should want to know where and when his grandmother was vaccinated or what he said on his sixth birthday. Was it relevant to his life ? Was it amusing ? Was it edifying ? Was it necessary ? With remarkable ease he came to the conclusion that this kind of rubbish was none of those things and ought not to be set down and he should ignore the precedents. His idea was quite different. Suppose, he said to himself, a man was to address himself quietly and comfortably to the reader in a relaxed, genial sort of way, as he might in a letter to an old friend – suppose he was to take the reader into his confidence and confess his joys and hates, but not too much of the latter for no one ought to fill a book with hatred, and in truth the man had rarely felt that horrid emotion – suppose he were to write a nightcap sort of book which the reader could dip into at his leisure and smile and sleep for a little while then wake up and read a little more and so on, suiting himself as he went – suppose he did that, would it do ? People might sneer and say such a book was a poor little scrap of a thing with no weight about it at all, but then did he care ? Wasn't that what he wanted ? He thought it was, he thought he would be quite happy to leave behind such a visiting card when he packed his bags and left, as he knew he must shortly do. He would prefer such a light-hearted record to the solemn tomes written about other writers with all their dull delving into unimportant details of their lives and their ridiculous panegyrics about their work. There would be something brave about the attempt that appealed to him.

The man was now clearly pleased. A smile lit up his sad face and he squared his shoulders and sat up very straight at his desk. It would be a strange experience reviewing his own life, but a salutary one. He was determined not to spare himself but to face up to his own mistakes squarely and not duck the consequences. He knew there were going to be some sticky passages where he had not always acted as he ought to have done, but what he hoped to achieve was a perspective he had of necessity lacked while he was engaged in life's battle. He was pretty certain that the rough and tumble was for the most part over, that he was now on a plateau until the end of the ride, and he thought he was in a good position to describe the journey he had made. All this decided, he proceeded in good spirits to consider how exactly he should write his account – should it be chronological, should it be written in the third or the first person, should he attempt to judge his own books ? Little by little he drew up a list of rules he would adhere to, a list of things he would need to know, a list of letters he must keep back from other people, a list of this and a list of that until his desk was littered with papers and he had to sit back and mop his brow with a white handkerchief embroidered in the corner with the initials W.M.T. . . .

There! I have given the game away. But then, dear reader, I expect you guessed at the beginning. At any rate, it doesn't matter, for the first thing our man learned was that subterfuge is out of the question. If a man is going to write his own life then he must say who he is and what he is about and not skulk behind pretty literary devices. Why be afraid of that " I " ? Is there anything disgraceful in it ? Those who address us as " one " immediately become two in my opinion — the person they are and the person they are pretending not to be. I will have none of that. If my letter to you young 'uns is to be of any value, honesty is the best policy. I shall be dead when you read this — perhaps for a very long time — so why should I care about preserving any illusions ? You must take me as you find me, as those of us who are sure of their own worth are always saying at the tops of their voices. Well, I am not at all sure of mine but I know there is no other way. I daresay I shall digress — I daresay I shall get on hobby-horses and gallop away furiously — I daresay I will get hopelessly involved in

matters that have nothing whatsoever to do with my life, but you may be sure of one thing and that is – nothing shall be contrived. I shan't reject episodes because they ain't suitable for your mama to read, though I may omit details nobody has any right to know. I heard a few sniffs then – I can hear somebody saying the fellow is at it already, a-covering up before he has even begun, telling us in his roundabout way that he isn't going to mention the six bodies in the cellar, or his wooden leg, or the disappearance of his son in mysterious circumstances. You are wrong, sir, for I shall enthrall you with blow-by-blow accounts of every single murder I have committed, you can be sure of that, and as for the wooden leg how can I help boasting of how I led the cavalry charge at Waterloo ? No, what I meant was of a different order of things – private, intimate things that ought never to be bandied about and, please God, will never be written about. But I shall play fair – when anything comes under that heading I shall run a red flag up and then you will know it is decency and modesty that brings me to a halt and not cowardice. I can't embarrass other people in the writing of my own life, you know, and you ought to remember that, nor do I believe such proper scruples get in the way of truth. Stuff and nonsense.

Where shall I begin ? Immediately, there is a difficulty for I can't remember being born no more than you can. This is where we ought properly to have my mother's testimony, but I think I have heard it enough times for you to trust me and not bother that lady, who is at this moment in the next room giving her maid the most famous telling-off about how her clothes – my mother's I mean – have not been packed for travelling in an adequate fashion. Since my mother is forever travelling the maid has all my sympathy – those clothes live in a frightful state of readiness all the time and are a fearful responsibility.

But to return to my birth: I was born in Calcutta on July 18th, 1811. You are entitled to know that much but I refuse to go into how I was premature and the dreadful worry I caused during the first months and all that sort of sentimental twaddle that my mother would pour over you were I to tear her away from the maid and the clothes. Let us say where and when I was born and that is enough. You will get to know my mother very well indeed in these pages, unless I am mistaken, so I need not in any case trouble you with too close a sketch of her at my birth, and as for my father all I know of him is second hand so I cannot enlighten you there. His name was Richmond Thackeray and he died when I was four years old. His family came from Yorkshire and he had followed in an established tradition of service in India. From what I have been told he was a tall, kindly man with artistic leanings – dear me, he sounds like a tree – who would, I believe, have been a good father if he had lived. I was an only child, though I was entranced to learn later in life that I also had a black half-sister, my father following local custom and having a native wife. Only think of it – a little black Thackeray! Perhaps, if I had stayed in India, we would have become good friends and my childhood would not have been such a desperately lonely business.

There are going to be such long pauses in this narrative, that I already know. I have sat here fully half an hour wondering at the truth of that statement regarding my childhood for I don't want to overdo it and I don't want to blame anyone or hurt my mother. When I say I was lonely, from which you may rightly infer that I was unhappy, I don't mean to suggest I suffered any real hardship or that I was regularly starved and whipped and turned out on cold nights clad only in a few rags. Nothing of the kind, but there are more ways than one of being miserable if you are a child. The facts perhaps speak for themselves and support my claim: picture a little boy of five years old taken from his mother and sent thousands of miles from her to relatives he had never seen. Picture that same little boy as a loving, soft, gentle kind of creature used to his mother's tender embraces and to the warmth and ease of a life in India – picture him suddenly in England where it was cold and grey and nobody knew him however good their intentions. You don't need much imagination, I think, to weep for him. Though I remember very little of the voyage in the *Prince Regent* beyond putting in at St. Helena and having Napoleon pointed out to me by my black servant who

told me he ate all the little children he could lay his hands on, I do remember the awful bleakness of life without my mother, and the dreadful suppression of the grief I felt at the parting. I don't think I cried much, except at night

under the blankets.   My Aunt Ritchie was able to write with conviction
that I had settled down well and seemed quite happy.   How easily we adults
judge a child " quite happy "!   He only has to prattle a little and smile when
you pat him on the head and sit quietly at mealtimes and say his prayers
sweetly and we know he is " quite happy ".   Nobody tries to divine the
desperate anxiety to please that lies behind the prattle, the search for approval
that lurks behind the smile, the fear in the silence, the deception in the
prayers.   We are determined children are quite happy if we know they are
well fed and sleep in clean beds and that is that.

My mother says she is sure she wept much more than I did and swears I
could not wait to be off on my exciting adventure in the big ship.   Perhaps
she had to think like that because the truth was unbearable, or perhaps the
sending away of small children from India to England was so commonplace
she really thought I did not mind.   All I know is that even thinking about
parents parting from children can set me off blubbering to this day.   The
abstract pathos of such partings attacks me where I am weakest and I can't
compose myself. When I am a party to such a farewell, oh how the eyes do
stream!   Leaving my children to go to America was one of the most frightful
experiences of my life – that ocean, those thousands of miles, the uncertainty
of it all, the not knowing if I should ever see those dear trusting faces again.
There you are you see – out with the handkerchief and I shan't get anything
done if I carry on like this.   At any rate, part from my mother I did and
survived but I don't want to hear anyone saying it made a man of me and
that all children ought to be made to stand on their own feet for I don't
believe real independence comes that way.   Staying in a loving home with
loving parents makes for strength, not weakness.   I'm sure I could have
stayed with benefit another few years with my mother and her new husband

and travelled home later with them, but what is the point in dwelling on it ? Let me tell you instead the romantic story of my stepfather, Henry Carmichael-Smyth, whom my mother married in November 1817. She had met and fallen in love with him when she was seventeen, long before she saw either India or my father. He was an ensign in the Bengal Engineers and as such deemed unworthy of her daughter's hand by my mother's mother. She was told he was dead, he was told she had married someone else. Broken-hearted, she was sent to India and there married my father. One day, he announced a charming fellow was coming to dinner – and in walked my mother's long-lost love! Who says fiction is more fanciful than fact ? Every day amazing coincidences like that go unremarked, yet were they written down they would be condemned as absurd.

So there we were – my mother blissfully happy in India with her darling Henry and I lost and sad in England. Of course, I wasn't sad all the time, no child is. My grandmother Becher and my great-aunt Becher, at whose house in Fareham, Hampshire, I was received on arrival in England, were kind to me and I might never have suffered any agonies at all if they had not chosen to send me to a frightful school in Southampton run by a Mr. and Mrs. Arthur. I think they are dead now but I don't care if they are not – they deserve to be named for allowing such brutality to exist in the name of education. What a time we Indian children had of it, pitched into a regime of bad dinners, terrible cold, caning, chilblains and nobody to turn to except newly acquired relatives who for all we knew had sent us there knowing what it meant. I have never sent my children to school but if I had you can be sure I would have examined the establishment very closely indeed before consigning their tender souls to it. But people don't, not even good people – they take other people's word for it that Mr. Arthur runs a good place and the price is reasonable, and that is how Miss Brontë's Lowood and Mr. Dickens' Dotheboys Hall flourish. Nor am I sure that famous establishments are necessarily any better than the hundreds of small unknown places – look at Charterhouse. Hasn't the Duke of Wellington called it " the best school of them all " and yet didn't I find when I got there that it was hardly better than Mr. Arthur's purgatory ? I tell you I cannot bear to think how easily parents are duped, nor to find how they grow to believe that punishments they themselves have experienced and wept over are somehow right and necessary for their children. How can it be that generations of parents forget their past misery and condone the continuation of it ? A mystery if ever there was one. I say for my part loudly and clearly that it can never do children any good to subject them to cruelty and that it ought to stop and that I won't have it and that really I had better return to the point at once.

The point was, even in the first bad times at Mr. Arthur's it wasn't all misery. Quite often I was tolerably happy and certainly extremely contented for all the non-school days. My aunt Becher bought me many presents and took me on delightful outings into the countryside and I took great pleasure in finding birds' nests and other boyish pursuits, and I know that from the earliest age the beauties of a landscape or the splendours of a fine building were never lost on me.   I was very fond of the house where we lived in Fareham High Street – it had a high sloping roof and a narrow porch with low front windows opening onto a pleasant fruit garden sloping to the river, and I know it made me very happy to be there.   Fareham was a Miss Austen-like village peopled by retired naval officers and spirited old ladies who played whist, and it suited me perfectly then.   Where there was love and affection I flourished and forgot to cry for my mother – it was only at school I despaired and wanted her arms round me.   Though I was glad to leave Arthur's – how did it come about ?   Did we tell and were believed ?   Did something finally strike our relatives as not quite right ?   I don't remember – though I say I was glad, I was sorry to leave Hampshire and the Bechers for the Ritchies and London.   Children don't like change – they like to know where they are and who they are with and any disturbance of the *status quo* makes them anxious.

As it turned out, it was a move for the better.   Dr. Turner's School at Chiswick, though leaving much to be desired, was a considerable improvement on Mr. Arthur's, but better still I was now near cousins and in touch with a family life I greatly admired and envied and was eager to share.   John Ritchie had married my father's sister and at that time lived with his wife and children in Southampton Row.   They made me very welcome and I delighted in their company, and though all the children were younger than I they were better than adults and good fun and took the place of the brothers and sisters I did not have.   I wonder, looking back, if the Ritchies ever thought me a nuisance ?   We never see ourselves as being any trouble at all – what, where is the trouble in feeding a huge boy (I was 3 feet 11 inches at the age of six, don't ye know, and heavy in proportion) at least three times a day ?   Where is the self-sacrifice in squeezing another in on a visit to the play ?   Please God I returned these unrecognised kindnesses with my enthusiasm and gratitude.

I have no doubt that those two years, from 1817 to 1819, from the age of six to eight, of which I have such scattered recollections, most of them dismal, in some way formed my character for the rest of my life.   You will think I am off my head but I am quite convinced I am right.   From when my mother returned to England in 1819 I saw things quite differently.   I had a home to which I went in the holidays and I was therefore secure and untroubled even when I was troubled, if you see what I mean.   My time of trial was over, never to return again in quite the same way, and I was glad of it.   I suppose during those two years my mother had become a myth, a fantasy, to which I clung but which eluded me.   When she was restored to me, when I saw her like a beautiful, smiling angel in front of me, it was the realisation of a dream. It was as though nothing bad could ever happen again. Oh mothers, what power you have! Who knows but that all the wickedness in the world comes from men not having good mothers. Mine protests she would have been quite happy to die after our re-union, such was the ecstasy of beholding me. If partings fill me with anguish, reunions with loved ones are a joy unparalleled.

I entered Charterhouse at the beginning of the long Quarter in January 1822. That establishment was, I believe, at the height of its reputation, which is doubtless what attracted my mother. Do you remember your own schooldays, friend, and do you still think I am making a fuss about nothing when I protest yet again that I hated 'em? I can hear to this day the rasping voice of Dr. Russell as he shouted, " Thackeray, Thackeray you are an idle profligate shuffling boy." Well, was I? I was frightened, I know that. The whole place was run on fear. Every blunder was punished twice over – once with the torture of Dr. Russell's ridicule, once by the lictors with their bunches of birch twigs, and I know which I preferred. That man seemed to single me out for the full weight of his sarcasm – perhaps because I was big for my age he could not resist it, and then again, because I was not small and snivelling, he may have felt it made no impression on me, he may have ignored my burning cheeks and the tearstains still visible upon them and looked only at my eyes, which he seems to have found permanently insolent. Do you smile and say again this harsh discipline was necessary and did me good ? Then there is no hope for you. It did me no good, and furthermore it hindered rather than helped the learning process. The teaching at that school was bad, I am sure of it. Consider the system that was used: instead of masters in the lower forms we had a praepositus, or monitor, that is to say a boy like ourselves who was deemed the cleverest and therefore capable of teaching us. Often he would be the weakest and therefore his task was quite impossible and chaos was the order of the day until Dr. Russell heard the din and came to bully us into obedience. In such an atmosphere it was difficult to inculcate any love of learning. We learned facts by rote, we copied things slavishly, we recited tables and verbs and poetry like parrots, and all the time our hearts beat wildly within us with terror that we should miss our turn and be found out and punished. I believe I would have been a good and industrious student if I had been treated as a human being capable of appreciation instead of as a helpless animal.

I was not altogether silent about my ordeals, writing home at frequent intervals that I really didn't think I could bear it much longer, and that I didn't see why I should. Nobody took any notice. Gradually, I became resigned to my ill-luck even if I never accepted it, and learned like everyone else to concentrate on those things that made my imprisonment bearable.

The first .was holidays. Oh the bliss of arriving at that day so heavily circled on the calendar! I would become feverish with anticipation as that happy day approached when I would take the coach to Ottery St. Mary in Devon where my parents had finally settled. I didn't care how long the journey was, nor how cold I became — sometimes they had to lift me down from that Exeter coach so benumbed was I with cold — but I was warmed through and through with enthusiasm. Coming back was dreadful of course, but there was another day of release to circle the minute I arrived in London. Then there were books, which provided another kind of escape, ever available.

I don't know that you will be impressed by my reading material but I can't help that — I relished those stories I read and if I could have the desire of my heart it would be to write a story which boys would turn to for the next thousand years. What were they? Why, *Manfroni: or the One-handed Monk* and *The Adventures of Corinthian Tom, Jeremy Hawthorne Esq. and their friend Bob Logic.* What titles! What tales of stirring adventure! If you sneer, you make a big mistake — you are looking at these boyish books with old eyes and you can't possibly see what I saw, you can't hope to be spirited into a land of blood and thunder where melodrama was the order of the day. I can't see that they do any harm either — they provided me with what I wanted at the time and led me by degrees to more wholesome fare. I have seen the same thing happen with my children — before they learned to cherish Mr. Dickens they devoured all kinds of worthless stories and I didn't object. If you would feed an infant you must first get him to open his mouth and he will only do that at first for the sweets and goodies and not the healthy, less enticing morsels.

Almost more than the stories, I loved the pictures. I would sit at my desk screened by great dictionaries and books of Latin and Greek turning the pages of one of my beloved stories, staring for hours at the illustrations. They were such odd pictures — I can't look at them now without wondering what on earth I admired, but I know I did admire them and that they excited me in some strange way. They were not Art, they were not Life, they were extremely lurid and even ridiculous but I loved every line. They took me to places I had never seen and tallied exactly with my imagination. I would sit transfixed looking at a picture of Jerry and Tom watching the irons being knocked off the malefactors' legs at Newgate previous to execution, and the horror of it would bring me out in a cold sweat — but how I cheered up when the next plate showed our heroes at Tattersalls and how the blood pounded through my veins at all I saw. I'm not going to claim that here we have the seeds sown for my own illustrious career — I don't think I wanted to imitate what I had read — but the love was there and the interest and the attention. I knew I could not live without stories and pictures and that realisation was the first rung on the ladder, even if I did nothing about going up it. I think I did write some stuff for the school magazine but what it was I can't remember and should be surprised if anyone else could. I didn't slave in secret over any manuscript at any rate, though I admit I tried my hand at drawing, now that is true. I always liked to doodle, right from when I could first hold a pencil properly, at the age of four or five. One of the first things I did when I came from India was try to show my aunt Becher what my home was like by drawing little pictures of our house in Calcutta and my monkey looking out of the window and Black Betty drying her towels – my pencil told it better than any words. I had, I think, a good eye for line from the beginning – my horses looked like horses and excited the admiration of adults.

An ability to draw a little looks like genius in a small child, it is so easily understood. I have noticed that if little Charles can draw or play a tune on the piano or sing with perfect pitch then he is sure of popularity for his talent is plain for all to see or hear and twice as impressive because he is small. I liked the praise and I liked the applause more. I quickly found at school that being able to draw earned me a reputation as a good fellow that was of inestimable value. Most of the time I was drawing lines that were not there

– caricatures of masters and suchlike – but equally in demand were spirited renderings of pictures I had seen in books like *The Mysteries of Udolpho* or those of Walter Scott. You have no idea how we improved the frowning plates at the beginning of our school books that announced " A Latin Grammar – for the use of schools " and so forth with our moustachioed heroes brandishing swords. Briggs Minor and I, the Michelangelos of the fourth, were greatly in demand for this enlivening work. Our talent put us cosily in the middle of a circle of friends that made school a less horrible place, and we exploited it for all we were worth.

I know I even made it work for me in the following fashion: suppose I wanted a something-or-other from my room and was much too lazy to go and get it then what did I do ? " Gardner, I say young Gardner," I'd shout, " if you'll go up to my room and fetch me down so-and-so I'll give you half a crown." Gardner jumped upstairs immediately and returned in a trice with the desired object. " Now you know young Gardner," I would say very solemnly, " you know that I can't give you half a crown because I haven't got one to give, but I'll make you a drawing of a horse which is just as good and worth more," and I did and the drawing was beautifully made and young Gardner never complained so why should you say I was unscrupulous and wicked ?

Friends have done more than make school bearable – they have throughout my life made the world a less grim place. I urge you, young Tompkins, to make friends wisely as I have done and not stalk a lonely path believing you are self-sufficient. There is no doubt I was a most gregarious fellow, enjoying company hugely and getting on easily with most people. I could always be depended upon to join in whatever was going on and to give as good as I got. Pleasure to my certain recollection always came first and was indeed necessary to my wellbeing every mortal day.

I think the greatest pleasure of my schooldays was the play – bless me, how I lived for the play! I remember even the loathsome Arthur took us out once to the play and the intense pleasure I derived from that visit made the two succeeding dreary days pass in a golden haze. What was it I so enjoyed ? I confess – the women. Long before those goddesses had any other meaning for me I admired them for their beauty. I went to gaze innocently and was spellbound long before I also ogled these ladies. You who live now cannot possibly imagine how beautiful the actresses were in the reign of my King, George IV. You young lads only think you have seen beautiful women but I know I did and won't be argued with. Where is a paragon to match Mrs. Yates at the Adelphi, or Mrs. Serle at Sadlers Wells ? The mere memory of their dazzling loveliness makes me swoon. When I look at what is set upon the stage today it makes me weep for the deterioration of women – the paint is so visible, the clothes so wrinkled, the voices shrill and cracked. Ugh! If only I could take you by the hand, young Walter, and show you just for a minute Duvernay as the Bayadère – oh there has never been anything like it. Even the theatres aren't the same – nasty smelly dim unhealthy places full of bored cackling old people not to be compared with the magical palaces of my youth so subtly scented, thronged with sophisticated audiences who knew what they were about and including the very sophisticated yours truly. Lord, I can experience now the excitement of going to the play from Charterhouse without the least trouble. Getting ready to go wasn't like getting ready to go anywhere else for who knew what might happen, who might look your way or throw a flower into

your lap. (Be quiet – I know nobody ever did but don't spoil a boy's romancing.) The curtain seemed an interminable time going up but who cared when there was so much to look at and all the time that feverish atmosphere of anticipation filled the lungs and heart to bursting. I swear I died every time the orchestra struck up with the overture and bit my nails and sat on the edge of the seat and drew my breath in sharply as the first glimpse of the stage was revealed. Instantly I was transported to another world and lost all sense of place or time so that at the end I had to be pulled down brutally from my cloud and beaten back to life and even then I would go home and to school the next day not quite sane.

I am aware that there is very little in this account of any work I did or of any noble influences. I don't mention praying much or reading my bible or worshipping good men or earning pats on the back, do I ? It is all stories and drawings and visits to the play and holidays, and I have not even mentioned eating for that is going to sound worst of all, what a glutton I was, I mean with my love of tarts from the school's pastrycooks. Do you know what I think ? I think I was a remarkably amazingly staggeringly normal ordinary schoolboy. There is no getting away from it – you won't find any significance in anything I drag up as far as my literary career goes, though I suppose if I had turned out a great soldier I would have been able to relate the story of how I got my nose broken in a fight, or if a politician there are a few examples of double-dealing that might have stood up well, or if an orator of tremendous power I might just have been able to recall an instance or two of speaking out. As it is, I was nothing and nobody and don't care who knows it. If anyone dares to dredge over the first sixteen years of my life and come up with startling revelations then take no notice of them, I have told all – unless you wish to hear about the brace I had fitted on my teeth in 1827 – and all is nothing and everything, and I don't know whether that is a good thing or a bad thing but it is the truth and all you are going to get.

Chapter II

RELATES HOW YOUR HERO ATTENDS THE
UNIVERSITY AND WHAT HAPPENS THEREAFTER

HAVE in my possession still two sketch-books – quite ordinary drawing-books with blue and white marbled paper covers, the kind they sell cheaply at any stationers – and sometimes I think they contain all that is to my credit before the age of one and twenty. One belongs to the Charterhouse period of my life and the other to the Trinity College, Cambridge, epoch. The school sketch-book is a jolly affair, flimsy, not much in it but what there is – pencil sketches of French officers trying to arrest ferocious brigands – makes me smile and that can be no bad thing. The Cambridge book is fatter and contains more elegant drawings of churches and villages around the town – Granchester and Coton and the like – but it gives me half the pleasure. I cannot look at these sketches without regret – not for what they are themselves but for the way of life they represent. If I learnt little at school I stoutly claim it was the school's fault, but if I benefited scholastically very little from the university then I am not conceited enough to lay the blame on that venerable institution.

It was never my intention to waste my opportunities when I enrolled as a pensioner at Trinity in the Spring Term of 1829, but which young man of your acquaintance actually *intends* to idle his days away? Don't we all intend to win College prizes? No, at that age we are convinced it can all be done – we can play and sing and somehow score brilliantly in the examinations. We go up knowing that there are twenty-four hours to the day and that we can therefore parcel all that time out neatly and get everything done. But we can't – or I couldn't. The wretched day would not organise itself. I would end up in bed at three o'clock in the morning in a state of total bewilderment as to what had happened to prevent me doing six hours' serious reading and attending a lecture or two. Did I not get up

at eight and breakfast modestly and open my books on the stroke of nine ?
Certainly I did, so what the devil went wrong ? Why, Carne dropped in
and we had things to discuss over a little refreshment – opening books is
tiring work at eighteen – and then Hine came by and told us about something
we had to go and see at another fellow's rooms and so we went and then it
was not worth coming back for lunch so we proceeded in a merry party to
eat and drink and then the sun shone so brightly we had to have a stroll –
exercise is healthy and essential – and the stroll led to a small game of cards
which spread itself to dinner and after dinner we had to recuperate and test
a bottle or two then – well, it was three in the morning.   Don't it sound
awful ?   Well, that was the worst kind of day and I own there were too
many of them but there were others much better in which I tried to work.

I went back to Cambridge once not so long ago to lecture and you can be
sure I made it my business to go and stand in the Great Court of Trinity and
stare at the three ground-floor windows on E staircase which I inhabited all
those years ago.   It was a strange feeling in which time seemed mixed up
and unreal so that I was not even sure that I had ever been there at all, or on
the other hand that I had ever left.   The place is so old, so many men have
passed through it without it changing in the least, that one more human
being spending a scrap of time there seems irrelevant.   I remember I was
sensitive to this continuity the day I arrived, and filled with an ambition to
have my rooms pointed out to succeeding generations as Newton's were
pointed out to me.   The excitement of simply being part of that tradition
was tremendous – how eagerly I marched round those quadrangles, how
invigorated I was just by the sight of the buildings, how my spirits soared at

the prospect of living in the midst of such beauty and nobility.   It seemed
perfectly easy to live up to it all – I never doubted that Cambridge would
inspire me to great heights.   How many have found before and after me that
for some puzzling reason things do not always work out as we expect ?   I was
seduced by the grandeur and loveliness of that place into thinking I would
reflect it without any effort.   If I had been put down with my bags into
some scene of black ugliness, if I had been pitched into a squalid basement
with no light or air and nothing but filth and meanness around me then how
I would have stormed and shouted and said I could learn nothing in such
circumstances, that learning could not flourish under such oppression, and
how mistaken I should have been.   Learning has nothing to do with
surroundings – indeed, surroundings are not to be acknowledged, they are
dangerous things, liable to creep up on you and convince you that you must
be matching them.

Does all this sound like an excuse for a poor performance ?   I don't intend
it as such – I am only trying to show you how I loved Cambridge and yet
never did myself justice.   The noble thoughts and aspirations were all there
filling my young breast to bursting but nothing much came of them.   I had
not yet learned how to apply myself without firm direction and there was
no one at Cambridge interested in giving it, though I do not mean that as a
rebuke.   I ought to have been able to manage my own affairs but I couldn't.
I floundered about helplessly even on my industrious days in a panic of books
and papers not quite sure what I was learning or what syllabus I was following or what I was supposed to do at the end of it.   I might eventually have
struggled on to dry land if I had been studying a subject less exact than
Mathematics where there is no room for manoeuvre, but as it was I drowned
in a sea of Algebra and Trigonometry.   To this day I don't think I rightly
understand the principles underlying either, yet everyone seemed intent on
assuring me that I did and that there was no need to begin again.   I wonder
who ever convinced me or the authorities that I had a mathematical
aptitude ?   My stepfather is fond of telling the story of how I took to Euclid
at the age of six like a duck to water, but I cannot remember any affinity.

None of this matters now, yet I can't help going over it as if it did.   I
don't think my mother has ever quite got over her disappointment – that is
part of the fascination of the subject.   She had such high hopes of my career
at Cambridge and could never accept that I had chosen to come down
without a degree.   I suffered the most awful pangs of guilt the whole time
I was there on her account.   When I began, I resolved to keep a daily
journal and send it to her but that quickly became an intolerable burden
since I could not fill the pages with what I was really doing and my attempts
at subterfuge became woefully obvious.   I dreaded her letters back when
they became inquiring and critical, and disliked being driven into a defensive
position.   I suppose it was the first difference we ever had and I was nervous

of displeasing such a beloved mother but we can't always please them, can we, not if we are to keep our self-respect. I have no sons but even if I had twenty of them I hope I should have been tolerant of their independence and not tried to push them the way I wanted them to go. It is different with daughters, poor souls. How many ways can a girl go even when she is a genius like my Anny downstairs? Life is a cruelly constricting business for women, firmly set in a domestic sphere with little chance of any intellectual advancement. A girl can study and become just as proficient as her brother but then she is doomed to stand by and watch him put into practice all that she has learned. One day women will go out into the world — how I have not the slightest idea — and astonish the menfolk. Do you recoil from such a disgraceful notion? Why? Have you not looked about and listened in the drawing-rooms of England and been astonished at the unemployed female talent there? Think what they could do, what they could be, were their shackles taken off! Whoa! You say, we don't want the place full of Joan of Arcs, it ain't comfortable, and no more it is and that isn't what I meant. All I want is to see a place for women in our society that doesn't mean they have to stand by and be ordered about by men who half the time are their inferiors. There. Think about it.

It sounds as if I could make a speech or two on that subject and I do believe I could. There was a time when I shouldn't have minded becoming a great orator, declaiming in front of a rapt, respectful audience on matters of national importance, but Cambridge rather cured me of such hopes. I had my go there at spouting in the Union like any other young hot-head and oh lor did I make a mess of it — my face still grows hot thirty-odd years later when I remember how I blustered and blundered and retracted and stuttered about the character of Napoleon. I don't know that I regret this lack of talent for public speaking, though I admire it in others. It is a dangerous game these orators play — I think at university in particular we see fellows who we know in our heart of hearts lack weight standing up and making brilliant speeches and influencing people to go with them when we know that Jones, who cannot speak half as well, is really getting to the truth and ought to be followed. At eighteen, performances matter so much — we want to look impressive and sound impressive and have ourselves acknowledged openly as impressive. Nobody, at that tender age, is interested in quiet, solid worth, nobody gets much joy from knowing they have privately done something noble, not if nobody knows about it.

I was no different. Appearances were of prime importance to me as I flashed through day after day of that intoxicating existence. I don't think I was ashamed — I am disposed to be self-indulgent about a young man's experiments in life. Why apologise for playing at fencing every day for quite two terms? Who cares that I was a terrible dandy, spending hours planning new clothes and prancing about in them looking, I am sure,

altogether ludicrous ?   I remember several waistcoats of killing design with
the greatest affection, not to mention a cloak lined with fur that I was
perfectly convinced transformed me into a suave romantic stranger the
minute I wrapped myself in its capacious folds.   *O vanitas !*   All is vanity –
and quite harmless at that age surely.   It is only in the very young or the
very old that vanity seems disgusting – though I think there is nothing more

charming in the whole world than a two-year-old girl, I don't like to see her
fretting over whether her ringlets are arranged properly, and though I like
to admire a well-endowed matron of fifty, I hate to see her with rouge up
to her eyebrows or the *décolletage* of a girl half her age.   Then, vanity is
repulsive; but around the age of twenty there are a few years when it is not
only excusable but natural and even wholesome.   I like to see young people
at a ball eagerly displaying their wares, not knowing that their real attraction
has nothing to do with clothes or hair or paint but with their very youth.
Their uncertainty is what is touching, not their red dresses or their tight

trousers. I hope people looked at me as I trailed so proudly round Cambridge tripping over my ridiculous new cloak — I hope the old ones looked and smiled and shared my innocent pleasure and did not condemn me for a peacock with an empty head, for it wasn't empty. On the contrary, it was teeming with thoughts and ideas, it was in a turmoil, it seethed perpetually with new discoveries as I floundered about trying to find a niche.

Did I find one, at Cambridge ? I'm not sure I suppose I did, or if not one then several and that was half the trouble. Do you remember from your own college days the desperate anxiety to find a niche ? How lucky the rowing men are, knowing exactly where they belong, exactly what to do, which rituals to observe, what stance to take up! I had half a mind to join them and was only stopped by the embarrassment of having to admit that though as big and strong as any of them I had not the foggiest idea how to row. I envied them their untroubled days tied firmly to their boats and their river, obsessed with clearly definable roles and not caring that there might be other things in the world. Or there were the real scholars, men who before they were twenty were buried so deep in their work that they drew all the sustenance they needed from it — the libraries were their temples where they fell down before a god they worshipped and understood. The rightness of what he is doing never bothers a young man who has found his niche — he asks no questions, entertains no doubts, suffers no qualms or pangs of guilt. Contrast such felicity with my own case, and that of the majority of undergraduates. I did not know where I was going or what I wanted to do. I jumped from one group to another, trying every activity and finding none of them quite suitable, and all this without the firm anchor of any course of work I liked and was enjoying to the full.

My attempts to remedy this unhappy state of affairs — no, not unhappy, I was far from that — this unsatisfactory condition, let us say, were various and desperate but altogether useless. Let us establish first of all that I had a conscience, and that I exercised it of my own free will not just because I had a watchful mother. It troubled me that my work did not progress as it ought so I deduced at first that I did not work hard enough and that I would have to attack the problem ferociously. To do so I had to learn to overcome that malady which has bothered me all my life — laziness. If I was not cursed with being of a lazy, idle disposition I would not have worked nearly as hard as I find I have done. I do so like to stay in bed of a morning — that is, I did until I reached the age when I could not sleep. At eighteen I slept where I fell and was like a tortoise coming out of hibernation at each awakening. Since nobody at Cambridge paid the least attention to this affliction, I had to devise ways and means of getting myself upright at a reasonable hour. This involved bribing the porter with a sixpence to wake me up, which he truly did, but I simply went back to sleep again. I tried making infernally strong tea with several spoonfuls in the pot to keep me permanently awake but of course it did no such thing. I bought an alarm clock but regularly slept through the hideous din, though my neighbours were shaken out of their beds and cursed me from one end of the college to the other. Sometimes I would manage by all these devious means to begin my day at six a.m. but it

never lasted more than a week at a time, however much I lauded my own virtue and swore I enjoyed the fresh morning hours. Next – since I was clearly incapable of surviving that kind of rigorous regime – I tried working at the other end of the day but that was even more impossible for the distractions were endless. There was always something irresistible going on in the evening and I was a gregarious fellow, as I have told you. I found I was stuck with working during normal daytime hours, and if I could not manage to succeed within them all was lost.

In a sense, all *was* lost before very long. I tried – indeed I did – to adopt a systematic and steady course of study but it went too much against the grain and I was left pursuing an erratic course, one day working ten hours at a stretch and another doing nothing whatsoever. You can guess which variety of day was more frequent. My chief stumbling block was Algebra – how I hated Algebra. I have mentioned how I did not understand the underlying principles but it was worse than that – I couldn't understand anything at all. My struggles were Herculean but some little part of my brain is forever shut to Algebra, and to Trigonometry too. Finding the

n^{th} term of $a + b$ and that kind of thing does not make my spirits soar and so I would turn instead to some poem of Percy Bysshe Shelley and forget all about my first commitment.   I know what you are going to say and I say it myself — why did I not change my subject ?   Why did I not read something else ?   It is a puzzle to which I do not rightly know the answer but I expect it is all to do with what was wrong about Cambridge for me — nobody directed me or watched over me, least of all my tutor.   I was expected to get on with what I had begun and it was my own fault if I did not.   Then again, change needs energy and I was short of that commodity, so I staggered on, knowing I was going to make the most awful hash of the first examinations and dreading the revelation that would be to my mother.   I tried to prepare her by warning her I was bound to do poorly and offering her a variety of convincing excuses, but I knew she would be mortally offended by her brilliant son's lack of success.   A small part of me was deluded enough to think it might yet all turn out well — who knew what the day of testing would bring ?   Such comforts are all that are left when you know you are a dud.   Of course, I did badly — they put me in the fifth class and my mother was appalled, prepared though she was, and I was ashamed and resentful. That small boy cry of " It wasn't my fault! " welled up inside me and I could hardly stop myself from uttering it and fixing on a scapegoat.   I made a great deal of my illness before the examinations, describing to my mother in the most graphic detail all the agonising symptoms, and I told her repeatedly how hard it was to work eight hours a day with one's mind at a continual stretch.   Haven't you stood outside an examination-room and watched the candidates go in and don't you know which one I was ?   Yes, the wild-looking fellow arriving half an hour late with his clothes all undone and his pencils broken and his spectacles mislaid, and I don't know what other signs of strain but all of them together.   What remorse I suffered as I sat there staring blankly at the papers while all around composed men of my acquaintance, who had only the night previously vowed that they knew nothing either, were bent double industriously filling reams of paper.   It was a most humiliating experience, one that I was determined not to have repeated.

There are some lessons in life that are salutary and the earlier we have them the better, but I don't consider that ignominious failure is ever good. Failure cripples, it produces a lack of confidence so total that very often, if it happens early enough in life, the failed one never recovers.   This was not the case with me, but it could have been.   I have confessed I wanted to shine among my peers and it hurt to do quite the reverse, but I had enough consolations to enable me to weather the temporary storm.   I dug my heels in, looked around and saw there was a great deal I enjoyed at Cambridge that made up for my lack of academic honours.   After all, I might have stuck in my rooms day after day and somehow banged Algebra into my stupid head

but then I would not have tried my wings in other directions and what a lot of fun I should have missed.   I can, with hindsight, go further than that and say more – if I had worked and kept my head down I should not have helped to edit *The Snob* and therefore I should have missed my first journalistic experience, with what dire results for the world!   What ?   You have not heard of *The Snob*, that famous literary and scientific journal, every edition of which sold out immediately ? You have missed a treat. It happens I have kept all seven numbers, seven double coloured sheets, mere slips of things but bursting with vitality and humour.

I am, of course, joking. Undergraduate humour is all the same – I daresay I could go out on the street now and buy much the same kind of thing in any university town, and that you could too when and wherever you read this. I know I fell off my stool laughing at my own wit when I sat with the other editor composing the material – oh how we shrieked and clutched each other and could hardly see for tears of mirth. It is hard to say which pleased us most – our attempts at satire or the straightforward slap-stick. We sold it for 2½d a copy and prided ourselves on value for money. It was packed with solemn thoughts such as " Asparagus and poetry are equally worthless when forced ", and little ditties that mocked the current style like " Ode to a Casting Net ":

> By the pond's pellucid stream
> My casting net
> Will soon be wet
> Beneath the moon's pale beam.

Well, I didn't write it but I still think it is funny even if you are already half way across the room throwing the paper out of the window in exasperation. Nor did I have a hand in our serial " Moll of Wapping " which made me laugh most of all, or " An Essay on the Great Toe, together with the Nature and Properties of Toes in General " in which the delivery of a certain famous man was mimicked. No, my claim to fame was a poem called " Timbuctoo ", which may or may not have been a satire on Daddy Wordsworth, complete with notes for your edification. As it was my first published contribution I really think I am entitled to quote it now:

> In Africa (a quarter of the world)
> Men's skins are black, their hair is crisp and curled
> And somewhere there unknown to public view
> A mighty city lies called Timbuctoo
> There stalks the tiger, there the lion roars
> Who sometimes eats the luckless blackamoors
> All that he leaves of them the monster throws
> To jackal, vultures, dogs, cats, kites and crows
> His hunger thus the forest monster gluts
> And then lies down 'neath trees called cocoa nuts.

It went on for another verse or so and the sport lay in extremely erudite annotations which I suppose I can't persuade you to put up with ?   I thought not – but I can assure you my contemporaries thought it was splendid.   I was in a public house soon after this issue came out and there – oh heady stuff! – I heard some fellows I did not know and who did not know me actually quoting bits of my poem to each other and saying how good they thought it was and how clever and wondering aloud who the author was.   I drank in their praise faster than any liquor and was consumed with pleasure.   It seemed to me the most happy of combinations – to have done something I had loved to do and be congratulated for it.   I would like to say this experience stimulated a desire to write more extensively but I know it did not – I never thought about writing at that time.   Nor did it occur to me that this might be a way of earning my living because I never thought about that either.   I spent money freely because I thought I was always going to have enough – the thought of earning what I spent – of having to earn in order to spend – would have been shocking to me.

Knowing what came after, this easy style of accounting was a bad preparation for what followed, but I don't know that I regret my extravagant behaviour – or only in one respect.   I did not think of myself as having expensive tastes, whatever my mother said.   I dressed well, I kept a good cellar – I was proud even then of my taste in wine – and I decorated my rooms with tremendous flair, but I thought all these things justified and I still do.

Perhaps there was no need to have new curtains hung in the latest fashion on a brass rod, or to have my mantelpiece painted marble, but these were innocent and not really costly joys. I spent a lot of money on books and would argue that the laying down of a good library was an investment from several points of view. When they come to sell my library – though God forbid for I like to think of it staying in the family – when they do, they will find several volumes from my Cambridge days which proved to be bargains. At the time, Hume and Smollett bought uncut in thirteen volumes for £3.3.0. seemed expensive, and a Mitford *History of Greece* desperately dear at 5 guineas, but they have more than held their value and given me many hours of instruction and pleasure. I can't call it " wasting money " as my uncle Frank was inclined to term my hobby. This uncle was appointed Holder of the Privy Purse by my mother and it was to him that I had to apply for money. This irked me – I longed to have my own Cambridge banker – but I must say that Uncle Frank always paid up whatever the demands upon him.

How glad I am, as I sit here confessing for all I am worth, that I have earned enough money with this inkstand and pen to leave my girls ten thousand a-piece and my wife a comfortable income. If I had not done so I should have gone to my grave haunted by guilt at the memory of a patrimony thrown away during my Cambridge days. I speak not of money spent on clothes or rooms or wine or books but on play – on gambling – on the throw of a dice. Now that the poison has long since been purged from me I can hardly recall the force of the compulsion that drove me to gamble with such passion, such excitement, such disregard for the money involved. My mother, who suspected all along that the fripperies I listed could not account for the vast sums drawn, always maintained that I was led astray and that it was my unfortunate choice of friends that was responsible for my disgraceful behaviour. She would have it that her good, honest, worthy son was the lamb led to the slaughter and that he could not help himself – a happy fiction, which I cannot hide behind. Haven't I told you how I was a vague, floating kind of fellow, always open to suggestions, ever willing to make up numbers for anything at all, only content in the middle of a crowd going somewhere to do something?

My mother was wrong to blame any friends of mine for my recklessness – such a lad would always find his way down the primrose path. The penalty of an irresistible curiosity about everything and everyone is that the bad must be encompassed as well as the good, otherwise the phrase has no meaning. Nobody is curious about something they already know is dull or exciting, angelic or wicked – that is what has to be found out. Nor can anyone tell a really curious person that the thing he is curious about is dreadfully boring or unwholesome or that he will not like it – all that must be experienced before the curiosity dies. I knew perfectly well that gambling was odious and that it would do me no good and that I ought to keep well away, but I was drawn by the very fact that it was disapproved of and therefore dangerous. I had no doubt at all that when I had given it a try I should be able to say that was another veil removed and leave well alone and that is where I was mistaken.

A dissertation on the fascination of gambling may be repugnant to you, and indeed I am not equipped to give one even if I have made my young self out to be an old roué. I gambled pretty fiercely for a few years and then with an almighty struggle pulled myself clear and I have hardly indulged since, so you see I was one of the lucky ones. How frightful it would have been in the days when I was down to my last sovereign if I had been tempted to put it on a spin of the wheel or the turn of a card! It makes me quite sick to see the horrible desperation in the eyes of some of the impoverished wretches round a casino table — you know just by looking at them that this

is not a game but a matter of life and death, not just for themselves but for others connected with them. When they lose, how are they going to face going home to the wife and crying children ? How are they going to buy food and pay the rent ? It was never like that with me and I like to think that if it had been I should even then have had the strength of character to stop. The worst I ever knew was guilt at having to tell my mother, or at least Uncle Frank, and though that gave me an unpleasant few hours every now and again it did not exactly torture me. I was even indignant at my mother's reproaches – what, did she want me to be a milksop ? Was I to have no fun ? Didn't she trust me to be moderate ? Well, no, she did not, nor did she trust my dependence on others and she was quite right. It was perfectly easy to dupe me – I was a card-sharper's joy, so innocent and honourable and believing everyone else to be the same. They must have laughed heartily when they had done with me – the thing was so easy. I believe these men travel round likely haunts looking for just such a simpleton as I was, ready with their drafts and banker's orders to be signed, ever on the hunt for ready prey. I have often, since my own day, seen a young man hovering near the table as I did with that sweet inquisitiveness I recognise at once, and I have seen those dark, hatchet-faced villains move silently in his direction and oh how I have wanted to rush up and say my dear young sir, when these men invite you to a quiet private little game in a back room don't go, don't be taken in by whatever flattery they are bound to use, for they are going to fleece you with a knife every bit as sharp and ruthless as the shepherd cuts the sheep's coat. But I don't move. I stay where I am and I watch the young man eagerly go off with his executioners and I say nothing. Protection is no good, you see, it doesn't work. The battle must be fought alone against all such temptations. In gambling, I had discovered another weakness which had to be corrected as painfully as idleness. My interest in Rouge et Noir was so powerful that nothing could keep me away from gaming houses at that time.

Now how did I break the spell ? I wish I had some formula to pass on to others that I had discovered was infallible. I know it took a long time and that long after I had grown to despise and hate my obsession I still frequented those places. I told my distracted mother at regular intervals that I had put Satan behind me, but I had not. The more unsatisfactory my work, the more attractive gambling became. The more I lost, the more convinced I was that next time I would win – is that not the common cry of the gambler ? It was not until I was involved in work that excited and interested me and among company that stimulated me in other directions that I weaned myself from that disgusting sport, and that was after my Cambridge days were over. I look back and shake my head and wince over the amount of money lost, which I refuse to tell you for fear you will stop reading immediately, but all the same I still say it was a necessary process. The world being what it is, and I being who I am, I should have tried gambling at some stage in my life and I am glad it was at Cambridge and at that point.

It makes me uneasy that I am painting such a dark picture, unrelieved by any lighter touches, as though I spent my youth struggling with my soul and finding it wanting. I don't seem to have included any vignettes of happy,

carefree hours when all was right with the world, do I ? There has been
enough of the bad company I kept and the bad pastimes I took to but little
of the good friends and pursuits. I have noticed that when a man resolves
to be honest he almost always sees honesty as meaning the cataloguing of his
faults as though virtues had no place. Perhaps modesty ought to go hand in
hand with honesty – I don't know, but I must at least set the record right
and briefly touch on happier moments. As you will expect, these were in
the midst of friends. I did occasionally enjoy long walks up the river alone,
sketch-book self-consciously in hand, and I liked long hours sitting in the
window reading on my own, but they were not the highlights of my
existence. These came among good friends, men my mother might approve
of, having good conversations about worthwhile topics. I don't mean those

smoking parties with everyone singing and bawling and trying to pretend
they were having a good time – to do me justice, I always thought those
gatherings stupid and left many such a gathering of my own free will, bored
to death by the vulgarity of it all – but quieter meetings with Edward
Fitzgerald or William Brookfield or John Allen. I was very happy then,
among men I loved, sharing thoughts and opinions with those who possessed

sharper minds and keener faculties than I.   It humbled me to be their friend, worthy of their time, and I would come away strengthened against those faults of character I have told you about.   Sometimes we would pray together before we went our separate ways and I almost came to believe that " more things are wrought by prayer than this world dreams of ".   I would go out into the Cambridge night and walk slowly to my room, an arm about dear Fitz's neck, feeling purified and solemn and quite sure that tomorrow I would start on a new course from which I would not deviate.   Contentment would make me calm and I was almost afraid to sleep in case that strange happiness fled.

I have had many friends since Cambridge but none as dear as those I made there, not men at any rate.   I really think I love Fitzgerald still, though I know he thinks I have betrayed him because I do not write regularly or visit him or show other signs of keeping friendship alive.   Need I ?   Is true friendship such a tender hothouse plant that it can only thrive carefully protected in a glasshouse, sheltered from changes of temperature ?   I hope not.   In my heart I love Fitz as much as I ever did – only circumstances have made it look as though I do not.   It makes me impatient that such store is set by the length and time and frequency of visits – if we have not been to see Brown in six months oh horror, what that shows about our estimation of him!   It does not seem to matter that in that six months we have been at death's door, have had the bailiffs in, have been twice round the world and are altogether exhausted with the demands made upon us.   Brown should have been visited, even if he lives three days' journey away and has no room to put us up.   I find this kind of reckoning ridiculous.   How dare the world judge my affection for Brown on the basis of hours, minutes, seconds spent with him ?   Ah, you say, but what of Brown himself ?   Does he understand his place in your heart as clearly as you do yourself ?   Is he as confident that he is loved as much as before, when he had constant tokens of your love, is he as sure absence is insignificant ?   Perhaps not.   I am sad to admit it, but perhaps Brown – Fitzgerald – wonders with you.   He wrote to me once accusing me of forgetting him now that I had other friends, a cry of pain to be constant to him, and I knew that in spite of my protests he had justification in part.   Though I swore then – as I do now – that I loved him as much as before, it was true that I no longer loved him exclusively and that others shared his place.   I was a little ashamed at the extravagance of my devotion to him once I had left Cambridge.   There, where such things are understood, where friendship flourishes and luxuriates in perfect conditions, it seemed natural to address him as " my dearest Teddybus " and to grieve if we were apart more than a few hours.   Friendship then was an intense affair, demanding total commitment, but in the outside world how can this exclusive character be preserved ?   Outside marriage I don't see that it can, and if Fitzgerald was disappointed by this then I don't see how I could help it. Never mind – we will meet again in hell and be good friends there when we have all eternity to enjoy.

There are some parts of my life that I have only to begin to look back on for the very atmosphere of rooms I lived in to come back to me, but Cambridge is not such a part. I remember where I lived and what I did and so forth but that time is strangely dead to me. Oh, certain golden days and moments I can capture again but I can't grasp the whole convincingly, I can't shut my eyes and be back there however hard I try. My memories are for the most part laboured and I am quickly tired by them. It may be that the restlessness that filled me then comes across the years and affects me in the same way, that I can't wait to have done with the telling of it any more than I could wait to have done with the living. I wanted to escape Cambridge, I wanted away from my mother's expectations, though escape to

where or what I had no idea. All I knew was that I was sick of trying to conquer Algebra and that all the benefits of a scholastic existence did not compensate for my sense of failure. Even if it broke my mother's heart I was resolved to have done with this charade and not be lured further by the belief that I could do better next year. There was to be no next year at Cambridge.

Chapter III

———————◆———————

IN WHICH YOUR HERO ENJOYS HIMSELF
IN WEIMAR AND EVADES THE FUTURE

NLESS society has changed a great deal by the time you read this it will still be considered an essential part of a young gentleman's education to travel abroad on some sort of tour. The Grand Tour that was so common half a century ago has given way to a curtailed version that is nonetheless an absolute prerequisite for a man of twenty-one or thereabouts. This is all part of the English pattern – first send him to prep school to get his crying over, then to public school to starve him into obedience, then to university to confuse him with a mixture of untold-of pleasure and unheard-of work, and then, before pushing him into one of several moulds, send him abroad ostensibly to contrast inferior cultures with our own superior one but really to sow his wild oats before knuckling down for life. I had followed just such a pattern – my career had been mapped out for me without any consent of mine. Consent ? The boy must be mad – what does he know of what is good for him ? The very idea is nonsense – actually *ask* the young shaver what he would like to do ? Absurd.

I did not think it absurd and I still don't. A boy ought to share in the planning of his own destiny for only with his eager co-operation will any good come of a fond parent's plans, yet all around I see examples of forcing that will end in unhappiness and ruin. Jones always wanted to be a lawyer so from the minute young Jones arrives he pins upon him his own legal aspirations and it is no good the young fellow shouting, " But Papa I want to be a soldier – I like to fight – I hate books." Heresy! Wash his mouth out with soap! Your father wanted to be a lawyer and his father would not let him so you will be one and be glad that you are and that is that. And when young Jones grows up and has a son he seizes on him and says he will be a soldier and his son may cry and say, " Papa I hate fighting – I love books

35

— I want to be — " Well, I don't want to hear what this second young Jones wants to be because it isn't a bit of good, he is going to be a soldier. Sometimes it goes the other way and is even harder to escape. Bloggs is a well-to-do wine merchant and proud of it. He has built up an excellent business and wants to pass it on to his son. He wants his son to be exactly what he was and any contradiction is treated as high treason with a strong line in " what-was-good-enough-for-me-is-good-enough-for-you ". Ain't it pathetic ? Why can't young Jones be a soldier or a lawyer or whatever he

feels called to be ? Why can't young Bloggs admire his father's business but politely decline to enjoy it ? I wish someone would tell me why not.

In my own case it was not quite like this. My mother wanted me to get a brilliant degree as a first step to she knew not what — her ideas were fixed only so far. Though a strong-minded lady she was not a bully, and once I was old enough to speak for myself she was perfectly willing to use reason rather than force. I, on the other hand, was in the difficult but not unusual position of having no discernible talent for anything in particular nor any desire to become one thing rather than another. Remember I was still a man of means — modest perhaps, but still real, still with that small fortune in the three per cents waiting in the wings for when I came of age. There was no pressing necessity to decide on a career and I took full advantage of this happy state of affairs. Why rush me, I pleaded ? Why insist I should carry on at Cambridge when I was so manifestly unsuited to the particular study I was engaged in – what was the harm in looking about and thinking about it and then returning later when I was clearer in my mind about certain issues ?

I really think that is what my mother thought would happen, In letting me leave Cambridge to spend a winter abroad she thought she was giving me the opportunity to come to my senses. Once removed from " bad influences " I would see the virtue of study, return to university, redouble my efforts and in no time at all emerge with a gold medal. I am ashamed to say that while still in England I led her along to think this would happen, carefully concealing the delight I felt at the idea. She would look at me fondly and say to my stepfather that I did look pale and tired and that I had undoubtedly outgrown my strength and that I would surely benefit from a period of rest and recuperation. Perhaps her face clouded just a little when she remembered my previous excursions abroad – to Paris in the Easter vacation – and how my letters home had been full of trips to Frascati's, the well known gambling house on the rue de Richelieu, not to mention merry parties and more " bad influences ". I should never have written so openly of my jolly dancing lessons and the excitement of visiting the *Comédie Française* – if I had confined myself to comparing Notre-Dame unfavourably to Exeter Cathedral I might have alarmed her less. I would never have got away from Cambridge if I had suggested a winter in Paris – *quelle horreur !* But in mooting the notion of some as yet undecided quiet little place in Germany I overcame her alarm. I don't think I was deceitful about it – I didn't specify any particular place or say exactly what I intended to do – but I suppose I did go on rather about the necessity of learning German and do nothing to off-set the assumption that it was all going to be very steady and wholesome and in fact rather dull.

At any rate, it was agreed, and off I set in July 1830, fresh from my examination disaster, shaking Cambridge off my heels like an exuberant young puppy and with no intention of ever being brought back. I went first to Rotterdam and then made my way down the Rhine first to Coblenz and finally across to Weimar. I travelled with some vague friends but I felt alone all the same and savoured the experience to the full. I may somewhere have said, returning perhaps hot and tired from some exhausting journey, that I am bored with travel, but if I have, I take it back, and certainly at that tender age I loved it. Even now, I like to go to some new place, be it only a little village in England, I like to see places for the first time and learn the landmarks and sample the life there. I feel at peace when I travel, as though whatever worries are mine belong to someone else and until the train stops or the boat ties up I need be dragged down no longer. In 1830, I was hardly in need of this anonymity that I craved in later years – thoughts of returning to Cambridge or not sat very lightly on my young broad shoulders – but all the same I experienced a lightening of spirits and a freedom from care that excited me.   A Cambridge friend called Schulte introduced me to the delights of watching duels and also to those of drinking German wines afterwards – one night I drank six bottles at a go and am bound to confess such indulgence had a bad effect on my internals and strengthened my conviction that French wines were better.   There was plenty to satisfy me in that Rhine journey – every day the landscape changed a little and there were endless glimpses of towns and villages that I had known only as names on a map.   I sketched furiously, especially the old bridges and churches, constantly striving to capture with my pencil that beauty which made the Rhine almost the equal of the Thames.   If you have never travelled out of your own country you are greatly to be pitied, for the sense of adventure it gives is unequalled.   Passing through foreign countries brings a heightening awareness of your own background that exhilarates and illuminates.   It was not until I travelled that I properly began to understand what England was, what it meant to me, what it gave me, how I was part of it, of the land and houses and people, and how it was part of me.   As I look out of my window now on a scene so completely English that it could be nowhere else in the world, I feel tremendous satisfaction that it belongs to me and that it is English and that I know, because I have travelled, what that means.   And if that isn't a speech for a patriot I don't know what is.

The more I think about Weimar – and I enjoy thinking about it because I was so happy there – the stranger it seems that I picked that little town out of all the places in Germany to be my home.   I recollect that a friend suggested it, but what possible requirements could I have listed that made him recommend Weimar?   It was in no way typical of any part of Germany, but rather a rarity, a quaint backwater existing almost in another century with a different pace of life.   Everything was in miniature, everything clearly defined and very stable.   Though it was small, it had every amenity and even a court where the reigning Duke solemnly held *levées* and balls.   I lived there with a respectable family and went daily to a German tutor, the excellent Dr. Weissenborn, with whom I made rapid progress.   The society of the place was good and easily entered and I even appeared at court in a pair of cut-down trousers, a black waistcoat, a cock hat and a black coat, looking like a cross between a footman and a methodist parson.   Afraid that I looked altogether ludicrous, I got my mother to send me out a yeomanry uniform which I wore with considerable panache and enough pride to have made anyone think it was a general's uniform at least.   I think I hoped that was exactly what everyone would think – the great English soldier General Thackeray, fresh from his campaign in – in – well, unfortunately there wasn't a war on anywhere at that time.

Don't take umbrage, will you, that I liked Weimar better than Cambridge ? Haven't I, after all, flaunted my patriotism ? No, it wasn't the place that worked magic and made me happy but rather the freedom to do what I wanted and be only in the widest sense beholden to anyone. And tne surprising thing is that when I write " to do what I wanted ", this is not a euphemistic way of describing endless days in bed and nights carousing. Far from it – my diligence was exemplary. I worked hard at German and when I was not struggling with the syntax I read Schiller and Goethe and other eminent German writers. There was a marvellous theatre there – seems surprising doesn't it ? – and I went almost every night to hear plays and operas performed in German. The social life I led was as much chatting with elderly Germans on suitable topics as enjoying myself with my own age-group – in fact, it was distinctly weighted in favour of the former and I did not regret it a bit. It was exactly the way of life to suit me – pleasant, easy, no responsibilities, sufficient distractions and entertainments, and a modicum of work to satisfy myself and my parents that I was not idling. I suppose it was a spoiled existence – perhaps that degree of self-indulgence in a young man not quite yet of age makes you angry but if it does it is your own anger you ought to examine, not my pleasure. I cannot think it was wrong to be so contented when it hurt nobody. Would it have been better to be back at Cambridge struggling away to do something I didn't want to do and doing it badly ? The puritan in you may say yes but I say no.

I kept a commonplace book at Weimar but it doesn't reveal the treasures
I thought it might — in fact, it rather embarrasses me and I am glad to be
able to hide it. You see what an advantage it is to be writing one's own life?
There is nothing sinister in it but a grand deal of high-flown nonsense of the
kind I rather suspect I regularly take young 'uns to task about these days
from my lofty position. There are stories, mostly unfinished, full of prithees
and thees and thous and very little else — snatches of plays that reveal no
talent for dialogue at all, and long extracts from German works that I
admired. Nothing worth preserving at any rate — except perhaps a poem
called " The Stars " that appeared in a periodical called *Chaos* which I am
not altogether ashamed of and which I print now to prove I did attempt the
serious:

> Now when mortal eyes do close
> Lo! their lids the stars are raising
> And on us and our repose
> Those bright eyes of heaven are gazing.
>
> 'Tis in vain ye countless stars!
> That discontented men would see
> In your glittering characters
> Fates and fortunes yet to be.
>
> That which we slumber and forget
> He, who gave me that sweet sleep
> Remembreth and watcheth yet!

Well, perhaps it does not read as well as I thought and I will have to start
emphasising my youth and inexperience, and that kind of defence is no
excuse so I had better be quiet.

I wonder if it is beginning to strike you as rather curious that I am
apparently about to get myself to one and twenty without there being any
mention in these pages of r-m-n-e? Not a single lady except my worthy
mama has graced my tale and I quite agree it appears unnatural not to have
fallen in love at least temporarily before now. What ailed the lad? Nothing
— only opportunity. I had not had much access to beautiful young women
before Weimar and if my thoughts ran on them it was without any direct
stimulus. It would be too pathetic, surely, to dwell on a young lady by the
name of Ladd who so bewitched me that I bought a pair of bronze candle-
sticks from her in a Cambridge shop — not even a novelist could make
anything of such meagre material. I had been admiring women for years
and years — always have and always will — but without speaking to them or —
rapture! — touching so much as a hand. Do you see a large red flag waving

above my head ?   I promised that if I could not be wholly truthful on any topic then I would let you know and that red flag is waving now because I don't consider it any part of my duty to burden you with unsavoury descriptions of certain exploits to do with the kind of women I would rather not have known.   Indications are sufficient, so I will indicate that while my relationships with proper ladies had not yet begun I had briefly made some hasty associations with improper ones and had been much excited and alarmed by them.   Women, in truth, were beginning to figure rather large in my life.

I thought about the fair sex almost exclusively at Weimar, even to the extent of warning my mother that I might at any minute appear with a Mrs. Thackeray on my arm.   Of course, I was not serious – I don't suppose I would have taken it so lightly if I had been – but it was true that there were two young belles in Weimar who between them kept me in that blissful state of being in love almost the whole of my stay there.   One was Melanie von Spiegel and the other Jenny von Pappenheim.

Old men like to talk of their past loves, especially those that caused them no pain. They speak so fondly of certain misses that held their attention for a brief spell, caressing their names, the Melanies and the Jennys, with an affection that reveals straight away that there was never any struggle there. I am no different. There have been real loves in my life that I am going to find it difficult to mention but I can tell of Melanie and Jenny with the greatest gaiety and many chuckles over my infatuation with them. Neither of them ever even glimpsed my soul never mind plumbed the depths. My love for them is hardly worth the name. Can't you see it ? They were pretty and gentle and wore lovely clothes and floated about Weimar collecting compliments and it was the done thing to be hopelessly enamoured of one or both of them. As a young Englander I had a certain cachet, though the old dowagers, in whom the place abounded, had given the thumbs-down sign when they had finished ascertaining that I was neither a Milord nor the eldest son of some vastly rich family. Still, I was endlessly obliging when it came to performing social functions like making up parties for this and that and the kind of old Hofmarschal of those days welcomed me and put no barriers in my way as far as admission to all the official functions went. It was his daughter, Melanie, rather than Jenny, who was the target of my adulation, though I would not have spurned Jenny if she had thrown herself at my feet as in my fantasies she regularly did.

I was only one of many who were smitten by Melanie's charms and I courted her, if you can call it that, in public but I fancied at the time I was both sending and receiving the most subtle messages of love. Didn't her blue eyes hold mine rather longer than anyone else's ? Wasn't that small smile unmistakably directed at me ? Wouldn't everyone be forced to agree that it was to my conversation, with its interesting comments on Schiller and Goethe and Faust, that she paid the most attention ? I'm sure they would, but I'm afraid the young lady married somebody else in spite of her quite clear preference for me.

I once saw dear Melanie, years and years after that winter in the little Saxon capital. It was in Italy – Venice, I think – in a hotel where I was staying with my daughters. I had been looking at the guestbook and noticed a name that I was sure was Melanie's married name. With some hesitation, and even a little excitement, I asked a waiter to point the lady out to me, and who do you think he pointed out ? A fat, silent, ugly matron in pale green eating a boiled egg. The cruelty of it took my breath away – I was distraught – I could not bring myself to effect an introduction though my girls, intrigued by the romantic memories I had entertained them with, begged and begged me to go across and shake her by the hand. It was horrible to see the changes time had made – not just in the features which had gone from delicacy to heaviness, nor the figure, once slender and now stout, but the whole spirit of the lady had dramatically altered. She had become ordinary, leaden, flaccid – the aura had gone as well as the beauty, and when my first shock was over I wanted to cry at the tragedy. You see how foolish I am – Melanie was probably perfectly happy, she may not even have noticed what had happened to her, and if she had why should she cry over it ? She could not stay eighteen and beautiful all her life, though I have known women who have managed to do so – to preserve in spite of the lines and white hair their loveliness. But Melanie had not and I could not confront her with my disappointment, I wanted to keep her locked up in my head as she had once been and not have my recollections smeared. Somewhere, I was convinced, we were still flirting with each other, she and I, on a cold winter's night as we were carried in sedan chairs over the snow to the palace, talking of this and that while we gazed into each other's face. If I strain my eyes down the long corridors of time I think I can still see us and how pretty we look and I am going to leave us there, safely buried in the past. The fat lady in Venice has nothing to do with that time and I shan't let her intrude and insist on bringing me up to date. The Melanie I knew is preserved how I want her.

There are other memories, not so likely to be challenged, that I have of that time – apart, that is, from the general memory of being happy in the most civilised way possible. While I was there, I met, or was received by, the great Goethe, and I bought Schiller's sword. There. Ought I not to go to my grave a proud man ? I really mean it – both things gave me tremendous pleasure. Though he had officially retired from the world,

Goethe at that time still met people in his private apartments and maintained an interest in everything that was new. I was in a state of great excitement when his daughter-in-law told me he would be happy to make my acquaintance and that he had already seen and remarked on some caricatures I had

done for her children.   We met and talked – he asked me questions about myself – nothing extraordinary happened but I remember his dark piercing eyes to this day and his rich, sweet voice.   I don't think it is wrong to be impressed by the truly great, or flattered when somebody important takes an interest in you.   It is not snobbery to be pleased at these attentions – on the contrary, it reveals a humility in the worshipper that it would be silly to condemn.   It is quite different from fawning on someone altogether worthless because they are in a position to do something for you, or simpering in front of a jumped-up nobody who has achieved nothing.   But Goethe in his own time was a legend, and in paying homage I think I did the right thing and that I am to be congratulated rather than despised for my obeisance.

It is more than thirty years since I lived in Weimar, thirty years of travelling round many other countries and experiencing many different societies, and yet I don't think I have ever come across such a simple, courteous place as that city.   Do I exaggerate in retrospect ?   Well, all memory exaggerates in one way or another, we can't help but select this from that and compare one year with another so that one is bound to suffer.   All I know is that I loved Weimar then and I love it even more now that it has long since vanished and that must mean something.   I might still have been there today, such was my affection for the place and its people, if my mother had not prised me out like a clam from a shell.   She had all the time kept up a constant refrain in her letters about the future, hanging it over me like Damocles' sword.   Though delighted that I was happy, she never let a letter pass without reminding me that this was but a transitional stage and I must think about what I was going to do next.   Mostly I ignored her insistent queries, continuing to fill my letters to her with ecstatic descriptions of plays I had seen and books I had read and so forth, but then she would write that I had not answered her properly and I could not have read her letter and so on.   The lady had to be answered – there could be no prolonging of my evasions.

Sometimes we can't remember why we made decisions that turn out to be important – why Weimar precisely ? – but on this particular score I remember very clearly why I resisted with a firmness that astonishes me my mother's attempts to send me back to Cambridge.   I was not a disobedient nor an ungrateful son – I loved my mother and knew she only wanted to do her best for me – but it seemed to me that all my life I had done what I was told and had not enjoyed it and that the time had come to stand firm.   I hope I told my mother so politely, and without insolence, but I would not be surprised if a high-handed tone crept in now and again.   The trouble was, I could not discuss a matter that touched me so nearly without passion.   I would sit down to write to her with my arguments neatly and logically arranged but then as I wrote I would grow heated and begin packing my guns with more powder than I had intended.   Eventually, I convinced the poor lady that she had no hope whatsoever of getting me to go back to Cambridge, either to take up my interrupted studies or to embark on any new ones. Wisely, if sadly, she recognised my obstinacy and turned her attention instead to the alternatives.

The irony will not escape you that among all the professions I considered the literary one was not among them, but then who, then or now, considers writing a profession that a gentleman might take up ? Nobody, and we literary men have only ourselves to blame if we are thought of as the lowest of the low. What do we do to raise ourselves in the public's estimation ? Nothing. We are not even a corporate body with a charter and rules and awards and all those badges of office that any estimable co-operation bolsters itself up with. Heaven knows I have tried, Dickens with me, to change this sad state of affairs but to no effect. We go on being a pack of money-grubbers, hardly distinguishable from tradesmen, and no self-respecting

mother wants to boast that her son is of the literary profession.   For myself,
it don't matter, 'deed it don't ma'am, but I am quite surprised to discover
how much I care about my brethren and their poor status.   In 1831 of
course I knew nothing about literary men, nor wanted to, for though I
enjoyed putting verses together and was appreciative of what other men had
written, it never occurred to me even to consider trying to make a living at
it, which when you think about it was just as well for I would surely have
failed.   In any case, how could my mother have accepted such a decision ?
Where were the rungs of any ladder to point out to her ?   Where was the
training ?   She wanted me to enter upon something she could understand –
something with clearly definable stages, that she could tell her friends I was
in the first or second or final year of and that sort of thing.   If I had said,
" Mama, I want to write a book," what could she have said but, " Son,
write a book by all means but join a profession first " – and do you know it
would not have been bad advice and I might still give it myself today.
Writing is a perilous craft, best learned on some solid foundation.   Luck,
and not merit, plays far too important a part for my liking, and then so many
factors are involved apart from the writing itself – the cost of publishing, the
distribution of copies, the notice of critics – all these uncontrollable elements
can kill a book, however good it is.   The literary profession, in short, is not
really a young man's game and I was lucky it did not tempt me at that time.

The truth was, as you may have guessed, nothing did tempt me, tucked up in snug little Weimar, protected from all the realities of the big outside world. Gloomily I surveyed the possibles, all of which, after five minutes' consideration, seemed absolutely impossible. Medicine was the worst option in my opinion — I could not bear the idea of poking and prodding people and cutting them up and I did not hold that profession in any awe. Rather the reverse — doctors are a lot of fools forever telling you to do one thing and then the exact opposite, revealing at every turn that they do not know what they are about. My mother had never had anything to do with them and I can't say I blame her, though I do not esteem her homeopathic remedies much more. I, on the other hand, never seem to have been out of the clutches of medical men for the last twenty years in one way or another and I think I can safely say that though I have come across several good and kind practitioners none of them has made me take back my original pronouncement. Perhaps in the future medicine will become a more exact science but until that day I will not alter my judgement. I was more attracted by another ancient profession — that of War, I mean becoming a soldier in the British Army. I suppose it was most unoriginal of me — half the population of boys want to become a soldier. It has all the attractions, being the most manly of all callings, full of honour and glory, offering glittering fame and promotion and public gratitude for those who demonstrate their valour as we all think we will. I was always interested in military life and in campaigns and had studied several in minute detail. I thought I should fit in well with a soldier's life since I liked company and had always got on well with my fellow men. My mother might perhaps have demurred on the usual maternal grounds of the danger but I think she would have come round pretty quickly. There was only one obstacle — nowhere in Europe were we fighting at the time and I could not bring myself to be a peacetime warrior — it seemed somehow to make nonsense of the whole business.

What, then, was left if I was to reject the academic life, and medicine and soldiering? The answer came in one awful word that I shrank from — the law. It sent shivers down my spine but oh how my mother loved the idea! It satisfied her craving on my behalf for respectability and eminence and even power and excitement. I don't believe there is any other profession that appeals quite so much to a mother. The law is so highly thought of, so wonderfully obscure, so hung about with impressive regalia. She saw me as Lord Chancellor within a few short years dispensing justice to all and sundry. I wondered, after I had mentioned the law, why I had been so stupid, for of course my mother leapt upon my diffident suggestion and would not let go. If I had had any better inspiration I would instantly have produced it to dilute her enthusiasm but though I cast about like a mad thing I could think of nothing. The church? No — that would have caused more trouble when I knew, or had strong intimations, that our ideas on religion did not exactly agree and my mother would have wanted me to be one sort of clergyman while I would have wanted to be another.   In any case, though my religion was sincere, I was not temperamentally suited to the cloth, and while that is not always a bar to entering the church — witness numerous friends of an equally frivolous disposition who have successfully made it their field — this self-knowledge held me back.   There was also the valid point that for a man of talent and private income — didn't I think I had both ? — the church was unacceptable for it was still thought of as a means of employment and advancement for those who had no alternative, and I did not want to lump myself with those unfortunates in the absence of any true calling.   That sounds unpleasant, put so bluntly, but any man of the world will know what I mean.

There was nothing for it but to agree to practise law, to get myself set up in somebody's chambers and begin on the dreary business of learning how to trick the rest of mankind.   You see, I did not have the right attitude from the start — I always thought lawyers a snivelling lot.   While at Weimar I dipped into a few volumes on civil jurisprudence and they made me ill — they were distinctly not for me — but what could I do ?   I was not rich enough to do nothing — though God knows I was a millionaire then compared to my position shortly afterwards — and I had to do something solid to escape returning to Cambridge.   I tried to console myself with the thought that it would all be new and I liked novelty, and I would be in London and able to partake in what I imagined was the dazzling social life of the place. It did occur to me that at Weimar I could live comfortably on my existing income if I was careful and escape altogether the horrible necessity of returning to England and work, but when I mentioned it to my mother she poured out such a torrent of objections and labelled the notion unworthy so I was compelled to forget it.   I must return to England and begin on some honourable profession.   It was inevitable.   I thought with shame of how my father, at my age, had been working for five years and how I was about to come of age with nothing at all to show.   In the summer of 1831 I left that gracious life in Weimar with a heavy heart and returned to England and the bar.   The die, I firmly believed, had been cast and there was no going back.

Chapter IV

◆

I AM PUT TO THE LAW AND REJECT IT

N the year 1832 I kept a diary, though why I chose that year
rather than others to do so is a mystery. Perhaps I thought
London life was going to be memorable, and that I must record
the glittering names that asked me to dine and wine, or more
likely I saw my majority approaching and the keeping of a diary
seemed a suitably solemn act. I know one thing – I wish I
hadn't, for the account that emerges is a miserable one, of which I am not
the least bit proud. I have kept other diaries since, in the same spasmodic
way that I kept that first, but none depresses me quite as much as that dreary
tabulating of indolence and extravagance. There is hardly an entry that
does me any credit, unless the telling of unpalatable truths is creditable, or
the open admission that I am wasting my life.

I hesitate to stand up on a post and crow about this, but will you not
agree that self-awareness in the young does somehow seem unusual ? I
didn't whine in that diary, only repeatedly upbraided myself for my bad
habits and gave way often enough to despair. It rather pleases me that I
knew good standards when I saw them and that I knew I was falling
hopelessly short by anybody's measurement. Complacency was one of the
few sins of which I was not guilty. Instead, an awful rage filled me that I
was so useless and passed my days in despicable pursuits which served only to
sicken me all the more. My unhappiness during those three years in London
spent play-acting at being a lawyer was far greater than any I had known
before or since. It is frightening to be so firm about it, as though happiness,
or the memory of it, is a tangible thing, but I feel quite certain that I am
right and my diary supports me. Thank God it came to an end and that I
have the comfort of knowing it did while I review it.

I expect you, who have followed this chronicle pretty carefully, will know what was the matter.   I was a fellow who needed to work, wasn't I, even when I appeared to do nothing but play.   I could not be happy idling about though I may have given every appearance to the contrary.   I might pass my days fooling about supposedly having a good time but when all was said and done I was not doing anything of the kind.   I saw around me, both in Cambridge and after, many a young lad who wanted only to prolong his pleasant, carefree, empty days but I was never one of them.   I was hungry for some more substantial nourishment than the kind of slops I filled myself with.   More than that – deception did not suit me and I was practising that art with a vengeance.   Do you think I ever had any intention of practising law ?   Of course I hadn't, no more than I had of becoming a mathematician. Studying law was a device to keep my mother quiet and put in time until something more congenial would turn up.   In my experience, anyone who conducts their life on such a faulty premise is making a mistake for which they will pay dearly.   Only consider – how often *do* things turn up to rescue us from our vacillation ?   Almost never.   If we choose to embark on a course of action which before we begin we find distasteful then no good will come of it.   I ought never to have agreed to study law, I ought not to have clutched at any straw to save me from Cambridge, I ought not to have deluded myself with the thought that there was no harm in it.   In going against all my own instincts I prescribed purgatory for myself.

Oh come, you say, surely the life of a young well-to-do lawyer was not so bad – did I really find it so horrible, was I truthfully so wretched, can I bring myself to stick to such strong terms ?   Well yes I can.   I hated it.   I was intensely miserable both in and out of working hours and quite distraught with my own uselessness.   I don't know if I can capture for you the exact quality of those years but I know I can feel it in my bones – with no difficulty at all I am once again in that room in the Hare Court, in the Middle Temple, where I studied under a certain William Taprell, standing at the tall lawyer's desk staring dully at some legal covenant, yawning my head off as I attempted to understand the jargon and looking for the first excuse to leave my post and go off on " business ".   The walk from my chambers in Essex Court to this place of work was one I made each morning with leaden footsteps, dreading the moment when I should be there, shut up in that close room with the fire spluttering and the air still save for the endless turning of pages and the low hum of lawyers' talk.   I wonder if the man who took over from me at Mr. Taprell's when I left thought it odd that the desk was full of drawings and caricatures ?   Still, you say, where is the hardship ?   Boredom, believe me, is the worst hardship of all – worse than any grinding physical labour or the lash of an overseer's whip.   Boredom is worse because it stunts the soul as well as the hardier body.   There is no trade quite so cold blooded as the lawyer's.   Legal terminology can reduce the most passionate action to dust – how often did I sit at my desk studying a suit brought against some man for

debauching a girl and find within a few lines that the wherebys and wherefores had robbed such an interesting idea of any fascination.   Mr. Taprell
had plenty of business, though most of it was of a drier nature even in the
first instance, and I found through usage that I too became so familiar with
the accepted phrases that they slipped into my everyday speech.   I saw that
within a few years I should become as doubting and sceptical and fussy as all
the other snivelling, cheating lawyers and I did not fancy the prospect at all.
What did Mr. Taprell make of me ?   I think I could hazard a fairly
accurate guess.   He probably laughed behind his sleeve at my arrogant ways,
for he saw how the profession would break me of them given time.   I am
sure he disliked me – I know I had an incurable habit at the time of thinking
everybody about me a fool.   It took me a long time to appreciate that older
people in the trade might know more than I.   I don't suppose I hid my
feelings – and he can't have liked my laziness and my habit of not turning up
pretty regularly.   It was only the occasional morning at first but then I grew
bolder and had a tendency not only to arrive late, if at all, but to depart at
frequent intervals during the day in the most tremendous haste with a sheaf

of papers under my arm as though I was off to consult a client on a matter of the greatest importance.   It can have deceived no one – I was not expert enough to be near clients but condemned instead to working my passage as a scribe – but nobody ever stopped me.   Perhaps they thought that given enough rope I would hang myself, or more likely they simply did not care. They left me to my own devices and I discovered ways to make the days tolerable enough.   I could see me spending eight months out of every twelve jogging through life like this – the vista stretched ahead endlessly.   It was enough to drive me to – exactly.

   In those days No. 60, Regents Quadrant was the place that most exactly represented for me my concept of hell.   It was where experienced gamblers met to continue their sad pastime and it was there that I was irresistibly drawn after my stupefying lawyer's day.   You see the reason – I needed excitement like a starving man needs food and where better to find it ?   It was a horrible excitement – I did not want to go, I loathed the company I found there, there was no fun to be had at all, only the familiar lurching of the stomach as I lost or won.   For once, my mother would have been right about " bad company " – it was bad, very bad, and almost all professional. Beside my regular visits to that place my Cambridge excursions were nothing, and were in any case quickly offset by the other more praiseworthy activities that I indulged in.   In London, I was a hanger-on when I was not at work – or, in the more elegant phrase of the time, " a gentleman lounger " – easy prey for any devilish sport.   I missed my Cambridge friends desperately and longed for that warm companionship that I had so lightly thrown over.   Sometimes I went back to visit the place and found the degree of hospitality with which I was received almost unbearable.   What, oh what, had I done ?   Would not any amount of agony over algebra have been worth such friendly arms round my neck, such eager happy voices in my ear, such a sense of belonging ?   When Fitzgerald came to visit me in turn I found it almost impossible to let him go and grew quite wretched as I sat and stared at the plate he had used and so forth – what a state his departure always left me in.   As I trailed round London trying to keep away from No. 60 you can be sure I put that question to myself a hundred times.   There was little to choose between algebra and the law but a great deal to prefer in Cambridge social life to London.

Now, when London seems to me the most friendly place in the world – when I can hardly walk down a street without meeting a friend – it is hard to believe the degree of loneliness I suffered.   It is a common enough complaint among people who come to live in this great capital and easy enough to understand.   The place is so big – it seems full of people all going about their business with absolute certainty – and the hardest thing of all is finding a beginning.   Remember, I had no real family in London – my parents were still in Devon – and I belonged to no clubs.   An entrée into any society worth having was therefore difficult.   My uncle Frank invited me to dinner – far too often as a matter of fact – but what did a young man almost of age want with stuffy, elderly dinners ?   I looked for pretty, perfumed notes from beautiful ladies inviting me to soirées but none came – indeed, once again I did not seem to know any ladies, and after Weimar the deprivation was cruel.   I often think these days when I turn down yet another summons to a ball or supper given by a lovely hostess that it is all a terrible waste when out there on the streets of London are hundreds of unattached eager young pups who would sell their souls for the scraps of paper I throw so carelessly into the fire.   As I walked aimlessly round the districts where there were theatres and cafés and clubs my only consolation was the conviction that one day I should be at the centre of all this life that attracted me so much.   I suppose it came to pass and I suppose for a long time I found it as exhilarating as I had hoped but now it seems worthless and I wish I could tell these young men out there not to fret for something that will not make them happy.

I would not like you to think I was entirely shut out from all jollification apart from gambling – far from it, for I went to the theatre often and in time frequented various low haunts with cronies who were stand-ins for my real Cambridge friends.   I think I saw Macready in almost everything worth seeing and heard Braham sing and dined and wined my fill.   As I look through that diary I think how crowded my days seem but I know they were not – I know there lies concealed beneath the apparent activity day after day spent lolling in Kensington Gardens or lying on my bed eating biscuits or just sleeping.   I was dying from inertia – I was in the great world but not of it – I buzzed around with all the other little bees doing nothing all day except mill about.   What made this condition worse was the certain knowledge that some of my contemporaries were already half way to being

important fellows and while I ambled about to no purpose they were furthering splendid careers.   Do you know that feeling – not quite of jealousy, though there is that tinging it, but more of awe and amazement ?

We who have not succeeded cannot bring ourselves to believe that so-and-so has not had an unfair advantage or that he has not cheated. We talk loudly of other men's " luck " when we know perfectly well that it was hard work and application and not " luck " that brought them into prominence. It is hard, as a young man, to be generous in our acknowledgement of another's success but I think I managed to conquer my envy and shame and enjoy their fame.

Charles Buller was just such an example of praiseworthy industry that left me gasping – oh poor Charles Buller, you will never know how impressed I was! Charles was only a little older than I but already he was a member of parliament and well on the way, we all thought, to the highest honours. How gloomily I compared the two of us – and since we both looked rather alike, being over six feet and both with broken noses, the comparison was one others made too. Charles was a Trinity man before I graced the College portals, but unlike me he worked hard and distinguished himself and was even President of the Union. He was a brilliant speaker – you see what anguish the comparison gave me – and one of the most charming men in the world. Well, he is dead, poor Charles, and the glorious promise of his youth barely fulfilled, and we, who were so far his inferiors, are left to remember and regret. I meant to give you a sprightly account of how I went down to canvass for Charles – what a mad, wild expedition it was and how I relished it – but it no longer seems fitting. I don't like to go over it when I can't bring those times back and the point is the same without me needing to labour it – I mean, Charles Buller and others near in age to me, were doing well and making worthwhile contributions to the world and I was nothing and nobody and likely to remain so. I spent my entire time thinking I should like to be famous and doing nothing about it but idle around reading novels. Unlike Charles, whatever was going on of national importance passed me by, though I remember walking one night to the House of Lords to see them come out after the second reading of the Reform Bill and forcing myself into solemn reflections on the perils facing our constitution. It was borne upon me that whereas at seventeen I had been well-informed for my age, I was approaching twenty-one knowing less than most men, and I was bitterly ashamed.

There was one event I was waiting for as eagerly as any man ever did and that was my coming of age on July 18th, 1832. Somehow I had all my hopes pinned on that day in the most ridiculous way. I lay awake imagining how I should employ my vast fortune – it is quite touching to remember my plans for that modest sum that in the event I hardly saw. I was going to be so wise and proper and judicious and get such satisfaction from apportioning one sum here for rent and another here for – ahem! – debts and then I would take a regular monthly income which I would never exceed. And of course I would have a little trip or two – wouldn't I just! My head was full of visions, half of which I thought would be realised when the magic day dawned and I was my own master. Does that not betray a terrifying conceit ? As though all the mistakes I had made and my whole disreputable way of living were the fault of not having my own money – as though I had been held back by the lack of it from virtuous pursuits. When the day for which I had been panting so long duly arrived what do you think was the first thing I did ? Drew £25 out of the bank of course and then went off immediately on a spree to Cowes. I spent a week there and then off I took myself to France for a real, long holiday.

It was fatal – but thank God I did it, or I might have mouldered forever in the Middle Temple, and when the crash came how could I have got out from that bog of a place ? In doing something so wrong I unwittingly did the very thing that was right and when I needed to be sure of what I wanted to do, I was. It was a divine deliverance taking myself to Paris the moment I came of age – I saw exactly what I should be doing and though I was still officially engaged with Taprell I did not think it would take me long to quit Hare Court and follow my natural inclinations – but without that long holiday at that precise time, without that foretaste of a life I loved, I don't think I should have got away. I had begun twice already – at Cambridge and in the Middle Temple – and backed out both times and I knew I couldn't go on doing that sort of thing, especially when to complicate matters I lost my fortune in the crash of an Indian bank only a year after I had come into it. The exact dates of my movements at this time, in spite of that diary at my elbow, are hazy in my memory – there seems a great running together of different strands which I can't distinguish so that I am unable to tell how I finally left the law and settled in Paris or when precisely this change took place or what everyone said or what I thought. But as I see it I spent most of 1833 – that fateful year in which I lost my fortune but found my feet, or so I like to think – in Paris, not quite making the break with London and the law but doing my best to hasten the rupture. Making plans a long way ahead has never been my style – I like to think about moving, I like to turn it over and over in my head, mulling the idea like wine, and then I pounce and hey presto it is all done and irreversible in five minutes. This is hard on those about me who receive only the briefest intimation of general upheaval and chaos but in those days I was more or less accountable only to myself and so this did not matter. At any rate, I never reached the stage so far as I know of announcing an official change of residence and the removal of traps and trappings from London to Paris – it was all very hole in the corner, dodging backwards and forwards and living in the most casual way possible. My mother became somewhat exasperated but bore up pretty well because she was encouraged by my enthusiasm for a new affair I was dabbling in – not that this same enterprise earned her entire approval but it was work of a kind and I seemed keen and was likely to do well and I suppose she had

become disheartened by my rejection of established professions and longed to
see me settled in something – anything.   Don't all mamas love that word
" settled " ?   Isn't it the most desirable of attainments, quite surpassing all
others in their fond eyes ?   She longed to think I was " quite settled " at
one and twenty and not bouncing about from one thing to another in a
disturbing way.   I have noticed the same tendency in myself with regard to
my daughters – though I repudiate entirely any suggestion that I want them
off my hands, nevertheless I do feel a mite anxious that they are not
" settled ".   I fight this tendency but it is there and it would be humbug to
deny it.   The odd thing was, that in my case I rather agreed with my
mother – I too wished to be " settled " and not in a state of permanent

suspense about my future.   I hardly dared hope, but I know I thought a
wonderful career might be opening up for me and I was excited at the
prospect.
   Well, I have teased you enough and made a great deal of very little.   What
was this amazing job I have hinted at ?   Why, nothing more impressive
than journalism – and now how you toss your head and look the other way,
for if novelists are of low standing journalists are totally discredited and ought
not to be let in a respectable household without a reference.   Let me say
that I understand your honourable standpoint, speaking as one who has
suffered the most vulgar abuse from that species, but nonetheless I hold my
head up high and say that a good journalist writing in a worthy newspaper or
magazine is fulfilling a role in our society that it would be foolish to condemn.

I don't mean the penny-a-liners with their tittle-tattle, but the serious correspondents who have our interests at heart and have things to tell us that we would do well to know, whether it be what our rulers are doing in parliament or where we can see some brilliant new work of art or the appalling conditions that some people labour in that we knew nothing about. Everybody loves news so why do we scorn those who bring it to us ? I never felt any embarrassment about being a journalist and I still don't – it seems a perfectly proper occupation to me, as prone to malpractice as any other profession but wholly admirable when it is well and honestly done. There I rest my defence.

The estimable organ in which I had invested my talents – and not only talents but wait a minute – was the *National Standard*, a literary journal launched at the beginning of 1833. Now if you are keeping your wits about you, you will recollect that at this happy juncture I was still a man of substance so that I had no need, as I did later, to sell anything I wrote in order to eat and drink. I was able to contribute reviews in the most earnest way possible and enjoy it and not worry about striking the right note and all that kind of thing – and most important of all I was far from hard pressed for time and so I could do my best without hurrying. That was my introduction to journalism which I rather think was important – I have a suspicion that if I had only started to write when earning money had become a desperate necessity that two things would have happened, both harmful. Firstly, I should not have been interested in little literary journals just starting off that didn't pay well, if at all, and therefore I should not have learned my craft under the best circumstances, which I did on the *National Standard* – I should have been aiming at the top end of the market and trying to impress and failing. Secondly, I might have found nobody interested in me and my ego would have suffered another crushing blow. As it was, since I was eager and had money, the *National Standard* was more than glad to have me as a contributor rather than more experienced writers asking high prices and beyond being flattered by the appearance of their material in print, and I was happy to oblige. Indeed, the fascination grew so quickly upon me that in a very short time I had become proprietor of the magazine and co-editor and a very big fish in a small pond or paper.

If you suspect, before I have told you anything at all, that I purchased my own paper in order to give myself a good show then you are perfectly right and I shan't deny it, but at the same time I see nothing wrong in this. I had been bitten deeply by the editorship bug and what better way to try my hand ? My interest in journals and magazines of all kinds had always been there – I knew and bought them all and had toyed for a long time with the idea of becoming somehow involved in them, either as a contributor – vain hope – or in the production, which interested me almost as much. Does this surprise you ? Then you don't know what an exciting business the putting together of a newspaper is. It does not just put itself through your letter box on its own – the print does not jump onto the page by itself and the pages do not cut themselves and bind themselves alone and the illustrations aren't done on each copy by the artist – the whole process is extremely complicated and skilful and I am always astonished to this day that it can happen at all and at such speed. I remember being taken by my friend William Maginn to the *Standard* in London one Wednesday night where he showed me the mysteries I have outlined above and quite fired my imagination to have a hand in it all. Maginn's familiarity with this process – he was considerably older than I – was part of his attraction for me – I was impressed that he had helped to found *Fraser's Magazine* to which I had on occasions surreptitiously sent articles which had speedily been rejected – I own to adopting Maginn as an idol for a while and to hanging on his words and to wanting his approval. He seemed to me so extraordinarily intelligent and witty and I was more than ready to condone his drinking habits and his taste in women and all the other vices that made him an unsuitable companion for a naïve young fellow. What more natural than that Maginn should be paid to help me with my newspaper ? I had the enthusiasm and the money and he had the experience – it was a perfect relationship.

It was the *National Standard* that held me to London while my heart longed to be in Paris. I felt that if I could devise a way of somehow being in Paris and yet still produce the paper then I should be truly happy, and to that end I convinced myself that what the paper needed to lift it above the others was a Paris correspondent, for which post I applied and was pleased to accept myself. Now I had it both ways. The *National Standard* was published each Saturday morning by Thomas Hurst of 65, St. Paul's Churchyard, sometimes supervised by the Paris Correspondent and sometimes not, but always packed with that worthy person's contributions. I was quite sure that within a short time it would knock *Fraser's* into a cocked hat and then shouldn't I be run off my feet turning down famous writers and arranging for bigger premises and so forth ? There were a great many magazines around at that time – still are, I suppose – but there seemed no reason why they should not all flourish if there was enough capital. Ah – that was the sticking point. I know now, with the editorship of a powerful magazine behind me, how slim my hopes in 1833 were bound to be. The truth was, I did not understand about capital. Capital is what does for young 'uns who mostly don't have it and don't understand its importance and think flair and taste and energy can make up for it, which they decidedly cannot. To start a magazine you need enough capital to continue to produce it without earning a penny – mark that, not a penny – for six months at least. Do you reel back in shock and disbelief? Then don't start a magazine. The costs are enormous, no matter what the paper is sold for. You need a mass circulation to be able to sell it cheaply and as you don't have that to start with, and wouldn't be assured of it if you did, you need to draw on capital to keep the price low and pay your printer's bills and your paper costs and your staff's salaries.

I did not know about all this though I daresay Maginn and others tried to enlighten me, but since I found the employment delightful I don't suppose it would have made much difference until facts spoke for themselves, which they began to do rather quickly and frighteningly with the crash of that Indian bank. I saw my whole existence in peril and could hardly bear it – no sooner had I found an occupation I thought both congenial and respectable and likely to earn me money than I was cast out into the wilderness again. Could the *National Standard* survive on its own merits and pay its Paris Correspondent ? No, it could not, so what was that worthy gentleman going to do ? And that was where being in Paris made all the difference – all I cared about was staying there and so the die was cast (yes – again). I would stay – I would give up the law and scratch around for a way of keeping body and soul together. I resolved to become a humble student of art and to live among those who thought nothing of poverty and to forget for the time being my journalistic aspirations. I tried to see it as a silver lining to a black cloud – the becoming an art student I mean. Hadn't I always wanted to study art ? Now that I was thrown into it by the failure of my other enterprise and my new penury ought I not to be glad ? I don't know that I either put or answered these questions very clearly but I know I was not too depressed or miserable and that I made a pretty good job of facing up to the sudden change in my expectations.

When one pattern in our life breaks down it takes some time for another to emerge, especially if the tendency is towards indistinct patterns in the first place. Are you one of those who arise, every day, at seven-thirty, breakfast at eight, travel to work at nine, break for lunch at one, travel home at five, eat dinner at six and retire at eleven-thirty, every day, with unfailing regularity ? Would it cause you the deepest unease if you did not sit in the same seat on your way to work and at the same table in the same restaurant where, every day, you eat your excellent lunch ? I suppose, if you are that sort of person, you have your holidays for next year already booked and tickets for the Christmas pantomime in six months' time already taken and your children's schools arranged while they are still crawling. I know there are millions like you and I ought not to doubt that such people exist simply because to me a regime like that is abhorrent. I see it has merits to live by the clock and I am sure it is healthy and wise, but I should hate it. The most I have ever been able to pin myself down to is having a home and going to it every night when I am near it. I don't like sameness and that is a fact — I like infinite variety even when it proves wearing and leaves me exhausted. Now, I am not sure whether my temperament has led to my disorderly way of living, even as a family man, or whether events have made my life hectic and therefore I have adapted to this pace. I know that even as long ago as 1834 in Paris I watched with a sort of horror a certain monotony enter my life and I immediately resented this imposition that had somehow been put upon me. The old erratic system of dashing backwards and forwards between Paris and London with all sorts of irons in interesting fires gave way bit by bit to a settled period when I was living with my grandmother and going to the Atelier as faithfully as any clerk.

Let me say straight away that my grandmother and I were always incompatible so it ought to have been clear from the start that for me to consider living with her was sheer folly, but that was the first lesson I had to learn after I lost my money – in short, beggars can't be choosers. Well, I was no beggar but I had very little money and my grandmother was exceedingly wealthy and willing to provide a home for me in Paris and I would have been a fool to turn such a convenient arrangement down. Except, like all such arrangements based on convenience and nothing else, it did not work. Living with relatives never does, no matter whether you are host or guest. I have lived with my grandmother and hated it, with my parents and been crucified with boredom, with my mother-in-law who almost drove me to suicide, and with my cousin who enraged me. I have come to the conclusion that a bed under a railway arch is preferable to luxury in a relative's house. It is something to do with the degree of politeness required conflicting quite impossibly with the degree of familiarity assumed. You can't quarrel with relatives comfortably when you are tied to them by blood for the rest of your life, though I have had a good try at doing so – they almost always turn up again even when you have all said unspeakable things to each other and it becomes very tiresome. I have tried to take a strong line with unpleasant relatives in later years but as a young man I thought they had simply to be endured. My grandmother would have tried the patience of a saint. She was my mother's mother, who had married again after my mother's birth and returned from Calcutta a wealthy widow suddenly in search of family affection. Her name was Butler, Harriet Butler, and she was as cantankerous a creature as you are ever likely to meet though in later years, when I didn't have to live with her, I grew quite fond of the old madam. Even when I was completely under her thumb I could not but admire her absolute determination to have her own way no matter what the consequences. If you lived with Harriet Butler, you lived her way and there was no argument about it. This tyranny extended not only to meal times and what we ate during them but to who sat on which chair and whether the windows would or would not be opened and so on, but also, and rather alarmingly, to the conduct of our own personal lives. My grandmother thought she had the right to know every single thing I did because she was providing me with food and lodging – and not only what I did but what I thought. I would have been quite happy to voice my thoughts if only she had not also required that they should agree exactly with her own and any discussion was understood to be out of the question. We clashed time and again over absurd

things with me mostly swallowing my anger out of respect for her age and
status, and my grandmother therefore considering that she had won every
round.   Since at the beginning of our stay in Paris we lived in a boarding
house in the rue Louis le Grand you can imagine the entertainment we
provided – my grandmother didn't care in the least if anyone else was
listening – an audience only encouraged her to be outrageous while it
inhibited and constrained her poor grandson.   I writhed under the stripes of
her satire and cringed at the public expression of her wrath.   Don't think
that I went on putting up with this humiliating state of affairs simply because
of the money – no, it was because I thought I discerned underneath all the
bluster a very real warmth and kindness which she for some reason could not
show, and I think I was right.   My grandmother was a good lady when all
was said and done, but she did not suffer fools gladly and as she had a lot
about her I suppose she mistook me for another.

We moved eventually into pretty furnished rooms in the rue de Provence
where I endeavoured to assert myself a little more strongly, and to absent
myself as often as possible for meals.   The good old *National Standard* had
gone the way of all flesh and I was now the fully fledged art student I had
longed to be when I had the choice.   Lack of choice was beginning to
dictate my life – I had no choice but to live with my grandmother if I wanted
to use my own small pittance for other things, as I did, and no choice but to
go through the three years' apprenticeship to be an artist if I wanted to be
able to hold my head up and show I was doing something, as I did.   At least
I was not in London – at least I was released from that servitude and not
before time.   But yet again I was on a treadmill of my own making which

I was rapidly beginning to think I did not like much more than the others. The difference was, this time I had no choice. I had to succeed as an artist or find another way to make a living. You know my history — what was I fitted for but the life of a gentleman, the very life now closed to me ? I don't ask for your sympathy — I know I was still extremely fortunate and that I had never known any hardship and so forth — but only for your understanding. I am not even saying that it was a bad thing that I lost my money — it may well have been the best thing that ever happened to me — but I want you to appreciate the shock that an abrupt change in fortune brings. Though I insist I took the bad news well, I was nevertheless shocked and even excited and elated — does that seem nonsense ? Well, it was true. The depression about my financial condition was strangely slow to grip me. I find it is the same with most tragedies, of whatever kind, in my life — I take them well and everyone remarks on my cheerfulness and I appear philosophical to an admirable degree, and then several weeks or months later and I begin to shake and groan with anguish long after everyone else has forgotten the matter. I fall into the deepest delayed despair which is all the more violent for being pent up, and it is then, when it is least likely to be available, that I need consolation. Thus it was with the loss of my inheritance and you shall see what resulted in the next chapter.

Chapter V

---◆---

MY INHERITANCE IS LOST
BUT A CAREER FOUND

THERE I was, dizzy with the delights of painting in Paris and quite convinced for a short while that I had found my true self, but how much good was it doing me ? We had all been convinced for many years that I was a genius at art but this talent had never before been put to any test nor measured against others. Well, I quickly discovered that it was as I had suspected – I was a much better drawer than a painter, which was the reverse of the average student. My sense of colour was not good enough, though I rather jibbed at this realisation just as I never like to admit that my narrative flow in novels is not as good as it should be, though I know this perfectly well. With a pencil I was moderately accomplished but with a paintbrush I did not make much impression. Very soon, I had enough canvases to roast an ox by and grew disheartened at my lack of progress. I would spend hours copying my favourite paintings in the Louvre and then begin to wonder what was the use – I was only ever going to be second-rate. I couldn't see myself ever selling any of my efforts nor completing the three-year apprenticeship, though I kept this quiet. I could not help but contrast my lack of enthusiasm for what I accomplished in the way of painting with my eagerness for even the most puny of literary efforts and I began to ask myself – though never directly or in any formal way – whether I was wise to continue along my chosen path. I grew disgusted with my own artistic endeavours and for a whole month, after a year of trying, I lay on my bed and read novels as a protest.

You are not the only one who recognises the danger signal – I did too. Hadn't I always sunk into apathy at the first obstacle ? Didn't I know that a state of sullen despair would quickly follow if this listlessness was allowed to continue ? Nobody was going to stop it except me – my master at the

65

Atelier was about as interested as my tutor in Cambridge or Mr. Taprell in Hare Court.   If I wasn't going to get on with my art or my maths or my law then they saw it as no concern of theirs and quite right too – I had to make my own decisions and mistakes.   I prayed to God to make my fingers do what they did not seem able to do of their own free will, and meanwhile I was off again casting about for some solution to this mess I had got myself into.   Since I had no money to speak of, I must find work if I was to leave the life of art student or else I had to go home and throw myself on the mercy of my long-suffering mother, which I did not in the least want to do.   I tried very hard to get myself appointed as foreign correspondent in Constantinople for the *Morning Chronicle*, but though I did my damnedest the thing did not come off.   Heaven knows what good I thought I would do there but the very name Constantinople seemed to solve all my problems.   Flight is always attractive when things go wrong, especially a flight that is paid for and has a purpose.   I saw that job not only as a year's employment but as the probable basis for a book with illustrations – a Picture Annual that London publishers would fight over.   There you have in all its touching pathos my first avowed ambition, one that was to grow into an obsession within the next few years. Don't you find it curious that I saw myself as a travel-writer rather than a novelist, that my fantasies revolved round illustrated descriptions of places rather than an imaginative work about people ?   It was the art connection you see – I still saw my way with pictures and not words, for all my hankering after journalism.   I am glad that, in the end, I satisfied that first ambition several times over even if it will not be those books I will be remembered for, if I am remembered at all.

It proved impossible, while this kind of struggle was going on within me, to continue to live with my grandmother.   How could a fellow hang about all day under her eagle eye ?   The lectures became frightful as I gave more and more evidence of my disheartened state until at last I could stand no more of this old lady's criticism – did she not see I criticised myself and was not at all proud of my indolence ? – and resolved to give up my comfortable quarters and take myself off to a garret like my companions.   The minute I mentioned this possibility my grandmother began to try to placate me but I was adamant – going off to a garret and independent poverty suited my mood exactly.   I have no doubt that she thought my threat was idle in any case and was quite hurt and surprised when I carried it out and moved my few belongings to the rue des Beaux Arts where in truth I was always in dire straits for money.   It only needed a little thing like a doctor's visit to use up all my available cash and plunge me into debt until the next dividend day – for you see I still had a tiny income, not more than £100 a year. Once I had made the break I was much happier, there was no denying, and began to look about me for literary or artistic employment.

I was lucky in that I knew quite a variety of people in Paris, both French and English, and with a word dropped here and a word dropped there I was able to put myself in the way of a few small commissions.   I did some translating and a few lithographs and that kind of thing – all hand-to-mouth as a style of living but then I did not care about that for the time being.

That was rather the point – I was by this time twenty-four and you know what happens to fellows of that age in the normal run of things – they get big ideas, don't they, ideas about things they want and can't afford, ideas that might or might not include matrimonial plans of a kind that prove deuced expensive.   It was only a matter of time before the few francs I was earning would no longer be sufficient and I should need a more regular and larger addition to my tiny income.   Should I fall in love and wish to marry my poverty would be an insuperable stumbling block – unless my future beloved should be an heiress and that was too much to hope.   In fact, the girl I set my heart on, the poor darling, proved to be almost as penniless as myself and it was plain from the beginning of my infatuation that were it to come to anything I must shift for us both with all speed or languish forever a bachelor.

I met Isabella Shawe in Paris towards the end of the summer of 1835, at that time I have told you about at some length, that is when my fortunes and career were at their lowest ebb.   I can remember first seeing Isabella but not the circumstances of that meeting so you are spared the ins and outs. Of course, it was love at first sight as you would imagine in the case of such a romantic devil as myself, and I went off at once into transports of delight, unable to eat or sleep and all the usual symptoms.   I am not being cynical or

sarcastic when I say I loved knowing I was in love – I found it enjoyable
not to want to eat but only to smoke a little and lie on my bed daydreaming.
There was no agony in my attachment except that I could not wait to be
married and, as you are aware, wait I must.   There was a degree of certainty
in my choice all the same which supported and succoured me and which I
find, looking back, rather surprising – my confidence, I mean, that it would
all come out alright and that Isabella was the girl for me.   You would have
expected a period of doubt would you not ?   After all, discounting my
admiration for the Weimar ladies, I had no experience of women or romantic
attachments and ought by rights to have entertained at least a few follies
before finding a mate – but it was Isabella straight away and never any
hankering after anyone else before then.   If that touches your heartstrings,
I meant it to.   It spoils the story, but I intend to confess before I even have
us married that our happiness was shortlived and therefore I must extract for
you every drop of feeling.   I haven't three score years of married bliss to
look back on and take you over and point out the highlights, so I am forced
to bathe our few years together in the strongest light and derive what pleasure
I can from the little we had.   I regret the lack of a happy, steady, long
married life more than anything else in my whole existence – I would not
have swopped domestic felicity for all the money or all the literary success
in the world.   A man needs a wife to come home to at night – or this man
does, and has felt the want of it.

Isn't it splendid that in 1835 I had no inkling of these gloomy thoughts
I am having in 1862 – and haven't I somewhere in these pages said exactly
the opposite – I mean about wanting to know what lies ahead ?   How awful
it would have been to have had second sight then when my head was full of
plans for ten children and a town house and a country house and long
evenings by the fire.   As it was, I was blissfully happy plotting and scheming
to get married – which included finding work that would support such an
increase in my household – the thing was impossible otherwise.   My
enthusiasm was, I rather fear, a terrifying business and may have scared my
poor little Isabella half out of her wits for what a torrent of words I poured
out at her, never stopping to hear her opinion because I assumed it coincided
so precisely with my own.   I daresay she was astonished at the rate I travelled
at, talking so freely of children before we were even married, and of being
married shortly after we had said hullo.   I wanted everything to move along
at the most rapid rate imaginable and it only now occurs to me that my poor
love might have liked a longer and more gentle period of courtship.   Oh
how impetuous I was, rushing headlong into such a serious business, never
pausing to consider what damage I might do to more tender spirits than mine.
Did I stampede and exhaust my beloved? Did I drag her along panting to the
altar when I ought to have been offering her my arm and ambling along
sedately ?   Did I make her heart thud and head roar with the speed of my

proposal ? I believe I did all those things, and I believe too that I may have paid a greater penalty than is fair.

No more riddles: I met Isabella in the middle of 1835 and I married her a year later, which was six months longer than I had intended. The delay was not really due to the finding of employment – that fell into my lap very satisfactorily at the right time – but to the evil machinations of my mother-in-law, may the devil take her soul. Well, I smiled when I wrote that silly, melodramatic line and of course like a good Christian I would not wish eternal damnation on anyone, but all the same I am afraid there is some truth in the sentiment therein expressed. Mrs. Shawe is without doubt a vicious woman and nobody knows it better than I do. She dominated her five children in the most shameless way, especially the girls, until none of them knew what it was to have a mind of their own. I ought to have detected her cruelty at once but I did not – she simply seemed a rather strict, strait-laced widow when I first visited her in a boarding house in Paris where she and her children had lived on the small Indian army pension that was her only income since the death of her husband. The boarding houses of Paris are full of such dragons, all cleverly eking out a miserable pittance in the most marvellous way and meanwhile keeping their eyes open for the main chance. Mrs. Shawe may have thought she was on to a good thing when I first made an appearance in her daughter's life but since I never tried to hide anything she was soon disillusioned and from that moment on did all she could to break off any match. I ought, at this distance of time and with my experience of life, to be able to forgive her but do you know I can't ? Yet I appreciate her anxiety over the financial aspect for I know that when a rumour reached me in America that one of my own daughters was bent on marrying a penniless, invalid curate I was half mad with rage and wrote home the most violent letter forbidding any such match. Of course she was right to be concerned about the welfare of her daughter and of course she would have been perfectly correct in insisting on some security first – which I would have been happy to show her – but I see no justification for poisoning my loved one's mind against me nor for making her utterly wretched about leaving her mother for me. If all this had been founded on the deepest maternal love it would have been excusable, but I think that so-called love was revealed for what it was when tragedy hit us – that love was hollow, that love was self-interest, that love was a mockery and not worthy of the name.

I am always doing these things back to front – all the difficulties of our engagement, all the horrors of awkward relatives, and yet not a word describing Isabella herself. The truth is, my wife is not easy to describe, or rather the quality which drew me to her defies description. I can tell you what she looked like – or better still enclose one of my own drawings – but I am miserably aware that my wife looks very much like many other young ladies, that there is nothing startling about her when you take her feature by feature and that you will think it idle boasting for me to swear that she was perfectly beautiful in my eyes.   Nor was it simply the case of beauty being in the eye of the beholder – Isabella *was* beautiful, though I don't deny it was that kind of beauty which is not usual and which I have always singled out wherever I have gone.   If this beauty is elusive it is because it depends on a certain sympathy of the spirit between the individual who possesses it and he who admires it – and I am no good when it comes to clothing sentimental thoughts in fine words.   Let me try again – with her eyes shut Isabella would not have been beautiful for it was through her eyes that her beauty shone, it was from them that her purity and tenderness and sweetness shone forth and captivated me.   She had about her that goodness and quiet dignity that immediately attracts me to women, and with it a spark of feeling that belied the gentle exterior.   I don't go for statuesque damsels with marble complexions who flash and glitter in company, but for the modest maidens who hardly have the impertinence to think themselves pretty

and would no more attract attention than swear. If the lady I am struggling to describe sounds a goose then I can only say she is not — Isabella and all those sisters of hers in the world are perfectly intelligent with views of their own but they do not exhibit their cleverness for all to see. Their eyes are more frequently cast down than levelled challengingly at others and the extent of their knowledge is not something they parade. There is nothing insipid or colourless about them because they do not at once impose themselves on others, nor are they lacking because they choose to listen rather than to speak. Critics called Amelia in *Vanity Fair* too good for words and therefore dull and irritating, but if that is the case the fault was mine and a descriptive one. Have you ever tried to excite people by describing perfect goodness ? It doesn't work — I notice Dickens in this respect is no better than I — goodness won't get itself pinned down on paper without overtones of sickliness whereas evil, or at least waywardness, makes an imprint straight away. The very qualities we try to define are those that shun definition and we end with a great many superlatives adding up to nothing much. People won't accept that degree of saintliness without resentment, or a sneer of disbelief, and even when they do they are liable to be bored by a character so blameless.

Isabella, then, was like Amelia in many respects and I don't apologise for trying to describe her. I will add that she was pale and thin and delicate-looking with beautiful red hair, large eyes and the sweetest smile in the world. She was of a timid disposition to those who did not know her, though perfectly capable of boisterous good humour with those who did. She did not offer her opinions easily but had plenty when she was drawn. I suppose I was attracted not only by her appearance and behaviour, which coincided exactly with my idea of how a lady should be, but by her evident admiration for me. Oh heady stuff! Would I have survived if she had appeared to scorn me ? I don't think so. Would I have been interested if she had appeared uninterested ? Hardly. I remember she played the piano the first evening I met her in that frightful boarding house, and when she got up from her seat and turned blushing to her small applauding audience and her eyes caught mine — I remember that though I was admiring her I had the distinct impression that she was admiring me, though not in any spirit of coquetry, which was quite alien to her. Is there a man who does not love to be admired every bit as much as a woman ? I hope I talked sensibly — I know I thought my wit prodigious that evening and every sentence a gem of sarcastic genius. Isabella listened so humbly and patiently to everything I ever said, gazing adoringly up at me until I swelled with pride. Her whole aim seemed to be to please me and make me happy and I think that remained her object all the time we were together. But she was not spineless or docile in an uncritical way — though it cost her a great deal of effort and distress she would and did uphold her own values where they clashed with mine, though in truth these clashes were insignificant, hardly worthy of the name.   She would hesitate and her smile would fade and the colour come into her cheeks and then in a quavering voice she would tell me what she thought was right or wrong about something I had said or done – it was a pretty picture and I was not above provoking what for her came under the heading of anger.   Anger ?   I don't think she will ever know what that is till the day she dies – anger, rage, bitterness, hatred – all those horrid things were unknown to my Isabella.   Her disposition was angelic and I was quite convinced I was the luckiest man in the world.

Except in my future mother-in-law, who was an exact counterpart to her daughter.   All through the spring of 1836 I strove to bring her to agree to a marriage between Isabella and I, but in vain.   She was obdurate – I was not suitable.   With what I thought of as exemplary patience I told her of the new paper I was now involved in but she moved not a jot in her opinions, though I emphasised again and again how I was to have a regular income of £400 and the venture was a guaranteed success.   I meant it too – it was no moonshine story to hoodwink her.   The paper in question was to be called the *Constitutional and Public Ledger*, launched by a small joint-stock company with my stepfather, Major Carmichael-Smyth, as Chairman.   I was to be the Paris Correspondent writing about art or politics or anything that took my fancy.   Laman Blanchard was to be Editor and Douglas Jerrold Dramatic Critic and all sorts of prominent individuals pledged their support. Do you blame me for being excited ?   Wouldn't you agree I could not have a better basis for married life ?   I sense some hesitation – you are inclined to see my mother-in-law's point of view and point out all kinds of clever objections – the paper had not yet started, it was not yet a success, I had not yet been paid so much as a farthing so why not wait ?   Confound you – people in love cannot wait.   Do you know what you are asking of a hot-blooded young man who has already been eating his heart out for six months ? It is inhuman – my mother-in-law was inhuman – you are inhuman.   That said, I now feel all the qualms I never felt then.   Oh yes, it was dreadfully perilous and really ought not have been allowed and I really don't know why my parents did not also forbid it unless it was because they knew what it was to have first love thwarted.   I was never so grateful in my life as I was then for their blessing.   It seems such a wonderfully generous thing to have done – to have told their only, rather unstable son to go ahead and marry the girl of his choice without raising a single objection.   I thank them for it from the bottom of my heart.

But back to that she-dragon, Mrs. Shawe.   It was unfortunate that the setting up of the new paper involved me in a great many trips to London and that I was therefore away from Isabella and her mother had her at her mercy.   Though I wrote daily what were words on paper measured against the vitriol Mrs. Shawe poured into my beloved's ears ?   All day that fiend harangued her on the wickedness of considering marriage with me until she quite wore Isabella down and threw her into such a state of nerves that her health threatened to give way. I was not very understanding — in fact, rather the reverse, growing irritable at the lack of letters from my girl and not asking myself the reason why they were not forthcoming. How could

she write what she felt in her heart when her mother watched her and tried to possess her ? Her notes — they really could not be flattered by the title letters — were stilted and short — not more than half a page at a time and that composed of mere pleasantries, which might have been written to anyone. Do you know, I have always been cursed with reluctant correspondents among my lady friends ? You won't find a single letter that could be called a love letter among my belongings when I go, and yet how I have poured my heart out on occasions — what passionate epistles I leave behind me ! I wonder if a certain person has certain warm letters of mine wrapped up in a bundle and tied with blue ribbon — letters full of the most tender sentiments in which my heart was revealed ? I don't mean my wife either, though she may have kept those first innocent letters and has them secreted some- where. I don't want to see them again, or those others to that other person, though I don't think I should mind if you or anyone else read them.   They are too painful for me to see again – I should blub as soon as look at them – but I daresay you would find them interesting.   They were honestly written and I meant every word and I am only sorry that I never received any to match them from my wife or from J – from somebody else.

Well, I scolded my puss and told her she had nothing to do all day so why could she not write to me properly ?   By properly I really meant improperly – I wanted her to shower me with a thousand paper kisses, as I did her, and confide in me her pillow thoughts, as I did, and yearn for a certain event openly and with desperate intensity, as I did.   I might as well have wanted the moon.   I had her health and the weather and how her mama protested I was very cruel to want to separate them.   It was very tedious replying to this kind of thing and I suppose I became bad tempered on occasions and looked for a little spunk, and then I had to apologise when my complaints met with tears.   If my Trot and I had been parted for several years – suppose I had gone to India and been half the world away – I do not know how our love could have survived.   It is foolish to say that true love can survive anything – I don't believe it can, not at the beginning before it has been cemented by the marital bond.   I am sure Isabella would have been worn away by her mother as water wears down a stone even if it took as long a time – nor did she have the resilience to withstand this kind of persistent encroachment of her feelings.   I have always felt that her mother's forceful-ness was the start of her trouble – it caused her such unhappiness the damage may have been permanent, but then I suppose I was as much to blame with my lack of sympathy.   What a curse it is when life is not simple.

Isabella's little red-polled ghost pursued me everywhere I went in London throughout the newspaper negotiations, making me thoroughly miserable. I became so utterly love-sick that I resolved to marry whether the paper came out or not – we could live in London with my parents who had just settled in Albion St. and trust to selling illustrations and to Providence.   I really believed that if I had to be without my wife much longer I should go mad and rush to Paris and drag her away from her mother by her beautiful hair.   In the event, it almost came to that.   To my horror – and that, for once, is an exact use of that phrase – a letter came during the worst of my depression in which Isabella seemed to want to withdraw from our engage-ment.   She accused me of cruelty in wanting to separate her from her dear mama – as if I intended any separation apart from the bedroom and surely that was reasonable even if it might be thought coarse of me to be so blunt. I almost died with rage and disappointment and absolutely would not accept such a cruel pronouncement – if she was going to leave me she must tell me with her own lips and I did not see how she could.   What had I done or said to bring about this change ?   Nothing that I knew of – it was all her mother's doing and I had no intention of standing by and having my life ruined.   I remember with what violence I sat down to write on receipt of this calami-tous news — I could hardly bear to hold the pen or force my thoughts into sufficient order and decorum to write them down. I told her that if I had done or said anything wrong I did not know it and that I prayed every day for help in quelling any improper desires which might have disgusted her.

If my fault was passion, I considered hers a too great a care for what other people thought and I knew which I preferred. That kind of almost ungovernable emotion I experienced then comes rarely to me — only three or four times do I recollect being virtually demented, siezed by feelings so powerful that my mind and body become a turmoil and I don't see how I can live until the next day. You may have gone through your life without ever feeling this madness and if so you are lucky — it marks a man for all time. I feel I can trace in the lines of my face when I look in the glass these unforgettable incidents in my history — something happens to the very geography of the features during these bouts that changes them forever.

Lines appear while I grimace with pain that never go away again, deep clefts in the skin that are like valleys of unhappiness, always there afterwards however hard I grin.

My eloquence must have been greater than I thought, though how my strangled cries could impress anyone I don't know, for when I returned post-haste to Paris – as I was bound to – and insisted on seeing Isabella it was to find her already repentant of the step her mother had forced her to take. It was a time for resolution and strength and I surprised myself by bringing forth both.   In short – and I don't wish to drag over any more of the ugliness that preceded it – we were married on August 20th, 1836 – William Makepeace Thackeray aged twenty-five to Isabella Gethin Creagh Shawe aged eighteen with the consent of her mother.   Mark that last line – with the consent of her mother.   You will naturally wish to know how I persuaded Mrs. Shawe to give way but I can't help you for I don't rightly remember.   I know I felt inspired and that anger and passion lent force to my arguments but I don't know what I said.   Her consent was vital for Isabella was a minor and she must have known she held this trump card.   I expect she would tell you that I threatened to elope with her daughter and I may well have done but she ought to have realised I was incapable of dishonouring the girl I loved.   She may say, for all I know, that I had got Isabella's feelings to such a pitch that she was forced to give in for fear of her life – quite right – I am sure Isabella could have died if her love had been thwarted.   She – Mrs. Shawe – never let me forget the favour she had done me.   Later, when everything turned out so tragically, she was there with her ugly mouth shouting in the wings to tell me that she had told me so, that she knew this would happen, and so forth.   She does not realise that even if it were true – and God forbid – I do not regret our marriage then.

We were married in the house of the British Ambassador in Paris with only three people present and none of my family.   There was no fanfare of trumpets nor a stately procession of bridesmaids nor crowds of elegant well-wishers – it was a quiet, modest ceremony and I suppose it may have seemed a little pathetic.   Sometimes I have been passing a small church somewhere and seen just such a couple as Isabella and I made coming out with only a few rather awkward looking companions and the charm of it has almost engulfed me in tears.   I can't help thinking when I see young couples like that almost on their own what an awesome thing marriage is, and how the wonder of it is obscured by pomp and ceremony just as a beautiful flower is hidden in a mass of wrappings.   And do you know it is the same with that other tremendous occasion – it is the same with funerals if you will forgive me bringing that up at such a sentimental point.   How often have I stood on the edge of a hastily dug grave with a friend or two while a rough wooden coffin is lowered into the ground and been overcome by the emotion it stirs in me, and yet how often, standing among crowds in deepest most splendid

mourning with black horses tossing their magnificent purple plumes in the background and a gold casket being lowered down the same way – how often I have felt that emotion diminished. Simplicity ought to be the keynote if the feeling is to be kept – and I have done preaching.

At last, among all this prattle, I have told you something worth telling, for the love of a man for a woman is always worth telling. I was the happiest man in the whole world as I drove off with my wife – my wife! – after our wedding. I didn't need coins thrown at us, or rice, or ribbons tied to the carriage – my happiness was decoration enough. And Isabella ? Oh, she was happy too, but more tremulous and even tearful and not so absolutely confident, but I had enough of that commodity for both of us. What a marvellous, altogether wonderful thing youth is.

Chapter VI

———◆———

A CHAPTER OF DOMESTIC BLISS
IN STRAINED CIRCUMSTANCES

INTEND this to be a pretty chapter before all the darkness that must follow it, but I at once find myself in a common predicament, which is the impossibility of successfully describing bliss. Happiness I might have a stab at, but bliss is beyond the reach of the pen. If I floundered and struggled and was desperately embarrassed trying to delineate goodness and was emphatic in the belief that it could not be done, then how much more despairing must I be faced with the prospect of attempting to convey that delicious atmosphere of my early married life ? I shall fail, I know I shall, but do you know what consoles and gives me courage ? Why, knowing that I have it to describe, that is what, for don't you see how unbearable it would be to hark back to a time that was never as perfect as I now make out. There is nothing worse than that whining self-pity for something that you know in your heart of hearts was not what you are now cracking it up to be. It gives me such joy to remember how happy Isabella and I were in our rented apartment in the rue Neuve St. Augustin – nobody can take it away from me or spoil the memory of it with grudging doubts as to the authenticity of the picture. We were blissfully happy – that is enough.

It is enough – it ought to be enough – but on the other hand those kind of statements mean nothing. I am expecting too much of your imagination to give you an address and say now you can see it all. You can't, and I shouldn't be able to either. Let me give you certain sounds, certain tastes, certain tableaux and see if you can then begin to piece together for yourself the whole picture. (Nobody will be able to accuse me any longer of being an old cynic only interested in writing about the horrid things in life after this noble effort.) First, the noise of an organ-grinder playing quavering tunes that stop and start rather abruptly and never seem to turn into any recognisable melody, or perhaps it was just that I fell asleep again after these tunes woke me.   I don't think the organ-grinder positioned himself deliberately under our window but he always seemed to choose that place and gave us with the greatest regularity our morning serenade.   Then the carts trundling past – it was a noisy thoroughfare you see – each with a different sound to its wheels.   Sometimes I would almost imagine we were ourselves on some delightful journey, such was the feeling of motion that the passage of the carts gave me.   And as to smells – we seemed near all the most delicious patisseries in Paris, though in fact we were not.   Nobody stays in Paris, it seems to me, without inhaling first thing in the morning that warm aroma of croissants and bread baking in every second building in the place – I tell you it was that message to my stomach that finally hauled me into the land of the living.   Then we would sit in a dishevelled state at the open window with a table between us on which we had the breakfast just sent in and there would be a good deal of shy smiling on one side and rather more boastful grinning on the other and hours and hours would pass in this disgraceful fashion.

It puzzles me a little to think what we did that made the hours so long and yet the days so short.   I know we spent eleven out of every twenty-four hours in bed and that I grew fat.   I, of course, was working, supposedly writing and drawing for dear life, but what was my little wife doing ?   I don't know – our housekeeping was a sketchy business which can't have occupied much of Isabella's time but then I didn't require it to – I was quite happy if she brushed her hair half the day and played the piano the other half. She did play the piano a great deal and sang, both perfectly charmingly and entirely for her own amusement.   When I try to picture our sitting-room I find the scene full of that piano and hardly anything else, except a rather fine clock that springs to mind and an old battered sofa where I would loll smoking a cigar and enjoying the impromptu concertos.   Not even the faintest twinges of uneasiness troubled me as to the fittingness of my wife so obviously playing at being married – I did not pause to consider whether perhaps I ought to take her education in hand and open her mind to other pursuits apart from hair-brushing and piano-playing.   Why didn't I try to share my own pleasures with her – in art and reading I mean ?   I don't know – it was not that I thought her too stupid but rather that since she did not have any interest or knowledge in these things in the first place it never occurred to me to involve her in what I was doing.   I suppose I did, in this way, treat her like a child and wanted only to see her amusing herself.   It was self-indulgent of me and unwise and I wish I had behaved otherwise. Isabella was there to be made something of and I never took her seriously. I loved her passionately but I thought it was enough to admire and pet and protect her, I didn't think that a diet of play would in the end lead to unhappiness – I thought it right that she should take her ease and please me for when the babbies came along she would be busy enough. Until then, I saw marriage as a prolonged holiday with pleasure as the purpose.

There we were, eating good dinners – of the sort that Paris provides without needing much cooking – drinking good wine and thinking good thoughts about future prosperity. We spent our money as it came in, confident that there would be more where that came from and do you know there always seemed to be a constant supply of small commissions. People

were fond of us – big Thackeray with his sweet little wife. I know how they felt – I am always doubly kind to loving young couples that have not yet lost the bloom off their marriage. Hands were stretched out to help and we were not too proud to take them. Our accounting was marvellously simple – I cashed the cheques as I received them and then went out and spent the money at once with never a thought for laying-by savings to take care of the long line of Thackerays that we hoped we would in time produce. I knew I had very little in the bank but youth is hopeful and I was very young and exceedingly hopeful. It was a hope built on my own energy and strength and – dare I say it ? – talent rather than on any actual evidence that I was about to earn a fortune. There was nothing in the least encouraging about the major event of that first year of my married life – the crash of the *Constitutional* and the loss in that wreck of most of my stepfather's fortune and what was left of my patrimony. Could anything have been more disastrous ? I don't think so, and yet I did not give way to uncontrollable grief or despair or anything like that. Instead I was galvanised into action and when that happens to a lazy fellow the results can be quite startling. I had all the time this internal conviction rumbling away that I could and would do something in a literary way and it was this that kept me going and overthrew any lowness of spirits.

Well, it was a time to take stock, that autumn of 1837. What, after all, had I done up to then to give me this blessed confidence ? Almost nothing – so little I don't know how I had the impertinence to presume I might eventually succeed, but ain't it lucky I had ? All I had to my name was a good deal of hack-work done with a total indifference to who wanted it – any magazine could have me for a price. Review a book ? Certainly – how much ? Write a Foreign Letter ? Charmed – pay by the line. Criticise an Art Exhibition ? Done – a flat rate if you please. Contribute a few drawings ? Delighted, dear fellow – name your sum. I wasn't in the least choosy who wanted me or for what publication, though of course human nature being what it is and mine especially I had my preferences. Can you guess what a journalistic snob prefers ? The *Morning Chronicle* was my favourite journal in which I was extremely pleased to appear and be read by serious people – oh my ! – but it was reviewing for *The Times* that made my heart swell. My reviews weren't signed – hardly anything I did was – but it didn't take long for anyone interested to find out who had written them. There was Jones in his club settling down in his favourite chair with a glass of very fine port beside him and opening *The Times* and reading my review, which naturally caught his eye straight away, and in no time at all he was tapping Brown on his shoulder and disturbing his sleep to ask if he knew who had written this uncommonly fine article ? Good heavens, Brown would be bound to say, though with something of a sneer for Jones' ignorance, that was done by Thackeray – haven't you heard of him – promising young man, everyone talks of him. That was how I imagined my name being bandied about London anyway – I convinced myself in addition that I was developing an unmistakable style which nobody could imitate, or only at their peril, and to some extent I was right. I am not saying I am proud of the stamp I put on my work but only that it was individual. I prided myself on being

forthright and honest and in taking a strong line about almost everything –
vigorous attacks were my speciality – I thought I lashed about with words
in the most magnificently effective way and should I choose to be sarcastic
then watch out. Many years later, somebody dug up these early bits of work
of mine and reproduced them and oh didn't I almost cry with shame at my
arrogance! The most frightful scorn distinguishes them all, the most

confounded confidence, the most ludicrous impatience with everyone's talent
except my own. I didn't see how this kind of excess only succeeds in
antagonising the reader – either that, or rousing in him the utmost contempt.
Strange to say, nobody ever reprimanded me at the time – no editor told me
to slacken off a bit – but then I suppose blistering articles make good sales.
I wish I hadn't overdone it – but those days are long ago and I have learnt
to be more circumspect and tolerant and that young puppy who laid about
him with such force is no more and I mustn't be too angry with him for he
knew not what he did – not really.

There was another stream I was following at the time which turned into
a big river before very long and was the deliverance of us all – I mean,
writing stories. The journalism earned our bread and butter and could not
be done without, but the stories were nearer to my heart and much less

boldly done. I couldn't always be as savage as I was in my reviews and I found it more interesting to try to write good original work than to permanently be scathing about other people's which I thought was bad. Somewhere there must be a record of the first story I ever had printed – you would think I would know the date of the publication off by heart but I don't. I know I wrote a steady number and that most of them were printed without attracting any undue attention. *Fraser's Magazine*, which I had admired from the beginning, took a good few tales and it was in their pages that the *Yellowplush Correspondence* appeared in 1837.

Now that was an interesting sideline that unwittingly did me more good than I knew in putting me higher up the ladder. It began as the review of a book on etiquette by a linen-draper called Skelton – don't you see the fun in store as soon as I write that down ? – but before I had finished it emerged as a series of articles supposedly written by a cockney footman called Charles Yellowplush. In these, what had begun as a bit of satire at Mr. Skelton's

expense turned into a humorous account of the life of a footman which so caught the Editor's fancy that I was asked to do more. What easy work! If only everything had tripped off my pen so lightly and been laughed over so much as dear old Yellowplush. I can't resist giving you a taste of what it was like so that you can see the sort of thing I found fun. How about this description of Yellowplush in Paris:

> About three months after, when the season was beginning at Paris, and the autumn leafs was on the ground, my lord, my lady, me and Mortimer were taking a stroal in the Boddy Balong, the carridge driving on slowly ahead, and us as happy as possbill, admiring the pleasant woods and golden sunset.

My lord was expayshating to my lady upon the exquizit beauty of the sean and pouring forth a host of butifle and virtuous sentaments sootable to the hour.   It was dalitefle to hear him.   " Ah! " said he " black must be the heart my love, which does not feel the influence of a scene like this ; gathering as it were, from those sunlit skies a portion of their celestial gold, and gaining somewhat of heaven with each pure draught of this delicious air! "

Well, it was the most awful nonsense but it did work up to a point in that I caricatured the masters of Yellowplush and their manners as much, if not more, than Yellowplush himself.   But it would not do as a career, these attempts at satire and these reviews – they still left me regarded as merely a competent critic and an amusing writer of articles and I wanted more, much more, than that.

Where was the way ?   Do you suppose there are not several thousand young men asking that question in quiet desperation at this minute ?   I know I asked it all the time and came up with different answers all the time too. I thought the solution to all my problems would be some regular appointment to a newspaper which would give me a salary and experience and leave me in my free time to write fiction.   I tried hard to get a post as a sub-editor or some such position on the *Morning Chronicle* but without success.   I wonder what would have happened to me if I had obtained this place ?   Though I promised myself not to indulge in " might-have-beens " that is one avenue that I have half a mind to explore.   Would I have become an editor in time and been totally absorbed in newspaper production ?   Would I have settled in some small English town and edited the local *Patriot* or *Examiner* or *Morning News* ?   And how would that have changed me – would I have ceased to be in a permanent frenzy producing every sort of writing and opted instead for control over other people's ?   We don't know what changes in circumstances do to us or how much we are affected by the kind of life we lead.   That edge of dissatisfaction, that restlessness, that desire to make a mark – they all might have left me if I had settled into regular well-paid employment with strict hours.   Would I have been happier with none of my books written but my domestic life perhaps sheltered and calm ?   There is no way of knowing but I wonder how many of you have been as tormented as I have sometimes been by that kind of speculation.

There being no job forthcoming – though I did not stop expecting to be offered one for many years – I turned my attention instead to another goal. What I needed to establish myself I decided was one good hit – one full-length work of some sort that would catch on and sell enough copies to make me the darling of some publisher.   In this supposition – that a hit is necessary to haul you up among the giants – I was of course absolutely right.   I suppose there are some writers who have made their reputation by slowly and steadily adding a long list of unknown books to their name, but all the greats that I can think of have made their name famous at some point almost overnight and that was what I resolved to do. At least I was honest about it, openly confessing that I intended to try to hit the public, but how was the problem and here I departed a little from that honesty, though not sufficiently to disturb you. I looked about me and what kind of book did I see making money? Books about villains – absurd, blood-curdling yarns that glorified the villain's life. Scoundrels were not painted as they really were but dressed up with their brutalities kept in the background. How far we have travelled from Fielding's day when vice could never be mistaken for virtue, and yet it is Fielding who is often called immoral. There were a whole collection of novels in the 1830s that came under that heading – ridiculous books about confessed murderers and such like – and I decided to write a story that should portray the criminal and the life of the criminal and the morals and standards of the criminal as they really were. It was my first attempt at something more ambitious and better than anything I had yet done and I had high hopes before this tale – *Catherine* – was done.

I shan't let this become a catalogue of all my literary efforts – how weary you would grow if I did. There were so many years to come before I achieved that ambition of hitting the public that were I to list everything I wrote until then you would marvel at my obstinacy. For ten long years I laboured away scribbling stories long and short before I found one that satisfied everyone – myself, the critics, the public. There is almost something a trifle indecent about such a prolonged apprenticeship, as if the labourer was not suited to his work if it was so hard to turn out a good product. Some writers have within them stories they have to tell that will admit no denial and others again have a fount of inventiveness and others burn with one passionate idea that must be spread – I can only say I fall into none of those categories. I have to manufacture what I want to write about, driven only by the vague compulsion to the act itself and a fascination with the written word. I need to experience before I can write, and to think after I have experienced before passing whatever I have learned on to others. It was hardly surprising that as a young man who had experienced very little of importance I should not yet be ready to write anything worthwhile.

Fortunately, I had no time to brood on all this, nor to philosophise. However much I look back now and talk in this solemn way of what sounds like burning ambition (don't it?) I was actually living in such a turmoil making ends meet that I don't think I ever put two thoughts together at any one time about either my career up to then or my prospects. Indeed, so little faith had I in this ambition that I longed to be bound by a contract and *made* to write. I was forever searching for some publisher to sign me up and force me to deliver the goods or be imprisoned for failure to meet my obligations. Life was a scramble made all the more hectic by my decision to move permanently to London from Paris even before the final nails were in the old *Constitution*'s coffin. It was obvious by March 1837 which way the wind was blowing and I wanted to be in a comfortable position to weather the crash when it came, particularly as Isabella was in an interesting condition. My path for the time being lay in journalism and I was far better off in London picking up work than in Paris. Besides, without a salary I didn't see how I could support a wife and family in Paris whereas in London we could for the time being live at 18, Albion St. where my parents – thank God – were then living. Leaving Paris was hard – it seemed so much sunnier and happier than fog-ridden London – but it was necessary and I still had my little wife who I loved more dearly every day, so what did it matter ?

I don't, to this day, know how much it *did* matter, but I have my suspicions. Life was harder in London, for both of us. Our bohemian existence vanished to be replaced by an anxious regime of attempted order and discipline. The strain on Isabella was tremendous – there was her lazy husband who had until now only been too happy to lie in bed until noon

suddenly roaring his head off if breakfast wasn't on the table at eight sharp. In the evenings it was worse – I wrote so hard for magazines during the day that at night I positively had to have some pleasure and off I would go seeking distraction to the Garrick Club. My membership of that institution wasn't new but until then it had meant very little – now it became a daily fixture. I was no longer content to lie and listen to Isabella's piano-playing of an evening – I had to have conversation and company among my peers at that infernal club. If my conscience had troubled me – but I am afraid it did not – I should have quietened it as all we men do – by re-assuring myself that a woman likes to stay at home by the fire with her baby and welcomes an empty house because it is restful. And my little Puss made no word of complaint – she didn't ask me to stay at home more often or chide me for my absences. William worked hard, did he not, and was entitled to play – but so were you, my love, so were you. I thought, you know, that our love was strong enough to withstand anything fate cared to send me and looked for terrible outside events to test us, never suspecting the enemy within our gates. How could I be neglecting my wife when I loved her so much ? If anyone had told me that I did I would have punched them on the nose.

A family man is quite a different creature from a merely married man – it isn't at all the same thing. Our first child was born on June 9th, 1837 and I swear that I changed immediately into that awe-inspiring mortal – a Family Man. It was a girl whom we named Anne Isabella, born with the minimum of trouble and fuss in spite of all the matrons' gloomy predictions as to Isabella's strength and so forth. There proved nothing wrong with her strength – she produced Anny as easily as is possible and looked the prettiest, pinkest mother you have ever seen.   I suppose this very ease made me think everything would continue in the same fashion – I thought the hardest, most dangerous part over and never gave a thought to any difficulties to follow.   The mother was healthy, the baby even more so, what was there to worry about ?   I suspect I missed many hours of screaming but then I was rushing here and there trying to keep us solvent and there was nothing deliberate in that.   Nobody could have been a prouder and more devoted father, but what can a man do the first year except coo and rock and generally get in the way ?   Though I loved to stare at my little daughter's face and never tired of tracing her development, I own to a certain ennui after half an hour of her solitary company.   Sometimes little Miss T. would scream incessantly for five hours at a stretch then suddenly stop, making me wonder what are the mysteries of children and how are they moved.   Once she could walk and talk I had my part to play but at first I felt her an encumbrance – it seemed much more natural that her mother should hold her.   A man with a baby in his arms is an awkward creature – he looks old, so tall and big and heavy holding something so tiny and fragile and all the ladies are surely right to cry give the child back to its mother, do!

The truth was, we were in desperate straits for money and now that I was a Family Man whose responsibilities sat heavily upon him I could not regard this position lightly.   When we did have any money, it proved fatal to have it in the house for fear we would use it for something not strictly necessary. We had to have our own house, but the rent of 13, Great Coram St., modest though it was, almost proved too much for us when we moved there at the beginning of 1838.   There was no one to shield us from the realities of household expenses then – oh God, how they mounted up those darling taxes and the charming servants' wages!   It was hopeless entrusting money to Isabella – her innocence in such matters only exasperated me and all attempts to instruct her in judicious economies failed.   I think it was then that I hit on the primitive method of keeping only five pounds at a time in the house and eking it out to the last farthing before daring to draw any more, always supposing there was some to draw.   If I sound amused now, I was not amused then.   Poverty as an artist in Paris is one thing but poverty as a Family Man in London was another – especially with another little Thackeray on the way.   Don't tell me that I never knew the terror of real poverty, that I was never in the shadow of the workhouse so it is absurd of me to mention the word, for I believe the desperate struggle to cling on to a little wealth can be almost as fierce as trying to stay alive at all.   The abyss below seems bottomless when you are on the edge – there is so far to fall compared to those poor souls already half-way down.   I tell you I had nightmares about what would happen to my wife and children should I die leaving nothing.   The spectre of them becoming paupers haunted me for years and my suffering on that score was no less real than the suffering of a man already destitute. It made me tremble to see how happy we were and to know how threatened that happiness was by our financial position.

I worked like a tiger at that period. All sorts of mad schemes to make money filled my head — letting our house, or part of it, or taking a lodger — something of that kind was in order to tide us over. My main source of income at the time was *Fraser's Magazine*. I was such a regular and popular contributor that I worked myself up to threaten to strike for more wages when I found James Fraser paid more to certain other writers. I have never been more terrified in my life than when I wrote off nervously asking for more money — suppose he said no and be damned to you for asking? Nobody who has not been involved in a strike knows the horrible fear that arises upon considering that the outcome may not be a rise but being paid off altogether and then the humiliation of having to say you didn't mean it and will after all work for the same pay and perhaps ending up begging to be allowed to stay for less! All this went through my mind but it did not stop me trying, and thank God more money was forthcoming, making me rather ashamed of my bullying ways. The extra I was paid came just in time to pay for the expense of a doctor and nurse at the birth of our second daughter, Jane, though it seemed to me they were hardly necessary, so easily was she born, except to give Isabella re-assurance. She was born on July 9th, 1838 — I never forget the date even now when she has been dead so long that you might think the date of her birth would seem insignificant — in the middle of that summer heat which makes all right-thinking men long to have themselves and their suffering families out of London. Oh, how I longed to get away from the intolerable heat which seemed to stifle me and to generate, I swear, a sluggishness of mind and spirits that in any other place would not have lasted an hour. But any kind of move for the family was impossible with a new-born baby in the house, and I could only afford to go alone if it were a business venture properly paid for.

Shall I admit straight out that I spent a good deal of time that year and the next scheming to organise vital journeys out of London? Well, I did, though you would be wrong to deduce from that admission any lack of love on my part for my wife and children — quite the contrary — I was always wretched when I was away and felt as if I had left my heart in Great Coram St. and could not function properly without it. That said, you must believe me when I tell you that work was well-nigh impossible there. We lived in an atmosphere of domestic chaos with myself at the centre of it. However sternly I gave orders that I absolutely must be shut up in my little room for three uninterrupted hours morning and evening, they were constantly disobeyed. How often did my wife come in to ask me some trivial thing that she had convinced herself I would know the answer to? How often did Anny trot in to pull at my sleeve and request in the most delightful gibberish

that I should draw pictures for her ?   How often did all three of them – wife,
child, baby – tear in all roaring their heads off because of some dreadful
calamity happening that only I could resolve ?   Then the noise – it is
impossible writing now in this quiet house to imagine how the walls in
Great Coram St. vibrated with noise – with babies crying and bells ringing
and servants shouting until I was unable to write two consecutive sensible

words.   Nor was any order ever imposed on this scene – food was burnt and
served hours late, clothes remained unwashed till the last garment was worn,
beds were tumbled in and out of with all speed – it was the nearest thing to a

madhouse outside Bedlam.   Of course, I exaggerate, but only so that you may catch the unmistakable flavour, which might not come across if I diluted the mixture with the occasional quiet day upon which everything turned out well and Isabella grew pink with pride that she was after all managing to become a good little housewife.   I could never reprimand her seriously for her shortcomings — how could I be so brutal when she was so well intentioned and tried so hard and was so loving to husband and children and servants alike ?   Nor did I in any way regret the advent of children — on the contrary, I marvelled every day at Anny's genius — she was a noble little thing right from the first and a constant source of pleasure.   But I did begin to blame my home circumstances for my failure to produce that hit I had my mind on, and to look for peace and quiet somewhere in the universe to accomplish more than the articles and reviews to which I was obliged to restrict myself.   I was always behindhand with these bread-and-butter writings and always thinking of novels and travel books and other ambitions, more attractive projects that it was impossible for me to begin on.   I struggled on with *Catherine,* my first attempt at a short novel on the lines I have told you — that is, to reveal villainy as it is — but my heart had gone out of it long before the thing was finished.   Wasn't that often to be the case in the future and don't all writers know what I mean ?   The excitement of beginning is tremendous but oh, the tussle at halfway to keep going, and oh the boredom at the end !

I dreamed, in those years, of going off on my own to write a work of genius that would make me but I could no more do it than fly, though I did sometimes snatch a couple of days at an inn near Greenwich or Richmond, but that was all.   I don't know that I ought to regret that it was never possible to achieve greater solitude.   How many years have I had now when I have been protected from all noise and rush and the need to earn my living ?   Too many, yet too little done.   I look back to those hectic years and cannot help but glory in the awfulness of the pressure and yet the quality of the work.   No masterpieces perhaps, but an abundance of sharp, observant, well-written pieces that betray no evidence of the circumstances in which they were penned.   I could not leave Isabella or I might have contrived to put my talent to the test in some hidey-hole.   She hated me to go away — increasingly as time went on — and I could never do so even under the most pressing business engagement abroad without tears and sighs.

Do you think you perceive a certain callousness in this gentleman ?   I know I do now, but did not then.   I confess to an impatience with Isabella's distress that I could not conceal.   This fuss about my travelling — and I shall tell you why it was necessary in a minute — became more acute towards the end of 1839, after the death of our little baby Jane.   Now, it was natural that Isabella should mourn — we all did.   The death of an eight-month-old baby who has not yet walked or talked is every bit as dreadful as the death of

a loved one with whom the closest contact has been forged. You may contest this – even think it absurd – but I tell you Jane's death appeared to us tragic and heartrending and the pity of it engulfed us. Don't be heartless and say we had another child and every prospect of more – don't remind me infant deaths are commonplace and to be expected – a child is a child and never replaceable. If I said at the time that I thought of Jane as something charming we were allowed for a season to enjoy, and if I appeared to acquiesce with God's decision to take her to Him, it was only my usual mask to hide deeper feelings of anguish and loss. I tried to think of her as an angel enjoying some higher state in heaven above where she would be eternally innocent. But Isabella ? She seemed to sink into a deeper melancholy with every day and could not be cheered or reconciled. A dreadful apathy seized hold of her so that she would sit for hours rocking backwards and forwards and weeping all the while. I hope I was patient and comforted her but perhaps I made matters worse by being even more active myself until the contrast was too painful for her. At any rate, it was a bad business and I was a fool not to see that making her with child again was not the remedy for her grief. I don't like to think that the third pregnancy so soon after the others was disastrous – surely not – Isabella seemed much happier once the baby was on the way and if I search in my memory I can produce many instances of happy days and outings that belong to that time – all simple affairs to be sure but that is where happiness lies. She was undemanding in that department – an evening wandering about looking at the lights and decorations for the Queen's wedding was quite enough to send her into raptures, a trip to Watford and a picnic in a field would be talked about for days, and listening to a good performance of the

Messiah produced such ecstasies of delight in my little wife that I marvelled at such innocence. I don't think we ever did anything more exciting than go to the seaside for the day, but Isabella seemed perfectly content and situated as I was it was as well.

When Harriet was born in May 1840 I really believed I might look for an end to the delirium in which I had been working to keep up with the commissions I had accepted. Though *Catherine* had long since been finished and published – without attracting much attention, though some critics were kind – I had hopes that another scheme was about to come off, which was a sketch-book, with commentaries, on Ireland after the fashion of the *Paris Sketch-Book* of a couple of years before. That volume had not been particularly successful but I managed to convince the publishers that this other would be better and that my name was so much better known due to my large output in magazines and newspapers that it would attract followers. Longman, the great publisher of the day, and Chapman and Hall, Dickens' publisher, were prepared to enter into a treaty with me, to my own astonishment. There was only one drawback. Can you guess? I would either have to leave my family for a few months – which was unthinkable – or take the whole tribe with me, which was equally unthinkable. The problem was a nice one, but whatever the answer I was quite certain the book must be done when I could get £300 for three months. I might even be able to break from the gruelling magazine work on the strength of it. To my relief, Isabella shared my excitement and was similarly preoccupied only by the whys and wherefores of the arrangements. I think I inclined towards a stiff upper lip and a parting for three months with perhaps my parents coming to live with my wife, but Isabella would not hear of it -- she absolutely would not hear of it and declared she could not endure such a separation. What was a man to do? I put off deciding and in the meantime another plum fell into my lap – well, not quite, I may have stretched a good way to pick it off the tree – for I went to Belgium to look at some pictures and did a little book about it and sold it to Chapman and Hall on my return. Wasn't that clever?

In the event, no, it was not. It was the beginning of a thick-headedness and stupidity on my part that I look back on with grief and remorse. Isabella did not want to go to Belgium even though it was a short trip – a matter of a few days – two weeks – what does it signify the exact length of time – the fact was I went off on my own with my wife's exhortations to stay ringing in my ears and the tears wet on her face and I hardened my heart AND I WENT. There. I won't hide behind any convenient truths about needing the money or having to go – I went because I wanted to. And I enjoyed myself hugely. What more could a man ask than the luxury of being paid to look at good pictures and say what he thought after he had taken a stroll in the sun and drunk some wine to lubricate the brain? I tell

you the freedom to do this was intoxicating and I revelled in it.   It seemed
to me that I had not been made to hide myself in Great Coram St. listening
to the howls and roars of children – how could anyone expect me to produce my best work in such an atmosphere ?   I wasn't a humdrum man,
dammit, and nothing was going to make me one.

Don't you hate me for my insensitivity ?   I do.   Why didn't I put myself
in Isabella's shoes ?   I don't know.   One look at her when I returned from
that Belgian trip ought to have been enough – I can see her still, sitting
there as I had left her, apathetic and miserable, tears forever cascading
silently down her thin cheeks, one hand languidly extended to touch me,
and I avoided that touch, feeling only irritation that she didn't rush to greet
me and fling herself exuberantly at me and kiss me with a pretty pink mouth.
Well, I sent for the doctor and he said what they always say – a change of air

would do the trick. Off we went to Margate, the entire family, taking Brodie, our good Scottish nurse, with me perfectly convinced that all that ailed my wife was some weird kind of indigestion. Sea air and plenty of rest and she would be fully restored to herself and no longer a worry to me – for that, of course, was the truth of the matter. I did not want to be worried – I did not want to face the seriousness of the situation – I grew absolutely furious at any suggestion that this frightful condition might be permanent.

Margate did its best for us. Our lodgings were in a charming little house on the seafront with all our windows looking towards the water and the door of our queer little sitting-room opening straight onto the beach. Nothing could have been more delightful. The sun shone, there was a refreshing breeze, the children were in marvellous humour and Brodie a devoted companion – but none of it did Isabella any good. Backwards and forwards I walked with her on my arm, pointing out the beauty of our surroundings, but she only stared dully and sighed. Night after night we sat together in the sitting-room while I tried to work in a way that ought to have been companionable but was more like imprisonment – every time I looked up there were those great tear-filled eyes staring pathetically at me until I could have hit her – yes, I could, for the most awful irritation and anger welled up inside me at what I thought of as stubbornness. Why would she not shake this languor off ? Why didn't she try, for God's sake ? I was reduced to walking full three miles away from this depressing atmosphere to get any writing done at all – out I went, when everything got too much, to a little bowling green where I sat in an arbour and scribbled away.

You see how far I was from understanding – you see how I invited tragedy ? But not till it was upon me would I own to it.

Chapter VII

---◆---

AFTER HAPPINESS COMES TRAGEDY...

E returned from Margate just as dismal as possible —
except for Anny who was full of merry quips about the
long way she had been. Often she made me smile even
when my humour was at its blackest, but Isabella was
immune to the child's charm. I think this lack of interest
in her children was what terrified me most and made me
determined that come what may Brodie should never leave us. I may have
said as much to our nurse — I think I was driven to it over an embarrassment
about wages due — but if I phrased my desperation delicately she understood
instantly and her loyalty never wavered. What did I do to poor Brodie,
asking such devotion of her ? A woman's heart is surely one of the most
beautiful things God ever created — no man can find in himself the depths
of compassion that can stir a woman. If I took advantage of Brodie I did
not do so without daily giving thanks for her sacrifice.

You will hardly credit it but — we went to Cork, where Mrs. Shawe and
Jane had long since taken up their abode. Could anything be more calculated
to bring about a crisis than organising the departure of a family for an
unspecified time to Ireland ? Do you know what such a move involves —
the sorting and buying and packing of clothes and goods and chattels, the
cleaning of the house to let it during the absent months, the endless to-ing
and fro-ing between ticket offices and baggage depots — oh it was a nightmare
and none of us equipped to face it. I went on telling myself the bustle would
do Isabella good as if even a well woman would not have found such upheaval a strain. She could hardly fold a gown and put it into a trunk yet I
persisted in the notion that she enjoyed the activity. There was no doubt
that I was obliged to go to Ireland to do my sketch-book — our finances
depended on it — nor was there any question of leaving Isabella behind in her

condition, but I own that another element besides necessity had crept into the argument – I did not want to be on my own with my wife. There, it is a shameful admission but there will be plenty of those before I am done. It was driving me mad being responsible for an invalid day after day and I was resolved that her mother and sister should take their turn. I wrote to them warning them of Isabella's lowness and asking that they should take her in hand and restore her to her former spirits. I expect they announced to each other that this was just like a man as they laid in stocks of beef tea and so forth but I did not care what they thought – I was beat. I don't know if I showed it or not, or whether Isabella noticed, but I know I felt the want of a shoulder to lean on and somebody to direct me. My mother might have helped, but she and my stepfather had taken up their abode in Paris and letters were inadequate. Indeed, they proved worse – they were dangerous, for when I described Isabella's attitude to my mother in one of them she in turn told a friend who told Isabella, who was plunged afresh into tears because she had let William down – not at all helpful. In marital affairs it is better to keep our own counsel I think.

We embarked on September 12th for the trip to Ireland, a journey taking some seventy hours and not the most comfortable in the world. Do you know the crossing? Treble the horrors of the sail across the channel to Calais and you will have something of an idea as to the feeling. There was not much provision made in those days for women and children – perhaps things have improved now – and it was upsetting to subject my loved ones to the rigours of such a voyage, but there was no alternative. Travel loses its appeal when worry over wives and babies interferes with excitement at the adventure – you can't be savouring the strangeness of the experience if you are concentrating on keeping a child warm or bolstering a woman's failing confidence. God knows I have had some frightful journeys with my family over the years, but none as terrible as that crossing to Cork, when I really began to doubt that we would ever survive. I only have to see one of those steam boats chugging out of a harbour, crowded with women wrapped in shawls and children held high to wave goodbye, to experience all over again that nausea which gripped me then, and I have to turn away in a hurry and grit my teeth and swear not to remember – but of course I shan't ever forget and perhaps that is my punishment.

We made a good enough show at first. It was a triumph simply to be all present and correct on board with our traps safely in the hold and the anxiety of getting away done with. I think we were reasonably merry that first Saturday night, congratulating ourselves on our fortitude at surviving the departure, and if Isabella did not respond to my high spirits – well, she had lost the habit and I thought nothing of it. I was full of talk about Ireland and the good time we would have there, away from the fogs of Great Coram St., and I described most vividly to Anny and Brodie and anybody else who would listen the beauties of a country I had never set foot in. Brodie was a tower of strength – she did all the things Isabella ought to have been doing in the way of comforting the children and had her own fund of stories besides. She shushed and rocked the baby to sleep, and wrapped Anny up tightly against the cold, with never a thought for her own comfort. Isabella would not try to sleep – she said she preferred to be in the fresh air above and though I thought the air far from fresh – fresh was too mild a word for such an onrush of icy air – I did not discourage her. Any decision Isabella made I had learned to welcome – any positive step away from her usual listlessness was a victory. Up we both went on to the deck and she clung to the rail and gazed down at the black water with a fascination that seemed inexplicable. There was nothing charming about the scene – it was very dark and cold and the noise of the engine and the pitching of the vessel were not calculated to soothe shattered nerves. But my wife seemed to enjoy it – she made no move to go below, simply stood motionless, without replying to anything I said, occasionally putting her head back as though to feel the wind on her closed eyes. It was I who grew bored first and urged her to go below with me and sleep while the sea was relatively calm and I remember I had almost to prise her reluctant fingers off the rail. If she had put up any protest beyond that tight grip I might have endured standing there for longer, but she said nothing and I was tired and stiff and badly wanted my bed so I led her to our cabin and insisted that we should rest.

I don't know what happened next – to Isabella I mean.   Did she lie
beside me, wide awake, her head full of the pounding waves, while I slept
and snored oblivious of her pain ?   Did she rise at last, stealthily, like a thief,
and perhaps look at me and even kiss me – oh pathetic touch ! – and creep out,
her heart beating with fright but her mind quite made up ?   I don't know –
she never told me – we never talked about it and I am left to surmise and
scare myself with all possible combinations in my imagination.   I don't know
which I would rather – that it was all done in a hurry in some fathomless
fury, or that it was planned and executed with cold deliberate calm.   Either
way, it was hideous and even now does not bear thinking about.   My poor
little wife, you see, went back on deck and threw herself overboard into that
foaming hell of an ocean.   Can't you feel the sickening thud as her body
hit the water ?   Can't you hear the scream she could not stop herself giving ?
And don't you cry out " Why did she do it ? " ?

I still do.   Even now, when her madness is a thing I have lived with for
twenty years, I still ask over and over again how could she do such a terrible
thing.   To us who are sane it is incomprehensible that an act so cruel and

frightful could be carried out by a loved one who only a few minutes before has been talking and smiling with us. It seems ridiculous, and yet there is the evidence, we must swallow hard and face it and say it was done and there is no help for it. Perhaps one day, when medicine is in a more advanced state than we find it today, the minds of poor mortals like my wife will be properly understood and instead of throwing up our hands in despair and horror we will be able to minister to them as we do to broken bodies. It seems to me that there is a trick somewhere that we have not learned – a piece of knowledge perhaps so simple that we have overlooked it – a remedy as straightforward as setting a broken arm in splints – only we do not know it. I don't believe that there is anything in God's law that forbids trying to understand the mad, nor that the devil is responsible for derangement and that those who suffer it ought not to be tampered with. God never intended that my little wife should try to kill herself, nor would He do anything but bless the wise man who discovered how to make her whole and well by whatever means.

I was a long way, on that ghastly night, from trying to divine any rhyme or reason in the awful deed that had taken place. I ought to have every detail of what transpired imprinted on my mind but I find it difficult to remember the exact sequence of events – I think it was the clanging of the ship's bell that woke me and that it took a long time for me to connect the general commotion with the absence of my wife at my side. Even when I properly regained consciousness I was not alarmed but only rather perplexed as to the disappearance of Isabella who I concluded must have gone to look at the children. I can't claim to any feeling of foreboding – it was curiosity that took me on deck and not terror – I looked in the other cabin on my way and was relieved to see all three occupants asleep in spite of the noise. What happened next? How was it borne upon me that I had suffered a dreadful blow? I don't know, I can't remember, I would only be lying if I were to take you step by step over a dramatic tale. Somebody must have told me a young woman had thrown herself overboard – I must have instantly thought of Isabella and connected her with this calamity but I can't be sure – I may have crowded to the rail with the rest, driven by eagerness to see if the body would be recovered before the terrible certainty that it must be my wife they were looking for occurred to me. I don't think I shouted or cried out in any way – I wouldn't have been heard if I had for there were people running pell-mell in every direction and order after order was yelled along the deck and on top of it all the wind howled and the sea roared and the ship's engine shuddered and ground to a halt.

Nobody expected to find the corpse. After all, how long had it taken for the ship to stop and how many miles of sea were there to search and how could the poor lights available hope to penetrate the absolute blackness? It was a tribute to the humanity of the Captain that any search was made at all and entirely due to the endeavours of this brave man and the crew of his lifeboat that Isabella was found after twenty agonising minutes, lying on her back, paddling gently with her hands. Do you see the contradiction ? She hurled herself over the rail but then she kept herself afloat instinctively and waited. It struck me at the time as almost shameful – as though she wanted only to draw attention to herself and had never intended anything else. God forgive me if that judgement sounds harsh – I was glad enough at the time to lift her sodden body from the boat and hold her in my arms. The shock was frightful – I could hardly meet her eyes or those of all those around me, and if there had been a dark place for me to crawl into and howl I should have fled to it instantly. All the rest of that night I lay awake with Isabella dried and wrapped in warm blankets, and now in the deepest sleep imaginable, at my side, secured to my wrist by a cord so that the slightest movement would awake me in case she tried to kill herself again – though this pre- caution proved unnecessary for I never closed my eyes. I know I was calm and quite rational. I lay and stared at the wooden ceiling above me and gave thanks that my wife's life had been preserved and that I had been given this warning before it was too late. I saw how wrong I had been to pass her melancholy off as some physical disorder and cursed myself for the fool that I was to have believed it would cure itself. Worst of all was the remorse that followed for my irritation and lack of sensitivity towards that sweetest of creatures and I swore that if she could be restored by devotion and care then she should have it in abundance. I was ready to go down on my knees and pledge myself to a lifetime of protection – nothing would be more important than looking after my poor broken companion.

The rest of that voyage I ate, I drank, I walked the deck, I made conversation, all like a perfectly normal human being when in reality my life was shattered. I found I could even laugh without any appearance of artificiality and that I took a lively interest in the weather and the people and all the other mundane things that you would have thought would be ana- thema to me. Nor was I striving to behave normally when inside I seethed or anything like that – I was disgracefully tranquil and even content. I wonder if the other passengers pointed me out and knowing what had happened branded me as a monster ? I wonder if they commented on my cheerful air and bland expression and privately expressed the opinion that I was an ogre to be so unmoved ? I expect if I had emerged gaunt-eyed clutching my hair they would have thought it only right and proper and felt somehow relieved. Well, I am sorry if I disappointed them but I could not act like a maniac when I did not feel like one. It may not make sense to you, but I remember a feeling of peace, of deep peace, as that ship plunged across the Irish sea with its pitiful cargo.

It seemed when we first reached my mother-in-law's house that matters might after all improve and Isabella's condition turn out not to be as serious

as her past behaviour implied.   There was some relief in arriving at a house
full of women all ready to fuss and cluck over my poor darling and I even
went so far as to imagine for a short time that Mrs. Shawe might not be so

bad as I had always thought.   She was the kind of woman who adored illness,
who loved the drama of it and the coming and going of doctors, all the things
I hated — and where she got all that procession of medical men from in that
God-forsaken part of the country I cannot imagine.   They seemed to arrive
by the score, driving up in their pony carts with their blessed bags, and all
pronouncing with the utmost confidence that all my wife needed was rest
and calm and a light diet and tranquillisers and restoratives, all of which they
were more than ready to provide at a high price.   Mrs. Shawe presided over
them like a queen, solemnly nodding her head at the most ridiculous
instructions and doing a good deal of tip-toeing in and out of Isabella's
bedroom in the most exaggerated fashion.   All the trouble was put down to
Isabella's recent confinement and Mrs. Shawe had a habit, when this was
stated, of looking at me in the most direct and disgusted way as though it was
all my fault.   However, I did not take issue with her but surrendered her
sick daughter to her gracefully.   I at least had the consolation of knowing
that my sister-in-law Jane, who never left Isabella's bedside, was kindness
itself and that while she was there, their mother could not become too
overbearing.

Meanwhile, the initial panic over, there was the original purpose of the visit to think about. Touring was out of the question – I could not either leave Isabella or take her with me, so therefore I was obliged to do my observing of Ireland from my mother-in-law's and bide my time. Though I was thus constrained, and in no position to play the tourist, an awareness of what that country was about did begin to seep through the walls of the house and into my bones, and I don't know that I greatly deepened my insight into it even after I had later spent several weeks travelling extensively about. I realised Ireland was a mystery, impossible to understand for anyone not born and bred to the strange contradictions of the country. Situated as I was, all that impressed me about the country was the physical beauty I saw all around. Nature seemed dominant wherever I looked and I could not decide whether this was due to the indolence or poverty of the inhabitants who, by the way, seemed remarkably unimpressed by the beauty that drew such verbal raptures from me. I found no pride in the magnificence of the landscape, only a kind of grudging acceptance of what God had given them.

I may say this magnificence stopped at the front door of my mother-in-law's house and any other house I happened to be in. I know from later experience that Ireland does boast some splendid residences and comfortable homes but none of them were in the Cork I knew. I wish you could have seen the stately drawing-room in which I spent most of my days – there was neither paper nor paint to the walls, only a coloured distemper holding the cracks that I spent many an hour tracing with my eye, and a chair had to be permanently shoved against a window to keep it shut else the very frame would have fallen out and half the wall with it. Every blessed stick of furniture had something the matter with it and there was no touch of luxury anywhere. In this hovel I spent most of my days, trying to shut out the incessant bragging of my old humbug of a mother-in-law, listening to the stout voice of Anny outside playing with the brats who lived at the lodging house next door and sounding twice as Irish as they did, and trying to work on a play that I had taken to as a refuge from my troubles. That play never came to anything but I remain thankful for the distraction it gave me and for the solace that the act of writing the words on paper provided. Work is the surest palliative I know – positively the only medicine that, taken in large and regular enough doses, can bring comfort to the sick and miserable. It don't much matter what the work is, nor the quality, just so long as you keep at it and go through the tasks you set yourself. How hard it is to begin when whatever is the matter presses in from all sides, but once begun, how quickly the load is lightened. I don't mean by that that the sufferer forgets – if you have a pain in your guts you cannot forget it, if your child is cold in his grave you cannot forget him, if your larder is bare you cannot forget it – but all the same the agony of whatever it is recedes and when the work is done the triumph of something heroically achieved provides new hope.

Luckily, I never thought to impart this piece of homespun philosophy to dear Mrs. Shawe who, I am sure, suspected I shut myself up in that wretched back room every day in order to drink or indulge in some other piece of wickedness. If I had begun by at least admitting that woman might have some few virtues it was quickly apparent to me that I had been lulled into a false sense of security by the convincing show of concern she at first managed to put on, for that was all it was – an empty show. She cared neither for Isabella nor her grandchildren, and as for me – she would have consigned me to purgatory rather than waste any sympathy on me. Her sole concern was the expense we had now placed upon her, though we were her own flesh and blood. She never let me forget what an obligation I was under for the shelter she had given us, nor did she fail to remind me at increasingly close intervals that I had brought my troubles on myself. I am afraid I hated her, and that this hatred has not been distilled by the passage of time. Her hardness made me long for my own mother, who would know how to comfort us all and never think of any distress we might be causing her. Indeed, no sooner had I written to inform my parents of the calamitous events that had overtaken us than a letter at once came back full of heartfelt sympathy and instant offers of help. The contrast was too painful and I began to feel an urgent need to rid myself of that tyrannical mother-in-law and take my family to Paris where we would be truly welcome.

The problem of how to manage this almost overcame me. I had not only a family to transport but a sick wife who needed constant vigilance and even then was quite likely to do something desperate. The doctors went on saying what she needed was rest and quiet but what rest was there with Mrs. Shawe roaming the house ranting and preaching all the time, and where was the quiet with the baby screaming and Anny roaring in our confined quarters ? I saw no evidence that Isabella was improving under this regime – her mind remained clouded and she either rambled on about incidents in the past or sank into that dangerous apathy I had grown to dread. I knew that the merest suggestion of moving her would have Mrs. Shawe screaming murder at me, but I thought that if I could drug her and do the journey by easy stages we might reach London in safety and then by degrees Paris. The loss would be irreparable in terms of money – there was nothing in the bank and my contract with Chapman and Hall was unfulfilled but there was no help for it. An Irish Sketch-Book was out of the question – better to cut my losses and retreat while I still had a shilling or two to get us home.

There was precious little humour to be found in that horrible situation, you will admit, but I cannot deny a certain malicious pleasure obtained by me in hoodwinking that harridan in the manner of our departure. I knew of course that I could not discuss leaving with her – though she plainly loathed having us she would be sure to holler and call me every evil name she could think of at the idea of moving her supposedly darling daughter and the doctors, who were all terrified of her, would back her up. She had already gone too far by pumping Brodie in the most suggestive manner to see if I ill-treated my wife and I could not bear to risk the scene I knew would be inescapable if I announced our departure. Part of me longed for that confrontation when I should unburden myself of all the resentment I harboured, but the other more sensible half knew that it would be a mistake and that I should regret it. Confrontations of that nature are all very well in novels – don't I enjoy writing them myself ? – but in real life they are immensely harmful and never provide the release expected, not for my kind of character at any rate. I am not a violent man – I don't remember ever hitting anyone since I was a boy and then only because it was expected and I had to pretend fury or be labelled a milksop – but there was about Mrs. Shawe a provocative element that might have led me to anything should the occasion arise. What a set-to we might have had! Claws out, face slapping, hair pulling, wild punches at each other in the sitting-room – oh lor I can see it now, with Titmarsh coming off worst and getting blood all down his vest. Well, I didn't risk it. Instead, I primed dear old Brodie, who was on my side and had herself suffered insults from that odious woman, and with tremendous daring managed to snatch my entire family away without so much as saying goodbye. I swear I laughed all the way across the Irish Sea just at the thought of her face when she realised we had gone, and only sobered up when I thought what poor Jane would have to endure. I haven't seen that lady, my mother-in-law I mean, since and I don't intend to. She can rot in – a very hot place anyway. I wrote her the most savage letter afterwards but I don't think I posted it -- or perhaps I did and she will bring it to light some day to shock you. If she does, please to remember my side of the business and see if you don't find it in your heart to forgive me.

We got to Bristol and from Bristol to London with about a halfpenny to spare, and that is no exaggeration. Thoughts of a financial nature occupied me almost more than those of a medical sort. Where in the world was I going to find the money to pay for the care Isabella would need ? It seemed so recently that I had been congratulating myself on reaching a state of near solvency – of almost being free from that nagging anxiety about where the next month's rent was to come from – and now I was back again, plunged into never-ending calculations all dependent on the rate of work I could keep up. That was another thing – what hope had I of working with a sick wife ? Who was going to look after the household and the children, and come to that, me ? I could not turn my hand to it though the thought made me smile for a few jolting miles – if I was not pushing the pen then all was lost and to do that I needed a modicum of peace. I sat and pondered and wondered what other men did in my situation. Thoughts of female relatives swooping to gather up my little ones to their comfortable bosoms crowded my head but the Thackerays were short on those, and I no sooner went through the brief roll-call than I rejected every name. There was really only one solution and that was to go to my mother till we all sorted something out, and I thanked God she was neither too old nor too burdened with other cares to make such a course of action unthinkable.

I longed, on that journey, and have never ceased to long, for someone with whom to discuss my predicament. I looked at Isabella who, since that terrible day when she threw herself overboard, had been increasingly given to smiling at me as though eager to please, and wished that I could talk about what we were going to do. Sometimes she looked so rational and easy that the words rose up to my lips and had to be stifled at the last minute and when that happened I swear her face clouded and darkened and she knew she failed me. A man grows used to sharing his thoughts with his wife and voicing his worries and the habit dies hard. There is no one else he can be quite so sure will defend him when he needs defending or prejudiced in his favour when in truth there is a great deal to be said for the other side. There is no one else so quick to suspect what is really on his mind when he hums and haws about something apparently too trivial to merit such attention, nor anyone so slow to lose the conviction that he will triumph when everyone else can see he is beaten. A mother, however devoted, is a poor substitute for a soul mate – she, poor lady, cannot rid herself of the blindness that comes from believing her son is *herself* whereas a wife knows her husband is *himself* and that she must never make the mistake of thinking she knows everything. As for children, they try, and mine have tried harder than most, but nobody wants to stand revealed before their children, nor turn for help to those they are used to providing with protection.   I tell you there is no substitute for a loyal and devoted wife, not even the most passionate of mistresses, though I have never explored that possibility.   A man who has had such a wife and then loses her remains crippled the rest of his days.

Well, it is a bleak prospect and it was fortunate that though I knew – any fool would have known – that I was in for hard times I had no idea that my wife would never be restored to me as we returned home that autumn day in 1840.   My head was full of plans for the future, all hinging on my mother taking on the children while I found a doctor who knew what he was about for Isabella and then a lodge somewhere in the wilderness for myself while I strove again for that hit that would make everything alright.   Does that disgust you – I mean that my mind still ran on thoughts of personal ambition when my wife was so ill ?   I hope not – I hope you have the compassion to allow the wounded man visions of beautiful fields as he lies in the mud of the battlefield – I hope you will lift the glass of water to the lips of the thirsty nomad.   How the devil could I keep going without dreaming of what would satisfy me ?   Nature, I think, has her own way of protecting us when the present proves unbearable – she lifts our eyes up to the horizons that rise above whatever carnage is about us and so hypnotises us that we can bear the pain.   Of course I sat and dreamed of the future – of course I dwelt on success and glory – of course I did everything except look at my pathetic wife and tell myself I was doomed from now on, and if that shows I am callous and self-centred then hurrah for that judgement.

But I prayed too – I prayed oh so hard that I should be given another chance to love my wife as I ought to have done and not fail her.   If I wept any tears at all it was for lost opportunities and for the way I had taken Isabella's sweetness and compliance for granted.   Only give me the chance and I would play another game.   I wasn't fool enough to imagine that if I got down on my knees and swore never to be a bad boy again then Isabella would be cured, nor did I think I had anything worth trading in for such a gift.   All I could do was bow my head and try to be humble and then jump up and work hard to do my part.   It never entered my head simply to sit about and wait for miracles.

We can't select parts of our lives and throw them away and say there, that part is done with and I don't need to tell you any more about it now that it is over.   When I took my little family to Paris on our return from Ireland it is true that my life from that time changed dramatically and that I never again knew the domestic felicity that had marked it up to then.   I was no longer in quite the same way a family man, even though my family was more important than ever to me and my ties with them strengthened.

Instead, I found myself once more on my own, aware that I had been singled out by fate for a role I was never designed to fill. Do you remember that I had never enjoyed being a bachelor ? Do you recall how eager I was to enter into matrimony and have a life-long companion ? All that had gone — I was back on my own and yet not on my own — free when I did not wish to be free and at the same time not at all free — I had two small girls to bring up and not the slightest idea how to do it, and a career on the edge of being made that looked likely to collapse. You know — at least, I think you know — and I know that it didn't collapse, but that is not what is important about a man's life. I don't want to be judged on my career — God forbid — I want instead that you should understand me, and you can't do that without appreciating the deprivation I suffered back in 1840. Isabella's illness was absolutely crucial to my happiness. I won't go on about it after this — no endless moaning, no attributing to it everything else nasty that happens to me — but I must say it with the utmost solemnity that the virtual loss of my wife marred my future most miserably, and you must always remember that when you are skimming over what follows. We all have other things in our past that explain our present and even help to predict our futures and that accident to my wife is the key to a great deal that befell Titmarsh.

Now I have lectured you long enough and promise herewith to rattle along at a fine old pace for the next few chapters to make up for the dullness.

Chapter VIII

———————◆———————

A RE-ADJUSTMENT

I AM not sure if I have even begun to impress upon you what a remarkable woman my mother is, and unless you understand that you will not appreciate how she became an anchor for a good many years until, in the way of anchors, she began to weigh rather heavy and I needed to separate myself to some extent from her. At the time of Isabella's illness she was a mere forty-eight years old, still outstandingly beautiful, still full of energy, still an authoritarian figure in my life and the lives of those around her. She remains to this day strong-willed and resolute but I fancy that age has begun to blunt the sharp edge of her determination. She is not a person who entertains doubts, which makes her an ideal mother for the very young – firmness is so re-assuring to the young especially when, as in the case of my mother, it is tempered by a large dash of gaiety and a constant supply of affection. She was never a dragon or an ogre – the very idea is ludicrous – but she liked everyone to do things her way and mostly people were content to bask in the glow of her vitality and do just that. At that period of my life – from 1840 to 1846 – I could not have managed without her. Not a word would have been written but for her willingness to stand in as mother to my children, and if you see no reason to thank God for that cheerful acceptance of a considerable burden, I do.

For some reason I was not able to dump my little family straight away upon my mother's doorstep so they stayed at first with my grandmother, Mrs. Butler, who very soon found them as intolerable a burden as they found her, but everything righted itself once they were installed in my parents' flat in the Avenue St. Marie. Both sides took to each other at once and I can't tell you what a relief it was to see my little ones lose that pinched, deprived look that even the ministrations of the devoted Brodie had not been able to keep entirely at bay. They knew at once that they were secure and loved and that nothing bad was going to happen to them if Papa went away, as he was always telling them he must. And they had such fun – my mother was inventive and original and my stepfather liked nothing better than a small audience for some of his more eccentric practices. They were taken out and about far more often than had been the case of late in London and they were stimulated beyond words by the warmth and life of Paris. In a very short time I knew I need have no worries about my daughters.

With my wife, it was different – there was no end to the worry in those first years of her illness. I have promised not to make a meal of that sad story and I shan't, but oh dear it all but finished me. I noticed I disliked hearing of other people's good luck but that I was delighted to hear of their misfortune and begged my friends to write and tell me quickly if they knew of anyone disfigured by smallpox or robbed of their jewels or some other disaster that any right-thinking man would have been appalled by. The trouble was, I was decidedly not right-thinking – how could I be when I had a sick wife that nobody would cure ? I took her from place to place all over Europe in the hope of receiving beneficial treatment but it was always the same – at first Isabella would seem to respond and my hopes would soar, but then inevitably her progress slowed down and in a very short while she would be as bad as ever. How I longed for some kindly, older medical man at the top of his tree to take me aside and explain to me exactly what was amiss and how it could best be put right. I would have taken any verdict like a man provided I was certain that it was correct, but it was never my luck to meet with such an oracle. I listened to scores of speeches by eminent doctors about my wife and none of them made sense. What I learned about her condition I learned through trial and error – in short, the hard way. I knew fairly soon that her illness was not physical – rest and good food and plenty of sleep soon restored her body. Her trouble was mental and even then not consistent, by which I mean she could be perfectly sane and lucid for quite long stretches of time before reverting to that frightening melancholia that characterised her disease. This being the case, would she not be better off at home with a nurse ? Would I not be able to look after her myself and gain some at least of the benefits of her company ? The answer turned out, painfully, to be no. At home, Isabella was dangerous precisely because she could appear so normal, and then one minute with a child alone and the damage would be done. Her mood could change without warning and any kind of responsibility was beyond her. She would never have harmed the children except by neglect but that could be frightful and then I had to consider the effect of the company of an unstable mother on two young girls. I thought it most extraordinary, and still do, that though of such a highly nervous disposition Isabella could also be stoical in the face of pain – it confused us all. I remember once she had a tooth pulled out as big

as an ink-bottle and did not even cry " oh! " and yet she could not apparently
cope with ordinary wear and tear and the demands of household and children.

At home or elsewhere was but the first stage of the problem – if elsewhere,
where ? I tried Esquirols, the famous clinic outside Paris, but it did not
seem right.   Isabella would beg me on my visits to take her away and
sometimes I did.   I remember, among the blackness, a spring day when I

walked across the fields at Ivry with her hand in hand in the sunshine with
flowers all around and the river glinting at our feet and her laughter, so
natural and unforced, warming me as I had not been warmed for months
and telling me that everything would after all be put right. We talked and
told stories and she leaned on my arm in the most engaging fashion and as I
looked down into her clear eyes I could not doubt that she was well. We

dined at a little gudgeon house and drank champagne and Isabella kissed me and flung herself into my arms, whereupon a waiter burst in upon us and would not believe we were an old married couple.   Only let this continue, I thought, and see if I shan't be the happiest man in the world.   For a while, it seemed my wish was granted but then the inevitable regression occurred and I was compelled to seek another cure, this time in Germany – oh what a business that was!   The sanatorium I took my wife to was near Boppard on the Rhine.   The treatment consisted of subjecting the patient to alternate showers of very hot and very cold water in the belief that the shock to the brain would restore the mental balance.   I had grave doubts but was persuaded to try it.   Isabella could not at first stand up to the immense sluicing of the water so I accompanied her into the chamber where it took place, looking perfectly ridiculous clad only in an old petticoat of my mother's.   I think it was the absurdity of the picture I presented that finally convinced me enough was enough – I must stop chasing after so-called cures and find a permanent home for Isabella.

Do you think the world is full of apple-cheeked ladies all waiting to look after mentally ill girls?   I think I thought something like that and was rudely awakened.   Looking after the mentally ill seems to bring out the very worst in people – they think that if the patient is an idiot she cannot tell on them, as if the unkempt hair and dirty clothes did not tell their own tale. Besides, my wife was not an idiot or a lunatic and it is not just pride that makes me say this.   I have seen lunatics, God help me, and my wife bears no resemblance to those strange, wild, violent women whom I have seen wandering half demented round the grounds of institutions.   To their ranks Isabella will never belong, for though not entirely sane she is not mad but rather belongs to that grey unmarked land between the two.   Nor do I believe, as some have tried to convince me, that she has no feelings and that I could lock her away and she would be quite happy – she would not, and besides she has her rights like you and I, the rights of a human being and a Christian.   There is nothing more likely to turn your stomach than the treatment of the mad in our land and I do solemnly believe that the plight of these lunatics is worse than any of the other evils we have in our midst.   If I have worked to leave my children well provided for how much harder have I worked to ensure that my poor wife can be looked after in privacy and comfort all her days.

A sniff, a weep, a shake of my head and come let us finish with this quickly – Isabella was lodged temporarily at Chaillot after I washed my hands of clinics and cures, and I took myself off to London and pastures new. Does that sound callous?   You don't think much of it?   Well, there are two things I can say about your high-mindedness – firstly that you can never have been afflicted with a sick wife as a constant companion and secondly you are not me, and that is the major difference.   I found that with my

temperament enforced seclusion with an invalid turns me into the monster
I am otherwise not. Now what good does that do ? Isn't it better to stay
kind and humane, doesn't it make more sense to do my best in my own way ?
I know some martyrs who would say no, it is still desertion, but I cannot go
along with them even if I admire them and I am not sure that I do. Besides,
financial considerations effectively prevented me from staying permanently
at my wife's side – I needed to earn money to keep her as well as my children.
My mother generously offered all she had but that " all " was nothing much
and I did not intend to take advantage of her kindness more than was
absolutely necessary. It was enough that she gave the girls a home until
such time as I could provide an alternative, and there would be no alternative
unless I returned to London and set about working like a demon to earn
everyone's keep. London was the place to be, unencumbered by sick wife
or small children, and I never doubted that my decision was the right and
only one.

Perhaps unwisely I returned to our old house in Great Coram St., sharing
it with my cousin Mary and her husband. It was not a particularly comfortable existence but we shared the rent and so I was provided with cheap
quarters at a time when economy was important. Mary was no better a
housewife than poor Isabella had been, but whereas in my wife's case the
cobwebs were nothing beside her cheerful welcome they loomed large in that
frigid household where I felt myself excluded. But there were alternatives,
namely my clubs and other people's houses, all of which grew to know me
rather well. Clubs were invented for men like me – men without a real

home who seek security in some other place where they will find companionship and good food and wine and not feel conspicuous. You reply, smartly,
that my case is feeble since I have told you how I was always dashing out to
clubs even when I had all those things, but there was a difference – before,
my club was a recreation, afterwards a refuge. Now do you see ?

There is no doubt I like to be known in some quarters – not in the street –
that is odious – nor anywhere public so that it becomes a nuisance – but at
my clubs I do enjoy being known. I like to walk up King St. knowing that
the minute I walk up those steps the doorman will sight me and have a smile
ready and my paper and if there is beans and bacon on the menu I shall hear
about it first. I like to walk into the smoking-room and have a place made
for me at the fire and a hand offer me my favourite cigar and another a drink,
and I like to know that my moods will not be misinterpreted so that should
I decline both and slump into a chair and go in for building castles in the
flames no one will take offence. I like all the little attentions and amenities
– the club notepaper, the inkwells always full, the ashtrays always empty,
the boy ready waiting to run messages, the newspapers and magazines laid
out for inspection – all those trivial things. I like the rules too – I like
knowing where I can speak loudly and where whispers are the order of the
day, I like knowing where to put cloaks and muddy boots and where to
sit to be served first and what time I may first come in and last go out
without inconveniencing anyone. In those early days, before I became a
gnarled old pillar of these establishments, I also liked to feel a certain
affection and deference on everyone's part – it made me feel important even
when I mocked it and I prized it highly.

I wasn't important in 1842, of course, not even in that tiny world. If
you want the truth I don't mind confessing that my obscurity troubled me
and caused me a good deal of teeth-gnashing. I had a reputation, but of an
odd kind and certainly not of the recognisable sort. I had, after all, been
writing steadily for some ten years in one guise or another and I should have
been most surprised if my varied and enormous output had not made some
impression. The thing was, I was known very well by those who com-
missioned work but hardly at all by those who read it, by which I mean the
public. This was due to never writing under my own name but always
either anonymously or under a pseudonym. Then again, if I had stuck only
to M. A. Titmarsh or to Fitzboodle, news of who that was would soon have
leaked out, but by employing some dozen or more names I spiked my own
guns – but there was professional cunning in my method for if I had used
the same name I should not have been so widely used. Everyone in the
newspaper world likes to think their correspondent writes only for them you
know. What I needed more than ever was that hit I yearned for when I
could throw off the masks and be myself thenceforth. It was to that end
that I worked and worked, churning out yards of copy and all the time

testing and trying a dozen different themes in the hopes that I would light upon the one that would make me. Perhaps you don't like to hear of such cold-bloodedness in art – perhaps you like your writers genuinely inspired all the time without a jot of calculation. I suppose they do exist, those fellows, but I am not of their number – I always have to put my books together and think them out first and if I don't the labour is tremendous. My only advantage in this respect is that I know what I can pull off and what I can't – or I do now, and quickly learned in the beginning, sometimes at great cost.

I don't propose to take you solemnly through all my mighty works – they are all there on the shelves if you are interested – but I ought to mention *Catherine* and *Barry Lyndon*, just to show you how wrong I found I could go – and *The Second Funeral of Napoleon* to show you that even when I succeeded nobody cared, and brought me to conclude that the system was rigged and Shakespeare himself would not have been granted a hearing.

Catherine was my first attempt at a full length novel, conceived to demonstrate villainy in its true colours, and I believe I have told you of the little noise it made. *Barry Lyndon* was altogether more ambitious, written in 1844 soon after my second visit to Ireland and the publication finally of that long delayed *Irish Sketch-Book.*. In it I attempted to put together several elements that I concluded made best-sellers – a hero who was a villain, a narrative that stretched across Europe, a setting that ranged from princely splendour to peasant poverty. Well, it was a disaster and I hardly got the thing underway before I knew it was going to be. It was a hotch-potch of different themes that did not mix and it lay like lead on my soul. The necessity of finishing this quickly detested book – it was appearing in *Fraser's Magazine* so there was no drawing out – pushed me into accepting a free berth on the *Lady Mary Wood* which was journeying to Egypt and back. I thought if I was trapped in a cabin the words would come out more easily but oh la! what a mistake. I moaned and groaned over every dreadful chapter and was bitten to death by bugs and racked by seasickness every line of the way. When I finished it somewhere off Malta I was entirely spent and almost cured for life of the desire to be a novelist. If someone at that point had put me at the head of a dashing magazine with a decided air of white kid gloves about it I should have thrown over my ambitions and jumped for joy.

But nobody did. I returned to London consoling myself with the thought that my journey had at least provided me with material for another travel book – *Notes of a journey from Cornhill to Grand Cairo* – and that my wanderlust was partially abated. All the same, I can remember how un-settled I was as I came back to that constant whirl of nothing-doing. I can follow myself up Jermyn St. – I had taken rooms there in preference to sharing Great Coram St. – and up the steps of 44 to my quarters above a chemist's shop. Ah how slowly I climbed the stairs, not really wanting to reach my room where a wooden table and a day's work awaited me. It was exceedingly plainly furnished, that room, with its rush seated chairs and painted French bedstead and nothing much else. I would breakfast off a penny roll and hot chocolate and then sit at that table and work my way through reviews and articles in a state of quiet desperation and then at night out I would go to dinners and parties, smiling and talking and bowing my way round the company until it was time to return to my garret. Am I trying to tear at your heart strings? Well, I won't succeed, will I, for it wasn't a garret and I was wearing a silk dressing-gown as I worked – but spare a small sigh for my loneliness. I missed my wife, I missed my children, I missed my home – all that was real. The irony of my position did not escape me – hadn't I cursed the domestic uproar that prevented me from working and yet wasn't I now cursing the solitude I had craved? An awful resentment began to build up in me – why should I be denied the comforts of a home and the joy of children simply because my wife was sick? There was no doubt that after a couple of years of this false bachelor existence I

longed to return to family life. I missed the small people consumedly – longing for them created a kind of muzziness and incoherence that prevented me working – and besides I came to believe I needed their good influence. There is nothing heartbreakingly persuasive about a child's innocence – when I took hold of Anny's hand or held Minny on my lap my whole life since I had last seen them would seem shabby and unworthy and it would come over me with a rush that they were my guardian angels and that I needed them by my side. Don't fear that I was up to any mischief in London on my own – no return to gambling or other sordid pastimes – but I did spend my days drinking and eating and whirling about whenever I was not working and it was this kind of giddiness I looked to correct. Every time I left my daughters in Paris – where I may say they were blissfully happy without me – I would bawl my head off at the pathos of the parting, and for a day or two the mere sight of children their age would set me off again. Once I was deluded enough to imagine I actually did see them and how I ran along the street and how I blushed when at last confronted by perfect strangers. I longed in equal measure for my wife – just for the sight of her and the rare moment of happiness if I was there to catch her good spells. It became my fixed intention to bring my entire family to London and install the lot of them in some double cottage in Hampstead or Hammersmith where we would all be together and yet separate. The stumbling block was money – I knew such a vision would need a lot of money to realise and however hard I worked and however much I earned I still seemed incapable of amassing sufficient capital to bring this happy state into being. But if I could make one hit — you see how I was brought back to that wretched hit that would not come again and again ?

I have always had a degree of perseverance if I wanted a thing badly enough and I did want my family about me before too long. I began, little by little, to raise my fees and was astounded when nobody murmured but paid up on the spot. I began also to write for a new low magazine called *Punch* that paid very well and was great fun. It took me a while to catch the tone of the paper but once I did — after a false start — I had the best vehicle a man could have for his talents and used it to the full. They gave me a free hand before very long — I could contribute anything I wanted — poems, parodies, caricatures, criticisms — they accepted everything and gave me security when I most needed it. Knowing that I now had a personal connection with a flourishing magazine — was indeed their main contributor and in a measure depended upon — gave me great confidence in a way that writing for ten or twelve periodicals never had. Don't think such permanence made me lower my standards, content in the knowledge that I would be published — not a bit of it — I *never* lowered my standards but was always aware that every single piece of writing could have been improved. Hardly anything left my hands without several attempts at improvement and when I finally did let a piece go that I remained dissatisfied with, it was only because the printers' boy would wait no longer. Nor do I altogether despise my efforts when I look back — it is all very well to despise journalism but some of it can be good, and of use, and amusing people is in itself a perfectly worthwhile occupation. Reading stuff in *Punch* you might think it was all run off in five minutes so easily does most of it run off the eye, but that is not so — I know I spent many hours over articles, just as long in some cases as I have over chapters of novels. Nor is the labour any less — the well informed, responsible journalists, among whom I number myself, take a great deal of care over checking their facts and sources and in reading round their subjects and that is hard work. No book I reviewed ever went unread or was skimmed through — quite the reverse, for I did not consider myself qualified to pronounce an opinion without doing the author the compliment of familiarising myself with his pedigree so that I could better understand the work in hand. I took myself seriously and my craft equally so, sometimes to the detriment of my health, and often my happiness.

I remember one piece in particular that upset me for months so seriously did I take it — a piece on a hanging I attended in order to decide for myself whether it was or was not a barbarous spectacle and advise my readers accordingly. It turned out to be a perfectly horrible experience but I was duty bound to report it faithfully with all the attendant emotions and I do believe I opened some people's eyes. Or another piece, on families emigrating — why, I cried for a week after I had been to the docks to see them go, and again I honestly think I told my readers something they ought to have known and did not and might do something about when they did.   I don't mean they would go and cut down the man waiting to be hanged or house the family driven to emigrate because they had no home – nothing so definite – simply that each individual, by feeling differently, changes the climate of opinion and that way society changes too, given time.

I suppose the above is a spirited enough defence of journalism but I suspect you think I protest a little too much, and I own that I do – journalism was not enough.   Even when I was happiest doing it, it was not enough – I wanted to be a novelist and would not be fobbed off with another career however tempting it was.   It did not satisfy me, that was the trouble – it was transitory, here today, in the dustbin tomorrow, whereas novels ended up leather bound and on shelves.   *O Vanitas vanitatum !*   There I have them, rows of them, shelves of them, and yet still I feel dissatisfied, except for a small corner of me that fills with wicked, conceited pride as my eye lights on one volume, or perhaps two.   Well, that is enough – it might have been none – I might have left nothing behind me and Dickens could have reigned alone.   I can remember in the summer of 1842 setting off to do my *Irish Sketch-Book* and thinking, when I picked up the Liverpool newspaper in the hotel where I stayed waiting for the boat, that there might – there just might – be a paragraph or two about a rather well-known London journalist on his way to Ireland and finding instead that it was full of Dickens on his way back from America.   I laughed at myself, but ruefully – why pretend that I did not think of Dickens a great deal ?   At one time I was obsessed with the fellow – which writer was not ?   There he was, at the top of the tree, *Pickwick* written at twenty-five, four more hits before he was thirty, a celebrated, acknowledged genius in his own time – good heavens, of course I thought about the fellow and still do – and I was envious, not of him but of his amazing skill, to which I hope I have paid sufficient tribute in private and in public.   Why, I could not do otherwise even if I did not agree he is a genius – and I do – for my children would not allow it.   They adore Dickens – didn't Minny read *Nicholas Nickleby* when she was happy, *Nicholas Nickleby* when she was unhappy, *Nicholas Nickleby* morning noon and night and at the end looked up at me and said, " Papa, why don't you write a book like *Nicholas Nickleby* ? "   Child, I could not if I wanted to – but do you know – I didn't dare say it to you then for fear of being misunderstood – I DO NOT WANT TO AND NEVER DID WANT TO.   There, does that shock you ?   Does it sound like sour grapes ?   Too bad, because it is true – I admire Dickens, I take my hat off to him, but even in those far off days when I was thirty-six without a novel written and he was a public figure with eight bestsellers, I still did not want to be him.   Do you know why ?   Then I shall tell you: Dickens is larger than life and I do not wish to be larger than life, I wish to be life.   The artist, in my view, must mirror reality adding only sufficient material of his own to make that reality clearer. He must not distort or disfigure for some purpose of his own, whether that may be to make us laugh or cry, or he will end with losing our trust and his work will seem a mere plaything that we need not worry about – the effect will be lost and the achievement spoiled.   Take, for example, Mr. Micawber in that wonderful work *David Copperfield*.   We laugh at Micawber, we point at him and roar with laughter, but when all is said and done he is larger than life and overdone and somehow the author patronises all men like him by making him a figure of fun.   How much better to sacrifice a few of the laughs and a little of the dramatic effect so that Micawber would be real and recognisable and not leave a nasty taste in the mouth.   You will not agree – you will say you love Micawber – you will say *David Copperfield* is far better than anything I have written and you will be quite right and can sleep easily because you have missed the point entirely.   Never mind – I will say what I like and to the devil with the consequences – the pathetic business in all Dickens' books is beautifully done but the characters otherwise are overdrawn and detract from the work. The Art of novels in my opinion *is* to represent nature – to convey as strongly as possible the sentiment of reality.

So, in my youthful – well, middling youthful – arrogance I had the temerity not to want to be Dickens. Good – Dickens was never in danger anyway for my talents, such as they were, were different. Cold-blooded again you see, totting up my own talents, but I'm afraid I did, so I must say so or you might as well have Jones writing this, dear good soul that he is. My style I knew to be flippant, tending towards the sarcastic and aiming for the satirical. I had plenty of fire in my belly when I warmed to a subject – furious diatribes were quite in order. I had, though it may surprise you, a degree of moral fervour – don't that sound ghastly – and a critical appreciation of the finer points of life. I had a keen eye for the contemporary scene, a quick tongue, a careful ear that could exactly catch the mood of the day. My style I thought commendable – use of language a model – no worries on

that score. On the debit side, I was weak on narrative drive, found the handling of time tricky, and though I was sentimental enough myself didn't find that kind of thing easy to write about. What was I to do, ambitious, analytical monster that I was ? How could I exploit my good points and overcome my bad ones ? What the devil could I turn my hand to ?

I think I could tell you precisely how I came to write all my other books, though I shan't except *en passant*, but as to *Vanity Fair* I am stuck. I don't exactly remember the moment of conception, though I remember the writing of it well enough, and I know that it began as a series of sketches on English society – that, you see, had become my background without me realising it. There I was, gadding about from one party to another, taking it all in and not realising that *this* – society life – was my natural material. I had become a social butterfly without noticing, accepting invitations here, there and everywhere with the greatest of ease, and after a very short time driven by boredom to amusing myself by making fun of it all on paper. I don't think I began frequenting balls and dinners as a cynic – I was excited enough in the beginning to be invited to some great person's house – but gradually I saw through the glitter and gold and read in people's faces the true stories of despair and depravity and the whole scene became one of peculiar fascination for me. I went home to my room and put my observations down and then I found they grew into character sketches and it struck me that with very little effort those sketches could be linked and I might have a novel on my hands, a novel in parts, a novel that would be so different and daring, dealing as it would with life as it was, that I would have that hit I craved. The idea made me tremble – so near and yet so far – so possible and yet so elusive – I can tell you I was in a half-frantic state as I tried to put it together, cautioning myself at every step not to expect too much and always to remember my previous failures. I think, though, that I knew there was an important difference this time – namely, my heart was in the subject. I was not contriving interest or putting together other people's stories – I was not inventing opinions and trying to give life to characters I knew nothing about – far from it – I knew them all intimately. How many Becky Sharps do you suppose I had seen in action before I ever wrote down her name ? How many Amelias had crossed my path ? Hadn't I witnessed countless scenes figuring George Osborne and didn't I know his father intimately ? You are going to ask me who exactly all these characters were modelled on and I am going to tell you on no one and everyone and refuse to play that game. It is true I thought of my wife and a certain other person when I described Amelia but that was only the starting point and then as I thought myself into the character all kinds of things happened that took Amelia a million miles from anyone I had known – and as for Becky, why the world is full of them – I have seen them young and old at every party I have ever gone to and I have never tired of reading their faces. It ain't difficult – it is

all there on their sharp little features, the whole sordid story, you don't even need imagination to interpret the expressions. I own to being pleased at the success I had with the Becky doll – and even more pleased at the device of pretending my characters were puppets manipulated for my public's benefit. That was a stroke of genius – the minute I had thought of it I felt happier – I was able to stand back and felt easy about the running of the story. I can't ever go straight into a novel without a thread to guide me – it comes easier if I am the narrator or some such trick, and I find it frees rather than hampers me however clumsy it may strike you.

I seem to be jumping the gun – we haven't got to the publication of *Vanity Fair* yet and I am allowing memories of it to swamp everything else – memories that I have already told you not to depend on. There is something not quite right about this – here we are, bumping along from event to event, adhering to chronology with the most awful solemnity, and what does it all add up to ? Not much more than the sum of those wearisome biographies I refuse to have written about me. In my eagerness to be simple and straightforward I am becoming a bore, falling into the very trap I confidently expected to avoid. What to do ? What did I mean to be about ? Well, I thought that in every man's life there ought to be information worth passing on without burying it in 800 pages of turgid prose. I thought I could amuse and divert you and perhaps even teach you a thing or two and find answering chords in your own life that might interest you. The trouble is, the thing hooks me – I get carried away constantly looking back and trying to make sense of shadowy images and I am making every little thing important – where is my sense of proportion ? Gone – telescoped to oblivion. There is a dreadful fascination in dredging through my life and lighting upon the high and low points – I am caught and could not leave it alone now if I chose however imperfect I know the balance to be. I must surely be able to make sense out of fifty-odd years – there must be a key that will unlock the door to understanding – either that or I am in the grip of some dangerous malady that afflicts the elderly, some fatal egotism that needs to be fed by the constant repetition of quite trivial details from the past. In a little while I know I am going to tell you about Young St. and my family life there and do you know I am already enjoying the prospect of displaying my ability to recall the exact rent I paid ? It is pathetic, but I can't help it – and I notice the same loving attention to the most boring facts in the past being paid by my contemporaries as they sit immovable in big leather chairs and reminisce for all they are worth. You don't care what the rent was, do you, or the name of my servant, or what I usually had for dinner ? No, of course you don't and neither should I, but only start to cast back in your own life and you will find the same joy in this kind of thing. I intend to struggle on, hoping that this strain will wear itself out and by degrees I shall come up with something worthwhile (oh well done Thackeray – the perfect excuse for a lot of mumbling and muttering!). In the meantime, the years are skeletons to hang my thoughts on and I shall rattle them before you in strict rotation.

1846 – a good year, but I wonder if I thought so then ? Somehow, I doubt it. I had my head down and did not see good fortune when it was staring me in the face – or perhaps it came disguised and I did not recognise it, used as I had become to blows of one kind or another. It was scribble, scribble all day and hob-nob every evening and only an occasional break for sanity. My thoughts at the time I know were pre-occupied with the bringing of my family to London rather than with the placing of *Vanity Fair* – the early chapters, that is – with a publisher, though in truth the two events had a connection. I am glad, all the same, that I did manage to bring my wife and daughters to London before the success of *Vanity Fair* made it financially possible – I wouldn't like to think that the matter had hinged

quite so much as that on money. What had prevented me had never been money, apart from the first two impossible years of that unhappy separation, but the responsibility that would be mine if I took my daughters from a happy home with their grandparents to a scene of domestic chaos with their poor father. Was I entitled to take the risk? I asked myself that question all the time and came up with conflicting answers every day. Anny was by this time eight years old and more my daughter every time I saw her. She would write letters that made me laugh out loud – " I am unhappy and don't know y " – Yellowplush to the core. She was a man of genius and no mistake, full of spirit and it was this that worried me. My mother was increasingly driven to report that Anny had frightful tantrums and that in many other respects showed a want of restraint and decorum. I wrote back that she must be disciplined, with the rod if necessary, but what a panic I was in the minute this sensible order left my hand! I fell immediately to thinking that my daughter's behaviour could only be the result of some kind of frustration and that life with elderly grandparents surrounded by fuddy-duddy friends was no life for a high-spirited young girl. My mother's influence I knew to be prodigious and that too gave me cause for alarm – there she was bringing up two sensitive intelligent girls to believe that the Old Testament was a verbatim report of actual events and I did not like to think about it.   I wanted to teach the girls what I believed and leave them to make up their own minds, not have them filled with the nonsense my mother believed and told that to think differently was wicked.   Very soon they would be more her children than mine – I would miss those formative years and never be able to make them up however many letters I wrote or however many flying visits I fitted in.   But however great my panic in this respect, I still for a long time held back, long after I was convinced that something must and should be done, defeated by the hows and wheres and with-whoms of the business.   I was a single man, a busy single man – how could such a person look after two little girls? I would need a woman, a whole tribe of women, for many years – not just servants but someone to be a mother and be with them night and day, and then if I found that someone, how would I get on with them ?   I dreaded the thought of depending on some harridan who would quickly realise her power and drive me out of the house (if I found one) and defeat the whole object of the arrangement.   I thought it would be preferable to have my parents, but my stepfather, neck-deep in some crazy new scheme to make his fortune, refused to consider leaving Paris and my mother would not leave him.   She was unwilling to surrender the girls and I had to take that into account too – I should be making her very unhappy, scant repayment for all the love and care she had given so unstintingly.   She would come and stay and still see them but it would not be the same and I should have torn a huge hole in the comfortable fabric of her life with them.

What was a man to do?   Sometimes I think those who go through life insensitive to the needs of others are the blessed ones – it is so tiring to be constantly setting off somebody else's pain beside your own, so continually sharing their anguish until any course of action becomes quite impossible. I know of nothing more wearing than knowing what is going on in some-body else's head and heart – I swear another's grief is much worse than our own.   How smooth the passage through life is for those who know only their own thoughts and fears – how swiftly they are transported, never having to stop and take on an extra passenger – how comfortable they are putting themselves first because it never occurs to them that there is anyone else waiting.   I have many times longed to share their carriage and cursed my awareness of other's thoughts.

Enough.   In 1846 I brought my wife and children to London and I shall enjoy telling you about the change it wrought in my life and How the Man was Saved just in time – saved from losing his family life I mean, nothing worse.

Chapter IX

———————◆———————

LIFE AT 13, YOUNG ST., KENSINGTON

I HAVE among my acquaintance several families who enjoy the pleasures of an ancestral home, a house rather grander than most set in the country with grounds and that kind of thing and inhabited over a period of many years by parents and grand-parents and great-grandparents, and I have always envied them — not for possessing the actual house with the wealth that implies but for the continuity it gives their lives. I should love to have had a Thackeray house, set somewhere near Harrogate where we hail from, not too large or imposing but big enough to accommodate a few friends in comfort as well as my family. I would have enjoyed all the associations — uncle Henry put that window in, grandpa built that summerhouse, great-aunt Lucy insisted on a lawn here — and the roots that go with them, and I would have enjoyed collecting lovely things to go into it side by side with the heirlooms, each with its story. What fun it would have been to have Anny sleep in some old bedroom of mine and watch Minny sit reading in the special corner beside the fireplace that was mine by common consent. How thrilling to point at an apple tree and say it was planted the day I was born and pick an apple from the bough, or push a child on a swing hanging from an oak I had climbed as a boy — well, I am a sentimental old fool and there is no family home, no oak or apple trees and no traditions. The recent Thackerays have mostly been rolling stones and to find the connections with property that I appear to crave I would have to go to India, where I might possibly discover a stick or two that my mother could endow with meaning for me. If my wife had remained well, perhaps my small ambition to begin such a home might have been realised, but as it is I must be content with this mansion I live in now. Who knows — it may yet turn out to be full of Anny and Minny's families and they will have the fun even if I did not.

At any rate, you see why 13, Young St. in Kensington was precious to me even though it was a mere stand-in for what I had in mind and never properly owned by me. The girls and I lived there from 1846 to 1854, the longest time I had ever resided in one place and a happy one. The house was nothing special — double-fronted, bow-windowed — but it was pretty and conveniently situated on the outskirts of London and reasonable at £65 a year (there — I told you I would tell you the rent). I settled on a room at the back for my study, a room with two windows shaded by a vine looking out on a medlar tree and some Spanish jessamines. The garden was quite big, full of heavily scented flowers — verbenas, stacks of flags, London Pride, blush roses — and it caught any sun there was. My bedroom was also at the back above this study, and above that was the schoolroom where such a lot of energetic banging and thumping went on that I could hear it even at two rooms' distance. That room became a positive menagerie — Minny kept two doves there, not to mention cats and a windowsill full of snails and flies. The rest of the house had the usual number of other rooms, though rather short on bedrooms with a governess (more about her later) and relatives occasionally staying for quite long periods. The whole was furnished in the most extra-ordinary style — a mixture of things my mother gave me, odds and ends left over from Great Coram St., and things I had picked up between times. It was, in short, a bachelor establishment, elegant in parts but mostly comfortable and decidedly shabby — we were quite likely to pour our tea out of an old cracked teapot into the most exquisite cups, or eat with a tin knife and fork from gold plate — well, not quite, but you know the sort of thing. The girls didn't care and neither did I, except sometimes when my soul cried out for beautiful things and a degree of luxury — but it didn't cry very often or very loudly and I didn't listen to it but instead treasured the new life I had been granted.

There wasn't a day I did not give thanks for the laughter and noise that my girls brought with them — after so long in chill rooms and other people's houses it was heaven to open my own front door and be greeted with rapturous kisses and smell the dinner cooking and feel part of a family. The joy my children brought me far outweighed the minor irritations and I was touched at how hard they tried to play the part of dutiful daughters, never seeming to mind my erratic habits of coming and going, nor the hours I spent shut up in my study. That study was one of their favourite places, though it was meant to be out of bounds. They liked to admire my pencils which I kept fiercely pointed and watched me cut nibs at a certain reverse angle I liked with rapt attention until I could not help but smile at the awe with which they were prepared to regard such simple operations. I hope they were not unhappy — sometimes I think I was too grave and unbending and that I did not pay enough attention to the needs of two young women. They didn't, God bless 'em, ever complain but I ought to have romped more with them and brought more life into the house. I once tried to say this but Anny put her hand over my mouth and laughed and persisted in mentioning only how I took them everywhere with me and how many interesting houses they saw, much better than being at home. That was true – I did take them everywhere. Hostesses inviting Mr. Thackeray during the daytime had to accept that their invitation was understood to include the Misses Anne and

Harriet Thackeray too. They never let me down, but discussed the weather with Mrs. Carlyle – who always had two cups of hot chocolate waiting – with wonderful gravity or poetry with Mrs. Browning with commendable enthusiasm, or their health with anyone who asked after it. They were marvellously catered for by these kind ladies – endless tea and jellies and cakes until they threatened to turn into regular fatties, or at least Anny did, taking after yours truly in that department. Minny was more like her mother and like her, delicate, which worried me – I took care that she should not be too tired or over-excited and that not too many demands were made upon her. She was not so clever as Anny but more *sympathique*, with a quietness and sweetness about her that the more robust Anny lacked. I always had the feeling – I still have it – that Minny must be watched over or the shadow of her mother will fall upon her – God grant that when she marries it will be to someone who understands that.

Isabella was not part of this happy household, though I looked to the day, when the girls were older, when she might be. My worries on her account were nevertheless largely assuaged by the discovery of an excellent woman in Camberwell, a Mrs. Bakewell, with whom I was able to board her. A week after she had been brought from Paris to stay with this Mrs. Bakewell the difference was remarkable and my heart lifted to see her look so well and happy – her hair shone, her clothes fitted her, she laughed as she used to and played the piano cheerfully. I went to see her in those days very often, and took the girls with me, though sometimes it was distressing for them – their mother hardly recognised them though I had seen to it that they were taken to visit her regularly in Paris. One day I had to tell them all about Isabella but it was not until they were older and less likely to be upset or frightened by the details that must of necessity come out. They accepted, when they were young, that their mother was a pretty lady they sometimes visited and that she wasn't well enough to live with us. If this state of affairs struck them as odd I don't remember them saying so – they grew up without a mother and didn't until later think it the least remarkable. It is never any good reading into children's lives thoughts that simply are not there except when adults put them there, or so I have found. Don't weep into your handkerchief because Anny and Minny were motherless – *they* didn't.

I wonder whether it was mere coincidence that my children joined me in 1846 and *Vanity Fair* came out the next year with such success ? Though the early chapters were already done before I moved into Young St. and resumed day-to-day family life, I wrote the bulk of the novel afterwards and I like to think that my new happiness at that time gave me an impetus I had missed. I don't suppose you will be convinced – you might even say rather sternly that if I had not been so domestically involved the book might have been even better. The strain was certainly there, but it was not the children who caused it but rather the endless juggling necessary in a household without a mother. For a while I thought I had solved that problem by having to live with us Bess Hammerton, a distant relation, but it simply did not work – she was no more a substitute for Isabella than water is for wine. What I needed, you see, was not just a housekeeper and chaperone but a fountainhead of feminine wisdom combining affection and discipline and tolerance with common-sense. Bess lacked this quality. As a housekeeper she was moderately satisfactory – telling servants how to do things was quite in her line – but as a mother she was a disaster. All she cared about was a vulgar keeping-up-of-appearances that drove Anny frantic – she was forever goading the child into rebellion by her vehement insistence on ridiculous points of order. She could keep the girls clean and tidy and healthy and see that their day outwardly ran smoothly but that was the limit of her contribution. She could not give them either the emotional or intellectual sustenance they needed, and I was not surprised that in a very short time they grew to resent and even hate her mealy-mouthed attitudes – I myself so loathed her that I took to having my breakfast in my room to avoid her presence at that tender time of the day. In the end, I told her to go – yes, straight out, amazing myself by my forthrightness, a trait in my character I had always thought I lacked. She went, in a huff, leaving me guilty but relieved. It was a case, however, of out of the frying-pan and into the fire – I had to have someone and there was no alternative but the dreaded governess. Have you ever been in desperate need of such a creature ? Then you will

know that all the hardship is not on one side.   Nobody deplores more than
I the exploitation of young, poor girls in that profession, but all the same my
heart feels for the employers too, especially when they are absolutely
dependent as I was.   I was always entering into treaties for some paragon –
miracle of sweet temper and so forth – and always ending up with some
whey-faced shrew, or worse still some pretty but utterly incompetent minx.
Oh, I wanted the impossible I agree – I wanted a girl easy on the eye but
not disturbing, if you see what I mean, and I wanted her self-effacing but
pleasant, and firm but not domineering, and happy but not forever giggling,
and so on.   I never found her, though one or two were not so bad.   After
Bess went, I first of all had a Miss Drury, clergyman's daughter, excellent
references – she lasted six months before it was quite clear to me, and I think
to her, that Anny had the upper hand and it would not do, and then we had
to go through the horrible business of dismissing her – tears, embarrassment,
pitiful looks – and finding another.   How my spirits used to droop waiting
for them to arrive – waiting to see this highly important stranger who must
perforce share our life but who we did not want – and don't think I did not

imagine her thoughts too.   After Miss Drury we had a Miss Alexander,
who was a nuisance but more successful – her main drawback was her
constant presence – she never knew when to withdraw and leave me to enjoy
my children.   If I came into the schoolroom and announced I had tickets
for the play who do you suppose had her coat on first, though she had not
been asked ?   Why Miss Alexander of course.   She had no tact – she was

like a leech – but she was honest and eager to do her duty and very adequate at teaching, so I had to put up with her, especially since chicken-pox raged in the house and I was knee-deep in work. In the end I grew so used to her that I dreaded her leaving – that is what happens, I am afraid – familiarity makes you grow fonder and it is such a relief to be at least settled and you quite forget you do not like the lady. I was forever giving my girls instructions to grow up quickly so that we could dispense with a governess, or threatening them with boarding school any minute when arrangements broke down and we were left temporarily with nobody except my grandmother who presided over us for some years and had her own decided views on the subject. I expect I will have to return to the question of governesses in this account before I am through with them – they did loom large as an aggravation – but you can be sure that my feelings never changed and that I don't end up falling in love with one of them or anything like that.

But I did fall in love, and no account of my life at this period would be complete without confessing that I did. If you see a large red flag waving above my head you will please to remember that I told you of my difficulty – that I wish to be truthful about delicate matters but not at anyone else's expense and not so that I betray anyone's trust. I wonder what the world will say about Jane Brookfield and I when we are both dead? Perhaps it will say nothing – perhaps that sad story will be buried forever, and rightly so, but I cannot leave it untouched however much I may wish to. My love for Jane caused me more pain than any other event in my life, not excepting Isabella's illness or the death of my child. It tortured me for years, and when finally the pain lessened to a dull ache and the dull ache to emptiness, I still never forgot or forgave the way in which I was treated. That statement will puzzle you – what the devil does the fellow mean? What is he trying to say – what kind of love is this that causes such a lot of bother?

It is damnably hard to be honest in a case like this. If I were back in Young St. in 1847 it would be so easy to laugh and introduce you to my friend Jane Brookfield, wife of my old Cambridge companion, William Brookfield. I would do it with such pride and so openly – this, I would say, is the lovely lady I admire most in the world, this is the kind, gentle woman my girls adore and whom I wish them to adore, this is the goddess I worship daily – AND I SHOULD SAY IT IN FRONT OF HER HUSBAND. Does that startle you? Do you believe instantly that I have been misleading you? Well, I have not, but the history of my love for Jane Brookfield is complicated. It is hard to be honest, it is even harder to begin at all. Let us begin with William, for it did begin with him. William was a clergyman, not entirely through choice but because it was the only way he could get on in the world with his large talents and small income. I resumed my friendship with him when I came back to living in London after Isabella's illness. He was a curate of St. James's Piccadilly and since I was virtually a bachelor our activities inevitably centred round William's home and not my rooms. He urged me to treat his home as my own — was forever inviting me round, asking me to stay, pooh-poohing my hesitation in case I intruded. I don't think I am mistaken in emphasising the warmth of my welcome and the insistence of my host's hospitality — I have asked myself time and time again if I have misrepresented the case and I am sure I have not, I am convinced I did not ingratiate myself or push in where I was not wanted, and I am sure the Brookfields would agree. We were friends and we loved each other — what is there to be ashamed of in that? I never saw Jane without William being present, I never paid her a compliment without her husband hearing it and I think enjoying the praise as much as she did. There was nothing in the least sinister about our relationship until other people made it so. We shared the same tastes and friends and pastimes so it was natural that we should see each other almost daily and write when we did not. I for one never thought for one minute that there was any need for caution because I never looked ahead, and even if I had I think I should only have seen us continuing like that forever. Was that stupid? Do you sneer and doubt my integrity, or at least smirk at my innocence? Well, I was innocent — I am to this day — I know I am an entirely honourable married family man and have no qualms about my own behaviour. It never occurred to me to reason thus: my friend's wife is beautiful and I love her and this love may develop into an uncontrollable passion and she will have to choose between us and she may choose him and turn me away and I shall be desolate and therefore I had better not be friends in case this happens. I don't go through life in that way any more than you do, and it is nonsense to suggest that we should.

The truth was, I needed a Jane Brookfield in my life. I have always liked the company of women and admired that sex wholeheartedly and I could not live without some sweet, pretty maiden around, if only for an hour or so a day. You know how I missed my wife — we need not go over that again — but you don't know how hard it was to reconcile myself to the absence of female company simply because I had no wife. Oh, I saw plenty of women as I whirled about from party to party and dinner to dinner — hordes of 'em — but I don't mean that, I mean I wanted feminine company in a domestic setting. Jane Brookfield provided it. She sat at the piano in the evening and played and sang for William and me, and smiled at us, and afterwards poured out tea in front of the fire and engaged us in that kind of pretty conversation at which women excel. I liked to be wicked and challenge her opinion simply to see the delicate flush on her cheeks and hear the spirited reply that she fancied was harsh and in reality was sweet and soft as music. But Jane was not entirely meek and mild — far from it, for she had a sharp intelligence that I admired. I think she was the first woman I ever met with whom I could talk freely and equally on any subject I liked

and I was quite astonished at how this exhilarated me. Now, I had not been able to do this with Isabella as you very well know, though it may have been my fault that I could not. Jane was something different – she was wasted at home. I fancied I saw in her the tragedy of being a woman in our society, condemned to a milk-and-water existence when her brain was equal to a man's and perhaps her ambition also, though it was set in no particular direction. She never expressed her frustration or discontent but I could see quite well for myself that she was trapped and longed to be free. She had no children – not at that time – and I think a woman without children is even more conscious that nature is in some way cheating her and that she is filling in her days in a way that revolts her creative spirit. She had her husband and a pleasant life, but that was not enough – minds like Jane's need more and I wished with all my heart that I could provide it. I set Jane on a pinnacle and pointed her out to Anny and Minny and did my best work with her in mind and William seemed to me to encourage me and relish my admiration for his wife. Our intimacy extended to Jane adopting the role of mother to my daughters on many occasions – it seemed so convenient that she had no children and wanted them and they had no mother and wanted one. Both sides were delighted with the opportunity to be of use and love each other and none of us thought this connection anything but fortunate. We were at their house or they were at our house more days than not and if people shot us dark looks and muttered among themselves even at that early date then I neither saw nor heard them.

It may seem I have wandered a long way from my main theme – that I have created an artificial stopping place in my narrative to no purpose – but I think I do have a point that I wish to make with the help of this enormous parenthesis. I am about to have my big success you see – about to shoot to the top of the tree with *Vanity Fair* and since the charge of being the most frightful snob was thereafter immediately levelled at me I wish you to see how firmly my feet were rooted in family life and how impossible it was, given my main concerns at the time, to become conceited. I may have gone hither and thither wherever I was beckoned – indeed I did for I was interested in grand society every bit as much as in the other sort – but I always came home to two small girls intent on cutting me down to size with the demands of their age. How could I possibly boast of my success with two pairs of grave eyes fixed on mine and much more interested in relating their adventures of the day in the garden ? How could I imagine a glittering ball was the height of existence when I had just taken a junior expedition to the Zoo and knew that was ? No, my family life saved me from any head-turning and I don't care what other people say. Isabella had always dreaded the effects of flattery upon me, but she need not have worried – I gadded about but I also prayed daily that I could make myself worthy of those two little girls who depended so much upon me. When I grew sick

and tired of wallowing in turtle and drowning in champagne there was
always mutton at home and two unaffected little companions to prattle in my
ear.   Thoughts of them were constantly with me whatever company I kept
and I had no fears of *Vanity Fair* so long as my guardian angels watched over
me.   Don't forget, also, that fate had arranged my triumph cleverly – had I

not been fourteen years in the wilderness before it arrived, was I not
schooled in disappointment, did I not value it for what it is worth – shallow,
transitory, a matter of chance ?   Oh clever Fate to so prepare your servant.
    There was nobody who knew better than I that the success of a book
depended upon a great many factors other than the contents.   Catching the
public's attention enough to make them like and buy a book is a chancy
business hedged about with ifs and buts.   Best-sellers defy analysis as I know
to my cost.   Do you suppose that if it were an easy matter of putting two
and two together there would not be millions of them ?   But in the literary
game, two and two are more likely to make nothing more than four and if
you don't acknowledge that then you have no place in it.   When *Vanity Fair*
began to come out between the yellow covers of *Punch* in January 1847, I
was in a state of panic about what should be done.   On the one hand, I
wanted puffs everywhere and advertisements and all that kind of thing – even
wrote to some of my influential friends craving their indulgence – but on the
other I did not believe that in the end that kind of publicity did much good
and began instead to want to play it quietly and let the thing gather
momentum on its own.   It was not simply a question of pride – though that

came into it – but rather a feeling that the public automatically resent an over-sold product and that it is better to keep mum rather than beat the drum. Either way – silence or noise – there was a risk and I knew perfectly well that try as I might I could not eliminate that and so I sat still and hoped for the best. It was some consolation that my name had recently been bandied about with the publication of a Christmas book called *Mrs. Perkins's Ball* that had sold very well – only 20,000 less than Dickens you know! It was my belief that this small success would do me some good and that my serial in numbers being brought out so soon after it would attract at least as many readers.

If you think that the day the first number of *Vanity Fair* appeared, people danced in the street and cried Hurrah for Thackeray you are mistaken. Nothing much happened at all for several months while I sat at home praying for a miracle. Perhaps the first chapters are not so striking in any case, or perhaps all serials need a few episodes out before anyone wants to pass an opinion, but for whatever reason we were well into the summer before, with the greatest caution, I began to hazard a guess that I was made. Even then, it was critical rather than pecuniary success and that irked me – all very well being clapped on the back but I wanted gold in the hand as much if not more. There was no general salvo in my direction even then, but people began to rush to pay me compliments, especially the ladies – I do believe it began with the ladies, bless their hearts – and then shortly afterwards the sales increased, though slowly, so that I began to think the book would do everything but make me money, and believe me, if I wanted one thing more than fame or critical success it was guineas, shoals of them, guineas to pay off my debts. The fact was, being not so poor as before, I had unwisely indulged in some railway speculation and got my fingers burnt badly and it was for that sordid reason – except I don't think the making of guineas *is* sordid – that I watched the progress of *Vanity Fair* so closely. I don't think I was sure I had arrived until I saw this in the July edition of the *Athenaeum*:

NEW WORK BY MICHAEL ANGELO TITMARSH

This day is published price 1s. with
Numerous Illustrations on Steel and Wood

PART VII OF

VANITY FAIR

Pen and Pencil Sketches of English Society
by W. M. Thackeray
Author of Mrs. Perkins Ball etc.

Now is that not just like a publisher – I mean to start to advertise once
the book is acclaimed a success ? I shall never understand them – they will
only ever shout from the rooftops what everyone already knows. But once
this advertisement had appeared I think I knew I could uncross my fingers
and start to enjoy the applause, if only I could find the time with each
coming month's episode waiting to be done. The excitement was dreadful
– half way through each month I would become half-frantic as I tried to
meet the deadline and vow that the following month I would write two
episodes early on so that I should escape the terror of believing I would

never finish towards the end – but I never managed it. Somehow I could
never get ahead of myself but was always engaged in a life-or-death struggle
each month, continually surfacing for breath then plunging down again into
the whirlpool of work. It quite astonished me that the words I wrote made
sense when I read them, considering that I seemed to throw them onto the

paper in any kind of order.   Confusion was the order of the day and yet out
of that confusion came – dare I say it ? – a work of genius.   Now, I am no
genius, I do know that, but *Vanity Fair* does strike me in all humility as an
above average sort of book and therefore there is the distinct possibility that
while writing it I was transformed for a season and mistook confusion for
inspiration.   Perhaps I over-reach myself in this estimate of my powers but
I know one thing – I have never been confused since, never had to control
anything except boredom during the writing of another book, never felt
crazy, only lazy, never been carried away by that powerful internal momentum that hurtled me through *Vanity Fair*.   Is that a frightful admission or
not ?   I rather think it is a sad one at any rate – sad to realise that all those
millions of words written since add up to a tiny fragment of the sum total of
Vanity Fair.   My first novel was my best – incomparably the best, though I
retain the hope that future generations will rate *Esmond* higher than my own
does.   I confess it disturbs and puzzles me that I have never been able to
come near my first novel since, and yet there is Dickens trumping his aces
all the time.

I hope you have read *Vanity Fair* – I rather think you must have done or
you would not otherwise be reading this – but if by chance you have not then
stop and do so and come back when you have finished.   I don't intend to
discuss that book or question you about it or any other of my books, but it
would be amusing for you to have your own opinion before I pass on those
of others at the time it came out.   London is full of good-natured fools who
the minute anyone cries " Oh! " are ready to echo " Prodigious! "   It did
not take me long to distinguish between real critical appraisal and empty-
headed flattery.   A few people were discerning but most were donkeys to
whom I graciously inclined my head and shut my ears.   Among the critics –
oh I shall have such a lot to say about that breed! – opinion was divided.
The book came out in volume form in the July of 1848 and at once the
difference in the opinions of the reviewers was shown to be startling.   I don't
wish to embarrass you by flaunting a scrap-book of cuttings like an aging
actor, but you will perhaps permit me to give a general résumé.   As a general
rule, those who supported the book did so not because of its literary merits –
though some found a few – but because they saw me as a mighty moralist
who portrayed vices for the benefit of mankind, and those who hit out at it
did so because they thought the sentiments expressed in the book were
corrupting and based on some grossly distorted vision of society of my own.
I must say that for them to speak of distortion was rich – I hardly recognised
my characters in the hands of some of the more passionate critics.   The
usually sensible Bell in *Fraser's Magazine* announced that, " The people
who fill up the motley scenes of *Vanity Fair* are as vicious and odious as a
clever condensation of the vilest qualities can make them."   Dear me, where
could Bell have been living ?   Then Forster in the *Examiner* talked about

" unredeemed depravity " and thought it " overloaded with exhalations of human folly and wickedness ".   Mr. Rintoul in the *Spectator* went even further, arguing that my preoccupation with the seamy side of life implied " a want of imagination and large comprehension of life " and that because of this it could not be regarded as a fiction of high art.

No man ought to write a book and allow it to be sent for review unless he clearly understands that it is comparable with putting his head on the block and asking the executioner to take swipes at it with his axe.   I had been a critic myself for more years than I cared to think about when my turn came up with *Vanity Fair* and I knew perfectly well what a perilous business reviewing is to reviewer and reviewed alike.   I hold it to be the task of the reviewer to clear his mind of his prejudices and read the book carefully with due attention to the author's professed aims and then to record clearly and without malice his own opinion of this book together with some indication of what it is about.   No reviewer can do more but most do rather less.   There are many – I have seen them at it – who pick up a book, look at the name of the author and say, " Oh, Thackeray indeed – never liked the fellow, don't believe he can write in spite of his success which I do hear has gone to his head, ought to be taken down a peg or two," and so forth.   Reviewers like that are not worthy of the name – the only consolation is that any reader with sense can spot them straight away from their sneering tone and rate them accordingly.   More dangerous is the reviewer who is con-scientious but sees his review as a means to air his own opinions regardless of whether or not they have anything to do with the book.   Sometimes, I know, it is hard to resist the temptation to say what you think of French art when you have before you a book on one French artist and there may indeed be a place for general comment – it may add to the reader's knowledge and enjoyment and be not altogether irrelevant – but such care has to be taken not to swamp the actual book under review entirely.

My complaint – and in truth I had no complaints for my success satisfied me and made me marvellously tolerant – my complaint over the reviewing of *Vanity Fair* was that none of the reviewers, be they ever so eminent, stopped to consider my purpose in writing that novel and yet God knows I had made no secret of it.   I wanted to show a set of people living without God in the world – greedy, pompous, mean and perfectly self-satisfied for the most part and at ease about their superior virtues.   To put in more humour or pathos to lighten the darkness, as some critics said I should, would have been to defeat my object.   As to whether I falsified anything why it was quite the reverse – I did not make the picture nearly black enough or reveal half of the more sordid things that go on in high society.   Suppose my hands were not tied by my own sense of decency not to mention the conventions of our age, can you not imagine what a book I could have written ?   Oh my stars!   I showed only the tip of the mound of filth upon

which our most glittering members live and it made some fastidious gentlemen scream enough — what would they have done if I had brought an
avalanche about their ears ?   I say those who decry me for an impostor and
my book as warped lies are humbugs — I say they are the most awful hypocrites and ought to be made to eat their words — I say they shudder for
nothing and that they know perfectly well my portrait is true and just and
not in the least cynical.   As to the charge that what I wrote is so wicked it
cannot be termed art — poppycock.   Art is style, not content, and I challenge
anyone to prove *Vanity Fair* is lacking in style.   Art is truth, and I challenge
those critics who savaged it to prove that *Vanity Fair* was not truthful — but
they know they cannot.   Instead they bleat that I have viewed society
through a warped glass and picked only upon the more disreputable aspects
and that I ought to have concentrated instead on the pure and good.   Why ?
Have we not scores of ladies busy turning out novel after novel on the theme
of purity — busy writing about good little girls like themselves to whom
nothing horrid ever happens and whose minds and hearts are full of romantic
nonsense from morning to night ?   Ask yourself what good those novels do —
ask yourself how honest they are — ask yourself if your view of life can be
equally narrow and confined.   I hate and detest the wickedness I meet every
day in *Vanity Fair* but that does not make me push it under the carpet and
pretend it is not there.   To reform we must first reveal and that is all I did
in my book.

   I still grow warm on that subject I am afraid, but then I have suffered
more than most from critics and I suppose that even when I am writing of
Vanity Fair I am thinking of what I endured afterwards with *Esmond* and
other books that nobody liked.   I felt that there was an antipathy towards me
from certain quarters which meant I did not always get a fair run, and it
bothered me.   The praise I received for *Vanity Fair* from these people in
the other camp that I have in mind was grudging and I, who had always
been charitable towards their champion, regretted it deeply.   Who the devil
am I talking about, say you — why, Dickens of course say I, Dickens and his
followers, and don't think I imagined it.   I am not saying they were openly
jealous or that they did not want me to succeed, but there was a lack of
enthusiasm on their part which saddened me.   What do you think I always
did when I read something of Dickens that I admired ?   I jumped in a cab
and went and clapped him on the back if he was in reach, and if not made do
with boasting about him to anyone who listened.   I remember reading No. 5
of his *Dombey and Son* and being so carried away that I stuffed it into my
pocket, rushed down to the *Punch* office and slapped it in front of the editor
saying something along the lines of how stupendous it was and what power
the man had and how I could not compete with his genius.   My followers
were infected with my admiration and behaved likewise, but when all
London rang with my praises did I hear one word from the Dickens camp

that was not cautious and equivocal ? No, I did not. It may be, of course, that Dickens did not like or approve of *Vanity Fair* – I don't know – I didn't ask him – but I would have preferred him to speak out like a friend and a man and not mutter against me in private.

I own I am a sensitive fellow about certain things – things like honour for example – and I don't apologise for it. Anyone who likes can attack me for my looks or my lack of talent and I shan't complain but I won't stand for slurs on my honour. I am a gentleman and see no reason why I should be ashamed of it, and I adhere to the code of a gentleman and expect those I consort with to do the same. If that sounds pompous pause a minute – what do I mean by " gentleman " ? Not an aristocrat – you know perfectly well I am not an aristocrat – nor a wealthy man – wealth cannot buy manners – but simply a man who lives as a Christian and practises the virtues of truth, modesty and chivalry to the best of his ability. A gentleman does not cheat, a gentleman does not lie, a gentleman does not take advantage of others, a gentleman does not push himself – oh there is no end to the high ideals of a gentleman but in fact no gentleman could exactly define what quality is at the core of being a gentleman – he simply knows it. It was this understanding that was the basis of the quarrel I had at this time with John Forster, Dickens' right-hand man – which is to say, I thought I was accused of acting in an ungentlemanlike way and I would not stand for it, especially coming as it did from a quarter that was behaving in a churlish way towards me. I thought I knew spite was behind the attack and that even more than the slur provoked me.

Raking over old quarrels is surely a pathetic business – I ought not to do it – but the emotion I can feel even now on the subject tells me it was important and must be dealt with. It was trivial enough on the surface – it won't take six lines to tell. I caricatured Forster in a series called *Mr. Punch's Prize Novelists* and Forster took offence. Now, I don't know what grounds he felt he had but I thought my piece witty and justifiable and certainly never worried about possible repercussions for as that kind of thing went it was quite mild. At any rate, Forster was offended and told a mutual friend, Tom Taylor, that Thackeray was " false as hell " for writing it while posing as a friend. Those were his words – " false as hell ". Tom told me what he had said, and I immediately snubbed Forster and he in turn raged against me anew for snubbing him. It is embarrassing to recall what ensued – we were in the middle of a schoolboy fracas before anyone knew what was happening. Dickens was called in as mediator – the letters flew backwards and forwards – and it was ridiculous and I was sick of the whole business within a few days. Well, for once in my life I may have taken things too seriously, but I could not bear, even in a moment of anger, to be called " false as hell ". I was not false and would not have it said that I was by anyone. The truth was, Forster should not have said what he did,

Taylor should not have passed it on and I should not have taken his words to mean what they did. We all in the end professed sorrow – there was an official reconciliation – but there remained a shadow between us that was never quite dispelled. It made me see that success brings its own perils – how else could I explain the sudden disappearance of my popularity? Twelve months before everyone had liked me but now that I was well on my way to being an important man enemies appeared on all sides, making me think it was better to be obscure and liked than famous and hated, very often simply because of that fame.

This will not do – the outlook was not really so bleak for my new-found fame also brought me new friends and admirers whom I would not have been without. Here is a pretty tale to end this chapter: one day when I was working frantically on a number of *Vanity Fair* the manuscript of a new novel was sent round to me by William Williams, a literary assistant in the firm of Smith, Elder & Co. I groaned at the sight of it – there was positively no time to read other people's work when I had my own to write – but I took it up, out of curiosity, resolved only to read a page or two and before I knew what was happening I was entirely lost. The novel was *Jane Eyre* by someone calling themselves Currer Bell – I say calling themselves for I was sure the author was a woman. However, man or woman, the book was fine, the style very generous and upright – and some of the love passages made me cry. I believe my praise helped to get this book published and I am proud if it is true that I helped Miss Charlotte Brontë when she needed it. Her appreciation was fulsomely expressed not only by her written thanks but by dedicating the second edition of the book to me in the warmest terms. I blushed when I read it – no, I can't repeat it – and not least because it included a delineation of my character that I hardly recognised. Miss Brontë knew me only through *Vanity Fair* and from that had deduced that I was some kind of avenging angel sent to scourge the weak and wicked –

humph! She did not know the rumours her gesture would give rise to, for didn't half London cast me as Rochester the minute they read both dedication and book ? Poor lady – she was far more upset than I, unaware as she had been of my sick wife and need for governesses! I would have teased her about it but nobody teases Joan of Arcs.

There – I have told you all you need to know about my great success. Wasn't it quickly over, even though you thought I would never get to it ? There I am, on the pinnacle, and not knowing it. Not knowing it ? Well, of course I did not know it – I thought *Vanity Fair* was the beginning, I thought I should get better and better, I thought a golden age had opened up before me. It would have been insupportable if I had known the truth.

Chapter X

———————◆———————

VANITY FAIR AND THE TOP OF THE TREE

I DON'T think I have ever been in a more confused state of mind than I was at the end of summer 1848. As soon as *Vanity Fair* was finished, I took myself off to the Continent for a holiday, leaving my girls to the tender mercies of their governess, Miss Alexander, who took them to stay with her family and went up in my estimation because of it. All the world could see how tired I was, but only I knew how jaded I felt. I was not at all sure whether I was well or ill, happy or sad. The minute I had the leisure, and no demands were being made upon me from printers or children or hostesses, a kind of collapse set in – I could hardly get myself out of bed but got no pleasure from resting there, nor felt at all refreshed after hours of sleep. I was listless, and apathetic, seeming to have no interest in anything except the the past – night and day I was pursued by images of the characters I had created in *Vanity Fair* – I talked to them in my head and listened to them and thought of what they might be doing and was more than half way to forgetting that they were neither real nor still in circulation. I had done with that book but it had not done with me – everything in it was as fresh and vivid as if it had just happened the day before. It was as if the backbone of a pair of stays had been removed – there was no longer anything to hold my slack and shuddering body together. I was utterly cast down and under the influence of the worst blue devils I had yet encountered. I would sit for ages staring at the sea without so much as the will to walk along the promenade, wondering what was the matter and why nothing pleased me, and for the first time I had an inkling of how my little wife had felt during her first illness. What was the point of anything ? Why bother to get up at all ? Who cares ? Ah – there we had the crux of the matter in my case – who did I want to care ? My children ? Good heavens no, they cared quite

enough already.   My mother ?   She had never stopped caring.   Who then ?
Why, someone whose initials were J.B., that's who, for only a part of my
malady was due to fatigue.   The rest was due to the sense of loneliness and

isolation that swept over me as soon as I began my holiday, for what fun is
there in a holiday if you have no kindred spirit to share it with ?

My allegiance was by then entirely given to Jane Octavia Brookfield, and
all pretence that I still had a wife who would one day be restored to me was
quite over.   Oh, Isabella had not died but she had long since ceased to care

about anything but her dinner and her glass of porter and her piano – go, stay, die, prosper – it was all the same to her, and if I visited her less and less it was not because I forgot her but that I saw she forgot me when I was not there. I would sit listening to her play her little tunes, smiling so gaily at me, looking so young and I would think it was foolish of me to continue to prolong this agony. It was my duty to provide for her and see to the best of my ability that she was happy, but beyond that I need trouble myself no longer about loyalty – she did not know what it was and sometimes, at the beginning of her visit, I don't think she knew who I was. Why should she, when before her appeared a grey-headed grizzled old man in place of the William she had known ? She stayed forever at twenty-five while I aged a century between each visit. I meant nothing to her – no, that is unfair – she never obliterated her William from her fuddled mind – she always in the end remembered and was affectionate, touchingly so, but if I did not come she did not realise. I continued to visit out of duty, not hope – that was a fact – and a reluctance to face up to the truth. I needed a woman at my side, but it was not going to be Isabella however hard I clung to my memories.

Perhaps I was fated to fix upon the unattainable, for why else should I substitute in my affections my sick wife for the wife of someone else, equally impossible to have ? It looks perverse, don't you think, and my explanation that it was an accident sounds weak. For a long time, I had not cared that my new love was a hopeless one – I protested that it was enough to love her as a man might love a sister and that therefore it did not matter that there was no future in it. My interpretation of " loving " was admiring, caring, enjoying, sharing, protecting, not possessing or caressing or any other awkward present participles that you may come up with. I did not want to own or touch the lady I professed I loved – I did not even want her to myself, so I was lulled into a false sense of security and felt myself beyond suspicion. But then what happened ? Under the guise of brotherly love another emotion began to stir, one I was quickly helpless to control, though it frightened me – I began to feel passion towards Jane and the more I told myself it was nothing of the kind the more I trembled when my eyes met hers. (Run up the largest red flag you can find, for I intend to have my say, whatever taboos there are on this kind of discussion, so far as examining my state of mind goes.) I swear I did not deliberately start to think of Jane differently – it would have been folly, tantamount to putting my neck in a noose – but somehow this desire grew inside me until I could hardly bear to be in the same room with her. I struggled desperately to subdue my feelings – I tried every kind of trick to rid myself of them – but it was no good. Well, you say, you ought to have straight away broken the relationship off and never seen the lady again. I knew you would say that and I have my answer ready – why should I ? Why should I have withdrawn when I knew perfectly well that however agonising my love for Jane became I WOULD NEVER DO ANYTHING ABOUT IT. There – that was the point. I was the father of two children and I was quite safe. To break off the friendship would have been an admission that I could not control myself and I knew that I could, so why deprive myself of the dearest friends I had in the world ?

For months after I realised the real state of play, and I cannot put an exact date on when that was, I was still ready with virtuous assurances of irreproachable conduct and meant them but oh lor how I suffered! Whenever I was alone I thought of Jane and felt that if I should lose her I would despair of life and go hopelessly off the rails. It seemed to me that there was nothing wrong with Love – Love proved God – it must be good. I thanked William again and again in my prayers for his confidence in me, and swore that I would prove worthy of it. Humbly I went on adoring Jane and thanking her husband for allowing me to torture myself with his full approval, but I suppose even I would have revolted against such a cruel regime if it had not been for the absolute certainty in my heart that Jane reciprocated my feelings. I had only to look into her eyes to see that she shared my agony and to know that I had not imagined that she loved me too. Where, you may ask, is my evidence for this apart from absurd talk about eyes ? I admit straight away that I have none – Jane never committed herself on paper – but it makes no difference – I was not a love-sick youth who persuades himself that every woman in the world is in love with him but a man of almost forty who cherished few illusions. Jane Brookfield loved me as surely as I loved her. That is all I can say without overstepping the bounds of her trust and betraying confidences that ought never to be betrayed.

I don't know how long this would have gone on if someone had not whispered into Brookfield's ear that he was a fool and kindly pointed out to him the interpretation the world might put on my almost daily visits to his house. When I returned from my holiday, rested but still gloomy, I was closer than ever to Jane. In the autumn, I stayed at Clevedon Court with her and I think it was during that blissful time that some who shall be nameless remonstrated at our intimacy and pushed Brookfield into saying we must return to a more acceptable level of friendship. He said I wrote and visited too much and that I must not write unless I was written to nor visit unless I was specifically invited. My anger was matched only by my grief – how could I survive on the meagre diet now given me ? Feverishly I watched for the post, and when a sad scrap of a letter from Jane came what a torrent of words I had ready to release. Perhaps you will despise me for accepting these terms – perhaps you will think I ought to have said, " Very well, sir, if that is how it is to be, goodbye and be damned to you and your wife " – perhaps you would only respect me if I challenged Brookfield to a

duel and ran him through with the sword Titmarsh wears for such dramatic
moments.   All I can say is that if you go in for such melodrama then you
know nothing about Love.   Love makes you content with anything – Love
means you will sell your soul for the merest glimpse of your beloved and wait
months for a meeting.   I raged against the injustice of Brookfield's edict but
I accepted it because I had no choice.   My only consolation was to pour out
my heart in verses which I sent to Jane.   I received none in reply.   Her
letters were mundane, full of what her husband had just said or done, or of
instructions about how to care for my health – I hated those miserable
grandmotherly letters and yet I could not do without them.   The sight of
Jane's handwriting on an envelope made me happy for a whole day.

It was, of course, much worse for her.   It is no part of my business to
pry into the Brookfields' marriage but I will ask you to consider whether a
clever, sensitive lady can be happy with a much less clever, overbearing
husband who constantly disregarded her wishes and I think you will answer
that she is not likely to be.   I alone know something of the misery Jane had
to endure and I will keep my counsel.   She submitted to our separation, as
I submitted, because there was no alternative.   We could both have made a
bargain with the devil and fled together but there would have been no place

in the world far enough to hide from the shame we would have felt at the
wreckage left behind.   There was no way that we could see of overcoming
the obstacles between us so I went on yearning for Jane and making myself
more ill than I already was.   It came as the most almighty shock in the
middle of my unhappiness to be told in the strictest confidence by Brookfield
that Jane was expecting a happy event the following spring – my God how
I started at the news, how I changed colour and mopped my brow and
longed to be anywhere except in front of Brookfield in Brookfield's drawing-
room.   It was so unexpected – after all those years of childlessness to be with
child now, at this time, when she loved me – oh it was insupportable.   My
jealousy was almost uncontrollable, my resentment ugly, my horror un-
feigned.   Month after month I had to watch the body of the woman I
loved swell with the child someone else had sired.   It made no difference that
the father was her husband – somehow it was indecent, awful, bringing to
mind nightmare images that haunted me.   Could I accept this blow ?   I had
swallowed hard when told to curb my excessive adoration – could I swallow
this camel ?

Gradually, I grew calmer and began to share Jane's happiness.   She had
longed for a child and had almost begun to despair.   Now, in the midst of
her sorrow that we were parted, she would be happy and it was wrong of me
not to share her happiness.   And Brookfield too – he was my friend and I

ought to be glad for his sake — but what a tangled web it seemed and how I groaned at the prospect of ever finding a way to unravel it. A child would cement that union, and afterwards there would be three little angels between Jane and I, by which I mean my children and hers. Who can damn their children by acting selfishly as we would have been required to do ? Not us — we cared too much. So on I went, visiting when I was allowed to, sharing Jane with whoever happened to be in the house at the time, watching her from afar and making polite conversation, wondering how I put up with it, and then afterwards, when this charade was over and I was alone in my room, building her every glance into something significant, clinging like a drowning man to the touch of her finger tips as she bade me goodbye or allowed me to escort her to dinner. It was monstrous — surely they saw that it was as well as I ? Why did William not bar the door to me then and there ? Why did they allow me to think that our friendship could go on as before ? There may be all sorts of reasons but you cannot prevent me from suspecting that Brookfield enjoyed watching me adore his wife and that she needed me as much as I needed her.

There are some subjects it is impossible to treat lightly and I am afraid that is one of them. Show me a man whose heart has not been seared by unrequited love and I will demonstrate that he has not really lived, that he has within himself wells of emotion and suffering that have never been tapped, that whole reservoirs of experience lie unplumbed and though he may be all the happier and more content because of this, he is less of a human being. I used to think, once upon a time, that if a man could find himself a good wife and a warm fire and fill his stomach and mind his own business then that was as it should be, that an even keel was the thing to aim for, but now I am convinced that it is the rough sea which moulds character — not deliberately sought, you understand, but encountered because a man has left the safety of the harbour and taken his chance. I don't think I would want to have dodged my own storms and tempests, however much I hated enduring them, any more than I would wish to have stayed a child. It is not that I think clouds always have silver linings or any of that nonsense, or that God deliberately chooses hardship to inflict upon some of us, but that we ought not to be afraid to take risks for it is through risking ourselves that we learn and if we are called upon to learn more than most why so much the better. I would say to you, go out, take everything that comes and never mind if you end up battered and broken in the process — you will know more, you will have more compassion for your fellow travellers and when you get to the other side you will be glad you made the voyage.

You see how any mention of Jane Brookfield turns me into the most fearsome philosopher ? I can't help it — even at this distance my spirits plunge when I think of that time and I am given to the most awful gloomy ramblings. The only thing that saved me then — and still does now when I am in that mood — was the antics of people about me who by some piece of pomposity or absurdity made me laugh aloud at their folly and think that the world was perfectly ridiculous and that I had better not take it too seriously. I remember on that holiday I told you about, after I finished *Vanity Fair*, I was so sunk in misery I remember sitting at my dinner table in the hotel staring dully at the menu when I heard a lady at the next table proclaiming for all to listen that she was not long for this world, that she was an invalid, that she could hardly swallow a morsel and then to my astonishment I saw her go through the most enormous amounts of food before relapsing into her dying state again. Such silliness appealed to me so much that I quite forgot my melancholy for a while — and discovered that was the trick. The more I listened and watched the more diverted I became and soon I was almost normal. The worst thing we can do when we are miserable is shut ourselves away and brood on it, nursing our pain like a sick animal and not using what makes us different from animals — our brains. The mind must work if we are to forget, and if it is to work we must give it constant nourishment and a chance to have something to work on and by going out and observing what is happening we do just that.

You won't believe how many times I told myself all this after the blow about Jane's baby. I resisted the temptation to keep to my room and sigh and instead went out as much as before, when I was not working. The very

grandest houses were now my ports of call but though I relished the chance
to meet Disraeli or Palmerston the glee that such occasions used to afford
me had gone. I was living with a black-edged border round me and no
mistake, and if the company I kept damned me for an aloof, sour sort of
fellow they were wrong only in the reasons for it. What do you suppose
was troubling me, apart from Jane ? My work, that is what. There I was,
talk of London, whole literary world at my feet, publishers hammering at my
door waiting for my next book and yet with the bat at last in my hands I
could not get up the strength to hit the ball again. *Pendennis*, begun on that
awful holiday, was making no progress at all even though the first number
came out in the November of 1848. I had begun it not entirely sure what
it was exactly to be about but with one or two characters in my head and the
sketch of a plot which I thought sufficient, for that was how *Vanity Fair*
took off. Unhappily, *Pendennis* did not follow suit – I wrote slowly,
assuring myself that every book could not take shape the same way and
consoling myself with thoughts that it was early yet and there was no hurry
and that I was still tired and why rush and so forth. I would not have
allowed the first part to appear, knowing as I did how uncertain I yet was,
if I had not been tempted by the money. *Vanity Fair* had cleared my debts
and the death of my grandmother provided me with a legacy that meant the
next year was covered but I had begun to look further than the end of my
nose and had visions of striking while the iron was hot in order to replace
my own lost fortune and thereby ensure the futures of my wife and children.
I know you are going to say that this approach was my undoing and though
I think eventually it was I had no fears at that stage – I would have written
Pendennis straight away even if I had not needed the money. What else can
a giant do but flex his new-found muscles, even if it is only to convince
himself that he has any ? There was nothing dangerous about this – my
standards remained as high as before and I had no intention of compromising
myself by trying to aim at a particular market or anything like that. But all
the same, it was horrible to be writing such dreary stuff when in the other
camp Dickens was turning out *David Copperfield*. I need not ask you if
you have read it – everyone has – it is beautiful. Friends said flattering
things, one even going so far as to say I beat Dickens out of the inner circle
with my *Pendennis* – oh what a lie, for Dickens surpassed himself and I was
the first to acknowledge it. But I am going to tell you something: I believe
David Copperfield was Dickens' best work and showed a great improvement
on what had gone before because he had taken a lesson from Another
Author's work. I thought he had taken a hint from *Vanity Fair* and greatly
simplified his style, to the benefit of the world. Dickens would never admit
it – at least, I don't think he would – but set yourself up as an impartial
judge and see what you think – you may be surprised. You might imagine
that, with *David Copperfield* running alongside me, I would be put on my

mettle but not a bit of it – I continued to jog along as before, slowly, with infinite pains, producing dreary chapter after dreary chapter.   Nor was it the poor progress I made that alone frightened me – I was terrified by the growing awareness that I could so easily lose the thread of the book I was creating even to the extent of forgetting entirely certain passages in it and names of characters and so forth.   Imbecility seemed just round the corner – I thought Anny would soon have to nurse an old man who rambled incoherently and needed his drooling mouth wiped at the corners.   It appalled me to find that there was no liveliness in what I had written and no

fun, which I suppose was at least consistent for there was neither liveliness nor fun in the author either.   My cavorting gave me no pleasure – swimming in claret was all very well but it do congest the lungs so and leaves the head heavy the next day.   After a day mournfully placing one dull word on top of another I would take myself off to saloons like burning furnaces where people were half frantic with the crush and I would lift a glass as big as a chandelier filled with exquisite liquors and drink it and listen to the conversation like some elderly voyeur wondering what on earth I was doing there. A lampoon of that time called me " a publisher's man-of-all-work " and said my main function was " to hunt out incongruities ". Was it right ? Was that all I was good for ? Even if small sparks of rebellion smouldered inside me at this estimate of my talent, I was almost bound to agree. I slaved away till seven o'clock each evening to hardly any purpose – the required number of pages were filled and that was that. After each number I felt fagged and unwell and could hardly bear the prospect of immediately buckling to and starting again. I couldn't withdraw – already I had made more money from the early numbers than I had with the whole of *Vanity Fair*, but I won't tell you how much in case it disgusts you to find authors get paid as much for bad books as they do for good ones. Books are business as much as any other commodity, you see, and publishers are businessmen and they are bound to hire you for what your last was worth so it is unavoidable that an author can sometimes be paid twice as much for a bad book as he previously was for a good one. The only saving grace in this situation is that it cannot go on forever and if this highly paid bad book flops then very little can be got for the next however good it is. If you think I took an unhealthy interest in the pounds, shillings and pence of writing when I ought to have been on a cloud somewhere seeking inspiration like a proper writer, then let me tell you that I have never met a fellow author in my life who was not similarly preoccupied and that the public has it all wrong. Why shouldn't we care about what we earn ? Why should we be ashamed to admit that though we wish to stir your soul we also want to make the inkstand pay ? I wouldn't have written for no return, you can be sure, and I don't in the least think that makes what I have written unworthy. Money, my dear sir, is an excellent spur.

All the same, it didn't seem to spur me to produce anything good and neither did my rival's superior performance. It was one of the worst periods of my life – worse than Isabella's illness because then, though the tragedy was great, I felt perfectly well and even contented, but in those early *Pendennis* days I felt awful and could see nothing ahead. Those are the times to beware of – those horrible troughs between the waves when we are sure we are never going to see the crest of the wave again. I had far rather be buffeted to pieces than left to flounder out of my depth, and it is more of a test of stamina, those grey grey days, than an actual storm. When I see myself sliding down into just such a stagnant pond I start flaying my arms around and clinging for dear life to the boat I can tell you, and with all the practice I have had I have become quite adept at avoiding these depressions.

Sometimes, of course, I fight away and what do you think ? It turns out that my enemies weren't blue devils after all but real illness and that all my struggling and failure to recognise what was really wrong with me made me more ill than I need have been. That was what happened in the autumn of 1849. There I was, back in London after a brief precious holiday near Jane Brookfield on the Isle of Wight, convincing myself that misery at the parting was the cause of my unwellness, not to mention a return to boring *Pendennis*, and all the time the spasms of pain and feelings of fever that I thought I was imagining turned out to be a genuine physical malady. This illness of mine was never that I know of accurately diagnosed but whatever it was it almost did for me and took up three months of my life, and I do believe it changed me in many unexpected ways so that ever after I was grateful for it. Does that sound unlikely, to be grateful for a serious illness ? I daresay it does, but wait until you hear what I mean and see if you don't agree it had a salutary effect.

I don't remember much about the beginning of the illness except that I collapsed and had to be put to bed and then what a fuss there was with doctors and so forth looming over me in bed where I lay not caring a fig for what happened. I swooned in and out of consciousness for days on end, aware of pains and aches and shivers, but curiously beyond it all as though I was watching myself from afar. Sometimes thoughts of my girls would surge into my head and then anxiety sharpened any pain I was feeling but mostly a kind of numbness, not at all unpleasant, gripped me and took away all my willpower. I don't think for a moment that when I was at death's door I fought to live – on the contrary, I said " Thy will be done " and meant it. Even when I was so near Death I was not afraid of it and I know that as I near it again, very soon, there will be no terror in my heart. Dying is difficult only for those who cling stubbornly to life and I don't think I shall do that. When my time comes, I will be ready and you won't find me shilly-shallying about the going. I remember just before my own flirtation with immortality going to visit an aged relative in Paris and gazing with a kind of grim awe at what lies ahead of all of us and thinking that I would not mind escaping it. There in bed lay an old lean grey pale toothless woman tossing and moaning feebly, struggling madly to avoid the inevitable even at that stage. How she fought, and how I marvelled at her tenacity and wondered if I would find it in me to do the same when my time came. May God be merciful to all of us.

Gradually I came out of that state of semi-consciousness where I had been indifferent to what happened to me and then I saw the dear faces of Anny and Minny quite differently and loved them anew. I lay for weeks trying to regain my strength, feeling only a wonderful new happiness that I was alive and loved and what a blessing each day was. I think it is true to say that though weak – perhaps because weak – I felt cleansed and humble and the awful pressure of constantly battling against troubles and worries had entirely gone. I didn't know what had happened to me or what was going to happen to me but my trust in life itself had returned. The sun would come up, the sun would go down and meanwhile kind people ministered to my every need. Oh the kindness in the world is astonishing! It seemed that every five minutes there was a knock on the door and a message and a present left for dear Mr. Thackeray. Every lady in London seemed to feel it her positive duty to make a jelly or a nourishing soup and send it to the

invalid with protestations of undying devotion. Do you think I tried to stop them? Not at all – I basked in this affection and counted the number of good friends I had and was grateful and I lay and thought how much had escaped my notice during those dark self-pitying days before my illness. My poor pounding head had been full of Jane Brookfield and *Pendennis* and very little else and yet all around me I had evidence of other friends and other interests and I had chosen to ignore them. I promised myself that it would not happen again – I would not shut my eyes and ears so firmly against the world at large.

When I was able to move about, I took myself off to 63 East St., Brighton to convalesce and there I enjoyed the luxury of lolling and lazing about. Every day I was wheeled out onto the pier, muffled in rugs and blankets, and every day I watched the gulls swoop down and heard their cries and felt the salt water in the breeze sting my cheeks and I wanted to jump up and shout with happiness – except I could not.   My strength returned slowly, perhaps fortunately, for my bodily weakness prolonged this restful period and gave me time to think about what I was going to do.   I found that I thought in a different way while I reclined in my chair beside the sea – not in that hurried, jumbled fashion that was my habit in London with a day's work pressing upon me but in a slower, clearer vein that made it easier to reach conclusions.   All the same, I must return to *Pendennis* – interrupted during my illness and not on the bookstands for several months – but I resolved to pick up that story and shake it and apply myself to enlivening the narrative so that people would sit up and take notice once more – and there you have the most marvellous result of all of my illness.   Ambition had returned when I thought it killed, or rather enthusiasm for my profession. Where before I had dreaded sitting down to work and loathed the very sight of pen and ink and paper, now I longed to have the tools of my trade at hand so that I could go to it with a will.   The old desire to write stirred in me and I knew it must and should have an outlet and that seemed a little miracle to me.   My joy at this discovery was tremendous – I had begun to think I was a fraud, begun to hate writing except as a means to earn my living, begun to doubt that I had any talent at all, and how I rejoiced to find that I was as eager as a young man of twenty to try my hand again.   I would not have been happy without my work – however rich and easy I would not have liked to live in the world without producing something for it to look at, and often these days I remind myself of this when I am inclined to grumble at the hardship of writing.   The re-awakening of the desire to write was one of the greatest comforts I remember.

I ought not to go on much longer about that illness of mine or I will be in danger of becoming one of those unfortunate people who can be seen to derive more pleasure than is consistent with the tale they are telling of their agony.   They imbue their illness with all the mystique of communion, seeking to make themselves holy because of what they claim to have suffered. Their illness is as important an event as their conception and their description of it about as accurate.   How the detail is piled on!   How they relish the memory of symptoms – the cough that tickled on Tuesday, the pain in the stomach that stabbed on Wednesday, the hot forehead on Thursday, the delirium on Friday, the aching limbs on Saturday, the sickness on Sunday, the rash on Monday and then we are back, quite exhausted, to Tuesday and

ready to start all over again.   In the eyes of these people, doctors are high
priests and every word they utter is sacred.   One doctor is quoted against
another with distressing glee, until along comes the one who told them he
had never seen such a bad case as theirs – worst in London – worst in his
experience – worst in medical history – and that you can be sure is the one

privileged to make them well so that they can become his prize patient.   As
for medicines – oh lor how they go on!   Liquids and potions and tablets and
powders in every colour and shape and form, taken by the day or hour or
minute with intense fervour, doled out with shaking hands holding silver
spoons until every nook and cranny of the body is crammed with something-

or-other, enough to enable an apothecary to live in luxury for a year. These people make it obvious that nothing so exciting has ever happened before but should you be bold enough to say this then the cries of unfeeling brute will rend the air and they will faint and be ill all over again and you had better watch out. The trouble is, this kind of person does not really wish to be well again. There is a certain wistfulness in their account of their illness that shows they have a nostalgia for it which cannot be admitted but neither can it be denied.

I have, I trust, made enough of my illness now – we come out of that kind of experience moighty foine moralists, expecting the rest of you to bow your heads and listen and give weight to our words. As you will be able to imagine, it had done nothing to improve the state of my affairs in several respects. Since *Pendennis* had languished I had to bring the numbers up to date and improve it at the same time, a chore I did not relish even in my new benevolent mood. I might long to hold a pen again and show the world what I could do, but for preference I would not have chosen to do so on a book in which I had lost interest. However, there was no help for it – financially I was far from free of worry and the more money I could earn the better. (And that, by the way, is another thing – how much less awful Real Illness would be if we did not know how expensive every feverish minute of it was. Worry over what illness is costing us sends more of us into a coma than I care to reckon. Only tell us someone else is paying for the doctor and the medicines and that our wages will still miraculously be paid even though we are not at work and look how quickly we shall recover.) There was one kind friend who discreetly offered me money to tide me over and I think that friend showed more sense than all the others who showered me with presents. He put himself in my position, you see, and that is worth far more than sympathy or condolences. If anything, my needs had doubled while I was ill – the girls grew as girls have an awkward habit of doing and needed more expensive things, and my mother aged, which no one can prevent, and needed more care and help, and my household was continually expanding to take in newly required assistance and nothing was ever limited to what we could afford. We lived well and I had no desire to change that, nor had illness frightened me into thinking that we should scrimp and save to be ready for the next bout. Not a bit of it – my new friend was called Optimism and Optimism would not allow me to give up my comforts and act in a shameful, terrified way. All my plans to save for the future did not extend to economising in the present. I would keep my easy way of living with the little luxuries I was used to and that was final, and do you know I am more glad than I can tell you that I took this broad view. Now that I have all this money and so little use for it, how dreadful to look back and find I had denied myself a carriage or the girls new dresses in order to save a few miserable pounds that in the end I did not need. You might say, in your clever fashion, that if I had found myself at fifty penniless and in dire need, then I might feel differently and passionately regret that unnecessary carriage and those extra pretty clothes, but I don't think I would because if I was in truth destitute what would those gimcracks add up to ? Nothing very much now, a great deal of pleasure then. I hope that demolishes your argument.

I went forward, then, re-charged and hopeful, though still with that slight ache round the heart on account of you-know-who that remained long after my health was otherwise restored. What, I wondered, had the next chapter in store in that department ? Whatever it was, I was determined to be of good heart and cheer and not allow it to wreck me. All the same, I own to feelings of expectancy – I will not use a stronger term – about my future. I was convinced that something important was in the offing but I could not think what it could be. Can you ? Then you are shrewder than I was.

Chapter XI

————————◆————————

A NEW PATH IS FOLLOWED

GOT back to my former health and strength pretty quickly and rattled about London in quite the old way. I preached away in *Pendennis* – more like a parson than a satirist – wishing to goodness that it was over so that I could get on with a new story that was boiling up in my interior and clamouring to be let out. Isn't that always the way ? The next book is always the one we wish to be working on, the next party the one we wish we were at, the next holiday the one we will really enjoy – but that is a good thing on the whole for if the future did not glitter there would seem no point in going on. I would miss that secretive feeling of knowing something different was coming along if it ever left me – how awful not to be entertaining hopes that some new idea was going to blossom into the perfect book and I am quite content to take along with it the following disappointment when it turns out to be a damp squib after all. That is all part of the game and unavoidable. Every writer would much rather write new things than plod along with the old, reworking it and trying to make it better, and I am no exception. A clean sheet of paper, a fresh pen and a new story – now there you have the attraction of the trade. Come back in a few weeks with the impetus gone and the paper scrawled over with crossings out and the pen broken and there you have the drawback. Ah well.

I returned, then, to my old pursuits, glad to be back, out four times a week like a gay dog, but I noticed a difference in how I went about both business and pleasure. It seemed to me that the old inveterate flippancy had gone and that in its place was a soberness and steadiness that I found remark-able and did not altogether like. Being flippant is nothing to be proud of, heaven knows, but it does indicate an attitude to life of which I approve. I thought perhaps it was merely age that had reformed me – after all, I was

nearing forty years of age then. An old man could not expect to find a joke
wherever he looked and certainly there were those who thought I ought to
consciously adopt an elder statesman air and think before I spoke and never
smile and in general set myself up as a fount of wisdom and not a very
cheerful one at that. Miss Charlotte Brontë, for example, was forever
taking me to task over my levity and urging me to live up to the image I had

cast myself in when I wrote *Vanity Fair*, and I know I distressed her by
declining to conform. She was a strange little lady, God rest her soul, with
a view of both life and literary purpose that was not my own. I did not
know her well – I don't suppose I met her more than half a dozen times –
but there was no mistaking the steel inside that kept that thin back ramrod
straight nor the passion that burned behind those large grey steadfast eyes.
I don't think she found much joy in the world, or that her faculty for
happiness was particularly developed and in all that she ever said to me I
don't remember ever discerning the smallest particle of humour. Perhaps
she did not have very much to laugh about, but then you know perfectly well
that has nothing to do with it – some men can laugh on their way to the
gallows and find even at that hour some scene that amuses and interests them,
while others can sit stony-faced surrounded by the gayest and most infectious
jollity. But if I quarrel with Miss Brontë's disposition I did not find it
nearly so trying as her perpetual longing for every book to be a crusade against
something and every author a knight in real life as well as in print. She
seemed to think that having said what I said in *Vanity Fair* the rest of my
life should be spent decrying and reforming the evils I had shown up, and
she grew quite angry if I jested about my mission. Jests of any kind were
not to her liking – she took them absolutely seriously and do you know, that
irritated me? I cannot bear such a desperately serious outlook, such a grim
determination to take every remark at its face value – it seems to me to show
a want of experience that I in my turn deplore. Nobody detests more than
I the silly chatter that fills and echoes through the drawing-rooms of
England until you come to believe nobody is ever going to make a remark

with any more meaning in it than " Is not the weather warm " and that kind of thing, but on the other hand it is absurd to let fly with a full-scale lecture in reply to a mild mocking sally like – well, like those I made in Miss Brontë's company which don't bear quoting.

I remember one evening especially when this good lady was at her indomitable worst, so much so that I longed to say something quite disgracefully facetious in order to shock her properly, but of course I could not for she was a guest in my house.   I thought that would startle you, for haven't you been remarking how this fellow waltzes round London accepting hospitality at every turn and yet, my dears, there is never a mention of him returning it.   Well, you are quite right – entertaining was not my *forte* in those days and I did everything possible to avoid it short of downright rudeness, though I would not like you to think that I was ungenerous.   The truth was that lacking a wife I also lacked a hostess, and it made it far harder for a man to organise social functions.   It was easier and more suitable to take guests to my club to dine and wine and I hope I did that as handsomely as possible, but naturally, she being a lady, I could not take Miss Brontë there and if I was going to entertain her at all it would have to be at home and as I could hardly have her on her own I had to invite friends, and oh my goodness we were in the middle of a dinner party before I knew what had happened.   What awful things dinner parties are when you are giving them, though from observing the delight they give my daughters these days I suppose some people don't think so.   The whole house seemed to be in a state of constant turmoil with frantic servants running here, there and everywhere collecting together all the necessary articles, half of which were too splendid to be in every-day use and were scattered round the establishment in cupboards and drawers and boxes.   The kitchen became a holy shrine and the cook a *prima donna* who could not be insulted by the request for humble eggs and bacon while she was so important and busy and consequently we all starved for days beforehand.   By the time the June evening came round when this incredible event was to take place I was in the most dreadful temper, stumping from one end of the house to the other, swearing loudly that this was the last time I would ever lend myself to such a carnival.   Anny and Minny did not share my fury – they were in transports of delight at all the excitement and activity, and since it had been agreed that their desperate pleas to be allowed to stay up could not be ignored unless I had a heart of stone, there they were sitting on the stairs all dressed up in muslin and sashes ready to ooh and aah at every entry.   Poor lambs, I fear they were sadly disappointed, unless the guests made more of a show than I thought they did. Miss Brontë wore some kind of dark plain dress and frowned at my little girls most severely as I led her into the dining-room, perfectly aware of how ludicrous we looked since I was so huge and shaggy and she, at my side, barely reaching to my elbow, was so diminutive and neat.   Nobody laughed you may be sure at the sight of us, and even the hilarity I felt was quickly squashed as a numb feeling of absolute boredom came over me. How dull it was to behave myself and give straight answers to straight questions and never

risk anything more interesting and how stupid the assembled throng became under such restraint, even though there were several wits among them. I sat and gazed at the smoking candles – everything went wrong you see – and at Miss Brontë's intense face and I almost yawned aloud, fearing my ordeal would never end. Manfully I struggled to give my whole attention to earnest matters of the day and to listen attentively to one dreary monologue after another. I wonder what Miss Brontë thought ? I wonder if she was as bored as I was or whether she thought the conversation to her liking ? After she had left I know I felt so miserable and dejected that I crept out of the house secretly before all the other guests had left and went to my club – a shabby thing to do but I felt so in need of stimulation that I absolutely had to go somewhere noisy and lively where I could relax.

Why did I invite that lioness at all ? I don't know – there was something about her that troubled me and something about our encounters that was irresistible even though they unsettled and depressed me. I expect I invited her because it was the correct thing to do as she was a self-professed admirer and knew nobody in London and my publisher was hers and brought us together – I expect it was simply a matter of manners. Besides, can any of us deny that it is an honour to entertain a best-selling, critically acclaimed

novelist, especially if the novelist is a woman ?   Though there was never
any possibility of me measuring up to her ideal, I was attracted by her
vehemence and intrigued by her attitude – I don't think I have ever met
any other authors who wilfully concealed their identity and did not wish to
have their work acknowledged as theirs or be complimented upon it.
Forgetting this command – that I mustn't mention her books – I once
introduced her to my mother as " Jane Eyre " in a joking way and oh my
stars it brought the heavens down about my ears !   If you could have seen
her expression of anger and contempt !   If you could have heard her ringing
tones as she upbraided me !   You would have trembled for me and not
without reason – I thought the incident would end in blows.   As a matter
of fact, it ended with Miss Brontë settling the account with an attack that
took me by surprise and puzzled me.   " How would you like it," she said,
" if you were introduced as George Warrington ? "   " Arthur Pendennis
you mean," ses I, laughing.   " No," she insisted, " Warrington I said and
Warrington I mean," and she gave me a look of such boldness that I was
staggered.   I, George Warrington ?   How extraordinary – she saw me as
George Warrington when I knew I was Arthur Pendennis, and if you
cannot make sense of that you will have to read the book for I can't do that
for you.

There is no denying that I took a perverse delight – for which I am sorry –
in shocking Miss Brontë by not living up to the high moral standards she
had saddled me with while at the same time struggling harder than she knew
to live up to them in my private life.   You will remember that before my
illness Jane Brookfield was announced to be expecting an 'appy event, and
in the way of such things the event had arrived and was indeed duly happy
and I think I was extremely miserable in the midst of all the jollifications.
My visits to the house of this dear lady had still been frequent, in spite of
that warning we had received, and I had come to believe that the birth of
the baby would after all cement rather than weaken our friendship.   After
all, a baby would be a chaperone of sorts – surely tongues could not wag over
two people conversing over a cradle ?   Surely Brookfield could not object to
his small child being visited and played with – why, everyone knew how
Mr. Thackeray doted on children.   So you see my new friend Optimism
influenced even that troubled department of my life and I went on seeing
Jane and admiring her Madonna look right up to the very day the babe was
born.   I was in the house the morning the pains began, hoping to see the
dear creature, and awesome it was.   I called before luncheon and was told
Mrs. Brookfield was indisposed and the doctors had been sent for, and I
can't tell you how I trembled and shook as I left my best wishes then made
myself scarce.   I fancy without knowing if it was true that I was more
agitated than the father – certainly I was unable to work or otherwise occupy
my mind and I waited for a message with tremendous anxiety.   It came in

the evening – a daughter, Magdalene, mother and baby both well – and when I had read it I wiped the tears from my eyes and dashed off a foolish letter to the little girl who had just arrived, then I sat down feeling tired-out and thought what a momentous day it had been. My tongue played around the name Magdalene Brookfield, trying ever so hard to make it familiar and to clothe it with a face and a form that I knew. What would this new person be like, and how would she think of her mother's friend ? It seemed so important that we should like each other, and if I am honest I must also confess that a small part of me considered her mine even though it was absurd. I told myself not to be so foolish but a voice kept telling me that if things had been otherwise, if . . . you see ? What twaddle – you will agree that at some time in my existence I must have been a woman so easily do I fill my head with sweet nothings. I am full of ifs and buts and might-have-beens, passing many a long hour indulging in this kind of ridiculous specula-tion and often hard put to bring myself back to reality. Well, in that particular case, it was done for me. One look at the happy mother and proud father was enough to bring me to my senses – Magdalene Brookfield was theirs and might yet do for their marriage what ten years' companionship had not. I, at any rate, must resume my old position and be obedient and

not give offence if I wished to be near my lady again, and after eight years'
devotion that was still my aim.   I ought to have seen that a child would
make Brookfield even more jealous of his position and even more determined
to stand on his dignity, but I did not.   I could not do without Jane, however
heavy my heart.   It would have been a kindness if I had been shown the
door the day Magdalene was born but I was not, and if it was not left wide
open to admit me, it swung inwards at the merest touch.   Do you blame me
for going in ?

I can't make sense, a decade later, of my apparent desire to be totally
humiliated, and when I review what led up to this shame I am filled with
anger at my own behaviour.   Oh how I hurt myself, how I plunged my own
dagger into my heart and twisted it and seemed not to care at the pain.   Life
is too short and precious for such self-inflicted torture, but I floundered about
doing everything except drag myself out.   I seemed to think that I had no
free will and that it was up to me to endure in silence.   Not even the death
of young Henry Hallam brought me to my senses as it ought to have done –
I ought to have been shocked by that disaster into looking at my own perilous
state and putting right those things that were wrong before I was cut down
myself, but on I plunged, making no better use of my time and energies than
howling like a lovesick calf.   I went to Cliveden for Henry's funeral with a
detachment most cruel.   Oh, I cried – who does not when the corpse is a
young handsome lad brimful of promise – but a dreadful coldness filled me
as I watched the black horses tossing their black plumes and moving slowly
among the black clothed assembly.   Henry was dead.   At any moment I
could be dead too.   The thought neither frightened nor impressed me.   I
was curiously unmoved, except by annoyance at all the old world mummery,
and when I left, I remained undisturbed.   I knew all about death – hadn't
I just had a brush with him ? – and there seemed nothing dreadful about it,
but do you see why not ?   Because I was not happy, that is why.   I was
going about outwardly cheerful and bent on taking an optimistic view of
things and giving thanks for all that was good in the world when in fact the
euphoria that had followed my illness had disappeared and I was as gloomy
as ever.   Another crisis was approaching and this time I watched it come
with foreboding, knowing that I would not get off so lightly, that this time
it would not be illness that attacked me but something much worse and much
more likely to be fatal.

I finished *Pendennis* towards the end of 1850 without feeling in any way
relieved of whatever burden it was that I fancied I carried.   My fatigue did
not lessen without the daily stint of words to write but, if anything, deepened
however fast I trotted round London a-visiting.   What was coming ?   Again
and again the certainty that something *was* coming would come to me in my
dreams and I would wake up with a start and the word " Brookfield "
ringing in my ears.   Yet why ?   Everything went on as before – I was

careful to conduct myself with decorum – nothing at all had changed except perhaps for the atmosphere between all of us, which was one of constraint. I don't mean just between Jane and William and me, though God knows we were always covering up what we meant by saying things we did not feel, but with the children as well – even in that arrangement there seemed an awkwardness, though the girls adored Jane. Perhaps as they grew older – they were by then thirteen and ten – they began to worry about their status in Mrs. Brookfield's eyes as much as I did myself, or perhaps they were more sensitive than I realised and saw their papa was unhappy and saw that it was connected with their friend, be she ever so dear to them. I know Jane never at any time lessened in her devotion to them and would have been distressed beyond measure at the thought of them suffering on her account. We never discussed the Brookfields – I could not bring myself to place such a responsibility on shoulders so young, and in any case there was a natural reticence on both sides which has always prevented it. I think my daughters knew what Jane Brookfield meant to me and I think they understood all kinds of other things without me saying a word and showed by their behaviour that they did, for which I was always grateful – delicacy is the most admirable of sentiments in the young I think.

I tried the old formula of a holiday before I hit on a newer and more effective remedy for misery. First I went to see my mother in Paris and then I travelled alone on the Continent, culling material for a humorous Christmas book I had in mind. I saw some wonderful examples of idiocy on that trip that refreshed me and set my pen dancing until I found myself wondering why I did not always stick to light-hearted tales for Christmas. It would not have made my fortune, for sure, but then think what an easy life I should have had and I could even have done all the plates myself at my leisure. I hope those Christmas books of mine don't die the death – I hope they stand the test of time and please people after I am gone – there was so much fun in the doing of them and why should I care if they are lightweight and don't stir the emotions much. Do we have to have our insides heaving all the time? Certainly not – I groan to think how I have strained after that ambition when I might have settled for less. Ambition is a curse – it has kept me on my toes for twenty years and hasn't done with me yet. I shan't die happy until *Dennis Duval* is finished and reckoned by all – yours truly included – to be magnificent. Do I dream about it? Of course I do – I long to hear the plaudits and know that they are true and if work can make them true then it shall. I fear far more that men should say of me that I did not care than that they should say I failed to try.

We have wandered off course but then I do not much like the course at the moment and neither do you and you have been pulling my hand so hard to tempt me into the next valley. I am not at all reluctant to jump a mountain or two and get there, but duty keeps me to the chosen path and we shall lose the way unless we adhere to it.   Don't I sound a stern moralist, worthy of Miss Brontë at last ?   Well, I am both — the flibberty gibbert that wishes to write jolly children's books and the gloomy old parson full of calls to duty and dire warnings of what will happen if they are ignored.   Sometimes one gets the upper hand and sometimes the other and if they work together what marvels result!   Which brings me rather neatly — too neatly you quite rightly suspect — to a project that did momentarily satisfy both callings and led me into an occupation that helped take my mind off my troubles.

It came about like this: I wanted, as you know, to make enough money not to have to worry about the futures of my wife and daughters. To that end, I needed to amass capital on sufficient scale to settle £10,000 apiece on them — this would give them a generous, regular income and make them quite independent.   Had my children been boys I don't think I should have felt the same anxiety — boys can make their own way in the world — here is one who did — but girls can do nothing to support themselves except drag out a miserable existence as governesses or piano-teachers or the like.   For a

penniless girl service or marriage is the only escape from the poorhouse and, of the two, I don't know sometimes which is the worst. The marriage-market turns my stomach it is so degrading, and the thought of either Anny or Minny reduced to accepting the wedding yoke from some odious fellow in order to have a roof over their heads disgusts and terrifies me. Until things change – and I don't see how they can – women must remain like lilies of the field and be cherished accordingly. If my girls were to have any freedom they must have money and if that money was not forthcoming from novel-writing – which it was not though we lived very well – then something else must be thought of.

I cannot exactly remember how or when the decision to put myself on the boards and take a big hat round afterwards came to me. No, I did not turn actor, though it was a kind of acting, but instead hired a hall and lectured. Does it strike you as odd ? It did me, but then it was all the vogue at the time and I couldn't help hearing how much money was made at the game and the more I thought of it the more attractive the idea seemed. I had always read widely and after my famous illness even more so, for convalescence is perfectly suited to long hours with a book propped up on the blankets. The eighteenth century was a favourite period of mine – hadn't that History of Queen Anne always been at the back of my mind ? – and all the eighteenth-century writers were well known to me. I had read Fielding and Smollett and Addison and Steele and Pope ever since I could remember, returning to them again and again when current writings failed to satisfy me. It was the work of an hour to see how I could make a series of lectures out of my passion – the title found itself before long – I should call them *The English Humourists of the Eighteenth Century*, and if I couldn't fashion an amusing and enlightening entertainment out of that then I should have been very surprised. My choice was a good one – I had the knowledge, which is of course vital, but even more important I had the enthusiasm for the subject – which I might add has not been killed even though I have given those lectures a million times. If any of you feels tempted to turn lecturer, let me urge you to choose as wisely, for if you pick on a subject about which you are half-hearted then you will sling an albatross round your neck that will stink to high heaven before very long. I still read Fielding and company and I still love them and I could still stand up and talk about them even though I loathe the sight of my lectures.

I might say the thing was easily thought of and boast how well equipped I was to do it, but the fact remains that there was a good deal of labour involved before those lectures were ready for delivery. The reading was a pleasure, almost too much so, for I would carry my humorists with me wherever I went and become so entranced with them that I failed to remember I was reading them for any other purpose than enjoyment. I forced myself to take careful notes to stop my eye rushing on and then I thought long and hard about my subject before I had the temerity to set pen to paper.   I tried for an easy, conversational style, just as I am trying now, for I saw no reason to bore my audience with solemn pronouncements. They would be there, if they were there at all, to be entertained and I saw nothing wrong in pandering to that desire.   I must first of all catch their attention and convert them to my way of thinking before I could tell them anything at all and so I laboured to keep my tone light and my argument simple.   I did not want a single member of my audience to say, " This is incomprehensible so it must be awfully clever and I had better not fall asleep or everyone will know what an ignoramus I am."   I wanted what I said to be true and simple and immediately understood, which is in my opinion only giving value for money and much the best way to proceed.   Those who hold that everything worthwhile is difficult to understand do not have my sympathy – quite the reverse – there is no reason at all why a reader or listener should be compelled to work hard to unravel what the writer or speaker means.   In my book, that is tantamount to failure on the part of the creator, and I will have nothing to do with it.

My confidence in my material did not extend to a similar confidence in my ability to deliver the same – ah, there was the stumbling block.   I have never relished speaking in public – no talent for it – not even a good voice – and though I would have a written script in front of me that was what my performance would amount to.   Large numbers of people scare me – sitting silently in rows staring at me that is – and I suffer such severe attacks of nerves that I make myself ill.   I believe Dickens for one feels quite differently – is stimulated and excited by vast concourses of people gathered to hear him – but then nature has endowed him with quite a different temperament.   I knew it would be my lot to shiver and shake and turn pale and all but run away and I wished the actual giving of the lecture by me could be avoided – but it could not.   People would come to fix their beady eyes on me and would not accept my material read by somebody else – it was part of the deal that the author himself should read what he had written. I wonder why ?   Why should it matter whether the author reads it or not ? Why should he be such an object of curiosity ?   I cannot for the life of me see why my dress and my expressions and even my nervous mannerisms should afford people such delight.   Why make a man into an animal in a cage at the zoo in order to appreciate his work ?   By standing there delivering his own words in person an author appears to thrill his followers in a way I do not wholly understand – or rather, I understand it in such a way as to make me shake my head in sorrow.   To meet an admired author and hold his hand and exchange pleasantries – yes, I can sanction that, but to turn up with scores of others and simply look ?   No – that puzzles me.

I don't know why I talk so loudly of scores and even hundreds for I remember clearly my terror in case nobody at all should turn up except my mother and Anny and Minny and Jane Brookfield. If I sweated at the thought of a huge crowd, how much more I dreaded an empty hall and the humiliation of addressing row after row of empty seats. There was no reason that I could think of why anyone *should* come and pay money to listen to me — it was an impertinence to think they might — oh help, cancel the whole thing! However much family and friends consoled me and promised support I persisted in envisaging nobody there at all and worried myself to death over the amount of money that might be lost in this miserable venture. How ironic it would be to lecture in order to accrue a large sum of gold and find instead that I had only succeeded in robbing myself and others of the little we had!

Arrangements were made, with many misgivings, to hire Willis's Rooms in King St., St. James's, and it was decided that tickets for the whole course of six lectures should be fixed at two guineas while for a single lecture the price should be 7s 6d. Don't it sound like children playing at theatres? It made me smile, even though it was a desperately serious business, and I could not help calling it my tightrope exhibition which I exhorted friends to come

and watch, sure of an amazing display of agility and fearlessness. The first lecture was delivered on the morning of May 22nd, 1851, a Thursday. What an awful occasion! My nervousness increased with every hour and when I am nervous, you know, I become horribly bad-tempered. Couldn't I have done with a little wife to soothe my brow and put my clothes straight and find my other pair of glasses and execute a hundred other wifely services! Anny and Minny did their best – they always did – but my agitation scared them and induced in them a pity for me that was almost my undoing. It was like going to war, except that I have never been to war and therefore cannot truthfully claim to know what it is like. I got into the carriage that was to take me to the battle unable to speak and quite convinced that I would not be able to produce a single word above a whisper. Suppose I could not read my writing when it came to the bit? Suppose – oh horror! – suppose I lost my notes even though I was clutching them in a vice-like grip and did not intend to be parted from them for a second? There was no end to the terrors my imagination produced until finally a great gloom settled over me and calmed my palpitating heart and made me fatalistic – what would be would be and there was nothing at all I could do about it that had not already been done. Amen.

I had taken the precaution of going round to Willis's Rooms a few days before to familiarise myself with the place of execution and test my voice by reciting the multiplication tables to a bewildered waiter who obligingly stood at the far end and announced he could hear every word perfectly, but all the same the place seemed strange and eerie that May morning. Have you ever been in a lecture-room before it fills up? Do you know what a dismal air there is and how disconsolate the lecturer feels as he paces up and down the echoing aisles? It seems impossible that there will ever be any chatter or laughter or human warmth among the dark brown chairs, or that the dusty, dim atmosphere will ever be charged with excitement. All is dead. The lecturer's footsteps are heavy and loud as he continues his restless walk and if he knocks against a bench or drops a book it is like a clap of menacing thunder. I was sick in my stomach with fright and angry that I had wilfully drawn down on my head the mortification I was sure would follow. I might, I think, have bolted like the coward I was if Fanny Kemble had not chosen to arrive early. How I startled her by the extravagance of my greeting – how anxious I was that she should not leave and come back at the correct hour – how I implored that poor lady to take pity on me and stay and talk to me to pass the time! You see how distressed I was? It had been a mistake to come so early on my own – it was not peace and quiet and contemplation that I needed to prepare myself, as I had thought, but distraction. It was absurd to be so alarmed but panic overrode commonsense and if it had not been for Fanny Kemble I don't know what would have happened.

She took me into the retiring-room adjoining the lecture hall and there she did her best to allay my fears. I can't remember what we talked about – the growing hubbub outside as people began to arrive entirely drowned any conversation – but I know I was glad to have someone to talk to and ever since I have made sure of company before a lecture. As the moment drew

CLIO

near for the wretched thing to commence I began to wish I had not left my written lecture on the reading-stand outside but that I had brought it with me so that I could take comfort from the weight of the paper in my hands and actually feel that what I was about to do had some substance. Any thought of going to fetch it was out of the question – the audience would think I was about to start – but as I wished aloud what I had been thinking the good Fanny Kemble offered to go and do what I could not. Out she tripped, as neat and quiet as you would wish an angel to be on an errand of mercy, but on arriving at the reading-stand, which I had adjusted to the height I needed, she found she could not properly reach the top and in her efforts to be as unobtrusive as possible she made little half-jumps with out-stretched hands hoping to dislodge the manuscript and catch it as it fell. Instead, she knocked the papers completely off and they scattered in all directions.   In tears, she gathered them up like battered sheaves of corn and brought them to me, hardly able to look at me for consternation and the certainty that I would surely tear her limb from limb.   In fact, she had done me a greater service than she knew, for it took me the rest of the remaining time to put the pages in order and the mechanical nature of this task restored my spirits.   I stepped out onto that platform fairly composed and prepared to do my best.

A lecturer, in my experience, does not really see his audience but rather is aware of a great many faces and bodies in one mass that he feels he would disentangle at his peril.   He takes care that his gaze is sweeping when he looks up, that he pitches it to fall short of or far beyond the first row, and that he never focuses properly on anything more risky than the edge of the reading-stand.   At first he follows his words with care, even if he knows them by heart, then as confidence grows he dares to rest his eyes by lifting them to another horizon, keeping his thumb all the time on the word he has just forsaken in case he needs to rush back to the safety of that written word. It took me time to become practised at this art and even now, were I to lecture again – God forbid – I would adhere to those simple rules and would never imagine that I could afford to dispense with my notes or that I could wave cheerfully to my great-aunt in row three.   All the same, once launched I noticed almost at once that the words flowed out of my mouth in a gratifyingly smooth way and that I hardly needed to look at my text and that I could time my pauses quite well and altogether did not appear too stupid.   The audience were not at all restive, as I had feared, but seemed intent on what I was saying, laughed at my jokes, and applauded most heartily at the conclusion.   What more could a lecturer ask ?

What indeed – I suppose I shook some two score hands afterwards, so eager were people to press in upon me with congratulations.   Did I like it ? Of course I did.   Did it go to my head ?   Absolutely – I grinned like an idiot and felt I had conquered the world.   Modesty may even have flown out of the window – but I hope not, not entirely – I hope I knew it was all luck and didn't boast too much.   Is it wrong to openly enjoy success, do you think ?   It isn't English at any rate – restraint is all in this country and I can't decide whether for better or worse.   Perhaps some thought my joy unseemly – perhaps they fancied that was the reason behind John Forster's slashing review in the *Examiner* two days later.   Well, I couldn't help that and chose instead to concentrate, like a wise man, on the next lecture.

Mr. Mitchell, the impresario responsible, was immensely gratified by the initial response and began straight away to make arrangements for more chairs and so forth next time. I was besieged by people wanting tickets and I own to a sense of pride that they should want them. The demand increased rather than abated during the remainder of the course and I finished up a much wealthier man as well as a much more famous one. I couldn't help seeing this unlooked for success as an omen, though my heart told me differently. Surely, I said to myself, whatever it was that you feared has blown away and you are at last on a new and easier and happier road. I said it, but I did not believe it, and you shall hear why.

Chapter XII

———————◆———————

THE MOST DREADFUL SCENE IN
WHICH I AM REJECTED IN LOVE

N July 10th, 1851 – let us have a few more dates in this chronicle by all means – a very 'appy family was seen to leave St. Katherine's Wharf, bound for the Continent by the look of the smart new dresses that some of them were wearing. Papa seemed to have a confident air and gazed around him with a smiling countenance that was pleasing enough but entirely eclipsed by the radiance of his two daughters, who would have been even more radiant if their new bonnets of blue and pink wreaths of acacia had been on their heads and not hiding their brilliant ribbons in a trunk. Papa said they would be mobbed if they wore them and would not allow it. They could not keep still, you may be sure, but fidgeted and jumped up and down and peered in every direction until an observer might have feared for their necks so severely did they misuse them. Everything was of interest to these two mademoiselles and Papa was constantly called upon to explain what that was and why this was done and where the other had come from until you might have supposed the poor man to be quite exhausted, but not a bit of it – he appeared to thrive on these demands for instructions and never lost his temper, which did not escape the notice of the other travellers who thought he might be a tutor. The crossing to Antwerp was horribly rough but all who witnessed the fortitude of the two little women marvelled at their cheerfulness in the midst of their sickness. They seemed determined that everything should be perfect and stubbornly ignored anything that quite obviously was not. Now, that is a trait that in adults can be tiresome but in children is always admirable and greatly to be advocated. At least, that particular Papa thought so and gave thanks for it and hoped that it would continue.

Well, it did. We rushed gaily from city to city on that long promised

holiday, always in a great flurry of packing which suited the children, though
in truth they were more like young women than children, which was what
had persuaded me to take them at all. They had pleaded for years to be
allowed to accompany me on one of my jaunts but I had held off until they
were of an age to dispense with governesses and nurserymaids and so forth.
At fourteen, Anny was indisputably fit to be a companion, but Minny, at
eleven, still teetered on the brink of the grown-up world and I had my
reservations about the wisdom of including her in the party. However,
I could not take the one without taking the other, so strong was the bond
between them. I suppose never having a mother they had loved each other
more than sisters usually do and had supported and cared for each other in a
way that brought tears to my eyes when I saw it. I remember once at
Baden going off on my own to have tea with a lady friend and rather un-
kindly leaving my two doves to fend for themselves in the inn and when I
returned, after a longer interval than I care to think about and certainly had
not intended, there was Anny with Minny on her knee reading her a story

in a motherly way to allay her fears till I came back. There was always that
goodness and sweetness on the part of Anny and that trust and dependence
in Minny – though I confess I could catch that younger one at a different
game sometimes which is not quite so edifying to relate. Anny was so good
and sensible and open whereas Minny was full of feminine wiles – she had

bags of little tricks and Beckyfied arts which she used most skilfully to make Anny appear stupid and dull without Anny even realising. It was all sweet cooing for Papa but very often cat's claws for Anny and the minx thought I did not see. I could not help but admire her sharpness, and did not hold it against her for I knew very well it was her nature and that she would never do Anny any real harm – quite the opposite for should any third party seek to exploit Anny's goodness her sister attacked on her behalf.

You will see, by this lecture, how taken up I was with my daughters and how fascinated by their emerging characters. Since my illness, and since they had grown beyond the nursery stage, I had indeed become much closer to them, just in time for them to become my friends. Each gave me something different, each filled a gap in my life until then. With Anny I could talk about books and art and was delighted to find her opinions informed and original. She tried her hand herself at writing and though her efforts did not then amount to much she clearly had inherited her father's prodigious talent. She was a great wag, if given the chance, but I clamped down heavily on any facetiousness, preferring that she should develop a modest, straightforward style first before she took any liberties. Wasn't I fierce ? But only for her own good and because I cherished her gift. It is my belief that Anny will take over where I leave off and keep us all yet with her pen and none will be prouder than her own father, even if he finds her stories too affecting for him to read sometimes. The girl has a feeling for people that amazes me – nothing in her dealings with others reveals how developed are her sensibilities. To look at Anny, the stranger would imagine that she was simply a plain sensible girl, eager to please but perhaps not over bright – oh stranger, little do you know how wrong you are ! Behind that fat face and lumpy body is a quick mind and a sensitive soul attuned to every change in the atmosphere. Anny's looks are homely – I would be the first to admit it – and make her try all the harder to please, almost as if she were trying to make up for them. Perhaps a mother could have helped her appearance by choosing clothes that did more for her, but I doubt it. She is not beautiful or graceful but who cares when she is so loving and good ? Certainly not I – I am as thrilled by my daughter as I expect Cleopatra's father was by his.

As for Minny – she is quite different and developed in quite a different way. To begin with, she is pretty and diminutive and rouses everyone's protective instincts. Her features are delicate – none of the Thackeray heaviness there – and her colouring light. Whatever she wears she looks attractive and walks and moves in general with grace. Whereas Anny is open and garrulous, Minny is reserved and not given to much chatter with those she does not know very well. Anny will engage a stranger straight away in conversation while at her side Minny will listen and stare and say nothing at all, not even if she is directly addressed. Anny volunteers her views on everything whereas Minny very often does not have any, or if she has keeps them to herself. Anny is gay and boisterous and laughs a lot, but Minny is grave and quiet and a smile has to be earned. I could not make of Minny the intellectual fellow I did of Anny, but then I could not make of Anny the comforter I did of Minny. Minny would come to me and sit on my knee, when she was very small, or at my side when she was bigger, and by her physical presence soothe my troubled spirit. Her calmness stilled my rages and steadied me in my depressions though no words passed between us. She gave no token of her love other than a cool hand placed over mine, or a cheek laid against mine, but I felt it all the same. Sometimes she was so like her mother in this silent tenderness that I feared to see it, and looked around constantly for ways of hardening her to life's blows. Please God there will not be too many of them. I am prepared to come straight out and trumpet from the rooftops that I have the two best daughters in the world, and if Tompkins is lurking about at this minute waiting to pounce then let me warn him that he must beware my wrath if he fails to measure up to them.

There came a day on that long ago holiday before the storm (ssssh!) when the sun came out and the views from our little inn at Wiesbaden were sublime and I remember very well sitting down with my daughters at dinner and talking to them for the first time about their mother. If it seems perverse to have spoiled a lovely day by broaching such a sad subject I can only say that it was the very perfection of the day that made it seem natural and right to talk of Isabella, as though the happiness we were all feeling provided a cushion upon which my hard words could fall and not hurt. They heard me in silence – not a question from either of them – but then

Minny's eyes filled with tears and Anny was much affected.   I don't think
I have ever felt so close to them or been more sure that the bond between us
was strong and loving.   We went on sitting there for a long time afterwards
and I felt that the girls had come to understand at last many things that had
seemed mysterious to them and with that understanding had come a compassion that was almost too overwhelming for me to bear.   Later, but not
much later, when it was put to the test, I could sense how deep it was and
drew upon it with confidence, glad that I had no secrets any more.   They
were golden days, those, looked back on fondly during worse times to come,
but all the same – dare I confess it ?   Will they forgive me ? – pinpricks of
irritation troubled me at being constantly in the company of two children.
The drawbacks were unsuspected – I never thought, when I set out, that
finding two rooms would be so much harder than one, or that if one of
those rooms was a mere cubby-hole then of course it must be Papa's.   I
forgot that young 'uns don't like every kind of food but like it regularly at
the most boring hours and cry if they do not get it.   I never realised that a
man with two children is treated quite differently from a man unaccom-
panied, and that he cannot go and look at a great many things he would like
to see but is obliged to visit many other attractions which do not interest him
in the least but positively fascinate the darling girls.   I underestimated the
stamina of my companions and overestimated their patience.   When I would
have liked to spend all morning in bed they were up, bright and eager for the
next treat, and when I wished to spend all afternoon in a museum they
yawned after ten minutes and looked rebellious.   I vowed I would never
bemoan my solitary state abroad again.   Still, I malign the little dears – we
had a rattling good time, especially in Switzerland which nicely combined
things for both old·and young, and returned to London in the best of spirits
and the best of friends.   They were quite content to let me go back to my
old ways after they had had such a big slice of my time.

I began, as soon as we got back, a novel of which I had higher hopes than
any before.   I shan't go back on my promise not to drag you through every
blessed book I have written, but it might interest you to know that I took
more care over *The History of Henry Esmond* than over any other, and that
there is more of myself in it than you would guess.   I knew, you see, that no
matter how well it sold and how many people praised it, *Pendennis* had been
dull and dreadfully stupid and I was resolved to put all that right.   My idea
was to write a story of thwarted love between a young man and an older
woman and set it in the past firmly enough to re-assure those who would not
have accepted it placed in our own time.   I intended the background to be
as authentic as I could make it, and the character of the hero to be delineated
with the greatest care and attention to detail.   I would write it in one go and
have it published in volume form immediately, thereby ensuring that I could
oversee the complete story and change what needed changing rather than

have to submit to the tyranny of the serial form with the attendant pitfalls it held for me. No writer has ever been more determined to give of his best than I was with *Esmond*, at whatever cost – and that cost was high. Henry Esmond's unhappy love affair paralleled mine in all the particulars that

mattered even if the circumstances were entirely different and when I wrote of Henry's misery I was writing from the heart, so much so that it is the wonder the book was ever finished and saw the light of day. If this were a novel I was writing, here is the point at which I should begin teasing you along and laying a false trail all the better to astound you when I pounced, but I have not the stomach for such games and had better say straight away that the reason *Esmond* almost floundered was because in the autumn of 1851, soon after I had begun writing it, my relationship with the Brookfields was abruptly terminated.

There. It is out. The blow fell, the cataclysm came, the earth opened up and threatened to swallow me – all was misery – my mind blacked out and I crept away to howl with pain. I cannot look back now and smile indulgently and say it was all for the best or shake my head and be amused at my agony or claim not to recall why I was so upset – on the contrary, if I have learned to forgive I have not forgotten the hell I experienced and I can at any moment plunge myself back into the anguish that was mine. I have learned to accept what I was forced to accept but I will never condone the cruelty that was practised upon me, which left an open sore on my heart that will never heal. Nor do I believe that my suffering made me a better man – it did nothing of the kind – it crippled me emotionally for years to come and embittered me and robbed me of any joy in life for longer than I care to acknowledge. I will not bow my head even now and say " God's will be done " for I am sure it was not God's will and that He had nothing to do with it – the evil-doing was all man's and perfectly avoidable. Too many wicked acts are laid at the door of the Almighty, too many horrible deeds are said to derive from Him, too much nonsense is talked altogether about Divine Will to cover up for man's unkindness to himself. I shan't say " it doesn't matter – it is all water under the bridge " – not a bit of it. My pain is indelible and only softened round the edges as the years have blurred the outline of what happened.

What *did* happen ? Now there is something God may claim to know when others do not, not properly, and I wish – without any blasphemous intentions – that He would take me aside some time and tell me. I don't rightly know what happened, I swear, and I am one of the principal actors. All I know is that I went to see the Brookfields as usual one September day – sun shining, leaves changing colour and all that kind of thing – and I walked into the most shocking row. I think Jane was alone when I first went into the drawing-room – yes, I am sure she was – alone, sitting by the fire with her back to me, crouching as though she were cold and twisting a handkerchief over and over in her hands. I thought at first she was ill, as she often was, but as I approached her, my arms outstretched, she turned away from the fire and I saw her dreadful pallor and tear-stained face and the pain in her eyes and knew that no illness could be responsible for this awful change. I don't think I had ever loved her as much as I did at that moment. Who could help but love a woman so beautiful, so wretched, so tender ? I expect I asked her what was the matter, or expressed my dismay and distress in some way, but she said nothing, she only wept in a manner that threatened to break my heart, then William came in and without addressing me or shaking me by the hand he stood with his arms folded and a scowl on his face and began abusing me directly. I have no intention of repeating what he said, or what I said either, for both of us used fierce language which we later regretted and is best obliterated, but you may take it that since we were both heated we did not pull any punches and the verbal fight was a rough one, quite terrifying our lady who sat looking from one to the other as though we were both mad. I suppose we were – mad with rage, each convinced that the other was behaving in a brutal and uncivilised way, each knowing where best to slip the sword in because he knew the other's weak points well. Have you ever seen best friends fight ? Then you will have remarked how much more vicious the struggle is than one between strangers. Brookfield and I had known each other twenty years, man and boy – we had spent millions of hours in each other's company – we were as close as brothers. Tearing Brookfield apart was like tearing my own limbs from my body, so what do you make of the cruelty with which I went about the task ? I called him names I hardly thought I knew and accused him of behaviour of the lowest sort, and he – well, he made it impossible for me to ever look him in the face again. We were both so horribly hurt you see – he by my apparent duplicity and I by his unjustified unkindness. There is nothing more dreadful that being unable to convince someone you love that you have not behaved dishonourably. I had never laid a finger on Jane or entertained an unworthy thought and yet he talked to me as if I were a common seducer and she a whore. Strong stuff, you will agree, but then he thought he was a cuckold and nothing either I or his lady could say could undo the damage. He thought the fault all mine – he trampled underfoot my protestations of innocence – he would have nothing of the sins I laid at his door, of the manifest ill treatment he had meted out. How many years had I paid court to his wife with his full approval and encouragement ? Too many – too many years spent obeying the rules, his rules, only to be turned off like a dog, because someone had poured poison into his ears. And yet, did they ? I have never been able to decide. Then, I certainly thought my good kind friend had been goaded and pushed into his course of action but now I rather tend to the opinion that his jealousy was Othello-like, a disease that grew upon him, nurtured by suspicion and nothing else. I suppose, if that were the case, he was to be pitied rather than condemned, for there can be nothing more frightful than that kind of canker eating away all decency and charity, feeding upon harmless images of Jane and I talking, Jane and I laughing, Jane and I walking arm-in-arm, Jane and I playing with his child – oh yes, I see the torment and feel for him, but all those years ago I was too busy weeping for myself to give a thought to Brookfield.

For myself, and for my dear sister, for Jane, who throughout all this unbelievable shouting sat shocked and stunned, too broken to do anything or say a single word. Frequently I thought she must be roused to speak in my defence, but she never did, she allowed her husband to vilify me without speaking at all, though I know I wanted her to and looked for her to come to my side, but she never moved. She was like a stone, inert and unresponsive, taking all the blows that rained down as though they were nothing. Since I did not know what had gone on before I appeared I had no means of knowing if she had already said her say, but I assumed from her defeated air that she had and that it had been hopeless and that she had not the strength for further resistance.   It only came to me by infinitely slow and painful degrees that she was going to stay with her husband and by her submission condone his outrageous suggestions.   If she had shown even the slightest indication of standing by me – the merest movement of her hand would have been sufficient – I would have walked out of that house with her in my arms and never returned.   All I needed for that act of glorious folly would have been a sigh, a wisp, of assent and I could have done the rest without ever looking back.   But no – no movement, no glance, no support at all for me, so that I was driven into thinking that she was part of the conspiracy too – in my wild grief I accused her also of setting me up.   The cruellest part of my humiliation was Jane's absolute silence.

Afterwards, I saw she had no alternative.   She was a dutiful wife and mother – oh, we have been over that many times.   I expected too much and was disappointed as greedy people are.   I thought love could conquer mountains and that ours would triumph over petty minded adversaries.   It did not.   I wonder how often love is defeated by convention rather than any other single factor ?   I dunno – it beats me.   I left that house sick to the stomach, never wanting to see either of them again, and then followed a terrible time.   What was I to do ?   Where could I go ?   How could I live any longer ?   I went off immediately into the countryside to spend my time raving in lonely hotel bedrooms, going through the motions of living quite mechanically where no one could see me.   The blackest thoughts filled my head night and day and no amount of striding about fields and lanes could get them out of my head.   It was the injustice of it all that hurt me most – I could not accept that what had been done to me had been done.   And as for Jane, why she was with me all the time, literally before my eyes, so pale and trembling.   She was there when I woke in the morning, she was there when I closed them at night.   She was there in my horrible dreams.   My violent rage against her for her part in this treachery soon softened into pity and anxiety for her.   How could she bear to be with William all the time, suffering his anger as well as her own anguish – my lot beside that paled into insignificance.   What could I do to help her ?   Nothing, nothing at all.   I talked in my head all the time to Brookfield, arguing most eloquently and rationally against the sentence he had passed upon us, but I knew I could not possibly venture to see him.   I had had my opportunity and allowed emotion to speak for me.   Again and again I went over what I had said, what he had said, and re-adjusted both to make better sense.   Oh how well we behaved in my imaginary conversation!   How polite we were!   How reasonable!   How quickly the whole business was settled – to my advantage of course – and how easily I could see us all sitting round a table afterwards laughing and eating and chatting as we had done so many, many times before.

Eventually, that pleasant little scene was enacted but not for many a year and when it came about it was a chastened trio who were the actors. I would never, in that autumn of 1851, have thought even such token friendship possible and I don't know that if I had looked into the future and seen us round that table I appeared to hanker after that I would have liked it. What did I want with compromises then ? The only solutions I wanted were final ones – either Jane or I or both of us to die, or Jane and I to be together and alive. I thought death the more likely of the two. Jane's weak constitution would never withstand the demands being made of her – her health, perilous at the best of times, would surely give way and a rapid decline follow. I know that is what I expected so I am obliged to tell you, but truth compels me to add, with a rueful smile, that Jane not only rallied but went on to bear two more children and gives every indication now of living to a ripe old age. I don't think I would like, then, to have known that happy news either, for don't you see gloom was positively necessary to me ? That inner peace which I had enjoyed when Isabella's tragedy hit me had vanished. There was no peace – I could not be still, not even when I limped back to London licking my wounds and had my family and friends around me. I haven't mentioned those friends very much, have I ? – it has all been the Brookfields for ever so long and nobody else rating a mention. I haven't told you how kind some dear ladies were – Kate Perry and Mrs. Elliot and Anne Proctor and Lady Ashburton – they were all kindness itself.

They were Jane's friends too and their hearts broke for both of us and without their help, particularly the Elliot sisters, I don't know how we should have happened. Those two ladies were our post-box you see – Jane sent notes through them and I replied. Does that shock you ? I thought at first that I wanted no part in such deceit myself – I thought I gloried in absolute silence – but then by degrees this unnecessary martyrdom lost its appeal and I lifted the ban I had myself imposed on any clandestine communication. What harm was there in it after all ? Jane's pathetic little notes were drops of water in the desert to a starving man – they were nothing but everything. And oh the sweet relief in being able to write, write, write what I felt – to put onto paper the words " I love you, I love you, I love you " – to abase myself in words, to tell her that I wanted to kiss her feet – and to remember with her the good times like those nights at Clevedon when she used to call out to me. I wrote to her all the time, and burned almost everything I wrote – scribble scribble and then burn burn in one feverish movement it seemed. The letters I sent were in French – not for safety's sake but because French gave me a freedom my own language suddenly did not. I wonder what she made of them ? I wonder whether she kept them and tied them up in blue ribbon ? I don't much care – they helped me then and that is all that matters. I didn't say anything I regretted, I know that, or make up anything. When I received her little notes how happy they made me, so happy that often I could not prevent myself riding off to trot on my horse up and down outside her house just to be near her. Did she look out ? No, she did not, but I did not care – she had written to me and I was near her and that was enough.

I couldn't help talking about my love to anyone close enough to listen. Those ladies I have mentioned were content to listen by the hour to my babblings, and Fitzgerald visited me and comforted me, and do you know who else was understanding and compassionate ? Why, none other than my own mother, who brought to me a sympathy most rare. She not only listened but she wept with me and then dried both our tears and offered wise advice from her store of worldly wisdom. She loved Jane too, you see, and saw how it was and what a trap we were all caught in and she made it clear that whatever we did we would have her blessing. Don't you think that was tremendous ? I do – I hope to God that when my turn comes I have it in me to do as well by my daughters. The benefit of good people like my mother partaking in the sorrows of others is, to my mind, incalculable, and I shan't ever forget it. They say real friends are revealed in times of trial, and they are quite right.

You will easily understand that this business upset our friends almost as much as it upset Jane and William and I. I don't know if the quarrel was the talk of London or not but I rather suspect it must have been and was lapped up accordingly by those who relish bad news, be damned to them. Loud voices carry in any house and servants hear and tell other servants and there you are – it is the way of the world and there is nothing you can do about it. Many hours were spent analysing the causes of our quarrel and many more deciding what could be done to help us, and in the end that good

soul Lady Ashburton took it upon herself to arrange a reconciliation between
us. Oh horror! Can you imagine how I viewed such a prospect? It was
repugnant, but it was pushed upon me and I did not want to be the party to
refuse. Aren't we all afraid of the odium that being unco-operative brings
upon us? It was useless to protest that such a meeting would do no good —
our friends insisted that it would. Jane was ill with worry — she could not
bear separation on such terms — we had only all three to pass the time of day
and she would feel better and the way would be open to further negotiation.
I held back in a kind of disgust until I could hold back no longer and bowed
my head to the inevitable. We met, at the Grange, the home of the Ash-
burtons. We met, with others present, and talked for a few minutes about

the weather, and then shook hands, Brookfield and I.   That was all.
Afterwards we went our separate ways.   Jane and William together, I alone.
Finis.

I need hardly tell you what a strange experience that meeting proved.
The atmosphere was not nearly so constrained as you might think – I only
had to be in their presence to remember how much I liked both Jane and
William and the affection for their company as distinct from their persons
was still there and made things easy.   The awkwardness was over what to
say, not in each other's proximity.   The air was heavy with significance –
each movement of an arm or inclination of a head magnified it tenfold – but
nothing important was said.   My eyes drank in every detail of that couple's
demeanour and when I parted from them I knew what I had only begun to
guess at before, that they were suffering more than I.   If anyone had told
me that, I would have spurned the suggestion and thought them insolent,
but if that meeting did one thing it showed me there were other souls in hell.
William looked worn and haggard and defeated – yes, defeated, beaten,
though he might be said to have been the victor – and Jane was worse
affected than I had feared.   There was no happiness there, of that I was
certain, and though I did not rejoice in their suffering – may Heaven help
me should I ever sink to that – it made me bear my own pain with more
patience.   The possibility that others had been wronged as well as I occurred
to me for the first time.   I had only turned the telescope on myself, and
looked though the wrong end at that, while beyond my range others needed
attention.   There was nothing I could do to help them.   William, I
gathered, was going abroad for his health and Jane would join him.   And I ?
Well, I was writing a novel, was I not, and I had better return to it and
apply myself and pick up the pieces of day-to-day living and attempt to
conceal that I was gadding about London with a great big hole where my
heart used to be and nothing but tears behind those big spectacles.   The
human being is infinitely adaptable and can take greater strain than you
would ever suspect.   Amen again.

You have heard me reflect before, and will be bound to hear me again,
that work is an excellent palliative and restorative if it can be once begun.   I
would hazard a guess that for me the writing of *Esmond* was more than that
– more than a way of occupying my mind and keeping me sane, more than
a dull daily duty that put hours in when otherwise they would have dragged,
more than a way of spreading balm on an injured soul by distracting myself
with higher things of the intellect.   Writing *Esmond* was more a catharsis,
a going into the deepest black tunnel and wrestling there and coming out at
last on the other side pale and dirty and weak but glad to see the light of day.
Nobody, strange to say, has ever been able to find in *Esmond* the power or
the pity which I thought were there – readers find only an odd tale of mis-
placed love and are untouched by it.   I jump ahead, but why not, to tell you

that when that book, put together at a harrowing time, came out it was quite killed by a review that appeared in *The Times*, a review of such shallowness and malice that the disgust I felt rose in my throat and could not be swallowed.   I did not care about the poor sales – weren't my publishers even so offering me a vast sum for my next book ? – but I felt the utmost contempt for the fool who had shut his eyes to all I had laid before him in that novel. It made me re-read my own work again to confirm that I was not as stupid as I had begun to imagine, and I was glad to feel reassured when I had done so and even to experience a sense of pride in my achievement.   The pain *is* there – the pain in love that is not straightforward I mean – and the pity, and the power of those emotions that we wish we did not have and try to suppress but in the end overwhelm us.   I did what I set out to do and that is all an artist can do.

In November of that year – we are still in 1851 although it seems to have taken a century to review the miserable events that took place in those twelve months – in November, then, William Brookfield and his wife left for Madeira to winter there as I had been told they would, leaving the field clear to me. Now why do I put it like that, as though life was a race ? What I really meant was that once they had gone the embarrassment that a great many mutual friends had felt at the thought of having us in the same room, whether by chance or design, was lifted.   I don't say people had not been inviting me if the Brookfields were invited, or *vice-versa*, and I don't say that I had checked every place I went beforehand to see if certain other people were around, but all the same there was a feeling of apprehension in all our haunts in London that was unavoidable.   Sometimes I would come upon Jane – at the theatre, perhaps – looking oh so thin and sad, though she smiled and nodded gamely enough, and at her side would be her husband and though I thought to have stifled all rage, a black fury would rise up in front of my eyes and blot out both of them. Or sometimes I would hear a laugh and looking round I would see Jane on the other side of a crowded room and though it did me good to hear her happy the most awful longing would come over me to go over and touch her arm and then I would notice William hovering at her side and there was nothing to do but turn aside with the taste of bitterness in my mouth. The secret communication went on between us but I grew to hate that sham performance – if we could hope for nothing I wanted the rules applied rigidly and the nails hammered in firmly.

When the Brookfields deserted the arena – oh unfortunate image again but then I suppose I did have the air of a tired old bull – all that kind of torture ended and I was grateful. The emptiness was dreadful but it was wholesome and healthy. Not even I could ride up and down outside an empty house in Cadogan Square when the blinds showed clearly there was no spark of life there, not even I could keep alive the minutest details of facial expression when I was not constantly seeing them. Jane's voice and ·shape were ever with me but nurtured only on memories they did not have the same power over me. I breathed easier without her disturbing physical presence and slept better. The longing continued but examining it cynically – and oh dear me how very cynical I was then – I recognised that part of its fierceness was due to the need for a woman, any woman, not just Jane. Nobody could do anything for me in that respect – I went about grinning from dinner to dinner and was introduced to any number of young, fascinating ladies but none of them fascinated me. None of them seemed to have any appearance beside Jane, none of them could put five words together without sounding trite whereas she had sparkled, none of them had any interest in me except as a scalp to collect whereas she – she made me believe every thought in my head was her especial property. Oh Jane, Jane – you see what you did to me, you see how you spoiled me for life ? It wasn't simply that you felt sorry for me, was it ? It wasn't just that I was passing famous and you liked the glamour of being with me ? It wasn't that I pushed myself and was too stupid to take the hint when you gave it me – it wasn't that, was it, because there never was any hint, was there, you never did cry halt or misinterpret my feelings, did you ?

My, my, ain't it remarkable how this old fellow can work himself into a passion within half a page of writing about someone he cared about twelve years ago ? Yes, it is, but then that is to ignore what happens to thwarted love in that twelve years. Perhaps if I had been eighteen it would all have been over within a few weeks of Jane going to Madeira and I should have found another heart to make my own ache, but I was forty years of age and old hearts don't mend so easily, and Jane was not just *a* passion but *the* passion of my life. It took years and years for me to even see her name without starting, and many more until I could look at her and not tremble. I think it is only within the last two years that I have noticed I am quite calm in her company – not indifferent, but calm and unflurried and able to view her dispassionately. She is still beautiful and intelligent but she is different – she has travelled a different road from me and I am no longer close. The regret for what might have been is still there, but hand in hand with it goes a detachment most cruel. I wonder if she feels it too ? I wonder if she realises a fire has been extinguished that can never be re-kindled, and if she does realise I wonder if she is relieved or sorry ? Do you know what I hope ? I can't help hoping that she is sorry. There were always three children, mine and hers, to put their innocent figures between the devil and me, and the wretched old fiend shirked off with his tail between his legs when he saw them, but now that I near the end of my life and see how love is to be valued I am not so proud of conjuring up that vision to stop me acting as I would have liked to have done. I know why I gave in, I know it was the right thing to have done by everyone's standards including my own, but I can't help thinking it added up to the most awful waste. Not to have taken that gift – the gift of fulfilled love – not to have heeded the voice within me that cried " do it, do it, don't think of the consequences " – it seems tragic. That voice only called once and I did not heed it. I know others who did, who wrecked their careers and prospects, who laid waste other lives in the process and I can't help thinking that even if they are damned in eternity they may consider it worth it. It is the safe harbour again you see – the tempest dodged and over we went across the rough water to the harbour. I shan't ever know what would have happened but I would say unto you little children gather your rosebuds while ye may – I would say that even if Mama and Papa say I am wicked. Isn't that a terrible admission ? But then remember I had seen a rose drop off the twig, and that the twig was now a withered branch and the nightingales sang no more.

Chapter XIII

———◆———

ENGLAND LEFT BEHIND AND WHY

I EXPECT you are longing to get out and about and see something of the world after all the drawing-room drama I have subjected you to, and so of course was I. Doctors make such a great fuss about advising you that change and fresh air are what you need – five guineas please – if you are down, as if we have to be told. Of course we know change is what we need but then where shall we go and who will pay for it and who will we take with us ? They don't go into all that and yet our inability to cope with all the arrangements – our total lack of initiative – our complete apathy – is what has sent us to the wretched doctor in the first place.

Now, it is a fact that a fellow can't lie in bed and mope if he has to earn his living and in my opinion that necessity, which we curse and think of as a great nuisance, might well be our salvation. When all other inducements fail, earning money does not. Cold and cruel, the need-to-earn-money pokes and pushes us so that we cry out against the tyranny and wish we might be millionaires, but when we are, oh how we miss that stabbing sword – not, mind you, that I am a millionaire or ever likely to be one now, but I am comfortably off and don't ever have to lift a pen again for money. It was not so in 1852 and I had reason to be glad of the spur I professed to find a curse, for otherwise I should have languished forever without discovering a way to that complete change which we all agree was well advised.

We have seen – that is, I have told you – how finishing *Esmond* was the first discipline that forced me to pull myself together, but that done, what next ? Usual answer to usual question – one of those pitiful little holidays, this time to Germany, where I found some comfort in the dark churches and tall gabled gloomy buildings. But afterwards ? Back to London and a lethargy that looked like submerging me. I felt old and beat – nothing

interested me at all and though I might laud the beneficial effects of novelty
in all its forms, I had grown to hate anything new. I would look at a new
person – perhaps handsome, vivacious, cheerful – rather like a traveller looks
at a leper, which is to say that I did not want to touch them for fear of
contamination. I was set in my ways and weary – oh leave me be, the old
cry, leave me to what I know, I refuse to be interested in anything else.
Didn't Swift swear that when he was old he would not fall into that awful
habit of closing the mind to anything new, anything that might threaten
opinions tried and tested and lovingly clung onto ? But when he wrote
about old age he was a mere observer and not a participant and knew nothing
of how it feels. I do, and did before I was truly old – I understand the
frightening drain on the energies of old people when so much effort is
required of them, and I can sympathise with that weariness of the spirit that
settles like a fog and is twice as dense.

Well, I went a-lecturing again – public demand I assure you – entire
population of the British Isles hammering at my door and begging me to
come to their town – no refusal possible. It was something to do, wasn't it,
and got me out of London and that shows you how highly I rated it. In all
truth, I think it was my own idea to try my hand at the universities and
nobody suggested it – perhaps I had in mind a stiffer test than I had yet sat,
just so as to prove to myself that it could be done on a bigger scale. At any
rate, it did me the world of good for I had the devil of a job getting permission
and the more a totally humiliating refusal seemed on the cards the more eager
I became to do it and the more eager I became the rosier the black old world
began to look. It is a question of will, you see – once you have the will to
do something – don't matter what it is – the life force flows through the
body and you are on the way to recovery. My boldness in applying to lecture
in the homes of lecturing was like cocking a snook at my troubles and all
troubles benefit from such insolent treatment.

I shall have to tell you the story of how I was granted a licence at Oxford
as a reward for putting up with all that moralising. I requested an interview
with the Vice-Chancellor of the University, to consider my application to
lecture, you see, and presented him with my card with some hope that the
illustrious name thereon inscribed would impress him. To my consternation
he merely said, with something of a sneer I fancied, " Ah! You are a
lecturer are you; what subjects do you undertake – religious or political ? "
" Neither," I replied, " I am a literary man." He looked thoughtful,
examined the card again, and said " Have you written anything ? " My
heart sank as I replied, " Yes, I am the author of *Vanity Fair*." Looking
stern he said, " I presume a Dissenter – has that any connexion with John
Bunyan's book ? " " Not exactly," quoth I, and then in some desperation,
" I have also written *Pendennis*." He said he had not heard of these works
but no doubt they were proper books. I scratched around for anything to

strike a chord and suddenly offered the information that I had also contri-
buted to *Punch*.   What in heaven's name possessed me ?   He had indeed
heard of *Punch* but only that it was a ribald publication so that mentioning
it had done me more harm than good, and I had straight away to talk myself

out of the damage.   In the end I had to give character references before
permission to lecture was granted for a limited period.   Do you laugh or
weep ?   That man, that eminent Vice-Chancellor who had heard of no
literary names younger than a century, later on denied that he had ever said
what I say he said.   It may well be that I have not given a verbatim account
of that ridiculous interchange but I can't see that in this case a passion for
exactitude would in any way affect the matter.   My report is faithful to the
spirit and tone of the conversation and I have not forgotten how I felt and
that is all I wanted to remember.

However, this amusing experience did me no harm – it never in the least
discomforts me that nine-tenths of England have never heard of me – and
I went on to lecture with considerable success.   I don't say the hall was
packed out, as it was in London, or that the applause was so loud or long,

but there were plenty of smiling faces at the end and some hands to shake and a feel of professional competence that had been lacking at that other show. I began to see what it would actually be like to go touring with my lectures and that is quite a different thing from popping out in a cab for an hour or two to some nearby place to talk to a gathering comprised mostly of friends, relatives and acquaintances. It becomes an unemotional thing – you can't feel emotional leaving a strange hotel bedroom and going to a strange hall – you have to pull up your sleeves and get on with it in a strict sort of way and that is both helpful and unhelpful. I saw that while I did not have it in me to do this job forever, nor any real enthusiasm or talent for it either, I could perhaps manage better than I had thought on a strange pitch and last out a good few innings before I was clean bowled. It was a tiring game, to be sure, but only on the voice and legs – that drained feeling that quickly followed the euphoria after my London lectures was absent after Oxford and Cambridge. I was glad to sit down and not talk, but I can't say I felt exhausted – no, I did not, I adapted to the performance quite well. The dangers I suspected lay in another direction – I envisaged a state of tremendous boredom after a score or so of lectures which might produce in me a hypnotic stare that would ruin me and a parrot-like way of repeating my words that a new audience would not stand for. Who is this puppet, they would cry, and with a great crash I would fall to the floor, strings and all. Well, if they had paid their money first who cared ?

There was one by-product of this venture that I liked and that was making kind new friends. Now isn't that a contradiction – haven't I just said I felt jaded and hated new people ? Wait a minute while I explain: what I meant was that I did not have the impetus to make new friends – that I did not myself make any effort – but that did not also mean that when the effort was made for me I would reject it. If someone else was prepared to pull me out of my dullness and positively lash me into life, then it would have taken even more energy to keep them off. I thought I did not want new friends, I resisted advances and made none myself, but when someone came along and did the work for me then I found I responded and liked it and again the world glowed. I couldn't go lecturing without meeting new people and some of these strangers turned out to be so wonderful to me that I was staggered by their enthusiasm and kindness and cursed myself for being a miserable old fool going about with my eyes shut.

I met, for example, Dr. John Brown and his family, when I went to Edinburgh to try out my powers further afield, and made of them lifelong friends. Do some of you sniff and say what of it and who is this John Brown that I make such a fuss about meeting ? Well, he is no one, to be sure, no halls of fame will ring with his name, no history book will include him in some small chapter on our century, but that does not matter to me – John Brown is a fine, good man and I am prouder to have met him than Disraeli

or Palmerston.　I can't tell you how my poor frozen heart thawed every time I was received in a home such as John Brown's and saw those kindly, smiling faces beaming at me so eagerly and was fed modestly by some London standards but with such tremendous hospitality on the part of the hosts.　I could not help but think of all the homes in England and Scotland that I did not know about where similar gatherings took place every day, where good humour and a fund of what I would call informed commonsense made them the best places in the world for a man to find himself, and I felt humble when I reflected that I had known nothing of them until lecturing sent me into them. Did it make me different or better? I believe it did both. I have never been sure that rattling around Europe on a tour is really an educational experience, except in the obvious sense of making the traveller familiar with geography, whereas I was early convinced that living in one place, as unlike the one where you normally live as possible, is the best way to shock you out of any complacency you may be in danger of enjoying. It is the same with towns – no good at all simply passing through and adding it to your list, as I was to do many times, but should you stop even for a few days and walk about freely and get yourself if possible invited into a few homes, then how the viewpoint changes and what amazement sets in when you see all this life going on that you knew nothing about. Afterwards, it is impossible to return home to your own little quarters without seeing those differently too and the turmoil that results is perfectly refreshing.

I was turning all this over in my head in an unformed sort of way – ruminating I suppose you might call it, like a cow chewing cud and about as stupidly – when a plot was set afoot to send me to America with my lectures. What do you think of that? Everyone said it was guaranteed to fill my coffers to the brim and then I could retire and write great books in comfort setting myself the highest standards. The thing caught my imagination, especially when I thought how it would only be an extension of Oxford and Cambridge and Edinburgh and look how those trips had temporarily invigorated me. There was no doubt an American jaunt was feasible, and that it might be just that great change I needed – my goodness it would, thought I – change of air, of countries, of habits, of people, of scenes, even to some extent of cultures – it would be one devil of an enormous, violent, tumultuous, rattling old change that would either set me up for life or finish me off. Was I game? Certainly I was, but I held back too, and the longer I went on thinking about it the more serious the holding back became. If only an enterprise like that could be organised in a day – Do you want to go to America? Yes. Very well, here is your ticket, off on the two o'clock train to Liverpool this very afternoon where your baggage is waiting in a cabin that has been taken for you on a boat sailing with the evening tide – no need to worry about your reception, it is all taken care of, nor about this end here, absolutely no problems. Only it isn't a bit like that. Going as far as America is I assure you fraught with every conceivable kind of problem, or so I have found and should be surprised if you did not. The plans went on forever – oh how I hate plans – they are a muddle to me, best left to themselves, or to people who understand them for I do not. Going to America is awesome in concept, daunting in execution, a positive gift to Planners.

First of all, there is the sailing. Which boat will you travel on ? There
are not so many ocean-going liners that you may take your pick – perhaps a
dozen boats cross a year and none of them are ever quite sure when they will
go till it gets near the time.   You can't arrive and take a ticket there and
then as it takes your fancy – the passage must be booked months ahead and
then confirmed when they give you a date.   It means predicting your
movements several months in advance and who can do that with any degree
of certainty in this perilous life ?   It almost beat me, that part – I do so hate
being pinned down to what I am going to do this time next year.   Then
there is the object of the exercise – how could I possibly go half way across
the world with my puny lectures without some kind of guarantees that I was
wanted ?   Vague promises of support are all very well if the cost of a ticket
to Oxford is a few shillings and the hire of a hall a few paltry pounds, but do
you know what it costs to go to America and stay there for six months ?
My dears, sit down, the shock will have you on the floor – about 500 guineas
if you are to do it in any comfort.   It will be at once clear to you why I was
in a state of extreme agitation at the very thought of risking my savings on

such a venture without some reliable assurance that my expenditure would not be in vain. Negotiations to secure that promise were like taking soundings in the Atlantic itself – the letters went backwards and forwards between one association and another until I quite despaired of anyone being able to give me the confidence I lacked. I would not go unless I was invited, but how could anyone or any representative body invite me without a trial, and how could I give a trial when I was so far away? It was no good me boasting I was a success here – it was equally no good my American contacts swearing I would be a success there – the truth of the matter was that neither of us knew and what could be done on that risky basis?

Slowly, by infinitely small steps, progress was made along this difficult path and the way to America opened up. The real stumbling-block, however, far more serious than petty practical considerations, was my children. Can't you guess how I felt? I knew that my mother would welcome them with open arms in Paris and that they would enjoy returning there for a few months without being in the least upset. They saw their grandparents regularly – trips to Young St. were frequent – and who could object to six months in Paris? No, it was not finding them a home that made me hesitate so much as wondering if I would be sending them to it forever. Going to America is dangerous, you can't deny it – ships sink all the time and it could be mine and then what would my little ones do? Did I have any right to wilfully risk depriving them of a father when they had already been deprived of a mother? Why gamble all they had on such a desperate throw – was it right? I could not even insure my life to give them financial security if my ship sank – believe me, I inquired most carefully into the matter and with my stricture it was far too expensive to make sense. A good many prayers went winging their way upwards about that time as I sought guidance to make the best decision. Was money a good enough reason, but there again, was money the *real* reason? It was – I only contemplated going to America to get rich and secure the future of my family the speediest way possible – but at the same time I hid behind that reason for all I was worth and never acknowledged I did until much later. It gave me the perfect excuse for pushing myself off, you see – if I absolutely had to go to America for the sake of the future of my girls then there was no need to feel any guilt at wanting to go for my own sake. I was sad and weary and I saw America as one giant bottle of medicine to be swallowed at one gulp then hey presto mark the transformation – but I would not admit it. Hope and fear, excitement and dread, confidence and doubt – all fought within me for precedence and meanwhile the weeks and months ticked by.

I was not idle during this time of planning – there were more lectures to keep my hand in and give me more practice. I went to Glasgow, a hideous smoking Babel in my opinion, enough to make me thank my stars I lived in London, and to Liverpool where 200 people self-consciously heard me out in the Philharmonic Hall built for 2,500 – now that was good for me, excellent training, and so was another trip to Manchester where I broke down in the middle of a speech before 3,000 ladies and gentlemen. What a good douche for a man's vanity! Oh horror! Can you imagine? Do I really need to go over that ordeal and tell you how the faces swam and my throat dried up and my heart palpitated violently and worst of all a violent blush suffused my owlish silly bespectacled face? What would you have done if you had been in the audience when the great Titmarsh's nerves gave way? Waited quietly, exuding sympathy through the pores of skin like the good people of Manchester, I hope, and then clapped like billyo when the old fellow finally managed a stumbling address. How thankful I was for such kindness, and how wary I was of it ever happening again for next time I might be jeered at and abused and howled off the rostrum so that I would never dare appear ever more.

It began to occur to me at one point that I was perhaps being foolish rushing off to America so precipitously – well, I know, it took months, but relatively I mean. Why go at all before I had exhausted the English side? Every day requests to lecture came in, from places great and small, and the money offered was tempting. With our excellent new railways I could whiz about the country in fine style and stay with friends at half the places and be back in time for dinner almost at the other half. No need to pack Anny and Minny off, no need for the discomfort of sailing to America in that horrid ship I didn't trust, no need for upheaval – ah, there you have it. I wanted upheaval, I didn't want to plod about England like some itinerant parson travelling his parish – it would do me no good at all. I would be

much too comfortable and eat and drink too much and nothing at all would change.

You see how I vacillated? First producing excellent reasons for not going, only to trump them by thinking of even better ones for going, and I continued in this ridiculous fashion right up to the last minute. This kind of behaviour naturally played the devil with my health, which was not very good at the time anyway – my mighty body was out of sorts with all the irregular living it had been subjected to while I travelled about lecturing and struggled to finish *Esmond*. Do you think that in the frame of mind I was in that I slept eight hours a night and had three wholesome meals a day and stuck to one bottle of claret in the evening and walked in the park often? No, I did not, and I paid the penalty. I felt awful, inside and out, so awful in fact that I could not contemplate going to America without a companion to look after me. Does that seem spineless? Well, I suppose it was, wanting a nursemaid at my age, but I shrank from having to arrange my own affairs over there and thought I was entitled to the luxury of a general factotum. The problem was – another, you see – the problem was the nature of the beast. I did not want a valet, although the idea was attractive for I like the small homely comforts a valet provides in the way of ever-clean clothes and hot drinks when you wake up and so forth, nor did I want an idle friend, but on the other hand I did not just want a secretary who would write my letters and lecture notes and nothing more. What I wanted was a congenial fellow of the competent sort who would deal with all the paperwork and arranging necessary but not be above doing the odd errand that was not strictly speaking his job. I wanted someone I would be able to talk to who would nevertheless recognise there were times when I did not want to talk at all. I wanted someone who was an equal but who would not mind on occasions being treated as an inferior if he was not always invited to the exciting places that I was. I dreaded above all else landing myself with some feeble fellow who would be more trouble than he was worth and whom it would be quite impossible to rid myself of because I could not cast a dog off so many miles from home.

I entertained visions, on my good days, of real friends like Fitzgerald accompanying me – absurd, even if it had been feasible – but this gave me the idea that I ought to look around among the families of my friends to see if I could not hit upon someone not unknown to me, with whose character and temperament I was already familiar, who might jump at the chance. By this means I arrived at young Eyre Crowe, the artist son of a family I had known many years, right from the days when I had lived in Paris. He was a dear boy whom I had known since he was ten – in 1852 he was in his mid-twenties – and with whom I had a good deal of common ground since he had trained as a painter. He had some talent, rather as I had had, and as long as his family were well off he looked likely to make a living in a small way, but the minute the Crowes fell on hard times Eyre's days as an artist were numbered and he was obliged to support himself in other ways. Who does that remind you of ? Eyre's great merit was that he knew how to be silent. There are people, you know, especially young people, whom silence unnerves – they think of silence as something they have to fill in, something that is uncomfortable, but Eyre was quite the reverse. He could settle into a silence and make it his own, and as for minding loneliness, why I don't think he knew what it was. When I put the suggestion to him that he should accompany me to America as my secretary he was extremely eager, but the thought of his mother held him back. She was very ill – some said dying – and he felt it his duty to stay at her side. I ought, I suppose, to have patted him on the head and praised him for the faithful son he was but I did nothing of the kind. Selfishness made me bold. Time was getting short and I absolutely had to have someone, so I used all my powers of persuasion to convince Eyre that there was no immediate danger and that he would do his mother no harm by coming with me. That good lady herself pressed my claims, in the way those sweet martyr mothers have, God bless 'em, and the thing was done. Eyre agreed to go with me and at once half the burden of the trip was lifted from my shoulders. He proved himself efficient and trustworthy right from the start and if it had not been for a certain – no, it is uncharitable and will give you the wrong impression if I criticise him before we begin and in truth I never had any real fault to find with that young man.

So there we were – yours truly in a devil of a state but the lectures arranged, welcome assured, children packed off and boat booked. All that was missing was any sense of satisfaction. You know what I was like at parting from my children – simply multiply those feelings of terror and distress a hundredfold and you will have some notion of what I went through. There was no question of standing up like a man and saying, " goodbye, I am going to America, be good till I get back " – oh my dear me no, it was all sneaky and off hand and the poor darlings did not know I had done anything more than gone to buy a book when it came to the bit. I could not face those tender creatures and feel their arms go round me for perhaps the last time and behave like anything except a blubbering old fool so I invented a little game of pretence to get us over the bad time. My mother was not so easily shaken off. If I was afraid, my mother was simply terrified and her weeping and wailing were frightful to behold. She spent weeks searching for a life-jacket to support my massive frame and when I reached my cabin, there it was in all its nasty oilskin splendour, reeking to high heaven. I don't think I could have put it on if I had tried for a week, but thank God I was never called upon to embrace its smelly arms. I expect you are smiling at all this ridiculous fuss, but I'm not ashamed – it *was* a big step and I don't see why I should hide from you my agitation.

I went up to Liverpool in October 1852 to board the *Canada* in a sober,

solemn mood, still untinged by excitement. Excitement has something
pleasant about it, I think, and there was nothing pleasant about how I felt.
All the preparations had made my leave-taking seem like a final one – I felt
like a pharaoh who has packed all his possessions into his pyramid ready for
the big voyage into the unknown and now all that remained was a last
prayer and amen. My sense of doom was heightened by a clipping from the
New York Herald which had reached me. That paper had taken a vicious
shot across my bows the minute my tour was announced – it talked of the
toadyism exhibited in America before every foreign celebrity and then it
went on to deny I was a celebrity in any case and to maintain that to fête me
as Dickens had been fêted was absurd, saying somewhere in the piece that I
was a cockney snob. Wasn't that a famous attack ? I didn't care about

being fêted, I can assure you – Dickens was welcome to the crowds and
cheers as far as I was concerned – but I was rather more disturbed about the
general hostility. Who wants to go where they are positively not wanted,
when all is said and done ? Not I, nor you. Making money was not
important enough to be obliged to subject myself to a barrage of abuse.
Would they throw rotten tomatoes at me as I landed ? Luckily, I knew my
newspapers, and I knew that the public does not always think what they
say it thinks and that until I had evidence to the contrary there was no need
for alarm. I may be over-sensitive in some respects but in others my skin
is thick.

It will not have escaped your notice that if it was October 1852 when I sailed for America it had taken me a whole year from when the Brookfields broke with me to get away. That seems a long time, quite long enough to make you think I could no longer be seeking change on account of the difference that episode had made in my life, but in terms of emotional bereavement I can tell you that a year is nothing, nothing at all. A year after the event I was still convalescent, still turning the corner after that grave illness of the heart, still finding my feet among the ordinary things in life. All that time, my heart had lain fallow, nothing was sown, nothing reaped, and only now could I bear the possibility that the soil might be replenished by the elements of time sufficiently to have some seed planted in its rocky depths. We must have that fallow period after a disaster – there is no short cut back to full production that I know of. The weeks and months of emptiness must go by or another disaster will follow. Haven't I seen many times the folly that overtakes those who leap from one love to another

convincing themselves that both are the same when they know full well that they are accepting comfort in place of passion ? Lest you think I adopt a smug, superior tone let me tell you a little tale before I get on the *Canada* and you with me: during that year I have talked about I received a letter from a certain young woman called Mary Holmes whom I remembered from my childhood holidays at my parents' home in Devon. I remembered her name and her face and that was enough – together with the address – to make me interested in her predicament. As I recall, Mary Holmes wrote to me about the printing of some poems of hers – or were they hymns? I truly forgot – at any rate, about publishing something or other. She asked my advice the way hundreds of others did and do – letters arrive by the shoal all the time from little Miss Smiths in the country wanting me to see their work – which papa or the vicar or a dear friend has told them is remarkably good – between covers. I always write back telling them not to waste their time unless they have a small fortune to dispose of, but in the case of Mary Holmes I couched my stern words in softer clothing and managed to find her a few compliments along the way. Why? I don't know – I suppose her innocence was so transparent and I was touched by it. Whatever the reason, the contact was made and a steady stream of charming notes arrived from Devon to which I admit I looked forward and enjoyed and then I indulged in mild speculation as to the personality of the young lady who wrote them. Do you see which way the wind was blowing and why I am telling you all this? Before very long, Mary Holmes was confiding in me that she would like to find a position in London as a music-teacher or a governess and she would so appreciate it if – if – but that was being too bold and she hardly dared say it – if, then, I could even tell her how to set about finding a situation. Some inner caution must have told me not to move too quickly, for I suppressed the urge to tell this sweet creature to come to us and instead offered merely to inquire among my lady friends as to whether one of them could accommodate her. I wonder what I wrote to her? I wonder if she could produce any letters from me with a tender phrase or two in them? Perhaps, but I don't think so. I was merely kind, and interested and anxious to help and there was nothing more to it, so why then did I suffer such a fearful disappointment when I saw Mary Holmes in the flesh, and what did that feeling tell me about myself that is at all relevant to this chronicle? Poor Mary Holmes, who wrote such lovely letters, was not a lovely object to look upon – red hair, red nose, ungainly limbs – and her goodness and skill at teaching music could not make up for her physical shortcomings. I rapidly ceased to be interested in Miss Holmes – disgraceful to admit, but better the truth. She remained in my mind only as an object-lesson I was badly in need of, she showed me first that I was far from being as uninterested in women as I claimed I was – or else why should I have been disappointed when she turned out ugly and graceless – and secondly that I was not as totally committed to the memory of Jane Brookfield as I liked to think. There was no danger of me inventing some passion so that I could console myself with another lady, but I thought I defined a much worse tendency – to glorify Jane until the possibility of any other woman became quite unthinkable. In congratulating myself on not falling for

someone else on the rebound, I was going too much the other way, and if
Mary Holmes did anything it was caution me to be careful or my misery
would become permanent when my nature did not require it to be

The *Canada* took on board a fellow lately given to a great deal of ruminating of the above kind when it took on me, and a pretty doleful picture I
might have made if it had not been for the arrival at the quayside of the first
copies of *Esmond* almost literally as I embarked. Oh what a smile illuminated
the old fellow's face then! How his dark brow lightened and his dull eyes
twinkled as he looked at the beautiful thing in his hands! And it was
beautiful – I beseech you to go and look at that first edition simply for the
pleasure of admiring the Queen Anne type and the thick paper and the
general arrangement of the work which was as much like the genuine article
as you could want. Of course, copying the style of a century ago had not
been cheap, but why should it be ? There was a deal of workmanship
involved and I did not expect to achieve high standards for nothing. The
printers had been faithful to my idea and for that I was prepared to pay and
if the public for their part were not, why they were the loser. I expected
Esmond to be a failure, but I saw no reason why it should not be one of which
I was proud. I took that first copy on board with me with the greatest

pleasure and affection – it seemed a talisman for the voyage, and more than that – an ending to a sad part of my life just as I hoped to enter another, better phase. All my pain was bound up in that book and with it firmly between my hands it seemed as if I could at last close it and if not forget, move onwards.

I don't say that because of the fortuitous arrival of *Esmond* my spirits were high as we cast off, but they were not as leaden as I had anticipated. Perhaps they would not have been in any case for there is something infectious about the atmosphere of a big sea-port that takes a man out of himself and makes him suddenly eager and keen to be off. I stood for hours on the deck watching the goods being carried on board, watching the curiously rich faces of the sailors, watching the groups of white-handkerchiefed relations come to see loved ones off, watching the gulls wheel overhead in anticipation of a feast, and watching the sea itself, cloudy and thick, swelling and heaving far away into the horizon. The land behind, those towns and fields, seem so tame and dull besides the tempting restless movement of the sea, and instead of being pulled back towards them I felt instead an urge to be gone. The sea promises so much when you are at the edge – there is no hint at all of that grey monotony, those vast empty sea-and-sky-scapes, that are to whip you into a sullen rage when you have been in the middle of them for days and days. The sea represents adventure and every one of us longs to be on board. Even if we know that in a day or two it will be a case of " steward bring me the basin " we can't help but be invigorated by the spray and the wind and all the bustle that surrounds a boat leaving the shore for another continent. We know, besides, that time will be suspended for the next two weeks and that we will hang between sky and sea, hardly existing at all, immune to all but the moods of the weather. We will be in limbo, out of contact with the outside world, virtually sealed off from wars and plagues and famines, and that can't help but be attractive except to those of us who thrive on troubles. That setting-off is in my opinion the best part of going to America, not to be missed even if it were possible, and I suppose one day it will be, I suppose they will find a way eventually of careering through that ocean in no time at all so that the traveller hardly spends a night on board and will have no time for the kind of reflections I had when I hung over that rail. If that day comes, as it surely must, then I pity the traveller. I would not like to arrive in America without a period of contemplation spanning the old world and the new and without a long spell of neutrality between the two cultures. I swear that as the *Canada* left the shore and set out on that long connecting voyage, I heaved a sigh of pleasure and relief. The die was cast – there was no going back, and I was glad because at last I did not want to go back – at last I had the courage to want to go forwards.

Chapter XIV

———◆———

A GREAT ADVENTURE UPON ANOTHER
CONTINENT WHICH RESTORES MY SPIRITS

THE voyage to America was pretty rough – a lot of wind against us, dark skies, not much sun – ship plunging like a porpoise most of the way – but I survived it quite well. I was lucky in my travelling-companions, though I don't remember all their names. Russell Lowell was on board, and Arthur Clough – pleasant company to while away the hours once they threatened to become monotonous – and of course young Eyre who had already proved himself a stout companion and with whom I grew more and more pleased. What I liked best about the voyage was the enforced rest and idleness for which, as you know, I have always had a taste and was much in need of at that stage. I was sick at first – I think we all were – but after my innards adjusted themselves to the rolling, pitching motion I was quite content to lie in my cabin reading, emerging only to dine and drink with the captain and the other passengers in the evening. And what did I read ? Why, *Esmond* of course, and yes I was pleased at what I found. The feeling of peace that came over me was wonderful – *Esmond* finished and good and nothing else hanging over me – and I think I was the last to become bored because of this self-satisfaction. All the same, a day did dawn in the middle of the second week when I was as impatient as the rest to have done with the sea and I too began plaguing the Captain for news of land ahoy. He took all the questioning with admirable good humour, assuring all of us that we were almost there, and then there came a dramatic moment in the middle of dinner, on the eleventh night I think it was, when quite casually he sent a sailor up to the crow's nest to see if anything was visible. The message came back no, nothing and the Captain went on eating calmly for half an hour and then despatched another inquiry and lo and behold this time a light had been seen and we were told that we would land the next day.   I was dumbfounded – how the deuce could a man tell to within half an hour that we were nearing America ?   How did he know when to send a sailor into the crow's nest ?   How had he kept a straight line and hit the correct spot and all so coolly ?   Were they magicians, these sea-captains, that they could achieve this miracle with the aid of a few

unconvincing looking instruments ?   I lay in my bunk that night puzzling over longitudes and latitudes and I thought I began to see a light, but I could not be sure.   It fills you with a sense of Divine Wonder when you actually witness this astonishing feat of ingenuity, for that is how my romantic self persisted in seeing it whatever the explanations.

The moment land had been sighted the entire atmosphere on board changed – there was an alertness where before there had been apathy, and a heightened awareness where before there was a dull acceptance.   We all packed our bags and had them corded up and went to bed hardly daring to sleep for fear of missing the tremendous sight we had looked for all these days and had almost given up hope of ever seeing.   Everyone must have their own private image of what they expect America to look like but mine I remember was strangely unformed.   I did not have in my head any exact description of that country, only a jumble of facts culled from books and from other people's reports.   I think I envisaged a land of fairy-tale splendour, a kind of promised land dripping with milk and honey and yet at the same time barbaric and untouched, full of savages and landscapes of grotesque splendour.   I would ask you, if you have not already been to that continent and plan to go, to list for yourself what you think you are going to find so that you may be staggered all the more by the reality.   America – the very name America – must exert the most powerful fascination over us for I have never known a country capable of producing such mixed reactions.   People love or hate it before they have ever been – they presume a level of intimacy with every inch of that immense country when they have not set foot in it – they pronounce on American habits and tastes and opinions when they have never met a single American, and mostly they are wrong. What, I wonder, is it about America that provokes such dogmatic rubbish, most of it hostile ? I don't know, but I suspect it is the sheer size of the place – we automatically resent the size and wealth of that mighty nation and so we seek to decry it.

I did not. I was not in the least interested in attacking a country and its institutions before I had been privileged to visit it. If I had needed a warning – which in all honesty I did not – a New York sheet that I had read in Liverpool would have sounded the alarm. It denounced my intended visit as " encouraging that already too numerous class of lecturers who first mulct the citizens of their dollars and then return to their own country to lampoon them ". Exactly so, and I despised those who behaved so rudely as much as the writer of that complaint. As I stood on deck that November morning craning my neck to make out anything at all, I was filled with curiosity and nothing more. We touched first at Halifax and then we went on to Boston, all the time with as much confidence as though someone had been holding a rope and pulling us in. I don't think it has ever been listed by anyone, but the sighting of America at sunrise must surely be one of the wonders of the world – up we came onto a deck whose humble bleached boards were bathed in a red-gold of the sunrise and there before us was a glittering apparition that nobody could have imagined. I am sure the inhabitants would tell me that Halifax is the most ordinary place in the world, but after 3,000 miles of sea and with the rays of that magnificent sun catching every piece of glass and gilt in the island and blazing it forth like some heavenly message it is spectacular. I choked with emotion – my eyes filled with tears at the beauty of it all, and at the marvel of all that land ahead. Who, coming across that ocean, could not be moved by the awesome nature of our world ? The spirits soar simply to discover that what we have been told exists truly does and a sense of triumph fills the traveller's breast.

At Boston the weather was hazy and we were not vouchsafed a similar experience, though this was where we landed properly and where we first stepped on to American soil. The bustle was twice that of Liverpool, or so it seemed to me, but then the boat had lulled me into a stupor and everything everyone else did seemed at the speed of lightning. I was quite incapable, myself, of doing anything except stand on the quayside staring while all around men dashed hither and thither roaring and shouting and throwing and pushing and altogether going quite mad. First impressions are dangerous things, but I swear that when I say the speed of America is what hits you first I speak the truth. Everything seems twice as fast as back home – they speak twice as fast and move twice as fast and give every evidence of thinking twice as fast. The English mind cannot cope with it at first, but then the habit takes hold and becomes attractive and stimulates the newcomer to liven himself up, even if it means throwing overboard the conventions of a lifetime. Such is the hurry in America there is no time for unnecessary courtesies –

none of that time-wasting flam we go in for – and so you are quite likely to find that you will not be allowed more than one " Sir " in a conversation, and a curt one at that, and as for " please " and " thankyou ", they are kept to a minimum.   It shook me to begin with, especially when such brusqueness came from a doorman or waiter, but then as I came to understand that this directness proceeded from that love of speed I mentioned and not from rudeness I started to like it.   After all, why not – aren't a great many of our manners unnecessary and not manners at all but the most awful sycophantic hypocrisy ?   It is refreshing for everyone to be treated as equal and within a very short time I was doing it myself and liking it.   The Americans are very *literal* too – I remember my first breakfast in Boston – I ordered boiled eggs and among the array of dishes placed before me saw a goblet filled with something I didn't recognise and also I missed the eggs.   " Where are the eggs ? " I asked.   " That's them in the glass."   " Well, but where are the shells ? "   " You didn't ask for shells."   Good gracious, I thought, no more I did so why should I mind that this fellow reprimands me as if he were an equal ?   And that was another thing – another first impression that was to prove lasting – everyone *was* equal as far as I could see.   I don't mean that there were not rich and poor, but that in treatment of each other no man distinguished between the two.   Sometimes I thought it was carried a little too far – I remember once taking a vest to a tailor to be mended and the fellow called out to his assistant, " This *man* wishes his vest to be mended," and then turning to me saying ," This *gentleman* will attend to you."   What do you think of that ?   It was perfectly possible for a man to begin with nothing and end up a millionaire or at least rich and have at his table the best families in town.   Now how could that happen here ?   It takes years and years of careful marrying and breeding and being honoured for a poor man to really enter society. In America, society as we know it does not exist – it is perfectly open and anyone who tries can enter it. Every man's expectations can be of the highest from the moment of birth. This encourages an atmosphere of liberality that is quite intoxicating to a desiccated Englishman who has moved in careful circles all his life and knows money is the key to nothing except luxury. I knew within a week that *Vanity Fair* could never exist in America and I thought that wonderful.

Indeed, I thought everything was wonderful, from the oysters to the cries of the newspaper boys, who were amazing, confident urchins with the most infectious grins – and as for the oysters, they were as big as plates and almost impossible to swallow at one gulp though I had a try for the honour of England. The Bostonians surpassed themselves in their hospitality but it was only a foretaste of what was to come through the whole of America. As a race, the Americans are the most friendly people I have ever met – open and eager to know you with none of that calculating reserve we get used to here. I own to twinges of embarrassment at the degree of effusiveness with which perfect strangers greeted me – the handshake so vigorous, the expression so animated – and I had to stop myself recoiling from this powerful friendliness. It became a constant worry that my timidity in that direction – I wasn't used to such demonstrativeness any more than you are – would be mistaken for hauteur or arrogance and I tried very hard to overlay any bad impression I might have made by being extra attentive to what was said. It would never do if word got round that Titmarsh was above himself. I thought of myself, though I had alas received no official letter of appointment, as an ambassador for my country and was therefore on the watch for anything that might be interpreted as a mark of disrespect. This meant that although I tell *you* freely and frankly what I thought, I guarded my tongue in company unless what I had to say was flattering. It was my firm resolve not to be tempted into passing unwelcome judgements in the manner of certain other visitors from England – I would have thought it an impertinence to spend some few months there and then write a book on the subject. There would be no American sketch-book, of that I was convinced.

In the event, it was fortunate that I had decided on that stand for I don't know where I should have found the peace and quiet to write, never mind the time. Every day, from the moment I arrived in Boston, seemed one long round of meeting people and being entertained and I retired each night perfectly exhausted and incapable of either reading or writing. I was not fêted as I believe Dickens was, but what a host of admirers appeared from nowhere, wanting to shake me by the hand and tell me that they had read my books and so forth. Friends I did not know I had entertained me and showed me their city and altogether accepted me as their own until I almost forgot the purpose for which I had come. I found it extraordinarily difficult to pull myself together and stop behaving as though pleasure was my sole purpose – why, New York awaited and I must get to it and earn my bread.

I went by train to New York, marvelling all the way at the amount of reading American men seemed to do on their journeys. Can you fancy an English grocer reading Tennyson or Browning on his way from Brighton

to Broad St. every day ? Of course you can't – a quick look at his newspaper and then a snooze for the rest of the journey. But in America the majority of travellers, on long or short journeys, read for all they are worth and I could not help but admire them.   I was already pleased with myself, you can be sure, for being such a seasoned traveller, full of boasts as to the nothingness of crossing the Atlantic, laughing in a superior sort of way at the shivers and shakes I had indulged in before that trivial journey. Crossing the Atlantic was easy, my dears, and going to New York child's play – enough to make me yawn and declare the whole business dull and boring. Ain't it amusing when people do that ? Pretend exciting adventures are all in a day's work, I mean.   It is a type of snobbism that appeals to me for it is so transparent. But all the same, I was proud of the comparative calm with which I viewed the prospect of attempting New York and I think rightly so for it is a terrifying place. Boston is a sort of university town, not dissimilar to Oxford or Cambridge in many ways, but New York is peculiarly American and quite unlike any other city I have ever seen.   I can't say it is beautiful because it is not, nor can I list any buildings that I would consider worth making a special journey for, but there is an atmosphere of hustle and bustle about it that either stuns or uplifts and is most definitely worth experiencing. I found myself in a daze most of the time – not sure where I was going or what I was doing – constantly finding myself standing like a statue while the rest of humanity crashed about me. Simple things like getting on and off a car seemed beyond me – I was too slow to keep up – and everywhere I walked the energy of those hurtling past me made me dizzy. It was as though there was something in the air that intoxicated me and made me sleepy, and indeed I have heard people say that the air in New York is quite extraordinary and takes weeks to become accustomed to for a European. I tried to treat New York as I would any other foreign city – walk about and look at places of interest I mean – but it defeated me. The plan of the town is exceedingly simple and sensible – all the streets run parallel and the buildings are divided into blocks so that the whole resembles a tidy child's drawing – but there seems no heart to it, or if there was one I'm afraid I never found it. No heart, and hardly any greenery, though every street seemed to end in a vista of the river – but what a river, quite unlike the Thames, much broader and more of an estuary all the way. I think my trouble was that I could not accept the apparent lack of gradual growth in that city – it was as though someone had banged down the finished article and that was that. Except that it was not finished – nothing in America was finished – everywhere I went I saw more buildings going up and such a lot of hammering and sawing that the air was filled constantly with the noise. Where would it all end I was always asking myself – when will these striving people be content and rest ?

I stayed in the Clarendon Hotel on 4th Avenue at the corner of 18th Street, than which there can be no noisier corner in the world, though the hotel itself is quiet and comfortable and was to my liking. I had an excellent couple of rooms there, but any hopes of writing in them were quickly dashed because of the constant interruptions. There was always someone pounding up the stairs to see me. It was almost impossible to write a three-line note never mind anything more serious. Does that sound like a complaint ? Well, it wasn't meant to be – the rush and restlessness of the place agreed with me – it was exactly what I needed and I was forever congratulating myself on my luck in coming. I was so tired of everything being staid and dull and planned and organised and timed and contrived and oh what joy to be in a country where spontaneity was the order of the day! I was quite prepared to go along with it as long as it would have me. How long that would be depended very much on those blessed lectures that were as yet unaired.

At the invitation of the Mercantile Library Association – may God bless 'em – I gave my initial series of lectures at 548 Broadway at the end of November 1852. Now where and what do you suppose No. 548 was ?

Why a church, that's what, and in the main street, that is where, though in
New York no street seems more main than the next so you are not to
imagine the Mall. I was quite astonished when the secretary of this
association – Secretary Felt – led me into the place with its pillared nave and

oak pulpit and indicated that this was where I should speak, in the first
Unitarian Church of New York. It did not seem quite right to be standing
up in God's house and earning so much money, though I was the only one
who seemed to think it queer. Evidently they had a different attitude
towards churches there – right or wrong I don't know – for I was quite
often in my travels to find religious buildings used for other purposes more
as though they were village halls than anything else. I would stand in the
pulpit sometimes and be tempted to give out hymn numbers instead of reading
my lectures and if the whole congregation – I beg your pardon, audience –
had with one accord gone down on their knees and begun to pray I should
not have been surprised. The only difference lecturing in a church in fact
made was that the acoustics lent my voice a flattering depth and resonance
I had long wished to possess and would have liked to take everywhere with
me.

The lectures went down very well, though certain newspapers did not
think so. The morning after my first lecture when I came down to breakfast half the dining-room were trying to hide the *New York Herald* with its

offensive report, fearful that upon reading it I should burst into an apoplectic rage. There was no danger of that – I was an old hand at bad reviews and though I damned the critic for abusing me, and regretted it from a business point of view, I took no notice of the jibes contained in them especially when I knew that those hundreds who had heard me had been undeniably satisfied and would by word of mouth give the lie to what appeared in some news-papers. I took comfort instead from the good reviews. It just so happens – doesn't it always ? – that whereas I don't seem to have kept a copy of that *Herald* attack – don't you dare produce one – I have a beautifully preserved cutting from the *New York Evening Post*. Listen to this:

> It was remarked by a gentleman in attendance at Mr. Thackeray's lecture last evening that if the building were to fall and crush its inmates the loss would put New York back intellectually half a century . . . They never remember to have spent an hour more delightfully in their lives . . . His enunciation is perfect . . . his voice is a superb tenor . . .

Stop! Consoling myself with yellow old compliments at my age – you will be disgusted and so am I, but I only wanted to prove to you that I did not exaggerate when I said my audience went away happy, and more important longing for more.

I don't like to confess how much money I made in New York – the amount was indecent. It seemed to rain dollars and whereas before, though ever mindful of my bank balance in all its varied states, I had not been given to exact calculations all the time, now I found myself continually multiplying and adding up in my head and gloating over the sums arrived at. My head was full of financial speculations and little else – I carried scraps of paper about covered in scrawls that told me I would soon be a rich man, and soon – more scrawls – a very rich man at this rate. My wife and daughters would be quite safe when my time came, though curiously enough I was less sure than I had been that this would be soon for I had never felt so well in years – all I needed was a new stomach to cope with the gigantic meals I was forced to consume and otherwise I was in good order. Two worries – my bank balance and my health – removed at one blow – wasn't that splendid ? I tell you I positively leapt up in the morning full of vitality and ready for anything. America has done nothing short of give me a new lease of life.

I remember very well wondering what to do with my recovered energies that I was not already doing. For months I had written and lectured and gone a-pleasuring all with a heavy heart and often feeling ill so that you will see I was used to that kind of daily round and could manage it even in adverse circumstances, and now that I was so fit and lively it did not seem enough. I would get up each day and visit people and walk about New York all the time sniffing the air like some underground animal that had found its way to the surface and was intoxicated by the delicious air.   Everything fascinated me – anyone observing me gawping at the soda-water fountains, dispensing their tumblers of liquid from metallic dolphin-shaped spouts for three cents, or at the steel-topped roofs that lined the skyline – why, they would have thought I had only just emerged from the backwoods.   Those two and a half miles of Broadway soon knew me rather well.   When I was not engaged on business I paraded that lively thoroughfare constantly, on the lookout for anything different and amusing.   This business, I might add, was no figment of my imagination – I had an interview with the publisher Harper and with various other gentlemen in the hopes of coming to some agreement on the vexed question of copyright.   I suppose you know the Americans can steal any of our books and rush out a pirate edition without so much as a by-your-leave ?   It was not only the fact that they did this during my visit with *Esmond* and sold it for fifty cents that annoyed me, but that they produced the text in ordinary cheap type and not the Queen Anne print I had designed.

At any rate, my feelings were those of anticipation and impatience – each day I was convinced I was about to embark on an exciting new project, as though being in America was not exciting enough.   I wonder if that country does this to everyone ?   Or was that my true nature – would I perhaps always have felt like that if things had always gone my way ?   My own cheerfulness and good humour startled me and when I looked in the mirror I was amazed at the alert fellow who looked back at me even if he did still have white hair. My energies were by no means absorbed by my lecturing and I looked around for another outlet, not necessarily a physical one, more something to interest me and provide me with a foil to my unnamed ambition.

I didn't satisfy this longing by myself — it was satisfied for me by the introduction I received to a family called the Baxters. Did you think I was going to climb Everest or swim the Niagara Falls ? Does it seem absurd that the mere introduction of a new family into my life should immediately calm me down and make me content ? Well, I can't help making myself look ridiculous by telling the truth. What I had really been missing in my reborn state was a House of Call — somewhere I could go and be received as one of the family and find companionship that suited me. Ain't I a simple fellow ? Without realising it, I had been starved for too long of the kind of friendship I needed — at all stages of my life I have found friends indispensable especially f-f-f-female ones. Ah! You see the light do you ? You want now to know about this family I was so careful to mention collectively — and you shall. There was a father Baxter, to whom the introduction was in the first instance made, charming fellow, and a mother Baxter, to whom I was taken immediately to pay my respects, charming lady, and some little girl Baxters who were perfectly sweet, and I think at least one boy Baxter — who cares about the boys ? — and one other Baxter, also a female, called Sally. She was then about eighteen years of age and the wildest, loveliest girl I had ever seen. I felt I had found my Beatrix Esmond and lost my heart to her. I knew the minute I set eyes on her that the Something New I had been seeking was found. I no longer rushed about New York aimlessly, but directed my eager footsteps to a certain Brown House on Second Avenue where I was ever welcome and ever sure of exactly that mixture of interest and sympathy without which I appeared unable to survive. My loneliness was gone, and if you think I can't have been lonely when I have just told you how high spirited I was then you don't understand that loneliness doesn't necessarily make a man miserable and depressed but can affect him when he is happiest and bursting to share his happiness with someone else to complete it. That, at any rate, is how I thought of myself when I invaded the Brown House — I wasn't in the least sad or pathetic, I didn't in the least want to clutch at the Baxters and moan and groan and beseech them to keep me company — quite the reverse — I was delighted with myself and America and wanted to share my pleasure with someone who could appreciate it.

Let me tell you about Sally Baxter, but first of all I have to spoil my story and tell you that she is dead. That was a terrible shock, I know, but I do not have the heart to play games with my memories of Sally, and if the risk I have taken in telling you the end of the story at the beginning makes you lose interest then you do not deserve to share them. The way in which Sally died, and why she died, don't belong to this part of the story, but the fact that she *is* dead does, for it colours everything I am going to say about her.   Once someone young and full of promise dies they immediately become framed in our minds as they were when we first knew them and I have no doubt that if Sally was at this moment a plump matron with six children on her knee then her image would not shine forth so brightly before my eyes.   Death, in that respect, is generous.   I can see Sally in the winter of 1852 all the clearer because she stands out against that black shadow, and when she laughs and smiles, a trifle maliciously, at me I am overwhelmed by the sense of loss even though she was never mine or even likely to be.   Lost opportunities, lost chances, lost love — again I am compelled to advise you from my own life not to throw away what life offers you because you are constrained by the manners and mores of your time.   Oh Sally Baxter, how I did love thee, and how I did fail thee because I was unsure and afraid and backward and responsible and once again frail and unworthy.

I suspected I should slip into that kind of nonsense but I could not run up the red flag in time.   I shall try, now that my throat is clear, to be sensible and informative and then perhaps you will forgive that display of sentimentality which was unintentional and tells you nothing at all about Sally Baxter.

Miss Sally Baxter was an American girl — self-evident but it cannot be stressed too much. She was an American girl and therefore quite unlike our own girls. Don't laugh and say all girls have two eyes and legs and — well, that they can't be any different from our girls because I assure you they are a different breed. An American girl has a freedom and licence that our own girls have not and this fosters in them a spirit of independence which emerges as boldness in no time at all. An American girl is allowed to speak her mind without restraint and to interrupt her elders and to refuse to agree with those who know better, and if you think that makes her sound perfectly awful and a little hussy I can only tell you that you are wrong. It doesn't do that at all — on the contrary, this permitted waywardness makes her all the more interesting. She does not grow up in a mould which has set millions before her into a lifeless, rigid pattern but emerges as a distinct person who had better be respected. As in all things American, no time need be wasted for whereas in our country her counterpart has often to be coaxed into speaking, the American girl needs no persuasion and springs fully armed into conversation. It took my breath away — I looked to right and left, to Papa and Mama, expecting them to remonstrate with this exhibition of girlish passion, but when I saw their smiling faces I got over my alarm and settled down to enjoy myself. I talked to Sally about everything under the sun and grew quite used to having my learned opinion scorned and derided and damned in a way it had never been before — you know it had not — Isabella never challenged me and Jane, why Jane, Jane was too intellectual and grave to do anything so daring or risky. I am not going to compare these ladies with each other — it would be a degrading as well as a useless exercise — but if I say that Sally was unique I hope you will understand me and not think that I speak to the detriment of anyone else. How, when all is said and done, could that be ?

I hope you are not starting to have your doubts about me, or beginning to nudge your neighbour and whisper that I seem to have forgotten I am one-and-forty. No, I had not forgotten, and because I had not I did something which I trust you will think as clever as I did. I nailed my colours to the mast straight away and invited everyone to stare, that is what I did. I told all the Baxters how I adored Sally — I said it in front of her and in front of them and I made it quite plain that she was the Brown House's chief attraction in my eyes. Aloud, I expressed the opinion that Sally was the loveliest girl I had ever seen and that my old heart was not safe, and I stressed the old. Mr. Baxter smiled and did not look at all anxious and Mrs. Baxter smiled and looked very fond and the little ones smiled and shouted hurrah for their sister. Don't you think I was clever to come out into the open and thereby make sure that everyone knew it could not be serious ? Don't you see how, if anyone ventured the opinion in private that Mr. Thackeray seemed mighty taken with young Sally, it scotched any suspicions when the family

were able to say, " Why of course he is – he's told us himself he's head over heels in love with her and we had better watch out." Quite Machiavellian on my part, don't you think ? I know I was proud of my strategy and congratulated myself on my forethought and suppressed that little voice inside that piped up, " Aha – you might fool everyone else but you can't fool me." No more I could, for any length of time. I was in love with Sally Baxter, in a kind of way, and it threw me into something of a panic and that is why I behaved as I did, to warn myself as much as anyone else. Would it be ungentlemanly to say that I think I loved the sight and sound of her more than the girl herself ? I hope not. I had never been attracted to high-spirited young girls that I know of, but Sally's extreme youth and her vivacity were definite factors in the feelings I had for her. I liked to look at her, particularly at one of those amazing American balls where she dressed, as they all dressed, in the most elaborate and colourful fashion, which would have been thought quite brazen and shocking and vulgar on this side of the Atlantic but seemed suitably happy and gay and right over there. Her dress, her hair, the way she laughed and whirled about – it captivated me. Later, when I was in Boston and wrote to her, I had difficulty deciding who I was writing to – it was borne upon me that I might admire Sally, I might be able to see her very clearly in my mind's eye, but what after all did I know about her ? We had talked and talked but almost always in public and never about anything that would reveal our souls – nothing so dreary. It was all opinions and views and it left me confused and uncertain as to the depth of my passion for Sally Baxter. I said out loud that when Tompkins came along and claimed her hand I should drop gracefully out of sight but all the while I was wondering whether I was·Tompkins after all. Men of forty had married girls of eighteen before and been happy – why not yours truly ?

It was in this state of mind that I took myself off back to Boston to lecture there. It may seem a waste of energy to have gone from Boston to New York and then back again, but in America everything must start in New York and receive the seal of approval there before it can be carried elsewhere. Once my lectures had got underway and were successful in New York then offers came in from other places and could be considered. I was happy enough in any case to return to Boston and see it all the better for having seen New York. It was a healthy place to be that Christmas time – snow a-plenty and clean air and a general countrified atmosphere which was pleasant. There were times, in Boston, when I thought myself back in England so very familiar did parts of the landscape appear. Friends were forever teasing me at my amazement over the civilised nature of their city, and it is true that whereas commonsense ought to have told me Boston could not exactly be an encampment after some 350 years of settlement I had nevertheless not expected to find it quite so mature. There was nothing strikingly new or brutal or makeshift about it and I suppose I was prepared for all three. Nor had I anticipated vegetation quite so English, though I knew of course that it was not called New England simply because the settlers there had come from our country. In short, Boston was not foreign, not in the least, and I was almost pained to find it was not.

I spent that Christmas of 1852 feeling somewhat homesick in spite of the kindness shown to me by one and all. Outside, the snow made everything pretty and as I travelled everywhere by sleigh or sledge and watched the little lads careering down the slopes on anything that would slide, I could not help wishing Anny and Minny were with me to enjoy it all. Next Christmas, I vowed, we would all be together and have tremendous fun – and I am glad to say that we were and we did. I thought about Sally Baxter too, and wrote to her, but tore up most of what I wrote – don't I always seem to do that when I write to ladies I care for ? – because I could not strike the right note. My words were always a little too warm, a little over-sentimental and I was afraid of appearing foolish. When I finally did send a note, it was mainly about what I had not written and therefore faintly ridiculous. I don't remember receiving any replies, not satisfactory ones at any rate, though I

have never in my life received any letters from ladies I have loved that have
been even half as free as the ones I for my part have written.   My ladies
have written only the most stilted notes which have on many occasions

rendered me savage and capable of flinging them into the fire in a misan-
thropic rage – except, puny as they are, they are always something and better
than nothing and accordingly cherished in a way they do not deserve.   I do
not think I have in my possession one single real love letter and yet I have
thrown my heart away at least three times and written scores myself.   Do
you suppose my own long passionate screeds inhibit my ladies ?   Or is it
more mundanely that none of them have a talent for writing ?   I dunno, but
I wish someone would tell me and put me out of the misery it plunges me
into to think the reason is perhaps that my feelings have never been reciprocated.   What a miserable old age I am going to have without any little
bundles of sweet smelling letters to untie and pore over – don't you feel
sorry for me ?   I do.

That time, however, it was not too agonising – not getting love letters
from Miss Sally Baxter I mean.   I was in fact quite delighted to find I was
suffering from that malady again when I had thought myself incapable of so
much as a blink if Venus herself should arise from the waves and beckon me.
I was quite content to toy with the idea of being in love, knowing full well
that this bore no resemblance to the grand passion that had wrecked me
before.   I think I was more concerned at the poor attendance my lectures
earned in Boston than not hearing from Sally – my livelihood, you see,
touched me more nearly.   It was partly due to the weather – the snow
discouraged people from coming out, or at least discouraged the sort of

people who would have come out, meaning the ladies and old fogies. The people of Boston I found pleasant and well read but on the whole graver and more decorous than other Americans and not so easy to catch. They had their own society which they were quite proud of and they were not at all sure that they wanted any part of anyone else's, even a poor lecturer's who had written a few books. It was obvious to me, at the turn of the year, that if I wanted to make money at the same exciting rate as I had done in New York then I must set off on more extensive travels and not confine myself out of laziness or shyness or both to obvious places like Boston. And I was glad to come to this conclusion, for I felt I was in danger of missing what else America had to offer and settling for a very small slice of a very large cake which was a dreadful waste. Far better to tour a little and see different things and open my eyes to what I knew was the vastness of the country. In Boston and even New York there is no awareness of the size of America at all — that eastern seaboard where the boats land is a trap to lull the traveller into a false sense of what the place is about and it is only when he goes west or south that the feeling nothing is different from home leaves him. The people of Boston who stayed by their firesides did me a greater service than they knew.

I packed my bags with a good heart and no resentment at all at the beginning of January 1853 and boarded a train for Philadelphia. Can I say a word in praise of trains before that one starts ? Without trains I could never have attempted America — the distances between towns are so huge that it would have taken me months to do a quarter of what I did in weeks if I had been limited to a carriage. My gratitude for this mode of travel is enormous and my debt incalculable and apart from all that why I like trains — I like sitting in some comfort, able to take a step or two up and down if I want, going at such a rate across the countryside and all without tiring man or beast. Trains inspire the most philosophical thoughts as they chug along so smoothly and rhythmically, and they are not beaten by the elements — though I was snowed up once or twice. I like the privacy of a railway carriage and yet the company of others with whom you do not need to consort if you do not wish, unlike on board ship or coach. I like being able to read and eat in some degree of comfort and I like the excitement of the whistle blowing and the steam billowing past the window and I like knowing the track is set ahead with no possibility of ruts and puddles and other perils of the road and I like being able to take as much luggage as I wish and most of all I like the sense of ease that you never get with any other form of travel — nothing strains on a train, if you will forgive the rhyme, except a machine and I am all for that. Do you wonder, with this enthusiasm, that some of my most unfortunate financial speculations were to do with trains ? But I don't want to go into that — on to Philadelphia and stand clear of the doors please.

Chapter XV

THOUGHTS UPON A FLIRTATION

REMEMBER thinking as I travelled south at last that the train was carrying me an awful long way from home, and being aware that once I left the north I should be out of touch with the boats which brought news from England. It may seem ridiculous to care about another few hundred miles when I was already many thousands away from Europe, but I felt acutely that I was breaking the only link I had and wished it wasn't necessary. Letters from my mother and the girls arrived pretty regularly while I was in New York or Boston, but once I left those places they obviously had to chase about after me and sometimes missed me and then what a fine state I got myself into imagining all kinds of disasters or convincing myself that I was neglected and that nobody cared. You can't over-estimate the value of letters from home when you are in a foreign country – the very sight of the postmark is enough to give the homesick traveller palpitations, and then how dog-eared the sheets become as they are read over and over again and how they conjure up visions of the desk they were written at and the box they were posted in until an unbearable ache sets up at the familiarity of it all. You at home can't get anything like that from the traveller's letters – oh yes, they are exciting and tell you things you did not know, but your imagination, be it ever so powerful, cannot have you sitting down with the writer in those strange places, and those letters can never be evocative, not unless you happen to have been there yourself. Letters from home call you back loudly and clearly and at times I had to put my hands over my ears to shut out the noise.

I was fortunate in my correspondents or perhaps I should not have been so smitten. My mother can cover endless pages with her doings that exactly catch the flavour of her life and leave me in no doubt that everything is going on as before, and at that distance the knowledge re-assured and charmed me

whereas in the midst of it I was irritated to death. Little Minny wrote sweet notes that went straight to my heart, but it was that genius Anny who kept alive the bond between us all. Her letters were nothing short of small miracles and I could not keep them to myself. What an old bore I must have been, producing the closely written pages at every turn and shouting to anyone who was with me, " Now listen to this," and reading out what I expect was quite an ordinary observation. Were people embarrassed by me ? No, I don't think so – I know I am never embarrassed when parents boast about their children's prowess if it is all done out of genuine admiration and affection. Anny wrote to me when I was out in America with such verve and wit that she brought tears to my eyes and I did not care who saw them. She so precisely caught her grandmother and her circle that I was moved to wondering aloud at such shrewdness in one so young, and yet there was always a fondness in her most clinical descriptions that saved them from being distasteful and made me want to hug her across the water. She and Minny liked Paris – I had had no worries on that score – and I was delighted to discover from the letters that the city was not wasted on them. Everywhere she went Anny's sharp eyes saw the kind of things I would have seen and she would turn in as sophisticated a vignette of some part of Parisian life as you could wish, but at the same time – this was her charm – she remained a child. There was one letter in particular that I laughed over and then wept a little and then laughed again, and that was one in which she gave an account of a splendid parade she had seen and confessed after it that she would really like to have been born an elegant aide-de-camp. The thought of my dear fat little girl standing in the Champs Elysées ogling those splendid soldiers and visualising herself in their uniform was both funny and touching and I think I read about it till I could have recited what she had written verbatim. I could hear her voice saying it and catch the wistfulness in her eyes and for two pins I would have jumped on a boat home that minute.

Except that once I was on a train for Philadelphia I could not. Instead, I looked out at the miles and miles of countryside through which we travelled and reflected that by the time Anny's children were grown up that land could not stay as it was. No one can appreciate the room for growth in America until they have taken a train ride as I did and seen with their own eyes the sheer extensiveness of the landscape. It goes on and on without a hint of a break to a horizon that seems limitless, and when you stop to consider that within this soil must lie untouched treasures of every kind and when you couple that realisation with the human energy you see exhibited at every turn, why then there can be no doubt that a mighty Empire is in the cradle and that one day America will be a nation more powerful than anyone here dreams. Don't scoff and say a raw country like America can never hope to match an ancient civilisation like our own – why not? All civilisations begin somewhere and I tell you with absolute conviction that one has begun over there, one that will be as great as Rome, as great as Greece, as great as the British Empire if not greater. There will be simply no stopping it, it can't fail, and I am not altogether sorry, patriot though I am, to think that when America triumphs we at home will have to eat humble pie. I know you will say in reply that I am confusing quantity with quality and that America gives no indication of attaining any intellectual or artistic heights without which no civilisation can gain the ascendancy and of course in one way you are right – America is still a cultural wilderness, a nation of upstarts with no roots where nothing has emerged to inspire the multitudes but that kind of thing must evolve slowly and given the right climate, and a hundred years or so, it will. That is why I was extremely careful wherever I went not to damn their pathetic treasures before their eyes – it would have been cruel and pointless to brand their pictures as brash and their statues as crude – they know it in their heart of hearts and when something better comes along they will say so themselves. This lack of refinement

might grate on English nerves but I hold that it is better to avert our eyes
than give offence and insult our hosts with the news that in Europe we do
things much better – of course we do – we have been doing it for nearly
2,000 years so it is hardly surprising.   Sometimes my guides would take me
to see some particularly hideous national treasure and it would be all I could
do not to shout " Burn it! " – they were like eager young puppies longing
for praise and yet knowing it was not deserved.   It would have been un-
forgivable to lash them with my tongue – better, I thought, to damn with
faint praise where comment could not be avoided.   Does that mean I am a
confounded hypocrite ?   Very well then – I am a hypocrite and quite happy
about it.

Philadelphia was a different city again.   It has a pleasant Quaker-like
cleanliness and stateliness, giving it a physiognomy of its own and I was glad
to have visited it, though the weight of my official welcome just about did
for me.   We sat down the minute I arrived to a perfectly dreadful dinner –
about sixty of us – speeches – interminable introductions – votes of thanks –
everyone very solemn and wordy – oh dear me.   I expect I looked glum and

insulted my revered hosts but I could not help it – no one could – no one could sit through that kind of thing without going into a trance. I knew that individually they would all be pleasant, enthusiastic people but the occasion masked their natural exuberance, more's the pity. It was a compliment to be so entertained in that grand hall by the city dignitaries but one I could have done without. I enjoyed much more the private party we had at Prossers, a nightclub in the town, where I was taken afterwards by some of those kindred spirits who, thank heaven, always seem to be about to rescue me. We sang all the ballads we knew and I expect I disgraced myself with my rendering of " Little Billee " and we drank a good deal and do you know in those circumstances I did not mind in the least being asked ten million times how I liked America – why my dear sir I love it and this is what I love best about it and you ought to know that by now.

· There was another thing I quickly learned to love about Philadelphia and that was the young Quakeresses everywhere – my goodness how beautiful they were in their grey or black dresses and those brilliant starched white collars and caps. The first time I saw them in the front row of my dull old lectures I almost dried up with astonishment. Have you ever dressed up the prettiest girls you know in those garments ? Do so, and you will share my admiration. Far from killing any beauty, the white and black perfectly frame it and add an element of purity – intentional – that has quite the opposite effect. No sumptuous ball-gown or elegant evening-dress can do for a beautiful woman what the Quaker clothes can do and yet in dressing like that they thought they struck a blow against the sins of the flesh – not so, not so. They flitted everywhere round that city where Liberty had begun constantly inflaming the populace with the desire to touch and own one of them, or so it seemed to me. I could hardly concentrate on the same dreary old words with such visions of loveliness before me, and whenever I looked up and saw a pair of steady eyes staring at me so gravely from that angelic setting I was done for. There was a little of Jane Brookfield in them all, the same spirit, the same calm, the same modesty, and those Quakeresses played havoc with my emotions. I thanked God that pipe was smoked out – and it was fortunate that it was for it would have been awfully easy to be tempted. You will hardly credit this but I was actually followed from place to place by certain young ladies who declared themselves so smitten by my charms that they positively could not let me out of their sight. One day I was walking down Beacon St. in Boston when I met one of these infatuated young persons and I heard later her father had come to take her home in a great rage. Dear sir, it was not my fault and I quite agree with you and I swear I did no more than politely raise my hat.

I earned a lot of money in Philadelphia – high fees – good audiences – quite enough to justify the journey. I daresay I could have earned even more if I had been prepared to go cap in hand to each of the editors of the

twelve newspapers in the city and present my compliments and flatter them
a little as I was repeatedly told a Mr. Buckingham had previously done.
Who the devil was Mr. Buckingham ? I don't know I'm sure – some
fellow who had done a lecture tour there before and had made it his business
to butter up the newspaper proprietors beforehand. I would have none of
that – my desire to make money had not gone so far that I was prepared to
grovel before such people, nor should they have wanted me to if they valued
a free press. They could come and say what they liked – I didn't care. The
manager of the lecture hall wrung his hands at my stubbornness and pleaded
with me to think again but I cried fiddlesticks and stayed in my hotel room
to no discernible disadvantage. I felt no guilt about how I was making my
money so long as I gave good measure and did not try to hoodwink people
or ingratiate myself with them. And I did you know – give good measure
I mean, even though I was very quickly bored to death with my lectures.
It was a strange thing that though I felt myself grow stale and weary at the
thought of speaking the same words yet again, I knew all the same that I

was getting better and better at delivering them, exactly like an actor does
at each performance. I made no concessions to the difference in audiences –
though I might be a million miles away from Willis's Rooms in St. James's
and from the elegant cultured throng that had gathered there, I gave
precisely the same lecture even if it did often strike me that there was
something a leeetle bizarre in talking to a crowd of nineteenth-century

country Americans in some remote village about the humorists of eighteenth-century England. Did they have the background to understand my lectures ? And if they did not – if half of them were there because they had read my books and the other half because there was nothing better to do at home – then was the material interesting enough in itself ? These were the questions that troubled me but I never had any answers, and if I supposed on occasions that I might as well have been speaking in Algebra for all my audience took in I never had that suspicion confirmed. The dear souls paid and came and sat intent and applauded and how could I ask for any more ?

I stayed two weeks in Philadelphia before dashing back briefly to New York to give a special lecture and to pick up my letters. I found it a workmanlike city, well ordered, clean, with a population of the better trading classes – but that nomenclature doesn't fit Americans – what I meant was that Philadelphia did not have any high society or academic circle but plenty of good citizens who worked for their living and were proud of it. I don't know that I should like to have lived there in spite of my admiration for the way the city's business was conducted. They have their Liberty Bell and Independence Hall – very fine – and their place in history but there is something missing that I can't put my finger on. Was it just home-sickness again colouring my outlook ? There is no doubt that by the end of January, the end of Philadelphia and three months in America, my enthusiasm was waning slightly. What should I do ? Take what I had and invest it at 8% then dash for home ? Or stay while the going was good ? I decided on the latter course – America is an awfully long way and who knew if I would ever make it again and popularity of the sort I was enjoying is an awfully delicate thing that might disappear when the next fellow came along – better to brace myself and soldier on. The problem was, which way should I go ? North and over the border to Montreal where it was rumoured there was a fine killing to be made ? Bring out the fur coats, Eyre, and go buy me some boots for we are off to the snowy waste. Or south to the steamy rivers and marshy lands of the Mississippi ? Put those dratted furs away, Eyre, and have some fine lawn shirts made up and order a straw hat or two. Or both ? Demn it, Eyre, don't pack nuttin' at all for I don't know whether I'm a-coming or a-going.

No more I did. I was in a kind of limbo, willing to go wherever fate blew me. Little things decided me – the right invitation at the right time and I was off, committed to a course of action that I didn't feel I had chosen at all, and only afterwards wondering whether it was the best decision. I rarely knew how long I was going to stay in a place or where I would put up – I just arrived and hoped everything would turn out for the best. Poor Eyre bore the brunt of my waywardness – he found the hotels and arranged the introductions and all without a word of complaint. Sometimes I was driven to asking myself if this impetuous man I had become was the same one who normally inhabited 13, Young St., where every day had its familiar pattern and things were done by the clock.   What decided me on the south, for example, on Baltimore and Washington rather than the north ?   I don't know — perhaps Eyre might — but at any rate going south was a whim even though I had an invitation.   America after all, I consoled myself, was the place to throw overboard tidy habits and indulge that tendency to erratic behaviour that I had always tried to restrain.

Once I had decided on Washington and afterwards the deep south — perhaps New Orleans — I was glad.   My bones were too old for the cold and American winters are much colder than ours (just how much colder I had yet to discover on another occasion).   I liked the idea of staying in the same country and yet basking in warm sunshine when only a day or two before the hail had battered against my face most cruelly — what luck to be presented with the chance to do it.   Then again, the more I travelled south the more likely I was to discover a foreign country instead of one which bore such a strong resemblance to our own.   Only one thing troubled me and that was a slight hesitation about the slave question.   In the north, slaves are not so apparent but in the south I knew that I should come up against that vexed problem and no escape.   Now, I had been warned by certain experienced friends in England that should I wish to be welcomed by all in America and should I wish my lectures to prosper, which of course I wished very much, than I must be most careful not to take sides in the matter of slaves.   They said I could not afford to venture even the most mild opinion and told me in no uncertain terms that all manner of things would be interpreted as significant — everything from singling out a slave to talk to, or going to a meeting about them, or indeed anything, however slight, that made me appear prejudiced.   I would instantly incur the wrath of the other side and the support of whichever side I chose to support would not make up for it. I had taken this advice and these instructions to heart, and in truth it was not so difficult as you might suppose.   You may remonstrate at my lack of sensitivity and wonder at the weakness of my moral fibre, but I felt it was none of my business.   I had not come to America to fulminate against any of their ways or customs or habits — I had come to lecture on the English Humorist and nothing else.   Nor, I am afraid, did I feel any great indig- nation about the slave question as a human being.   Is that a dreadful admission ?   You ladies who reduce yourself to tears at the mere thought of a little black piccaninny separated from its mother will think so, but I looked at it in a simpler and less emotional way.   There was nothing I could do about it and it was not my concern.   There were things in my own country that I ought to be much more concerned about and it would do nobody any harm if I confined myself to those.

I don't sound comfortable about it, do I ?   Well, I wasn't, but I tried hard to believe what I said I believed out of self-interest.   What I dreaded

above all else was my neutrality being put to the test. Supposing I saw a
white overseer flogging a black slave till the blood ran – what would I do
about it ?   Avert my face and repeat it was none of my business and hurry
on feeling slightly sick ?   Or suppose I saw a black slave-woman being
dragged screaming from her children and knew she would never see them
again – would I really say none of my business and let it happen ?   It made
me shake just to think about it and mostly I managed not to think about it
and to take care not to go anywhere near where I might be forced to think

about it.   The nearest I came to the kind of test I dreaded was on a journey
from Philadelphia to Baltimore when a Negro Eyre was busy sketching was
turned out of our compartment, or car as they term it there.   The conductor
spoke very roughly – " Get out into the first car, sir – sitting here among
white people indeed! " – and the poor man slunk out looking so abject my
heart went out to him.   What had he done ?   He was perfectly clean and
respectable and well behaved.   I know I shifted uneasily in my seat and
grew red with embarrassment but I'm afraid I did not make any stand.
Cowardice or commonsense, given my circumstances ?   You shall decide –
I know what I thought.   But as I went south, I was apprehensive about
how well this deliberate policy would or could continue to work.   I looked
out of the train windows at every station and saw the black faces begin
to multiply and saw that the situation here was quite different and I
feared for my opinions, but then I could not help noticing that though there
were black faces in hundreds, they were smiling black faces, happy black
faces, and black voices coming out of them roaring and laughing with every
appearance of being more than content.   I sat a little more upright in my

seat and did not cower so much in the corner and began thinking that perhaps I need not worry after all, perhaps I would not be called upon to perform amazing acts of heroism and end up a martyr to the cause of the slaves rather than live ashamed of my indifference. I promised myself that I would continue to look no further than was strictly necessary, and to listen to no more than was forced upon me, and to keep my conclusions for the most part to myself. Now who do you think made all this most difficult for me to do ? Who threatened to wreck my whole enterprise by his outspokenness ? Who practically had me run out of town because of his prejudiced actions ? Why, young Eyre Crowe, my secretary, my travelling companion – yes, that model of virtue, that shy, charming fellow, that polite,

quiet young man who I had thought incapable of saying boo to a goose or ever wanting to do anything so futile and silly. I confess I was never more astonished in my life than I was at the stand Eyre took.

I don't know that I had any inkling before I decided to take Eyre to America of his views on the slave question – I can't even remember him expressing any before we were confronted with it, and yet he must have said something for it was after all 1852 when we made our trip and that was the year of Mrs. Harriet Beecher Stowe's *Uncle Tom's Cabin* over which half the world was bawling its eyes out and taking sides and he could not have kept silent even if he had never read it. I recall Eyre buying the book early on our American trip and reading it in some railway carriage and being much affected and urging me to read it too. He told me I ought to – oh yes, he could be quite outspoken – and that it was my duty and I had to be quite sharp in my refusal before he would accept it as final. He brooded on that refusal with an awful intensity and clearly could not reconcile it with what else he knew about me, but I was adamant. Why should I want to read that upsetting book ? I knew perfectly well – everyone did – it was a *cause célèbre* – that it contained harrowing descriptions of torture and cruelty all of which purported to be true, and it seemed to me that such painful themes were scarcely within the legitimate purview of story-telling. Let Mrs. Beecher Stowe if she so wishes conduct an inquiry into the real state of slaves in America and let her publish her findings and let those who are interested read them, but let her not seek to conceal politics under the guise of fiction for I for one won't have it. I may say that when I later met this lady the sternness of my judgement upon her was greatly mitigated by her sweetness and charm and that I was forced to consider her book – which I still had not read – in a different light, but at that time I was violently against her.

I would have thought that my views on this subject were well enough aired during that altercation and that there would be no need to impress upon Eyre the importance of behaving as I wished him to behave since he was my secretary, and therefore I did not even think of forbidding him to do this or that – I trusted to his sense of obligation and besides that it would have been unthinkable to treat him like a child and forbid him to go hither or thither. However, in spite of my confidence in him, he went to hear the Rev. Theodore Parker, the anti-slavery champion, and his presence was duly noted and I expect made much of by those who make it their business to make capital out of such things. I was annoyed, but said nothing – I had already said it all – but when Eyre then took his sketch-book down to a slave auction room in Wall St. on our visit to New York and there attracted considerable attention to himself and therefore to me I was very angry indeed. He had thought he could slip in quietly and sit in a corner minding his own business and sketching whatever interested him, but in this he showed himself absurdly naïve. How could he not be the centre of attraction himself when he was the only young white man there ? Or when he did something so outlandish as draw in such circumstances ? Naturally, the traders suspected he was there for motives they had no sympathy with and an ugly little scene ensued during which Eyre was forcibly ejected. He attempted to stand his ground, and when he was obliged to give in and leave or be assaulted he spoke up and said – and here I own to a grudging admiration – he said that they might turn him out but they could not stop him remembering and recording what he had seen. He returned to our hotel in a dreadful state and straight away began to describe the degrading scenes he had witnessed, with slaves, especially women, being treated worse than cattle, but I stopped him and calmed him down and told him that not only would I not listen, I would not have him do any such foolhardy thing again. He was jeopardising my whole career in America by his involvement in the slave dilemma and I would not have it, no matter how hard he thought I was. In fairness to Eyre, I must say that he took me at my word and thereafter gave me no cause for alarm, though I suspect he despised me ever after for being weak and unkind. For my part, I thought he failed to see that the question was a much larger one than he permitted – it was all very well to be full of righteous indignation about Blacky being my man and brother and so forth – which I am afraid, Christian though I am, that I do not for one minute accept – but there are all kinds of considerations apart from the moral that complicate the issue. Those who signed the Anti-Slavery Manifesto here cannot contemplate the economic consequences of freeing three million slaves, nor will they stop to understand the slave-owner's viewpoint – the care and expense of slaves I believe to be prodigious and they cannot be cast off as we cast off our servants. In fact, the sum of unhappiness among our poor is every bit as great if not greater than among the slaves and it is no good hiding behind the virtuous pronouncement that at least they are free for what meaning has freedom in those conditions?

You see what heading south gave rise to? It was only when we were once there that I relaxed and realised I was not going to be called upon to take sides, and neither was Eyre, however much he might long to. We went first to Washington, which turned out to be like a German Spa in atmosphere and a conglomeration of styles architecturally. It was a very sociable place but somehow decidedly quaint, with echoes of Paris and London and even Rome about it. The lay-out of the town is French in concept — the streets are more like *boulevards* — but then you come across the Capitol that reminds you of Rome and churches that remind you of England and everywhere gardens and trees that reminded me forcibly of London. Though it is the capital of America, Washington lacks the dynamism of New York and is sufficiently rural in parts to make me think it would not be a bad place to live. The people there were charming and appreciative and very eager that I should like and respect their town. There is a square in Washington opposite the White House — which looks more like a country mansion than anything — where the inhabitants erected a statue of General Jackson by Clark Mills which is quite the most awful thing you ever saw and what a test for Titmarsh's famous tact! If I was taken past it once and asked what I thought of it in that frighteningly frank American way — frightening, you know, because they don't really want you to be frank — I was taken a score of times — every journey in the place seemed to lead past it — and I had a devil of a job not to point out that since the said statue was of an impossible man sitting at an impossible angle on an impossible horse there was only one verdict I could give: impossible. I developed a trick every time I saw it looming ahead and knew there was no escape, of beginning to converse very rapidly with whoever was on my left to avoid looking to my right and seeing that monster — either that or I suddenly went temporarily blind — grit in the eye — that kind of thing.

It was in Washington that I sat down with two Presidents of the United States in that homely White House and shared dinner with them. Wasn't that something to write home to my mother about? Except that no one over here is impressed by the American President in the way in which Americans are impressed by our Queen. Quite right, say you, turkey-red with indignation that there should ever be any comparison, but why not? Is our Queen greater simply because the crown is an older institution? I confess the veneration Americans have for royalty troubles me. Do you suppose it will fade as their own office matures? I hope so — I hope in a hundred years they have ceased to ooh and aah at a little lady in a glittering crown — though I haven't seen much glitter lately — and begin to take more pride in the democratic institution they have made their own. I know I was proud as punch to sit down with their thirteenth President and will cherish the memory as long as I live. A very nice fellow he was too, though not a literary man, but then who among our rulers are literary men? We are lucky if they have read a dozen books between them and if one turns out to be a novel why cry hurrah!

It was after we left Washington that I felt my travels were only just beginning even if saying that contradicts all I have said up to now. The area round Washington had seemed foreign compared to Boston and New York and Philadelphia, but once we left that behind I saw I had been mistaken — there was nothing substantially foreign about Washington when you travelled on and saw what the country south of it was like. Now at last, though it was February, the weather was lovely – springlike and warm with blossoms and flowers everywhere and, biggest treat of all, fresh bananas to eat. There was a lushness about the countryside that was almost over-powering and unlike anything we have here – mile after mile of greenery and colourful foliage and heavy scents in the air of we knew not what. The buildings grew sparser and more primitive and the towns smaller and more scattered – we thought Richmond a village till we went to Charleston and then Charleston turned out to be a metropolis compared to Savannah. I thought Virginia quite beautiful – like all the most beautiful parts of England put together and something else added besides – whereas Georgia was too flat and primitive both in vegetation and settlements to rouse my admiration. It was amazing how quickly the heavy wooded hillsides of Virginia gave way to the mud banks and red-coloured rivers of Georgia until you could have sworn you must have crossed an ocean or two to get there, but no, it was all part of the same country. I felt like a missionary as I sat on one of those white steamers chugging up the red river between great swampy stretches of grey flats and could not imagine that there could be anyone waiting anywhere along it who would have even a passing interest in the English Humorists of the Eighteenth Century. How absurd I felt, in my stiff gentleman's clothing, an unknown writer from a tiny country a long way away presuming to venture into this kind of territory to lecture! But you know it was staggering how, even when there were sand tracks instead of pavements, a score or more people would come out of nowhere and gather in some simple wooden shack and hear me speak with every appearance of understanding and enjoyment. Don't you think that tells us something about human nature ?

It really was a-travelling wandering about the south – and often quite perilous. Once, between Fredericksburg and Richmond on a steep gradient two stalwart Negroes had to arrest the train's movement downwards by periodical thrusts of wooden logs because it had no brakes. If it gives you a turn just thinking about it, imagine my terror actually sitting there experi-encing it – oh la! We stayed in the most incredible places, quite pleased with ourselves at our own daring. Some of the hotels were so flea-ridden – and I am an expert in that field – that we wondered if we would get out without being eaten alive, and when we took a stroll round about we could hardly credit that such places existed so poor and ramshackle did everything appear. We felt awkward and embarrassed because we stood out as different and even though the local people spoke the same language as us, give or take a vowel or two, it might as well have been double dutch for all the communication we had. All around us in these up-river places negroes moved slowly about their tasks and I could not help staring at their strange faces, the features in every case so different from our own, and wondering if it was wicked of me

to deduce that their very thick and squashed appearance signified a lack of intelligence that was innate. Simply looking at them perplexed me and filled me with feelings I did not want to have – I preferred to look instead at the young boys, who were like boys anywhere except they had an extra vitality and spring that was lacking in their elders. It amused me to talk and joke with them and I must say they were bright and friendly in return. Eyre, of course, would keep trying to spoil my pleasure at this innocent pastime by pointing past the boys to the sad creatures with their pathetic bundles waiting to be auctioned, but I preferred to dwell on the happy side, and concentrate instead on the children playing or the jolly smile of the Negro peanut-seller who, when I asked her after her health, said, " Thank-you, I'm mending smart." It is too easy to only see the misery and that goes for everything in life.

I did not give so many lectures in this part of the country as I had done in the cities, but then you would not expect me to have done. There was plenty of time between whiles to loll about and sit in the sun and yawn and sleep and eat and drink and smoke – the pace of life there was so slow that I doubt if anyone even noticed that I was idle. At first, it was agreeable, but then it grew tedious – there was no stimulation of any kind, no society, no theatres or clubs, nothing much to do or look at and over the whole area a cloud of laziness that infected my very bones. Perhaps there were people working hard, but I didn't see or hear them and felt myself to be part of a place where time had stopped. It was then that my thoughts turned more than ever to home and loved ones, though New Orleans, where I was told I would get good attendances from culture-starved folk, beckoned me, but I was growing tired of the south and did not relish the thought of the discomfort a six-day voyage to that city would involve. Yet again, I did not quite know what to do. It ought to have been a time for the deepest philosophical thought not just about the direction I should take in America but the direction I should take in life, but I found instead that the atmosphere of that place produced in me a languor and sleepiness that meant I never wondered about anything except what was for dinner. I did dream, though, both by night and day, but I am almost ashamed to confess what I dreamed about in case it disappoints you, for hadn't I left all that behind and wasn't I healed and hadn't America restored my vitality ? But whatever divided us, dear old times joined us, whereof the memory can never be effaced and out of which in the midst of recurring fever and unhappiness came running streams of old love and kindness. I talk in riddles – I dreamed of Jane Brookfield. Oh, they weren't violent, passionate dreams of the kind that had tortured me for so many months, but sad, vague, not unpleasant dreams in which I looked at Jane and waved to her and felt sorrowful. She had written to me in America – one of those stilted little notes I hate and would never reproduce for you for fear you would deride them – in which she said she was expecting another child and was well and hoped that I was. My other lady friends – the Elliot sisters – had written also and told me this news and said Jane suffered still but was composed. Well, I was composed too – composed enough to send instructions that two lilies should be delivered to Jane on her birthday, one for her and one for the new baby – but all the same there was a chamber in my heart still locked with the memory of her. Sally Baxter ? Don't be absurd – more and more that little flirtation faded from my mind.

I thought that I might set off for Canada and then return home in June or thereabouts, but as I dawdled about still in the south loath to leave the sunshine I received a letter, or rather two letters, that decided me on going directly to New York in order to be near the setting out point for home should I decide after all to go at once. The letters were from my girls telling me that my stepfather was very ill after some kind of brain attack, and then that he was recovered and there was no cause for alarm. I had the whole saga in front of me – it had happened weeks ago – anguish was useless and precipitate action pointless – but even so I lived through that awful time with them as I sat on that veranda in the south and shared their distress and wished I had been there. A general feeling of unease overcame me even though the final news was good, and I tormented myself with the thought that if it had been one of my girls and not my stepfather I should have been hysterical with worry and yet unable to do a single thing. How many days to return to New York ? How many weeks waiting for a boat ? My God, it was unthinkable, it was horrible, I had no right to stay a minute longer away from them all. As it was, I had failed my mother when she most needed me and heaven knows she had not failed me when I needed her. I fell to thinking of that good woman's distress and my irritation at her absolute devotion to my stepfather was replaced by a sense of guilt that I had not valued more the love that certainly joined them. I ought to have been there to hold her hand and provide a shoulder to weep on, and when I thought that Anny must have had to do that and perhaps Minny too a new anxiety crept over me — what if they should not be strong enough and collapse themselves under the strain ?

It was the impetus I needed — we packed up and set off back to New York in an almighty scramble. What a different journey back it was — the traveller who is pulled home and is thinking of other things sees nothing at all interesting — his sole concern is with the clock and timetables — and though I was not at all sure that I would indeed go home and forget Canada I was in haste to have frequent news from home and thought only of that.

Chapter XVI

---◆---

I GO HOME AND AM CAST DOWN AGAIN

NCE back in New York and within reach of regular letters, I calmed down sufficiently to give serious consideration yet again to going to Canada. I was so near, you see, and I wouldn't have to come back again – boats went from Montreal to Liverpool, or so I believed – and really it seemed a waste not to. By this time it was April and the winter over and I thought it would be ideal to return about June and take my family off somewhere for a long holiday. All my thoughts ran along these lines while I visited old friends and rattled around the town, but then what do you think happened ? Simply this: I was sitting in the Clarendon in that lounge sort of place where they read newspapers when there leapt out at me an announcement to the effect that a Cunard liner was sailing that morning and it was as if it was written especially for me. I knew I absolutely had to be on it, ridiculous though the idea undoubtedly was. In a state bordering on insanity, I rushed off to find Eyre and told him to start packing for I intended us to leave for England that very morning.. Without waiting to hear his reply, I was off down the stairs again and running down the street in the direction of the booking office in Wall St. I expect they thought I was mad – have you two berths left on the what's-its-name, sailing today – yes sir but sir it is about to cast off – never mind – I'll take them – be on the boat in twenty minutes – and off I went. I don't know how Eyre managed it, but he had our traps ready by the time I got back to the hotel and we were on board with minutes to spare.

I wish I could go everywhere like that – no fuss, no nerves, no agonising goodbyes – simply up and off. I daresay the friends I left behind me thought it extremely odd and rude, and not the way a gentleman ought to behave, but though I regret hurting anyone's feelings I think they are foolish to take

such behaviour as a personal slight and ought in turn to know me better than
to believe I would inflict one. The truth is, I am sometimes governed by
overwhelming impulses which I must follow or suffer appallingly from
frustration. An excitement overtakes me at such times that gives me a rare
energy and decisiveness and I feel twice as large as life and full of enthusiasm.
It was as if I was commanded or hypnotised – HOME, that announcement
oaid HOME – and by jove home it was.

Naturally, there were no leave-takings in the circumstances but I did
manage a hurried note to those whom my departure would most affect. I
wrote to the Baxters of course, asking them not to hold the abruptness of my
return to England against me, and promising to return soon. Did I mean
it ? Certainly I did – my fondness for America was entirely sincere and
besides I was grateful to that country. Hadn't I come to it jaded and
miserable, and wasn't I leaving those friendly shores cheerful and well ?
My health itself was sufficient proof of the good the trip had done me – it
was quite remarkable that almost the whole time I had been in America my
'ealth was famous. I hardly suffered at all from those recurrent attacks of
hydraulic upsets that had begun to plague me in England, and felt in general
amazingly fit. How do you explain it, considering that I ate gigantic meals
all the time – helpings over there have to be seen to be believed – and drank
copiously and travelled rapidly from one climate to another ? I dunno and
I don't care – I was grateful to be well and didn't ponder too much over the
explanations, though it did occur to me that perhaps I was well because I was
happy. It is a theory that doesn't, to my mind, bear much testing but it is
attractive all the same – that the mind can rule the body I mean. I wish I
could make it rule now – I wish sheer will power could remove all the aches
and pains from which I suffer and make me a whole man again – I wish
being happy here in my lovely house with my daughters was sufficient to
cure my ailments, but alas I can't say that it is. The process of ageing has
gone too far for any magic to work and I must bear with it and not complain
and be thankful for those faculties which are unimpaired. Memory is one

of them – my memory, except in some tedious instances, improves all the time and I count it a privilege to be able to recall so easily not just places and events but emotions and states of mind.   It is as though I had access to an enormous treasure-house where I can wander at will through the most varied and stimulating rooms, each one differently coloured and filled with priceless jewels.   I go to that house more and more often to turn another key and entertain myself for another hour and it seems that the house is so large that I shall never know it all – there will always be one little room tucked away somewhere up a hidden staircase that I shall stumble on un-awares and be delighted with and enjoy for a while.   Where would we old folk be without that house ?

No one could have been more astounded than myself and the poor exhausted Eyre to find ourselves on April 20th, 1853 actually under way and bound for Europe.   I said goodbye to America as it slipped out of sight with a good heart, convinced I would return again soon when I had fashioned another set of lectures and I looked forward to that day all the more knowing as I did that I now had friends and a house of call on that side of the Atlantic too.   There was a great deal to reflect on as we settled into the ship's routine and I found pleasure in formalising my impressions of the country I had just left, aware that when I reached London I should be asked for them.   Most of them I have given to you along the way, but I may have forgotten to tell you – oh such modesty – how popular I was and how this popularity had endeared Americans to me and how very much I approved of their simple, unaffected way of demonstrating it.   In England I do believe we are incapable of lionising the way they do in America – they have a hunger for the public figure that escapes us, by which I do not mean that we cannot fête and salute and otherwise fuss over a great man – of course we can – but not in the same way that the Americans can.   Now, I was not so blinded by my own success that I for one minute forgot my true status and imagined I was a Great Man, but the Americans had.   I think they could take any Mr. Jones and turn him into a celebrity if they had a mind to, always providing he gave them just a line or two to go on.   This effusiveness, with all its manifestations, enabled me to make an interesting discovery that I brooded on a good deal on the way home – namely, that being popular to that extent is not the fun I once thought it would be.   You know very well that success and popularity were things I once craved, but in America I came to understand the implications of it all should it arrive. There is a dreadful monotony about being popular – people's reactions are all so similar and how tired you become of them and how hard it is to appear interested in what have become trite observations.   Posing as a lion is exhausting – there is no privacy and no rest and I quickly tired of it.   Wasn't that a useful thing to have found out against the day when Titmarsh should become the toast of Europe ?

That brings me, rather too neatly I fear, to the matter that was troubling me most as we sailed at a spanking rate for home, which was – what was I going to do next ? Writing is not like any other job, you know – it isn't like the law where a man goes into his chambers and picks up the next brief, it isn't like politics where he canvasses for the next election, it isn't like business where he has this to buy and that to sell, it isn't like medicine where he goes round the hospital to see who needs surgery, it isn't like the church where he is ruled by sermons and services, it isn't like anything at all. The writer has to choose something to write about and that has nothing to do with wanting to write. Wanting-to-write produces nothing at all unless Some-thing-to-write-about comes along to help. Don't tell me that since I had just travelled about America I must surely have a wealth of material for a novel – of course I did, but novels are not made like that. I had to find a story – always the bothersome part – and the characters and then all that American experience would be of use. But did I want to write a novel ? Hadn't *Esmond* just flopped due to that bad review in *The Times*, and wasn't the moment unpropitious for another Thackeray work ? Already the success of *Vanity Fair* seemed a long time ago – *Pendennis* a lukewarm reception – *Esmond* a cold one – goodness me, my reputation was almost gone and there was Dickens enhancing his at every turn. It was not so much that I was depressed by this state of affairs as worried that my powers as a storyteller had deserted me, and then where should I be ? I doubted if I had the energy to sit down and concoct a story when none occurred naturally to me. That being the case, what work was there for a weary old horse ?

This question troubled me constantly – I could see myself returning home, to sit in my study and stare at blank pages day after day and the prospect terrified me.   I could, of course, start work on another set of lecture, straight away and solve financial problems for good, but you will appreciate that this hardly appealed after such a long stint.   In any case, though earning money was still a prime consideration it no longer obsessed me – there was enough in the bank by then to look after my wife and girls if my time should come and though I had set my heart on £10,000 apiece for them they would be safe from penury without it.   I was to sign contracts in the future because I could not resist the offers made to me – I thought it wrong and selfish to resist – but from that time when I returned from America my prime motive was never money.   I wonder if I wasn't always more ambitious than I cared to own even to myself ?   I think I found it humbling to discover that I wished so badly to do something that I could not always do – namely, write first-rate books.   It was hard to knuckle down and try when I was full of such fears and gloom about my ability, but it would have been harder still to stay my hand until I had once again hit upon a good idea.   It is easy, in retrospect, to say that I should have lain fallow for a couple of years and then who knows what richness might have been stored up ?   I took the other path – the one that led to any novel – in the belief that with sufficient work I could make it succeed.   I knew, coming back from America, that if I was asked to write a novel then I would write one even if I had no compelling story to come out with and it upset me that this should be true.

There were other things that upset me too though I hope nobody guessed. There I was, loudly proclaiming with the rest of the travellers that I was deuced homesick and glad to be nearing England and all the time I asked myself homesick for what, glad to be going home to – what ?   Well, my girls, naturally, there was no doubt about that, and my mother and my little house in Kensington, though in truth I was already thinking of moving from Young St. to something a mite more elegant.   Oh, it would be delightful to have two pairs of soft young arms round my neck and two smiling faces to hold next to my own and two chatterboxes filling my head with all sorts of nonsense – it would be delightful and I would cry a little and blow my nose and laugh and think it was the best luck in the world to have two such children, and I would look at my mother and that sweet smile would captivate me as it did everyone and I should experience a pang or two at the new signs of frailty that I noticed after each absence and on with the tears again.   It all sounds very sentimental, don't it ?   And it was, and I relished such homecomings.   I liked renewing my friendships and visiting old haunts and nodding and smiling my way back into the groove, but all the same – all the same, it was not enough – I had an 'orrible suspicion that I was homesick for something that did not exist, that I was speeding towards an emptiness that would not be filled, and a kind of dread filled me at what I should find. The trouble was, I knew I was homesick for the tenderness of a woman I did not have. I had a great longing to go home to – nothing. I would have to bear the occasional sight of Jane in William's company with another infant of his siring dangling from her knee. What sort of homecoming was that ? It was enough to sink me into a deep depression all over again and I found myself muttering under my breath whenever I thought about it – which I am afraid was often – and hoping they would have the decency to go into the country and hide their faces upon my return.

All this sounds as if I did nothing but brood in a singularly unpleasant way on that homeward trip, but that was not at all the case. It was only hanging over the rail enjoying the sun and wind – we had excellent weather – that I would occasionally think about what I was going home to, or at night before I fell asleep. Most of the time I was as cheerful as the next man and as infected as him by the excitement of returning to England. Returning to our country *is* exciting, there is no denying it – you find yourself straining your eyes for the first bit of land with all your might, and watching the water for hours on end with the silliest of smiles on your face. There is such joy in being sure of everything, in knowing that you will recognise everything and know what to do and where to go, in being familiar with every mannerism and phrase of your countrymen, in recognising small changes that only mean nothing has changed, in taking things for granted and settling down comfortably as into an old armchair. I knew that the minute I landed I should be ignored, that nobody would ask me what I thought of England or drag me off to have my hand shaken a million times.

I would disappear into the obscurity from which I had temporarily emerged
and heave a hearty sigh of relief at the prospect.

There was nobody on the quay waiting for me but then I had not expected
such a welcome and reminded myself as I threaded my way through the
groups of touching re-unions that this was not my real homecoming for my
girls were in Paris and I would have to wait for the arms-about-the-neck
that I have described so eloquently. Nothing, however, could dampen my
high spirits and I rushed straight from Liverpool and burst into Lady

Stanley's ball where my appearance caused quite a sensation. Hold on –
wasn't I claiming I wanted to be ignored and now here I am deliberately
attracting attention ? It doesn't make sense, does it, but if you had gone
with me back to Young St., to that awful lonely shut-up house, you would
have understood my need for gaiety and companionship and a shout or two
of greeting. I simply could not have dropped my bags in the hall and stayed
there, and if you are at a loss to understand what I mean then you have never
turned your key on a house which has been virtually shut up for six months
and smelled that peculiar smell that signifies dust, closed windows, silence.
I exaggerate of course – the house was in a perfectly acceptable condition –
but I don't exaggerate the shivers that ran down my back at the emptiness.
There were no loved ones listening for my step, no voices shrieking a
welcome, nothing but the sound of my own footsteps on the stairs, my own
cough as the close atmosphere caught at my throat, my own heart beating in
a way I had never noticed before. So I turned tail and fled and after a

little sleuth work discovered Lady Stanley's ball where I knew all my friends would be conveniently gathered and there I went.

There was a man came into the Garrick the other day – ordinary dull sort of fellow – and the minute he said he had just returned from America there was a buzz of interest and a crowd round him in no time full of questions so that he grew quite pink with all the attention and could hardly stutter out his platitudes. I confess I was astounded to witness this scene – isn't it ten years since I first returned from America and aroused similar curiosity and wouldn't you have thought that a decade was enough for the novelty to have worn off somewhat ? I wonder if it will ever become so commonplace to go to America that we will think no more of it than going to Brighton. I cannot see any evidence that it will, but perhaps one day a man will announce he has just returned from America and we will all yawn and say oh really and go back to reading our newspapers wondering why the devil this fellow has disturbed us to give us such a boring, everyday piece of information. If that has happened by the time you read this you will hardly credit that the very finest society in London thronged to hear my views on that continent from which I had just returned. I dined out on my experiences for weeks and weeks and grew quite fat not just on the food but on my own bloated observations. I may have grown tired in America itself of being asked what I thought of the country but once home I seemed to derive enormous satisfaction and endless pleasure from that very question. Not only did I not mind being asked, I minded not being asked – was deeply offended – positively craved an audience for what became a regular little lecture on the subject. I think part of the attraction was the chance to shock – people expected me to dislike America and when I made it quite clear that not only did I not dislike it I actually preferred it in some respects they were unpleasantly astonished. If, through ignorance or prejudice, an acquaintance made some disparaging remark about America or Americans I had the greatest difficulty restraining myself from being extremely rude, which would have been absurd when all that was required was a mild rebuke. I became the champion defender of all American habits and customs until it must have been very tempting for my hearers to tell me to pack up and return there if I thought so much of the place. I suppose I did indeed go too much the other way as we often do in such situations, human nature being what it is, and that I began without realising it to hurt certain people by my insistence on American superiority. Oh, I would say at some grand ball, oh you can hardly call this a ball compared to American balls, you can hardly think those pitiful dresses splendid beside American dresses (which actually I had thought vulgar), you can hardly think these scraps of food delicious compared to American food – and so on. Aren't you surprised I didn't provoke some patriot into giving me a punch on my already broken nose ? But then I could have done some punching myself, for there is nothing more maddening than hearing someone who knows nothing, who has no experience of the subject under discussion, pronouncing upon it as though they were an expert. If I was too staunch in my support of America I was provoked into it by the unjustified attacks made on my new friends by those who thought it fashionable to sneer.

My euphoria – delight at being back, gratitude that the trip had been so successful – was short lived. For a while I left my watch defiantly at New York time and went in for rather a lot of heavy nostalgia as I watched the sun go down in the west every evening and thought of where else it was shining. Immediately I was back, America seemed perfect and I forgot all the minor irritations that had bothered me from time to time. Besides, hadn't I always been well over there, and wasn't I struck down almost as soon as I got home by the most infernal toothache? You may laugh and say pooh what is an aching tooth – never keeps me at home – but all I can say is that my aching tooth – my three aching teeth – gave me the worst pain I have ever experienced in my life. My head was aflame with it – agonising – piercing – enough to make me scream out loud but then I could hardly scream at all for my mouth was jammed with creosote. What a sight I was! I lay at home in that dreary, lifeless house moaning and groaning and wishing I was back in America and trying ever so hard to persuade myself to go to a dentist. I don't like dentists, whatever they are like. The art of dentistry, like the art of doctoring, has a long way to go as far as I am concerned and I prefer to keep away from both, but in that case it was rather obvious I could not. The pain would not go away – couldn't eat – couldn't sleep – couldn't be seen in polite company. Coward though I was, the inevitable had to be faced and off I went to Mr. Gilbert of Suffolk St. after a large tumbler of – well, a little something to screw my courage to the sticking place. I had a shrewd suspicion that at the sight of those awful steel pliers or whatever they are called I should suddenly remember a pressing engagement and charge out into the street, or that if I passed that test I would let out a bull-like roar at the merest touch of that instrument, and the dentist would be unable to do anything and I would be known throughout the dental world – good God, do you suppose there *is* a dental world? What a comic thought – known anyway as a coward. In the event, I was rather pleased with my behaviour – sat firmly in the chair like a gentleman – opened my mouth – breathed deeply and after a terrible five minutes and a good deal of blanching and wincing the job was done. Marvellous – pain gone immediately – nothing quite like it. Isn't the removal of pain one of the most wonderful sensations? And don't we wonder why we hesitated when we were assured it would be so? Perhaps if I could face the thought of the surgeon's knife as I finally faced the dentist's pliers I should find a similar relief, but then you see *that* pain, the pain in my interior, is not there all the time and when it goes away I convince myself it will never return and there is no need for the knife.

At any rate, those black throbbing monsters were out and I felt much better, though the hole left behind for my tongue to constantly probe seemed as deep as the ocean and as bottomless. Teeth are confounded nuisances – nature orders things very badly in that department in my opinion – but once they are gone they are greatly missed. All the uncomfortable treatment had held me up from that reunion in Paris with my family for which we had all waited so long so I paused only long enough to be sure that the pain was not

going to return then I took myself off to France. My mother was living at that time at 19, rue d'Angoulême, a pretty street in a pleasant, lively area, and I remember reflecting as I stood on the step and rang the bell that it was jollier than Kensington and I might do well to move there myself. Who knew? I certainly didn't – hadn't the least idea which way the wind was going to blow and waited with interest to see. I expect I grinned like an idiot as I stood on that step but I felt uneasy inside – more like a returning lover than a father with my heart beating a little quicker and a shiver of excitement going up and down my spine and a nervousness overwhelming me that was difficult to account for.

I had to ring the bell twice but I was not at all alarmed by the apparent lack of response for I knew the reason. The girls were as shy as I was even though they burst with affection and I could hear little squeals and scutterings behind the door and I smiled and knew how it was and my own hesitation vanished with the need to resolve theirs. I banged on the door and asked if no one was coming and at last it opened and then we were all over each other. Ah, what a welcome that was! My chest tightens to think about it. The hugging and kissing and tears of joy went on half the day and

I shall never forget the shock of seeing my daughters for a few seconds as a stranger would see them and being delighted with them.   That distance is valuable, you know — we tend to take so much for granted when we live with our family and we don't see them as they really are and it does us good to be able to do that from time to time.   Anny had grown so tall and was so womanly that I could hardly believe six months could have wrought such a change in my gawky girl, and Minny was so pretty I was charmed and saw how in a few years she would have every Tompkins in town running after her.   Their very flesh felt so wholesome and that was another thing that startled me — the knowledge that physical contact of that kind could bring such happiness.   I felt, as I held them in my arms, as if I were a withered old plant that had just been watered, as if some area of myself that I had neglected had flowered all of a sudden.   Lonely old men of forty-two don't have many people a-hugging them and it is the thing they want most of all. I reminded myself of that when I saw G.P. — my stepfather, looking dreadfully thin and worn but smiling happily at the sight of me and ready to be embraced with the rest of them.   My mother, of course, had already been near squashed to death and then held at arm's length to examine and then squashed again and oh dear what an exhausting process it was!   Then the

girls must fly to the piano and astonish me all over again this time with the progress they had made and then I had to listen to their French and declare I would never have known they were not natives and then there were yards and yards of needlework to be examined and admired and so it went on. Their industry had been prodigious and it was all laid at my feet as if I were an ancient deity. Where all had been loneliness and depression there was love and pleasure and my heart was full. I tell you I would sacrifice any success you care to name for a family – there is nothing like it.

We all stayed together in Paris for a time, never quite believing that each morning we would once again see each others' smiling faces, and for a while I felt young again and when I walked under the chestnut trees or looked up at the domes of the Tuileries behind I was inspired by a deep contentment. Why do anything ? Why not simply relish my family life and enjoy its pleasures and just be ? I don't know why, but after a few weeks of this kind of idyllic existence I was as restless as ever and furious with myself for showing it. Life with my mother would not do – from a twaddling society what can you have but twaddling ? There. I have said it. The society in which that good soul moves constrains me unbearably – I could not stand the way my mother was adored and I was deferred to – it was not healthy. Nor could I stomach her particular brand of religion with its daily emphasis on the Old Testament. Anny frequently clashed with her over her views in this respect and though I silently applauded I could not hurt my mother or undermine her authority by publicly challenging her. I must, I thought, get these girls away and back to London and into a different life.

As usual, this was fraught with problems of what you might call the technical variety. How impatient I was that Anny and Minny – aged sixteen and thirteen – were not yet quite old enough to dispense for good with a governess – if we moved back to London as I wished to all that would have to start again, whereas in Paris there was my mother and an excellent French governess whom they adored. I did think of tempting her back with us but then how could I when the status of a governess in our country is so very different ? She was a pretty, charming girl who moved freely in any society she chose and was treated as an equal, whereas in London she would have been relegated to a position in other people's houses little above servant and there would be nothing I could do about it. Then think of the talk if I included such a ravishing creature – good Lord, there was enough talk when my governess was some old hag without lending any credence to rumours. No, it was out of the question – best to return to London on my own for the moment and sort out my affairs and then bring my girls home. Before I left I did however make them one promise, which was that we would all go and spend winter in Rome when I returned. Can you imagine the screams of delight ? The minute the words were out I almost regretted them for the reaction of my daughters was so violent – it made me tremble to be responsible for their happiness to such an extent and a little ashamed and I wished I had waited until I was quite sure it could be arranged so that if it fell through I would not have to face their agonising disappointment.

Back in London I attempted to look facts in the face, something which I consider myself quite good at. Though I no longer needed to write for money as if the devil himself was on my tail, it was still very welcome and the more I could make while I was able the better. I considered for a while getting up some lectures on America. This was urged upon me by several friends who professed themselves fascinated by everything I had told them, but I felt I could not attempt it without the help of my secretary, young Eyre Crowe, and he, rather understandably, had moved on to other things and was not available. Then again, whatever the lectures were about, they were lectures and would have to be delivered and oh I had had enough of that for the time being. It would have to be a book, unless I totally changed direction and did something quite extreme and unexpected like entering public life. I feel a trifle embarrassed at this distance confessing to the temptations of such a career, but in all honesty I must own that I entertained this folly. Perhaps it was something to do with my age – I felt, at forty-two, a need to contribute more to the sum of human happiness than I did whiling away a few hours writing for some folk. There was a strong feeling of duty and obligation in me that wanted room to express itself and I thought that I could bring a little experience of life and some understanding of its problems into a career as member of Parliament. What made me hesitate at that juncture was the knowledge that if I stood I should want to stand as an Independent and that this would be costly and a luxury I could not afford without substantially depleting the savings I had only just amassed. Caution pulled me back and I think it was as well.

To cut a long story short, I signed in June 1853 with Bradbury and Evans for a new book in twenty-four numbers, like *Pendennis*, for the down payment of £3,600 and another £500 from the Americans, Harper and Tauchnitz. No, your eyes have not misled you – don't rub them so fiercely – it was coining money and I was almost ashamed to tell anyone what I was being paid. But then, once I had sat down at my desk and wondered how the devil I was going to invent a narrative and characters that would keep me going for twenty-four numbers and add up to something at the end – why, then I saw it was worth every penny for it would be a labour of Hercules. The torment would be so terrible that it made me see I was a masochist, wilfully imposing upon myself this dreadful punishment. Hadn't I sworn, after *Pendennis*, that I would never do it again ? And yet here I was, embarking on an even more perilous undertaking. I had no plot in my head – not much notion what the book should be about – only the sketchiest idea of who should figure in it, and I knew perfectly well that without a strong thread I would lose my way. There was no deep well of inventiveness inside me waiting to be drawn upon – quite otherwise. Yet all the same, in spite of all this, the minute I had signed and it was done, I felt excited and that excitement had nothing to do with the money. I was on my mettle and committed to writing and I gloried in the feeling. Who knew what I should produce beginning again after a year's rest and in other circumstances that were more propitious? I thought I might find, happily settled in Rome's winter sunshine with my girls, a peace and contentment that might be the very thing I needed to haul myself up again among the giants. In fact, I know now both were fatal decisions – going to Rome and signing for *The Newcomes* I mean – but unlike some of the bad decisions that I look back on with amazement and wonder how I could have made them, I find those two easy to understand and I daresay I would make them again given the opportunity. Hindsight is a wonderful thing, but sometimes we can do without it.

We did not set out for Rome until November of that year, with the first number of *The Newcomes* safely out, but before that we had taken, my

daughters and I, a two-month holiday in Europe, mostly in Switzerland. The idea was that I should begin my new book in a restful atmosphere and the girls enjoy themselves at the same time but as I ought to have known, it did not work out quite like that. I don't remember much about what we did because the whole trip was overshadowed by the dreadfulness of *The Newcomes*. From the very beginning it was not good and I found it haunted me like a great stupid ghost. I fairly gnashed my teeth – the remaining ones – with ungovernable rage at the discovery that I could not make my characters live and for two pins I would have returned the money and torn my puny efforts up if pride had let me. But it would not. I stuck to writing a certain number of words each morning in the hopes that this discipline would of itself produce something creditable, but every afternoon would find me even more dissatisfied than the day before. Poor Anny and Minny had to bear the brunt of my anger with myself – I hope I was not too sour – I hope the scenes and people we saw were sufficient compensation for my bad temper. I know one thing – they were greatly amused and I was greatly irritated by the behaviour of all the Americans we met. Oh dear me what was the use of me saying Americans were just as civilised as we were when throughout Switzerland we saw party after party of them sticking their knives down their throats at every meal ?   I discovered that Americans abroad can behave in a way most injurious to their reputation and most mortifying to me.   What good was it standing by their modesty and simplicity when, in hotel visitors' books under the title " Destination ", they would write so boastfully and vulgarly " Over the whole damned lot " ? What was the point swearing they were as intelligent and clever as the most learned Englishmen when none of them ever seemed able to speak a single word of French ?   Yes, it was a very grumpy Papa who squired his daughters about, one who refused to admit the giggles were about him as well as the American tourists.

There is one other thing I must briefly mention before I take you to Rome – ain't you looking forward to it now ? – and that is an unkind stroke of fate. I think I have mentioned to you before how I wished some day to write a history book – still do – and how I constantly turned over in my head ideas for this *magnum opus*.   Well, just before I left for Rome, and when I was already deeply committed to the blessed *Newcomes*, a publisher made me an offer to edit Horace Walpole's letters.   Oh the hagony of receiving the perfect invitation too late!   How I should have loved to execute that delightful commission!   Imagine being paid to read Walpole's letters all day! Imagine the pleasure in researching the background and compiling an inventory of the contents and getting to know somebody so intimately.   I cannot believe – I *cannot* believe – that I am going to die without savouring these delights.   Good God, when I think that I may all this time have been better suited, both temperamentally and as regards skills, to the writing of history books or biographies I could jump on all my novels and reduce them to pulp.   Why have I held back from ever finding out ?   I dunno but oh how I wish I did.   Facing up to conundrums like that – often of our own making – is to me the hardest part of growing old.

At any rate, I had to decline, with deepest expressions of regret, and get my little army ready to march on Rome.   If you think winter in Rome sounds Romantic, if you sigh with envy on this bleak winter's day, only wait awhile.

Chapter XVII

---◆---

MOVING HOUSE WITH ALL THE
ACCOMPANYING IRRITATIONS

 NEW important person came into my life just before I set off for Rome and I was to be heartily glad that he did. It must have been obvious to you all this time that a man of my general helplessness when it comes to organisation could really do with someone constantly at his elbow to guide and protect him from the brutal realities of everyday living, someone to think ahead for him and show him how, by a little gentle management, a tangle of appointments could be smoothed out and an impossible day becomes merely a mildly busy one. I had tried all kinds of solutions to my problem in the shape of one kind of servant or another, but until Mr. Charles Pearman joined my household in the autumn of 1853 none of them were satisfactory.

I ought to say a word or two about Charles, who is no longer in my employment but of whom my family and I retain the happiest of memories. He was young and energetic when he joined me – indeed his youth almost decided me against him for I could not believe that one so young would be steady enough for the job, or stay long enough to give me the sense of permanence I required. His alert manner impressed me, however, and so did his air of intelligence. Though he was not of course educated to a very high standard, he wrote a good clear hand and I saw he might be useful in another capacity apart from that of valet. There was nothing obsequious about him, but neither was he cocky and I thought we might get on very well. The relief was enormous when this proved to be the case – Charles got us all ready for Rome with the minimum of fuss and thereafter was to look after us excellently.

For some reason which I don't remember, we went most of the way across Europe to Rome by steamer – don't that seem igstrawdinory ? I

wonder whatever can have been the cause of that long, slow, cold journey?
My girls again displayed their admirable fortitude in the face of hardship and
discomfort and were forever telling me through chattering teeth that everything was l-l-l-lovely thankyou.   When we arrived in Rome towards the
end of November we set up house in an apartment over a pastry-cook's – such
folly – in the Palazzo Poniatowski in the Via Della Croce.   Don't let the
word " Palazzo " trick you into believing we were living in style – every
second building in Rome is a Palazzo however small and humble and the
word has none of the connotations we give it.   Our landlady was a little old
lady called Signora Ercole who proved very kind but did not immediately
radiate maternal warmth and caused my girls some misgivings at first.   She
lived on the premises but quite separately – it was a rambling old place heated
by a brazen charcoal burner and full of all kinds of strange pieces of furniture
so that the general effect was more of a museum than a home.   Our few
belongings were rather overwhelmed by their surroundings and I worried
that the weirdness of the place made it insufficiently homely for a family,
but Anny and Minny pronounced it delightfully foreign and would not have
had it otherwise.   The rooms we had were rather inconveniently arranged –
I have a memory of finding myself squashed into a room much smaller than
I would have liked because that was the way it worked out and a man who
travels with two children has to be prepared for some sacrifices.   Still, I make
too much of it – we were all quite comfortable, even me, and it was much
better than finding ourselves in an hotel or guest house.

Almost as soon as we arrived in Rome I realised I had not thought
particularly carefully about what our day to day regime would be, or rather
I knew what I wanted to do but not my daughters.   I wanted to work on
The Newcomes in the morning, stroll in the afternoons, and dine with
amusing friends in the evening.   It was no part of my plan to play nursemaid
or chaperone to two girls and yet I discovered very quickly that, if I did not
take them, my girls would not be able to go anywhere and if they did not go
anywhere they became bored and restless and finally boisterous and noisy.
I alternated between remorse at subjecting them to my bachelor habits and
annoyance at their lack of appreciation – I had brought them to Rome,
wasn't that sufficient?   Well, no, it was not, not if they were to be walled
up in a gloomy old apartment with nothing to do and no one to talk to.
There is, after all, a limit to the amount of piano-playing and embroidery
that can be done – young things need to be out and about and I blamed
myself for not thinking ahead and contriving to bring with me some sort of
companion who could do just that.   As it was, we struck a bargain – they
would remain quiet and busy while I worked, and would retire obediently to
bed at a reasonable hour in the evening when I entertained or went out, and
in return I would show them Rome and make sure that they met people and
had fun the rest of the day.   I don't know that I put my case so bluntly, but

my daughters understood and cooperated and a *modus vivendi* was reached.

Now Rome is an interesting city enough but it does not compare with Paris for entertainment and sheer sophistication and I think we were all a trifle disappointed. We made ourselves familiar with all the sights but did not find that St. Peter's did what it was supposed to do to our hearts or that the Colosseum thrilled us or that all the treasures of the place impressed us. You will call this disgraceful but I think we liked the food best. We had it sent in to our apartment and oh, the aroma when we opened those food chests! We liked wandering about the narrow streets, too, and watching

the various craftsmen at work in their open fronted work-shops, and we liked watching the sunset over the dome of St. Peter's which was quite the best thing about each day. I tried to bring the place alive for the girls by going over as much history as I could remember but I don't know that it did more than go in one ear and out of the other. They were far more interested in listening to conversation than history lectures and accompanied me most eagerly on my social visits to the English contingent there. By far the most fascinating to them was Elizabeth Browning, who was then in Rome with her husband Robert and their small son, whose absurd name I temporarily forget. She had left London and that frightening father of hers and eloped with her poet at the great age of forty-two and was by that time apparently cured of her consumption and blissfully happy. Anny and Minny thought

this the most romantic story they had ever heard in their lives and had read all that lady's poetry and were ready to be her slaves. She was very good to them – talked to them as if they were equals and invited them to tea and so forth, but I fancied that all the same she disapproved of me and thought I should not be involving two young girls in what she must have considered a Bohemian existence unsuited to their tender years. Something of the same attitude showed in the eyes of those other two kind ladies, Mrs. Sartoris and Mrs. Story, and it saddened me a little to think that they could imagine I would expose my darlings to anything improper. I took the greatest care to see that they met only the most suitable friends and that at home they were as sheltered and watched over as if they were in Kensington. I confess it also made me a little angry that I was not able to enjoy my family without people censuring me for it. What, should I stay tamely in London out of misguided duty to my daughters ? Should I separate us more than was necessary out of some mistaken zeal for laws of propriety that were wrong in the first place ? I do not hold with the view that girls should stay at home until they are of age – fiddlesticks. It does children no harm, boy or girl, to travel and share other experiences than the narrow one they are usually confined to – there is such a lot of stuff and nonsense spoken about what is good for them. My daughters seem to me a tribute to my beliefs about upbringing and I defy anyone to say they have been damaged.

You might think from all that that I was read a lecture on the subject from the good ladies of Rome but of course I was not – it was only that sensitivity of mine that imagined their disapproval. We made quite a jolly party of expatriates that winter and I would have been lost without my fellow-countrymen for access to the Roman circles was not easy for a man with two young daughters. I made some friends, but not exactly families, and not exactly suited to young female company. I am struggling to be unprejudiced about those months in Rome and to give you as favourable impression as I can of the city when in fact I am incapable of doing any such thing – I find it hard to remember the nice parts because in truth there were so few. The trouble was, I fell ill as soon as we were properly settled and everything thereafter was blighted by my physical condition. God knows what was the matter with me but my insides played havoc and I had a fever and altogether I was in the sorriest of states. Have you ever been ill in a foreign country ? Then may the good Lord preserve you from such an experience, for it is quite awful and to be avoided at all costs. I wish now that I had summoned up enough strength to set off for home, or at least Paris, as soon as I felt the first symptoms of unwellness and I declare that if I were ever to be as unlucky again I should have myself strapped to a stretcher and swathed in blankets and shipped back to England post haste. It is not, you know, that I set any great store by English doctors as opposed to foreign ones – far from it – they are all useless and I don't see the point in distinguishing between them, but at least the devil you know is better than the devil you don't and at least they know you and your history and don't waste time treating you for ailments you have already had and are not likely to have again. Then when you are feeling ill it is so very tiresome getting used to new doctors and their ways – quite little things can be upsetting – simply the way they handle you or the angle they like you to be at before they examine you – that kind of thing. Your own doctor doesn't expect any small talk if he sees you are ill enough but a foreign doctor is always suspicious and is always sounding you out and trying to establish if you mean by pain what he means by pain and oh I can't be bothered with it. No matter who came to see me I was bad tempered and had no faith in them and knew I would just have to sweat it out, to use a vulgar expression.

There is another part to being ill abroad that is equally unpleasant and makes you long for home and that is the feeling that nobody cares and that you could languish on your sickbed and even die and nobody would notice. Now, in my case that was patently untrue – weren't my two daughters constantly at my side and didn't messages inquiring after me arrive every day from our friends in Rome ? Well yes, they did, but it was not the same as lying in Young St. and having my house practically besieged by anxious callers. I had only to miss going to the club for a single day to have a fuss made of me and should I turn down an invitation then there was an immediate outcry and a score of kind people wanting to know why. I confess I missed all that solicitude and could have done with a few of those broths and jellies that I affect to despise when they are available. Anny and Minny did their best and were very good little nurses but then that only added to my worries – I fretted to see them confined indoors with me, growing paler and paler when I had brought them to Rome to sun themselves and make up for all the bed-watching they had done the winter before with G.P. The biggest headache of all, however, was work – there I was, only just properly launched into *The Newcomes*, which was financing the trip, and I was so struck down that the effort of lifting the pen was agony. I lay there tormenting myself with thoughts of what a fix I should be in if I got behind with my work and hardly daring to contemplate the penalty. Whenever I was able, I staggered to my desk to keep the narrative going, afraid that if I did not I should lose the weak thread I had and be unable to continue, but there were many days when not all the willpower in the world could achieve a single line and I was compelled to give myself up to moaning and groaning. Anny wrote for me then, if I could manage to dictate a line or two – she sat at a marble table near the window doing me so much good by her very composure and wrote away while the pigeons perched on the deep window-sills cooed and fussed and outside the *pifferari* droned in the street far below.

A pretty pickle, don't you think ? It made me laugh to think of all the people in London looking out of their windows on grey December days and envying old Thackeray enjoying winter in Rome. I might as well have wintered in Hades for all the good it did me. When we got some cold weather I felt a little better and did a lot of work in a rush while I was able and consequently relieved my mind of that worry, but I was still cast down and plagued by gloomy thoughts and having to pretend I was having a good time for the sake of my girls when clearly I was not.

There was a moment, that winter, when I almost bolted, presented as I was with the perfect opportunity to do so. At the end of January 1854, when I was not so ill but still not quite right, I heard from Paris that my aunt Mrs. Ritchie, the same who had taken me in when first I arrived in England, had died. This event threw me into an almighty flurry and I had a great desire to go at once to Paris to be with my cousin Charlotte to offer her what solace I could. I was all for packing up and departing immediately and I think my girls were alarmed by the passion with which I declared my intention. Well they might be, for they could not be expected to divine the reasons behind it, which were twofold. On the one hand, going to Paris for such a virtuous reason would absolve me from my commitment to winter in Italy, and on the other I felt a genuine distress for my cousin and was overwhelmed by a strange feeling to demonstrate solidarity with her. Do you know what I think now ? I think my grief and agitation were due not so much to sympathy with Charlotte as to my own identification with the death of my aunt. When we are feeling low, as I was, and have been ill, as I had been and still was to some extent, then the death of anyone in our family serves only to herald our own and the shock as we come face to face with our own mortality makes us exaggerate the blow. We grieve for the departed, but we grieve also for ourselves and the two become so intermingled that we do not rightly know who our tears are for. If I could have jumped onto a magic carpet the night I heard the news and been whisked to Paris in a trice then I would not have hesitated, but as it was the complications arising from wanting to make such a long and arduous journey at that time of the year defeated my enthusiasm. After a day of trying to make suitable arrangements I gave up and decided it would not be sensible to trek off in the middle of winter arriving far too late to dry anyone's eyes. Better to confine myself to letters and prayers and wait until the spring to pay my respects.

I wish I had not listened to dreary old commonsense – I wish that had been one of those times when I gave in to intuition and impulse and headed for home however difficult, and then I would have escaped the next instalment of bad luck and salvaged something from that doomed holiday. But I did not and instead we stayed in Italy and moved to Naples where I had

high hopes that the change of scene and air would do me good and enable me to work to better advantage. *The Newcomes* was not going well – rumour had reached me that the public felt it stood still and I knew that I would have to pick it up and shake it in an attempt to give it life. The wish to do so was there, and the effort was not lacking, but that third vital ingredient, being a measure of inspiration or inventiveness or whatever you like to call that elusive quality – that was missing. I convinced myself that Rome was unlucky for me and that vitality would return to my body and my pen only if I made a clean break and took myself to pastures new and – hopefully – a more stimulating environment. We accordingly went south to Naples and warmth and took some jolly rooms overlooking the little island of Capri – and there things were immediately worse than ever. Are you losing sympathy with all this complaining? But wait until you hear what fate had in store for me and then I swear you must have a heart of stone if

you do not groan with me. I was ill again myself within hours of arriving – same thing, fever and stomach upsets – and then both my daughters went down one after the other with Scarltina. Oh Lord, what an awful business it was – no sooner did I get myself upright than poor Anny was prostrate with a fever so raging that it made mine look nothing. How terrified I was as she seemed to get worse and worse and not to know me and suffered so dreadfully and all the time I clutched Minny, who I knew was bound to succumb next and be much worse because she was so delicate – and all this in a foreign apartment where nobody knew us and with no female servant to nurse the girls and no contact yet made with any of our fellow-countrymen. I can hardly think of one mitigating circumstance about that horrible time except I suppose that we were not poor.

I am not at all proud of how I stood up to this regime of sitting with invalids – I had no talent at all for the task and was dreadfully ashamed of my constant feelings of impatience and boredom.   I would wake up in the morning and see the sun shining on that deepest of blue seas and I positively could not stand the thought of not being out in it but doomed to sitting at the bedside making ineffectual conversation and pouring out glasses of water and mopping hot brows – oh God how I hated it.   You, madam, will say everyone hates it, everyone detests sickroom work, but I don't think you quite understand – it is not just that I find nursing tedious but I declare it robs me of my masculinity and gives me no comforting thoughts of how useful I am being.   I don't feel useful at all.   I feel a confounded nuisance, unable to do anything right and in danger of making any invalid worse by my clumsiness and general air of restlessness.   I admire those sweet-faced souls who sit hour after hour so calmly and gently soothing their patient, but I am not one of them and it is no good pretending that I did my duty with a good heart.   My heart was black and rotten, begrudging every minute of this enforced enslavement, finding no joy in it at all.

Work was out of the question – it flew out of the window straight away and I watched it go with a sinking feeling, knowing I should inevitably fall behind with my instalments and that the consequences would be too awful to think about.   All the same, I could not do nothing – any watcher over an invalid has many hours to spend when they are not doing anything but on the other hand it is impossible to embark on any project which won't bear interruption.   Ladies sit and sew, but I did not fancy my hand at embroidery or knitting, though it might have amused my poor sick girls watching me have a go, so instead out came the pencil and I took to sketching to amuse myself and them.   I sketch people better than places, and as I sketch the oddest ideas come into my head and must be expressed in words and really before I knew it I was engaged upon a children's story which was later published under the title of *The Rose and the Ring*.   It is all nonsense, but I was very grateful to that little book at the time for the diversion it presented and was pleased to find that even when the girls were out of quarantine they still took an interest in it and so did some other little friends we made.   The making and illustrating of that fable helped me to stay sane when I at least felt there was some doubt whether I would – being both mother and father proved a task too onerous for me and I frankly confess I was unequal to it.   Did I show it ?   I hope not – I hope my poor darlings did not have to lie in their beds feeling guilty as well as ill.   I know it made me happy to see how each helped the other in ways that I could not and did the most menial jobs for each other with a grace and humility that touched me deeply.   Minny in particular looked after Anny with a devotion which astonished me and I began to think I had misjudged my little minx and that she had a strength of character I had not even begun to guess at.   There I was – still am – worrying about Minny being too frail for ordinary life with all its pitfalls and yet when she is put to the test, as she was then, she rises to the occasion every bit as well as her sister.

I haven't anything interesting to tell you about Naples – didn't see much of it in the circumstances – so I will pass on rather quickly to our return from Italy in the April of 1854. We stopped off at Paris to see the grand-parents, and then it was back to Kensington and frightful hard work to catch up lost time with *The Newcomes*. In the midst of such a work panic you would have thought I would aim merely at keeping other things ticking over, but not a bit of it – hardly were we back in Young St. before I was in the middle of moving us from there to Onslow Square, and for the rest of that year we spent our time uncomfortably divided between the two residences. Some people can move overnight – there they are one morning in their old house, eating breakfast in an easy kind of way, surrounded by all their belongings neatly packed and labelled, and lo and behold that same evening they are sitting down to dinner in the new house, equally undisturbed, everything already installed in the freshly painted new rooms. Naturally, there are no minor inconveniences such as the absence of curtains perhaps – the old curtains fit perfectly or else new ones have been measured for and ordered ahead of time. The floors are covered – no bare floorboards to annoy with their dust and creaking – and there has been no difficulty whatsoever in getting beds or pianos up to the second floor because someone has made sure doorways have been adapted accordingly. I can only say such people are too good for this world and that I do not number myself among them and that my removal to 36, Onslow Square from 13, Young St. was awful to behold. How the devil had we accumulated all those possessions festooned everywhere in eight short years ? How was it possible for it all to be contained in twenty chests and carried off ? Why hadn't someone sorted it all out and thrown half away ? I don't know the answers to any of those questions. All I can tell you is that moving caused havoc in my life and amounted to absolute folly.

Why, then, did I attempt it not once but twice ? At least I know the answer to that. When I leased Young St. I was a poor man measured against my contemporaries and was obliged to settle for a modest sort of dwelling which by no means satisfied my cravings even then for something a little more elegant. By 1854 I was in a position to satisfy that small ambition and I did not see why I should not go ahead and do it. You may call me a snob if you like but I shan't care – I *do* like pretty houses and admire fine architecture and get a good deal of pleasure from living in a building that has a certain line about its construction. Onslow Square was no gem, but it was distinctly a step up from Young St. and gave scope for improvement and was the limit of my income at the time. I wanted very much to branch out and console myself with a more beautiful house that I could fill with interesting objects and good furniture – a man gets tired, you know, of

living in a disorganised house full of stuff that was never hand picked in the first place. I knew it was no good adopting half-measures – shabby old Young St. was not going to be transformed by a new stair carpet or fresh wallpaper on the drawing-room walls or anything like that. It had to be all or nothing and I was determined to start again with an absolutely empty house which I could mould to my taste bit by bit.

Whatever happened ? I swore I would not move in until everything was quite perfect but instead I found myself one June day standing in the hall of my new house with carpenters still banging away, painters still at it, rubbish everywhere and only two rooms habitable, neither of which were mine. Furthermore, I had not a minute to spare to supervise operations – it was a case of move aside the rolled up old carpets and let me get to my desk even if it is still out on a landing and covered with a dust sheet. How many times have I said in this narrative that a man of my disposition needs a wife? Scores of times and yet never more than during moving house. I declare it was a nightmare from which I never thought I would awaken and if you read certain parts of *The Newcomes* and have a puzzled feeling that something seems not quite right then you will know that was when I moved and couldn't think for the hubbub.   Nobody seemed able to make decisions except me – the girls were quite useless having for so long practised the art of pleasing their father that they no longer knew what they thought themselves till they had searched his cross face.   I struggled on alone writing *The Newcomes*, then emerging to give orders as to the colour of the bedroom walls and then writing a little more, only to be distracted by the urgent necessity of deciding which room the largest tallboy should go in.   Everywhere I looked I found causes of irritation – even the green, damp, pleasant garden annoyed me because there was so much to be done in it and nobody doing the slightest thing except for poor Minny, who hoed away valiantly to no discernible effect.   My original intention – to have the whole house in pale green to give a bowery sort of effect – was in danger of being lost for want of a general director.   It was no good telling myself that in time everything would sort itself out and my idea! be attained – I knew it would not if I did not keep a firm hand on the little army of men crawling everywhere without the slightest idea of the overall effect they were supposed to be working towards. Thank God that when I did all this again – when I moved here to Palace Green – the lesson had not been wasted.   Whatever the cost, I do urge you if you are about to move house, to stay on in the old domain just a little longer until the last workman has packed his tools and gone for otherwise your enjoyment will be spoiled and a dreadful feeling of depression will overwhelm you as you reflect that you have made the most awful mistake. You have not, but the prevailing chaos will persuade you that you have.

Eventually, everything sorted itself out – now what an amazing word " eventually " is, sliding in five little syllables over an unspecified length of time and managing to imply by the ease with which it rolls off the tongue that nothing much was amiss.   Can you see behind " eventually " ?   Can you count the days and weeks and pinpoint the exact moment at which this word could truthfully be brought into play ?   I cannot – the English language is full of such smooth adverbs which convey the opposite of their meaning and yet I employ them as often as the next man.   " Eventually," I say with a wave of my hand to indicate nonchalance – " eventually, " I say with the air of one who has suffered much but can hardly remember why – " eventually " I say and you know I have reached a conclusion in whatever I have been telling you.   When I say " eventually " I am tricking you and you must not mind – I only mean by it that I want to hurry on and that is the most convenient way of doing it without plaguing you any more. Eventually, then, the house in Onslow Square was complete and I was tolerably pleased with it – only tolerably because it still was not my ideal, though moving a little nearer.   When everything was straight and I was not so distracted by the boring parts of settling down I enjoyed very much wandering about shops and galleries collecting beautiful things to put in my new house.   I found, when I arrived at this stage, that it did in the end lift

my spirits to have moved and I was glad eventually (ah ha!) that I had taken the plunge.

It was part of the same urge to shake my life up that induced me to go out and buy a horse and take up riding as a regular exercise. Don't laugh – or if you do, do it kindly. I was getting very overweight in spite of that Italian fever which had done its best to reduce me and the more I thought about the kind of life I led the more I believed that most of my troubles in the health department stemmed from my lazy habits. I did not walk enough or indeed do anything to offset the large quantities of food and drink that I daily consumed and it seemed to me that I would feel much better if I could persuade myself to do something more energetic than stroll to my club and slump in an armchair when I arrived there. I could not help but roar at my own pretensions, but all the same I persevered and played the part of an 'orse-riding fella with the greatest determination. Don't imagine me galloping like fury on a coal-black stallion with steaming nostrils and gleaming red eyes – no thank you – mine was a dull, brown beast suited to its sedate owner. I bought this cob from Carlo Marochetti, my new next-door neighbour, who swore this paragon of horseflesh was all that I was looking for. Well, perhaps it was, but that did not prevent it from throwing me the minute I mounted. To tell the truth, the stirrup leather broke under my weight but it was the effect that I remember best and the effect was a bruised and battered and greatly chagrined yours truly. With incredible courage however the daring Titmarsh re-mounted as soon as he was able and thereafter was often to be seen trotting along in the park quite convinced he cut a dashing figure and not at all surprised that he attracted so much attention. It would have done you good to see him, I do declare. The wind brought some colour to his pallid old cheeks and he held his back so straight because he knew he was being watched and every now and again he would smile an enormous smile just because he was happy to be out in the fresh air which he credited with amazing recuperative properties. Let us not mention his aching limbs afterwards or his cold-in-the-head or anything else unpleasant – he loved those daily joggings and that is all that matters.

Some day I have a feeling that this new art of photography that is all the rage at the moment will sufficiently progress to capture for us episodes in our past, like the little scene I have just described, and we will be able to hold in our hands or paste in our album proof that what we have said is true. What if I could put before you a photograph of me in 1854 on that 'oss, grinning away and doffing my hat – what if it was taken without my knowing it – what if it was coloured and exactly caught the pink in my cheeks and the blue sky behind – what if this small miracle was achieved ? Why, it would be a lie all the same, no matter how perfect the reproduction and do you know why ? Because it would appear to show beyond any doubt that I was happy and jolly and had not a care in the world and therefore it would misrepresent me to you. I don't know whether that matters or not but I don't like to think about it – I don't want you to know me from photographs but rather from the inner workings of my mind and no photograph will ever capture those. Wherever I go I am constantly mesmerised by the impossibility of reconciling what we can see of people with what we know of them – take that lady out there in the street, walking in such a sprightly fashion with her dog and nodding and smiling at everyone she meets. Would you guess she lives with a crippled widowed mother who does her best to make her life hell on earth ? Would you know she cannot bear to get to the end of this street for that will mean she must turn and go

back and that her liberty for today is over ? The world and the people in it are rarely what they seem and I know that this old man who writes now is more than most a sham.

In 1854, after I had moved to Onslow Square, after I had done my best to wake myself up from the lethargy I felt was in danger of engulfing me, I experienced a kind of terror at the thought of finishing *The Newcomes*. Now that will sound absurd when you are already well aware how I loathed that dismal novel and how it had hung over me for twenty weary months. But I looked ahead and I saw " Failure " written very large indeed and I did not know what I was going to do. A terrible hatred of writing grew upon me – the sight of paper and pen and ink nauseated me and I could hardly control my desire to throw the whole lot out of the window. At night I lay awake terrified that what I had written the day before would be lost and I should not be able to write it again or to continue without it and then all would be up with me. (And this weak, wavering creature was the same one riding his horse every day and smiling fit to burst.) I was jogging through my life not just through the park – the thought occurred to me again and again – I saw how I was running along deep in a safe rut and that if I wanted to get out of it I would have to swerve in the most dangerous fashion and risk overturning in my efforts to escape. I looked for a break in the rut but there was none – the hard-baked mud was high and solid on either side and in any case, if I broke out of it, how could I be sure that the ground either side was not slippery and that I would not slip down a precipice ? (And this troubled, tormented soul was still riding his blessed horse and grinning and grinning.) Every day I did my stint of writing, watching the end get nearer and nearer, and every day I dreaded the completion of the labour I hated. If you think it is wrong of me to reveal my private agony even so many years afterwards then I can only say that I share your distaste but that this does not prevent me telling the truth. I don't like revealing how little pleasure I took in my work – I don't like admitting I wrote without conviction or passion – but it must be done. I envy from the bottom of my heart those who have written all their lives at breakneck speed, scared only that their days will end before they can get down all they have to say – what joy it must be to escape those doldrums I know so well and never better than towards the end of *The Newcomes* – what bliss never to have to dredge through every event that has ever happened to you in order to find something to write about. And yet, and yet – there is some final good that comes out of such anguish for I firmly believe that without it I should never have known how deep and permanent my desire to write is, and if I had not known that, if it had always come easily and been a game, I don't think I would have valued the small measure of talent which is mine and I don't think I should now be trying with all my might to give it expression in *Dennis Duval* before it is too late. I nod my head at you sternly and say, " Consider only what you want to do, not what it is easy to do," and I hope you agree that makes me an Immense Moralist and worth a new chapter at once.

Chapter XVIII

AMERICA REVISITED AND FOUND WANTING

I FINISHED *The Newcomes* on Thursday the 28th June at seven o'clock in the evening and immediately I got down on my knees and said my prayers. Finishing a long novel is a solemn moment whatever the quality of the work and whatever attitude of mind the writer has adopted while writing it. I might have cursed the poor Newcomes all the time I was involved with them, but the moment I finished I was overcome with emotion and hardly knew whether to laugh or cry. If that does not make sense to you – if you suspect I am making an ordinary event more holy that it ever could have been – then go out and ask the first novelist of your acquaintance if he does not feel as I did. There went two years of my life – two humdrum, uneasy years in which I had done nothing to be proud of but two years all the same. I cried when I wrote the death of Colonel Newcome – sat and blubbered away in that sunny apartment in Paris where I had gone to finish my book – and though I had thought all the characters, including that old man, dull and windy, now that the moment had come to say goodbye I discovered I was remarkably attached to them and was ashamed of not valuing them more, and though I had despised myself for writing a book about nothing I found upon its completion that it had not all been about nothing. *The Newcomes*, when I came to look at it with a detachment I lacked while writing it, was about a perfectly good subject, namely the marriage-market of our times. No, I am not inventing this – look at that book and you will see that the theme, while not apparently the main one, is quite striking. Perhaps by the time you read this the same subject will be dreadfully old-fashioned and you will be able to understand my fury and disgust at the way our young ladies are paraded through society's drawing-rooms in search of a title and ten thousand a year. Mammon leers over each assembled throng, rubbing

his greasy hands with glee at the sight of so many bowed down in adoration, ready to tramp with his heavy feet again and again over the bleeding hearts thrown before him. I said I wrote *The Newcomes* without passion – I have condemned myself out of my own mouth for writing without any true purpose – but when I think back to how I stood many scores of times watching the playing of that horrible game and when I remember how I felt for poor Ethel, then I know that the inspiration for that part of the book at least was real enough. How many times had I admired some ravishing creature arrayed in her prettiest finery and watched her closely as she raised those large clear eyes, set in such a fine intelligent face, above the rim of her glass and caught the steady stare of a certain young man across the room ? Haven't I smiled indulgently at discovering her secret and privately wished her well and turned my old grey head away from such tenderness ? But wait – what is this ? – when I looked back, unable to resist another glimpse of happiness, she had lost her smile and stands confused and then in another moment she is smiling again but in another direction and in a different way – she is grinning in a fixed, deliberate fashion at a perfectly hideous old gentleman, old enough to be her father, and as I watch the grin turns her face into a distorted mask and do you know why ? Because that young man she so plainly adores is a struggling artist without a penny to his name and the old man is a widower, sir-somebody-or-other looking for a new wife and with £10,000 a year in his pocket pretty certain of getting one. She will marry him – oh yes, she will, you may bank on it – she will marry him and be applauded, for according to the customs of our time she has done the right thing. She may not even suffer very much or know what she has lost – she will imagine that her first passion was a most wicked weakness on her part and be thankful that it was spotted in time. That, sir and madam, is what I call immoral and I will say so to your face even if you have this day announced the engagement of your youngest daughter Arabella aged eighteen to Sir Creepy Crawly aged fifty-two and are feeling very pleased about it. Think what you like about *The Newcomes* – call it boring and shapeless and without direction – I may well agree with you – but there are things in it that are honourable and which I would defend and the exploitation of the marriage-market is one of them. It occurs to me only as I write this that I have echoed *Vanity Fair* in treating this matter, and that Becky and Ethel are but different sides of the same coin and my obsession which I have spoken so bravely about is nothing new and you may be sneering at me for re-working old material and dressing up mutton as lamb and I don't know what else. Well, we can't champion new causes all the time and that marrying-off business still goes on so I don't see that it would matter if I returned to it in a hundred books as long as I revealed another facet of the game and I think I did.

What does a man do when he has just written *Finis* under two years' work and drawn a straight line and is suffering from some kind of severe agitation of the nerves which he cannot rightly understand ? Why, he goes out and eats a good dinner and celebrates. It sounds rather fun, don't you think, but what would you say if I took you back to that night and pointed out to you a large rumpled sort of gentleman snoring in the front row of the pantomime, his face a little flushed and an awful lot of wrinkles creasing his brow ? What on earth took me there I don't know – didn't enjoy it anyway – whole thing was more like a funeral than a celebration. Nobody blew a fanfare of trumpets except perhaps a clown, nobody clapped me on the back and congratulated me, nobody said drink up except myself and I wasn't very good company. I never remember such a dismal end to any work in my life – no joy, no pride, not even much relief, just a sort of numbness and bewilderment and gratitude that I had managed it. Afterwards I went home and slept a long time and then drifted round Paris supposedly luxuriating in the empty days that were now mine but really hating them and wondering what essential element to my wellbeing was missing. It is a curious period in a writer's life – the immediate aftermath of a long novel I mean – and I for one have never known what to do with myself. I want to rest and yet cannot – I want to have a good time but don't know how – I want to talk about what I have written but can't find the words – and worst of all, the supreme folly, I want to start what I have just finished all over again only do it better. I felt I could not be well without writing – and yet God knows in the case of *The Newcomes* that feeling amounted to the most monstrous contradiction for I had never been well the whole time I was writing it. The minute I stopped so did the shivering spells and spasms so what on earth could I mean by saying that I needed writing to feel " well " ?

If you had whispered in my ear in the summer of 1855 that I would write at least two other long novels in the not-too-distant future I would have said that you were mad. I sincerely intended never to write another long novel again. My story-telling vein was quite worked out and without that to draw upon I had found to my cost that long novels are misery. No more long novels – that was how I felt. What then, a small voice asked rather querulously in my ear, but it was drowned by a great roar of irritation from within me that damned such enquiries. I wanted to shake myself out of that absurdly sentimental finishing mood so off I went on a six-week holiday before facing the future. You notice, I am sure, that the future is always something I talk about facing, or squaring up to, or dealing with – in other words that I appear to have this habit of regarding the future as something unpleasant that must be tackled in an aggressive fashion. Do you talk about the future like that, or is it a misty, hazy country that you see no reason to venture into till the sun clears the air and the way is before you ? Then I envy you – the future is best left to itself – you have learned the lesson I found so difficult.

A curious episode in my chequered history – can history be chequered or only careers ? dunno – took place soon after my return to London and I want to tell you about it the better to illustrate the stage my life was at. Inelegantly put, perhaps, but the blunter the better. At any rate – I suddenly became obsessed with the idea of solving all my problems as to what I should do in that blessed future I worried about so much by obtaining for myself a Government post. Well, why shouldn't I – everyone else seemed to. (Do you note the petulant tone and ain't it sad in a man of three and forty as I then was ?) I expect you remember my extreme embarrassment when I was a young man and tried the same dodge and failed, but then, when I was old enough to know what it was all about, I was not in the least

put out by any lack of success but rather made more brazen. When the secretaryship of our legation in Washington fell vacant I instantly applied for it to my acquaintance – friend may be too strong – Lord Clarendon, the Secretary for Foreign Affairs. No luck. Not a bit daunted I next asked Lady Stanley to obtain for me the Auditorship of the Duchy of Lancaster, feeling that £700 a year and nothing to do would suit me admirably. Needless to say, some other fellow was lucky. I don't apologise for feeling resentful that other men, not a bit cleverer or more deserving than I, were continually getting something for nothing while I worked like a demon for all I had, and I don't apologise for approaching what connections I had and attempting to use them because I know that I never carried this kind of thing to excess – I never put any real friend in a position where it was impossible for him to refuse, witness my refusal to ask Lord Stanley for a post when he became President of the Board of Trade in Lord Palmerston's Ministry. Cockadoodledoo! Such humility is admirable, I do declare. But after all this bragging, there *is* something I apologise for and that is for being a fool. What on earth would I have done in Washington as Secretary of our Legation ? Gone quietly mad I should think, or shipped myself back home within the year. And would I have been comfortable raking in the shekels from the Duchy of Lancaster ? Of course I wouldn't, not even if everyone else was doing the same. I don't agree with those sinecures and should I ever have come into Parliament I might have tried to do something about them. I can only shake my head at my own sulkiness and pure worldly envy and rejoice that no plum fell into my lap to quietly rot there.

Work was a necessity, that was the only certainty about the future that I had and now that I haven't much future I still feel the same. Work for money was still important in 1855 so I cast about for some scheme that would bring me pecuniary reward and internal satisfaction. I have always, it seems to me, had to make things happen and particularly at that time, when I was so dissatisfied and unsettled upon the completion of *The Newcomes*. Ought I to say that some people liked that novel and said kind things about it in case you imagine I went round London having bricks thrown at me by irate readers and get an exaggerated notion of my unpopularity ? It wasn't like that at all – indeed, at that very time, *Blackwoods Magazine* ran a series of articles on the works of Dickens, Bulwer-Lytton and myself in which some highly flattering praise came my way and at the end of the series when a kind of poll was held to decide who was the greatest of we three I was led to believe it was a pretty close run thing before that doubtful accolade went to Bulwer-Lytton. I said doubtful because those competitions are always absurd – who can judge literary merit ? It seems to me quite clear that only Dickens has genius as distinct from ability, but no heed was paid to that. Perhaps in that one instance Dickens' amazing popularity ran against him – perhaps those who judged thought vast popular support could not go hand-in-hand with measured critical acclaim. If so, they were mistaken. They were foolish to be piqued by Dickens' fame and following. I know that I never held either against the man – though I held other things – and that I was only amused when I had direct evidence of how strong his hold was. I remember once I was invited to a house-party at Watford to shoot hares and rabbits. There was a crowd of us agreed to go together from the Garrick, among them Dickens, but as we were setting off – all very jolly – a note was delivered from Dickens asking us to tell our hostess that he was extremely sorry but unfortunately he could not that day be of the party. As it happened, it fell to me to present Dickens' regrets and apologies and the minute the good lady heard the news I heard her shouting to the cook, " Martin, don't roast the ortolans, Mr. Dickens ain't coming." I have never felt so small in my life – ortolans for David Copperfield, thought I, but not for Arthur Pendennis by jove! Not much danger of me getting above myself with that going on, was there ?

Among all the schemes that fell through in 1855 there was one which attracted me greatly but nothing came of it. What would you say had been a fairly consistent ambition of mine ? Editing a paper or magazine of repute I think I may fairly claim. In 1855 I was asked to consider editing a sheet of general criticism after the manner of Addison and Steele's *Spectator* or *Tatler*. It was to be called *Fair Play*, and if it had been launched I should have started earlier and perhaps with better personal success on a path I was to go down too late in my life. What if *Fair Play* had been a *Cornhill Magazine* ? It could not have scored heavier but I might have been able to endure the position of editor better than I have just done. You thought I was going to give up might-have-beens and so did I but I can never quite resist the temptation. If *Fair Play* had taken off I would not have been obliged to go to America again and I don't know whether that would have been good or bad. Good heavens, off again about being " obliged " to do something I apparently did not want to do, as though choice did not come into it, and yet just a short while back proclaiming that I was always having to make things happen. I never seem to make up my mind do I ? Whatever the truth of the matter, I felt then that I had no option but to go to America to lecture because nothing else solid had turned up and the attractions of seeing some old friends and making a lot of money were the only ones about. I had no great hopes that America would recharge the batteries as I had had last time, though there was a little superstition mixed up in my decision – I had always felt well in America and I think I hoped that after almost two years of ill health that might happen again and be very welcome.

Hold on, I hear you cry – he ain't a-taking them old lectures is he ?   No he ain't, but you are quite right to be suspicious for I didn't know what the devil I was going to take.   In fact – in fact – oh I am so ashamed – I went again to America to lecture with no set of lectures complete!   Isn't that shocking ?   I don't know what I thought I was about, plunging around in the history of the last century as I had been doing, hoping I would hit upon a convenient subject.   I booked a passage for October 13th and yet all September I was frantically reading and copying notes in the British Museum with no subject attracting me more than another.

Everything that dreadful autumn seemed stacked against me – it was scramble, scramble to be ready in time and no Eyre to help me.   He could not come.   I don't think he wanted to and who can blame him – and I could not think who else to ask, but even more than the time before I knew I must ask someone – it was impossible to go alone.   A young fellow who would have done perfectly – Maurice Marochetti, the son of my neighbour – was prevented from accompanying me at the last minute and that left me in an awful fix.   My feelings of unwellness were so strong that I did not feel capable of chancing the trip alone and knew I absolutely must have someone to tuck me up in bed if I collapsed somewhere out there in the western hemisphere.   It was thinking about this – bodily comforts I mean – that decided me upon taking my valet Charles Pearman.   As a travelling-companion I did not know how he would fare, and a real friend he could not be because of the difference in our age and interests and – well yes, our station in life – but then Eyre Crowe had done very well without being a real friend either.   Charles was strong and fit and knew my habits and I decided that I would rather have someone ready to hold the spittoon when I needed it than able to deal with my business affairs.   I don't know that Charles jumped for joy but he didn't walk out on me and seemed reasonably intrigued at the idea.

There were the usual tremblings and fussings to be gone through before we boarded the *Africa* in Liverpool dock – no need to take you through another set of heart-searchings – but we all drew comfort from knowing that the thing had been successfully done before and were a little more confident than we had previously been.   In addition, I was not this time going into a void but to see kind friends like the Baxters, with whom I had kept up a sporadic correspondence and who would be sure to give me a great welcome. This was cheering, but I can't say that I went on board in a happy state of mind.   My head was full of financial calculations – so many lectures would pay off the house, so many more complete Anny and Minny's dowries – oh how unscrupulous I felt and how unseemly it was in a man who looks down on a seething ocean and contemplates a long dark voyage ahead!   I was terribly afraid that to go solely for money — and let us not be hypocritical with the ship's hooter sounding in our ears — to go solely for money was downright immoral. The first time I justified my trip on the grounds of positive necessity of one sort or another, and was drawn to America by a strong sense of adventure that needed satisfying, but the second time I went for money and that is all. I did not feel in the least adventurous — quite the reverse. Nothing stirred in my blood as the anchor was weighed — I felt nothing but guilt and brooded upon this to such an extent that I convinced myself no good could possibly come of the trip.

I could, if I wished, write you a famous descriptive account of that same trip and how it turned out but I don't choose to, and if that disappoints you, though I don't think it will, you can always go to my *Roundabout Papers* and find everything you want. Nor do I intend to take you chronologically through my itinerary as I did before — that would tie me down to an awful lot of repetition and where is the fun in that? The trouble is that whereas I managed to recall my first experience of America without too much effort and to make it fun for you to listen to — I hope — I find I cannot do that for the second tour. I don't have to look far for the reason: in 1853 I was enlivened and stimulated by America and whenever I remember that time my old enthusiasm comes back and writes my words for me, but in 1856 I was somewhat disenchanted with the place and when I want to talk about it, disappointment slows me up. Now was that America's fault or mine? I don't know — but I do know that every man who falls in love with a new country and broadcasts its virtues far and wide ought to visit it for a second time before opening his mouth. I don't think I looked upon America with different eyes that second time but oh dear me I was different things and reached different conclusions, most of them unpleasant.

I wonder if, that first time, I was so surprised, if you remember, to find any kind of civilisation at all that I did not stop to examine what I had found very closely, or to ask myself how I should actually like to live among the people I professed to admire so much. Did I really want to live in a country where familiarity was the order of the day ? I remember falling asleep in one of the streetcars once and when I awoke from my nap it was to find my newspaper had been taken out of my hands and was being read by the person who shared the seat with me. I suppose I must have looked outraged, though I made no sort of protest, for he shoved the newspaper back at me and said, " I thought I might as well read your paper while you dozed off." But on a second extended visit – ah, that is different. You begin to notice who has power and who does not, you observe how the people are governed and decide whether you like it or not, you catch distinctions of class that had escaped you before and then everything falls into place and you are either even more attracted or else you totally reject your findings. I found, to my chagrin, that America was at a stage of its political development that made it impossible for me ever to consider living there. The vitality and energy that I had found so refreshing upon the first visit proved not to be sufficient to give the country that stability and steadiness that I require in any society. That lack of a strictly stratified society, which I had found so invigorating at first, struck me the second time as dangerous – I found, particularly in the deep south, that I longed for a more balanced mixture but could see no signs of it emerging. Where before it had seemed to me a wonderful thing that a man could rise in a few short years from nothing to immense wealth I did not find it quite so marvellous that he could also acquire through that wealth immediate power. When I walked through some of the towns and cities I visited in the south and saw those black-finger-nailed, high-booted, cursing men and knew that there was nothing else and that they ran the place, then my blood ran cold. I daresay there are as many highly educated men in America as there are here, I daresay there are as many cultured, but the point is that not only are there far, far more of the other sort but that in many areas that sort rule the roost. American democracy is an extraordinary concept, fashioned with care and intelligence, but in operation it can be terrifying. Who knows what it might throw up one day ? I don't see built into their system the kinds of safeguards against the rule of jumped-up ignoramuses that I see here, and I tremble for the outcome.

What began that tirade ? You would far rather have a lyrical piece about visiting the Niagara Falls or something, wouldn't you ? As a matter of fact, I might have obliged but I never did get to see those Falls, though I trekked all the way to Buffalo and almost did. That was another thing – I didn't get to the Falls because of the weather which quite blighted the whole trip. I happened by pure chance to have chosen the worst winter for sixty years to tour America. Don't shrug your shoulders and say what is a bit of snow – you have never *seen* snow until you have seen American snow, mountains

and mountains of it and there to stay.   The blizzards were frightful – gale
after gale of hard driven snow even in the centres of the cities – and the drop
in temperature so extreme it quite literally took my breath away and left me
with icicles on my lips.   Then it lasted for weeks and weeks, for months
even, with never a sign of a break and the whole world frozen solid.
Railways could not function – horses unrideable – complete stoppage of all
communications quite often – a fortune spent on heating houses – oh there
was no end to the havoc that weather created.   Next time you moan about
our weather please to remember the American winters and put up with your
deprivations more cheerfully.

I was not, of course, equipped for this sort of thing but I quickly learned
the necessity of putting on sixty layers of clothing before so much as putting
my nose out of doors.   Many a morning the willpower needed to get myself
upright was so enormous it exhausted me and made me want to get back into
bed at once and go into another deep sleep and wake up on an English
summer's morning with the green trees nodding outside and a warm breeze
coming through the open window and not a snowflake in sight or a sheet of
ice anywhere.   It was pure wishful thinking – the cold continued all the
time I was in the north part of that continent and there was no escape.
People everywhere suffered frightful hardships – trains were stuck in drifts
and in order to keep warm the travellers had to burn the seats.   Nothing like
that ever happened to me I am thankful to say but I had my share of long
waits in awkward places due to the weather.   It was no small undertaking
in those circumstances to agree to make a journey of two days to lecture to

a handful of people and find that in the snow it took three days and that the audience was sadly depleted, their firesides quite naturally being the greater attraction.   The halls I lectured in were never very warm, though everyone did their best, and the draughts that snaked under the doors made sure that some part of me was always cold.   Sounds miserable, don't it ?   And it was, especially since I was frequently unwell.   I could tell you exactly what form this unwellness took if I did not fear it would disgust you and if natural reticence on such matters did not hold me back.   I wonder about our modesty though – it would be much simpler if I could describe in technical terms my ailments without having to camouflage my symptoms with vague talk of being indisposed and so forth.   I know I have often been puzzled and distressed myself when I have been told a friend is unwell, especially if that friend is a lady, and it is not until the whisper goes round that in fact the unwellness is an attack of vomiting following the consumption of too much custard that I can stop worrying.   I thought it might be a miscarriage, you see – and there, I have offended you, but I don't see why.   We ought to be able to talk freely about our 'ealth and not wrap it up in euphemisms.   I am sick to death of having to leave the room in something like disgrace when my stricture plays me up – why can't I be permitted to explain the agony and have done with it ?

At any rate, in America that second time I was often ill and though I managed most of the lecturing there were a few I had to cancel which mortified me.   Worse than the cancelling was the worry as to whether I

should – I hated letting people down at the last minute but on the other hand I hated thinking I might be better in time. It wasn't the same sort of thing as in Rome – I wasn't prostrate and clearly unable to do anything – it was a case of a few hours of minor suffering followed by another few of comparative health and that was how it went on. I was never sure if I was going to be well or ill and that played greater havoc with the bookings than a straightforward month in bed. Perhaps it would have come to that – perhaps I would have collapsed entirely if it had not been for Charles, who looked after me so well. I can't tell you what heaven it was always to have him there, turning down the bedclothes and making sure they were warm and clean, and getting me the right kinds of foods at the right time. Not much fun for him of course, but then nobody was having much fun – it was altogether a grim business and only worth enduring for the money which flowed in as before in the most satisfactory way. Oh what joy to find that before I was halfway through this ordeal I had paid off the new house in Onslow Square – it was mine entirely, every stone of it, and a capital investment – and had greatly increased Anny and Minny's inheritance. Is it wicked to feel triumphant at money-making? I don't know, but the elation I felt kept me going and that cannot be bad. I have enjoyed accumulating money and since I don't consider it has been at anyone else's expense or to the detriment of anyone else's happiness I don't feel guilty about it. I thank God that I was allowed the strength with which to do it and beyond that have no deeper feelings than gratitude. I am aware that I have told you several times before that I considered money no longer a major problem, but each time I said it I found that afterwards I could not imagine how I could have been so complacent. It was only on that second trip to America that I had any right to be – and even then you will find me continuing to do things for money long after I have supposedly made enough. Money continued to drive me not because I was greedy but because it seemed wrong, when it was offered, not to accumulate more. I was safe, my family were safe, and unless some catastrophe affected the whole of England we would all go on being safe, but was that a reason to turn down more money? I did not think so – I thought it quite wrong to refuse the chance to earn more when it was given to me and it is only now that I have the courage to say " enough " that I see I could have said it sooner. I don't like to think that I may have made my daughters feel guilty because I had to work so hard for them, or that they might have preferred a poorer papa who was with them more often.

I remember, in the middle of that second American visit, being made to realise just how much I did value worldly goods and how much I wanted my girls to appreciate their importance and I am more than a little ashamed of my extreme fierceness on the subject. I don't remember the exact details, but somewhere out there I received a letter from Minny, I think –

or possibly my mother, though it seems less likely – in which I was treated to a spirited description of Anny's feelings for a penniless curate with one lung. My, how I raged! I sat down and wrote back the most monstrous epistle in which I told my elder daughter that such an attachment was out of the question and not to be thought of and that she would just have to

break her heart if it was set upon such an impossible suitor. On and on I went, hoity-toity, lecturing her on the absolute folly of her ways and telling her that I had not worked like a slave all my life in order to support such miserable specimens as her intended. In no uncertain terms I told her that when the time came her husband must be able to look after her himself and that I would not do so. It turned out that it was all a tease and very foolish I felt, but suppose it had been true how dreadfully stupid my high-flown sentiments would have been! It makes me shudder to think how I mishandled what might have been a delicate situation – how might I myself have reacted to such a broadside ? Parental control is all very well but there are ways of exerting it that are less brutal and a good deal more successful, but we get carried away, we parents, expecting our children to understand that we do all for their sakes and not for our own.   We simply want them to be happy and happiness does not stay for long in a garret with a one-lunged clergyman.   I am told our house in Onslow Square shook with laughter as my instructions were read out but it might just as easily have shaken with sobs and then where should I have been ?   I would never behave like that now — no matter what kind of Tompkins came along I should behave with more charity and dignity and not deal so brutally with an affair so tender.   All the same, I don't believe my consent could be given to any match which meant either of my daughters would not be provided for by their husbands and I don't believe any man ought to ask for any woman's hand unless he can provide for her.   Who shouted out " remember 1836 " ? What the devil do you mean ?   Oh, I see — well, yes, but I was quite confident that I could provide for Isabella — I had a secure job — a job anyway — it isn't at all the same — mumble, mumble — very well, I agree no papa could have welcomed me and I did take a chance and ought not to pretend that my own marriage was financially sound.   I am growing old, you see, and part of growing old is the adoption of conservative attitudes. We become so horribly aware of the pitfalls in life and tremble for the young and can't recall what it is like to have no fear.   I will try my best not to criticise Tompkins when he comes and not to raise my sights too high, but then you see I do so want him to come and make my children happy before I go and if I can't last until my grandchildren come along at least I can enjoy the prospect of them.   I promise I will not jump down his throat but that I will welcome him and not be so bristly and — oh good heavens let us close this dreary philosophising and start at once on another chapter, even if it is at an awkward place.

Chapter XIX

———————◆———————

A LECTURE TOUR

LEFT America on April 24th, 1856 on board *The Baltic* after saying goodbye to the Baxters and my other American friends. We had a – hold on – just a minute – whoa there! What? Oh. I see. Yes. Well. Mm – best confess that question embarrasses me and I don't quite know how to start. At the beginning? Oh, very well, but why, when it is a dismal story – oh, *very* well, you shall have your way. Sally Baxter got married. There – does that satisfy you, does that explain why I do not mention that dear family in these jottings on my second visit? I don't know quite what happened – apart from Sally marrying I mean – but from my arrival that second time relations were never the same. I expect there is no " apart " – I expect the news that Sally was engaged to be m-m-m-married which greeted me on arriving in Boston was the cause of my joy at our reunion turning a little sour. I had known perfectly well that Sally would get married sometime, sooner rather than later, and you know I have told you how the flame she lit within me was a very small one compared to others that had burned there a long time, but all the same the news was a shock when it came. Was it before or after I was told that I decided Sally had not improved in looks – was decidedly past her best – wasn't anything like as handsome as I remembered? I made light of my feelings and mocked myself publicly for being spurned and congratulated the bride-to-be with a good heart, but all the same I never felt quite easy with that family again. I didn't go to the wedding, though of course I was invited and expected and so forth. I knew I was right not to go but at the time I felt I was wrong. The wedding was in New York and on the day set for it I was engaged to lecture in Boston, but that wasn't what held me back – I didn't value my lectures that highly. The real reason was ill health – I was in the middle of one of those bad spells I have told you about and wasn't sure whether I could manage the journey and stay upright and cheerful during the jollifications and oh what mortification if I could not and blighted the whole proceedings! I decided it was my duty to stay away and wrote to that effect to the Baxters, hoping that they knew me better than to take my absence as a sign of pique. I don't think they held it against me or were in any way offended but I went on worrying about whether I ought to have risked going and made the effort until the day of the wedding dawned and I was so ill I was vastly relieved not to have tried it. I don't know that I am very good at weddings – I don't know that I really wanted to be there or that the Baxters would really like to have seen me – I wasn't Family or even a very old friend but just someone who had drifted across their path for a while and to whom they had been kind. I saw Sally later, in the south, with her new husband Frank Hampden – a fine fellow – and thought how she had aged almost immediately upon marrying, but then American women do. At thirty-five they have a scraggy, wan, melancholy look reminiscent of greyhounds and I don't like it. Our women, on the other hand, mature with age in the most delightful way and grow softer and rounder and altogether more feminine. Poor Sally!

I know one man who was overjoyed to follow me on board *The Baltic* on April 24th and that was Charles Pearman. Poor Charles – how lonely and miserable he had been with nothing to do but wait on me and then lie on his bed until the next packing up day. I asked him once how he was making out and his eyes filled with tears – he was desperately homesick all the time and there was nothing I could do about it. It was no good me jollying him along or taking him on outings – he had enough of those when what he wanted was someone of his own kind to be friends with. He was a shy and timid man who would not dream of sallying forth on his own – whereas Eyre, when he was with me, would fill many an empty day by sightseeing or otherwise making the most of his opportunities, Charles never moved from our hotel. He was a good and faithful servant to me – looked after me devotedly when I was ill and it is no exaggeration to say that I might have died without him so extreme was my depression when those fits of fever and so forth overtook me – I swear I could not move hand or foot and many a time there would have been nobody aware of it. In addition to these duties, Charles proved to be a better letter-writer than I expected and wrote out my lectures for me in a beautifully clear, large hand which was easy to read. He was quick and smart in every particular and I never once would have regretted taking him if it had not been for the ennui that assailed him with such regularity. Some of you might think it was no concern of mine if my young servant could not make the most of a fine chance – you might say he was a lucky fellow to be taken at all and shown things in a new continent that many men much higher up in the social scale would have given their right arm to see, but if you think like that you have missed the point. Foreign travel does not of itself entertain the uncultured man – rather, it frightens and disturbs him and creates a kind of stupefied resignation which he finds difficult to escape from and which is pathetic to witness. I thought I understood Charles' predicament and felt for him but there was nothing I could do, except take him home as quickly as possible and watch him then take a retrospective pleasure in the whole experience. I had a shrewd idea – which was proved quite right – that once back in London Charles would blossom as a devil of a man-about-town on account of his American trip and that nobody would guess from the nonchalance with which placenames tripped off his tongue just how unhappy he had been.

It was a horribly uncomfortable journey home and I felt none of that cheerful buoyancy which had sped me on my way last time. I knew that when I got home I was going to devote myself to being ill for the whole of the summer and the prospect did not please me. Something drastic would have to be done to my innards and I rather thought it might be a case of out with the knife. Not jolly for a man returning home to dwell upon, was it ? Nothing was jolly except the sight of my bank balance which was truly gratifying and made up for everything – however creased with pain I could still manage a smile when I saw it. A large part of what I had earned I had left in America invested in railway shares and other securities – if I am purposefully vague about exact amounts it is because I have now reached the happy stage of being above discussing money matters – it do make me yawn so. Fancy me, consumed by blue devils but consoled by financial gain, lying at home most of the summer of '56 after that prosperous, odious tour, afflicted with fevers and spasms and pains of every sort and in every place except my tongue which grew daily more and more bad tempered. How horrible I was – don't know how my family stood it – don't know how they kept on smiling and soothing me when I did nothing but grumble. It is all very well lying still, feeling weak and dreamy after a bad illness, knowing that all you have to do is wait for your strength to come back as I did that time at Brighton, but oh dear me it is quite a different thing to lie racked with pain and not knowing what is going to happen. Nothing was ever right – if nobody was with me I accused my nearest and dearest of desertion and if I had company I wished aloud in the most boorish fashion that I could have a little peace and quiet. The doctors kept assuring me that with rest and calm and the steadiest of diets my condition would right itself but I did not believe them. I knew about the kind of illness which makes a man weak and apathetic but this unbearable restlessness was new to me and I hated it. I was not at all inclined to lie back on my pillows and smile and talk of angels – on the contrary, I scowled and roared and threw things about and behaved altogether like a spoiled child in a tantrum. I would obey the ridiculous instructions of my medical advisers for a week or so, keeping to my bed and living on gruel, and then I would say it was getting me nowhere and that I might as well have a bit of fun before I died and out I would go and gallivant about placing my faith in activity and pleasure. Stupid, wasn't it ? It was dreadfully hard on my poor girls, especially Anny who came out that year and was looking forward to parties and balls in her first London season. I

managed to escort her to a few choice events but I fear such efforts were merely tantalising — no fun being dragged off by Papa just when things were warming up but he was on the point of collapse and must rush home. I daresay it even put dancing partners off seeing this scowling old fellow hovering behind the girl they might have asked to dance if he was not there, forever pulling out his watch and clearly working out how soon he could drag her away. Becky wouldn't have stood for it, would she, but my Anny did and with a patience and sweetness that made me weep.

I don't know that I ought to make the connection too strong, but I think it was while trying to squire Anny about that I hit on another idea which induced me to accept a bribe of £6,000 for a book. I never went to a ball without thinking of that wicked little Becky creature I have just mentioned — how could I help it when I saw her everywhere, as bright and gay and scheming as if I had never written about her ?   It was strange always to be thinking of Becky while in the company of Anny and it was the contrast between the two that set my mind racing.   Suppose I were to attempt a serial showing the other side of *Vanity Fair* ?   Suppose I were to return to the theme touched upon in *The Newcomes* but opened out and made the main story ?   Suppose I wrote about real goodness and honesty and openness and altogether lauding the blessings of domestic felicity ?   Wasn't that what people were crying out for ?   It wasn't, to be sure, what I wanted to write about but there was no point in dwelling on that.   Dickens may write about slums and villainy and all their attendant horrors and everyone applauds and cries capital, but were I to be equally free and write about the anguish of a man in love with another man's wife and all the wrecked lives as a consequence then oh horror and off with his head.   No, it could not be done — another writer in another century may leap to the subject and open up the sluice gates but not this man, and I am not even sure that I regret the impossibility of attempting what I longed to attempt.   Perhaps it is better to stifle the impulse to write about those things our society decrees it is better not to write about — I don't know, but anyway I suppressed the urge and haven't regretted it.

So there we were — vague literary stirrings and the Forthcoming Serial signed for while I was still ill.   Same old story — might die tomorrow — purse never too full — nothing else to do — might turn out alright.   Are you as weary of it as I am ?   I had resolved to write a domestic saga, to put a new set of characters smartly through their paces, but which characters and what paces ?   Those vague thoughts I had had while escorting Anny did not materialise into anything solid beyond a desire to aim for something wholesome.   I began my new story along these lines at least three times and burnt all three attempts.   It seemed impossible to introduce any characters which my public did not already know and about whom I had already said everything there was to say.   At the end of *The Newcomes* I had hinted that I meant to go on with the history of J.J., but when I began this it proved to be too melancholy and I wanted a cheerful hero for a change.   In between bouts of illness I attacked pile after pile of paper in search of that Forthcoming Serial that did everything but come forth and I grew more and more frantic as time went on and still I could not get a start.   It was not good for me — that kind of sitting and thinking and scrawling and fretting plays the devil with a man already irritable — it soon becomes hard to distinguish between bodily discomfort and mental torture and the body and mind together go up in smoke.   It was no good — I could produce nothing and had to let the little I had managed — the few scraps I had salvaged from all those pages — I had to let them fall by the wayside before panic sent me quite mad.   Admit defeat, I told myself, admit defeat, for no good will come of this forcing, and so I shut up shop with an air of injured pride and sat and twiddled my thumbs and waited until I felt better. Would you say that showed admirable restraint of which you approve or disgraceful feebleness which, being strong yourself, you can only despise ? I don't think I felt anything much myself except a great weariness that nothing seemed to go right and try as I might I could not make it.

I had signed for the first instalment of this Forthcoming Serial to appear in the autumn of 1857 and therefore, having begun and given up a whole year before, I consoled myself with the thought that there was plenty of time to make up lost ground when I was really well. Unhappily, as 1856 wore on, I realised that this state of well being was never going to arrive and that I must settle permanently for something less. Lying up all the summer had achieved very little — I was stronger, the spasms came less often,

but I was not cured, not bounding about ready for anything. It was explained to me that unless the surgeons operated everything else must only be palliative measures — in other words, rest and diet and certain medicines would only relieve the symptoms and not banish them. Nevertheless, I decided that so long as I could' get about and enjoy a modicum of good health I would rather not risk surgery. Why ? Well, because it seems to me to be still in its infancy — too many people I know have died under the knife during what was supposed to be a minor operation and I don't want to be one of them, not while I can still manage. I shan't ever know whether I am right but we can't know everything — and now I promise I will be quiet about my 'ealth and get on to something more cheerful.

Once I was not so incapacitated it was obvious I could not go on doing nothing, and since I could not get my serial underway, and since I soon got tired of wining and dining and otherwise amusing myself, I decided to —

I hardly dare confess – I decided to go a-lecturing again. Oh fie, sir! Hasn't he complained without ceasing about this set of lectures, even more than the last, and hasn't he protested he hates 'em ? Is he a liar, this man, or a humbug, or both, or is he so conceited that he absolutely must hear his own voice again ? I shall tell you what happened: into my room while I was sick trooped a succession of delightful ladies who saw it as their duty to cheer me up. This process took the form of inquiring with the most delicate curiosity as to just what I had been doing in America and what it had been like touring that country – do, do, tell us about your journey up the Mississippi, dear dear Mr. Thackeray! – and though I grumbled and declared myself bored I did quite relish narrating my adventures and there is no doubt that it relieved the tedium of those long afternoons when otherwise I would have been brooding upon how I would much rather be out in the park. These ladies were cunning – if that is not too impolite a word to use – and when they saw me stop and heard me say " then I lectured " they would cry, " Oh do give us your lecture Mr. Thackeray," and their eyes would grow big and round with enthusiasm. Now, I am not so stupid that I succumbed to such blatant flattery even though I liked it and was in a low state and therefore in need of it – I did not succumb, but all the same I made a note of their interest, which I did not think feigned, and reminded myself that nobody had heard me lecture on the Georges in England and that it might be worth considering the possibility some time. I had some tentative inquiries made and when it looked as though more than a handful of London ladies might indeed pay to hear me, I began to seriously weigh up the pros and cons of my old game. It went something like this: on the one hand I had nothing else to do and wanted something but on the other I had had enough of this particular something. On the one hand it would not make me anything like the money I had grown used to in America but on the other it would be easier to make. On and on I went, looking at every advantage and disadvantage until I hit upon a positive reason for doing it that overruled all the others – lecturing in England would make my name more widely known and I had reason to find that satisfactory. A grand scheme was hatching in my head and I saw how a short spell travelling about England lecturing would fit in very well. We have not had much mystery in this chronicle so let us have a little now. I will not divulge my scheme till the lecturing is over.

I began not in England but in Scotland. The reason for this was that I thought Anny and Minny deserved a holiday after all those summer months cooped up with a grumpy old man and as I had good friends in Edinburgh who had frequently urged me to bring my family and as the girls had never been there I thought we might have an agreeable time killing two birds with one stone or combining business with pleasure or however you like to put it. They were very excited at the prospect but hardly had all the details been worked out and agreed to than disaster overtook us – my mother fell ill. If that does not make sense to you, think about it. My mother lived in Paris. Her husband was already ill on and off and quite incapable of looking after her. There was no alternative for anyone with even a grain of compassion but to go to her – and my girls had hearts as soft as butter. They

were obliged to forgo their Scottish adventure in order to take up a regime they had only just left off – first nurse Papa then immediately fly to nurse Granny with no proper break in between. It wasn't fair, was it ? But my girls in that respect are saints – Anny might flush upon hearing the news and Minny turn pale at suppressing her disappointment but in a minute there is a brave smile and some cheerful words and oh how I admire them – I, who, to this day, grow quite savage if balked of some expected treat and sulk and stamp and create a great fuss. Off the poor creatures went to the same sick-room routine in Paris choosing only to remember how good their Granny had been to them and how they loved her dearly. I went too, of course, but out of guilt rather than with genuine pleasure, and saw at once that although my mother was indeed prostrate and genuinely ill it was all nervous in origin. She had been worn down by years of watching over my stepfather, never permitting herself to do what she wanted to do because of the ever present need to consider his feelings, his desires. Yet G.P. was never a tyrant – the tyranny, if there was any, lay in my mother's own nature with its insistence on serving.

I lay awake night after night trying to work out a plan that would be good for the whole family but the complexities of this domestic situation defeated me. It made sense – it had always made sense – to have all of us under one roof, but with G.P.'s obstinate resistance to living in England and the complete impossibility of all of us moving permanently to France all else

foundered.   I searched my conscience hard to be sure I was not thinking of
my own convenience – could I perhaps move lock, stock and barrel to Paris ?
Once I would have been glad to do so – would have welcomed the excuse
to do so – would have relished the financial independence that made it
feasible –. but I found that at forty-six I had no desire to quit my own
country.   I was settled there for better or worse, I had a house I had only
just perfected, I had a small name I was proud of – no, even if it was possible
after all, I would not be moved to France for the sake of a stubborn stepfather.   By the same token, I would not compel him to move either –
convenience and prudence must take back seats to deeply rooted prejudices.
I did not *want* to move to France and live with G.P.   G.P. did not *want* to
move to England and live with me.   Amen.   So be it – but in the middle
of we two opinionated men were three women suffering because of their
gentleness.   Temporary solutions were all I had it in me to come up with –
the girls must stay and look after my mother while I went off alone to
lecture until there was a change of circumstances and a chance to do something more constructive.   I left them feeling pretty gloomy but determined
to put a good face on it and not torture myself with thoughts about how this
kind of confinement was not good for Minny.   She had survived before and
would survive again and perhaps it would not be so bad once my mother
was over the worst, as she looked likely to be fairly soon.

Let me say straight away that in spite of the inauspicious beginning I
enjoyed that tour.   The Georges went down much better at home than they
had done in America and I am bound to say that the difference lay in an
informed audience.   I thoroughly enjoyed being hissed in Edinburgh for my
poor opinion of Mary Queen of Scots, though I was startled at first – after
all, how many times had I given that lecture and made that remark and been
greeted by stony silence ?   I had grown used to lack of response and had
forgotten that there were people in the world to whom the very name of
that Queen was holy.   How I rose to the challenge of open disagreement!
How it stimulated me to come out with even more forthright opinions!
Why, those dreary old lectures took on another complexion straight away.
There is nothing worse than addressing a lot of dull-faced, neutral-minded,
grey people who are all behaving as if they are in church and must not move
a muscle unless the parson gives them permission, and there is nothing better
than talking to an assembled throng whose faces shine with eagerness and
you know that if you put a foot wrong they will be after you.   The lecture,
instead of being mere words, becomes a question of emotion and passion
and then how your voice rises and takes off and how excitement fills the air
and re-charges the system!   An evening like that is excellent entertainment
– there is no longer anything sordid or disagreeable about it – even the
financial transactions become perfectly acceptable, and where once it had
depressed you to be treated like a common traveller plying his wares now it

seems quite otherwise. They enjoyed it – I enjoyed it – they learnt
something – I learnt something – everybody is happy and let us go on to
the next place and bless our luck. Would that it had been like that in
America but I am afraid that to half the people there the four Georges were
as familiar as pre-historic monsters and nothing I could say could bring them
to life. With the Humorists it seemed easier though they were as unfamiliar
– dunno why.

There was the usual feasting and suchlike after each lecture, for which I
no longer had the same taste, the victuals not always being good for me in
my newly recovered condition, and my jaws being positively dilapidated
after America, but I bore up admirably and enjoyed these provincial suppers
on account of the company. If you are a London person that is bound to
strike you as odd – *company* in the provinces ? – what can the man mean –
everyone knows that Out There, in those strange places Beyond Town,
there *is* no company worth knowing – they are all up to their poor ears in
mud are they not and hopelessly dull and dowdy and really hardly know
what civilisation is. How that view got about I don't know – perhaps it was
a convenient invention by some London snob – but I tell you with absolute
authority that it is false and that there is more good conversation to be had
within a 300-mile radius of London than you have ever dreamed of and all
of it lacking the affectation which distinguishes our society here. Many a
time I sat sandwiched between two burly doctors or merchants or parsons
and reflected that I had heard more good sense talked in one hour than in
twenty among more fashionable folk. They are humble, those men of the

shires, not with a false humility but with a just appreciation of their own limitations. They talk about what they know about and that is that. They don't pretend to have heard of someone when they have not but ask about him with interest. They aren't competing with you all the time, or trying to work in some item to show off about, but merely treating you as one of themselves. This may sound as if they did not know anything, but they did — they were amazingly well read and their opinions were refreshingly free from that stale tinge of accepted praise or rebuke which characterises London opinions and comes from being too much in touch with what everyone else is saying. They reminded me, by their openness, that in London our values are often perverted by success — I would realise with a kind of physical shock that I had just been listening to a parson who got £150 a year and that I was getting more than that for a week and that discovery truly disturbed me. I could not argue that I deserved more for I knew that I did not — the parson and the doctor too and all those other people who shared my table all worked twice as hard as I did peddling my old lectures and suffering no greater aggravation than that mild ennui now and again. Nor could I argue that I provided a more valuable service — what, talking for an hour or so about four dead kings ? How could that possibly compare with the day-to-day routine of men who looked after the most demanding needs of a large flock ? I was an entertainer, that was all, and vastly over-paid, and something ought to be done about it. Our society is built upon such contradictions — no man has the certainty of a just reward for his labours while such incongruities as myself exist, and I can only say that I am surprised my existence does not arouse more resentment than it would appear to.

You can see from all this how I was pulled out of that slough of self-pity in which I was in danger of wallowing for the rest of my days — travelling the length and breadth of Britain as I did I was continually shaken out of any complacency I may have been feeling with regard to my position in life and forced instead to consider myself in relation to others. That sounds very clumsy and grand, but all I mean is that it did me good to meet people and see their way of life. There was plenty of time for ruminating as I jogged along between towns that I had hardly heard of, and sometimes as I stared out of the window of train or coach I would be struck by how different my life might have been if I had not been a metropolitan. I remember going to the little Cumberland town of Carlisle and being re-minded that I was once offered the editorship of the *Carlisle Patriot* in my early married days. I looked at the quietness of the place, entirely without hustle or bustle or any kind of thrust that I could see, and I wondered what would have happened if I had taken that post and gone to live in that sleepy place — suppose the peace had exactly agreed with Isabella and suppose — and that was what I thought about many a time. You may say, with a laugh, that I would have been bored to death in five minutes, that I could not have endured a life without the sort of company I now keep, but you do not know for sure. We all have different sides to our nature and you only know in me those which have the upper hand – you don't know that I might not have been perfectly content to be a big fish in a small pond – you don't know

that I would not have found more happiness and fulfilment in fathering a large family and giving myself up entirely to the most fearsome domesticity.

At any rate, given to this sort of philosophising and buoyed up by the success of my lectures, my spirits improved rapidly as I made my circuit as solemnly as some worthy judge. The only snag was my 'ealth, to which I promised not to refer but it do keep intruding so and is quite pertinent to this account. Often I had attacks of the spasms which obliged me to lie up, invariably in hideous hotels. I may laud the provinces for peace and company and kindliness but oh dear me the 'otels! I daresay there are many esteemed establishments that you know of in Hull and Bradford and all the other places I found myself, but I never hit upon them – it was usually my fate, when ill, to arrive at a dingy, cold, unwholesome hotel where everything I wanted seemed to be unobtainable. Then Home would seem heaven and it was all I could do not to give in at once and go there. But I stuck it out and completed the arranged tour and only went back to London when I was free of my commitments. Once back, I was immediately seized with a new disease of a different and more serious nature than my physical infirmities – I began considering the purchase of a country estate. It was a game I had played off and on for many years, one to which I returned whenever I was prostrate, and I saw that I could do it. What was there to prevent me buying a beautiful country house and some land ? I saw a house advertised for sale near Southampton – on Bevis Hill – six acres of land and so forth – and I thought how splendid it would be to play the county squire game in reality and not just in my head. But for once being forward-looking had its advantages – I saw myself stuck on top of Bevis Hill in my gaiters with Anny and Minny both off with some Tompkins and it was a most dreary prospect. Who was I, at my time of life, a man almost on his own, to shut himself off from the comforts of town which he would soon need more than ever ? No, it would not do – I was a town mouse and must turn to other hobbies if I wanted to move on, as I always seem to. Better by far to stay in London and try my grand scheme – try a new important venture – in short try politics.

Chapter XX

THE FUN OF POLITICS, THOUGH
IT TURNS OUT SHORT-LIVED

A LITTLE way back there, I was in the doldrums and didn't much enjoy obliging you to languish becalmed with me, but it gives me an inordinate amount of pleasure to know that before I arrive where I am now I have two rattling good adventures to tell you about. That seems astonishing to me – that things have been more interesting towards the end of my life, I mean, rather than at the beginning or in the middle – or at least that is the way it seems to me looking back. It gives me a great deal of hope that even now, when the port is in sight, I may yet look for a diversion or two to entertain me. Don't we all long for that little bit of excitement to make us perfectly content ? I know I do – I may have stated often enough that I can't abide change and upheaval but you must have deduced long ago that this is nonsense – that I thrive on it, particularly if it entails no effort on my part as to the onset of whatever scheme is involved. That was how it was in 1857 – Oxford was offered to me on a plate and I was immediately plunged into the most delightful hurly-burly – no, madam, I must disillusion you before we go any further for I see you think I mean the University wrapped up in blue ribbon, and instead I mean a parliamentary seat for the town.

Now I will not have it that setting myself up as a parliamentary candidate – except I didn't set myself up without being asked – was a new conceit born of too much money and applause on my lecture tour – quite the contrary, for I believe it to have been an idea as old as the writing one itself. Will you bear me out ? Do you not recollect that the idol of my youth was Charles Buller upon whose behalf I once engaged in a political campaign ? And don't you remember how I spouted at the Union and was mortified I could not do it better and looked to the day when I might ? And what about my interest in the Administrative Reform Society which I haven't even told you about for fear of boring you – and my disgust at the lack of gentlemen in American politics – and the – stop! All this justification for a perfectly normal ambition is both unnecessary and unseemly and I don't know why I went in for it, but I do feel it perhaps needs explaining because it must have looked to the outside world so sudden. I was a man of forty-six who up to then had shown no discernible interest in Parliament and no one was to know, except my nearest and dearest, how long I had cherished this political ambition in my 'eaving bosom. I think people wondered why I had not come forward before, but then they were not to know that I could not abide standing as anything but an Independent and that to do this I had to be financially sound. Parliament before 1857 would have meant a place as a Whig nominee and what was the good of that ? It was not in my nature to toe any line and vote as someone else bid me – if I went into Parliament I wanted to be a free-thinking individual who could consider everything put to him without worrying about those he was beholden to. How could I pledge myself to stop the corruption I so heartily detested if I was corrupt myself ? Don't tell me that the end justifies the means for I don't believe it – I don't believe that a member who has sold himself in order to get a seat can do any good in Parliament when he gets there. If I stood, I wanted to stand as an Independent beholden to no set of politics except my own and therefore I must pay every penny of the expense myself. I knew that the cost of the election itself, however it might turn out, would be prodigious and then if I was adopted, supporting my position would eat into my precious capital at a fine old rate. If I was in Parliament for the good I could do, as I intended, then I could not accept rewards when I got there and must be above reproach and oh what a costly business such virtues would be! I estimated that I needed £20,000 capital before embarking upon such a ruinous course and it was not until my English tour with the George lectures made me a pot of money that I began to see that goal was in sight and then I would be free to make the decision to stand or not. In fact, Oxford came before I was quite ready – I think I would have seen no reason to stop while the gold still flowed in and might have proceeded to the eight Henrys and the sixteen Gregories when the four Georges palled. I had become big business – was taken over by one impresario named Beale who provided me with a contract for fifty lectures and burnt his fingers rather badly as a consequence before he was done – in short, I could afford a flutter and the offer coming at the right time I resolved to accept.

I was quite unprepared for what happened but the abruptness of it all was part of the attraction. In the general election of April 1857 my friend Charles Neate, leader of the Independent party at Oxford, won the second seat in the city only to be disqualified – unfairly – for bribery, and another election for this seat, the other being Whig, was announced for July. Neate persuaded me that this presented an ideal opportunity for me to try the hustings – he argued that so perfect an opening was unlikely to occur when I wanted it to and that I must take my chance when I could and that I should forthwith stand against the Liberal nominee Viscount Monck, a wealthy Irish peer. What a state I was in! Oh my stars what agonising went on – what consultations – what pacing of the floor – what calculations –

what feverish counting of assets – what a to-do while I decided whether I should or should not. In the end, after a good deal of prayer and quiet meditation as well as all the public talking about it, I agreed and off I went to Oxford without delay where there took place one of the more bizarre episodes in my life.

You may think you know all about Oxford – ain't there a university there and don't that tell you everything ? – but you do not. Oxford isn't only a few dreaming spires and a pretty river and some colleges – it isn't just a place where young men go to study for a year or two and end up having a good time, or where old men go to bury themselves in books – it isn't at all like that. Oxford, as I discovered for myself and had never thought to see before, is two places. Any man who wanders through the part everyone has heard of – up the Isis, or through Christ Church meadow, or along the Broad – can see at a glance that here is a most beautiful academic haven, all fine architecture and green grass and hallowed traditions, but unless he strays off the beaten track and goes further south and crosses Magdalen bridge and continues beyond he will never know that Oxford is also another place, entirely new, entirely alien to the little heaven he has just left. Nobody outside the place seemed to realise that there has sprung up in Oxford a quarter crammed with artisan dwellings full of hard-working labourers who are busy transforming a university town into a mighty industrial centre. The two Oxfords do not meet – you do not find your dons and students among the labourers and you do not find your labourers sullying the pristine elegance of the university. Both ignore the other, one because it wants to and the other because it has to, and the result is a curious dichotomy that quite shook me. You will guess which Oxford was my natural habitat, and yet I can only say that when I was led by the hand and saw what I had been too ignorant and blind to see for myself, I knew which Oxford I would wish to represent. The labourers I was taken among could have no champion so long as the Whigs held both seats and I resolved at once that as an Independent it was my duty to take on their cause.

I am aware you may be smiling behind your hand and thinking it decidedly suspect that a well-known man-about-town such as myself should suddenly be supporting the workers and I concede you have reason to be suspicious, but nonetheless I assure you that my concern was genuine and my interest once engaged perfectly sincere. There was nothing inconsistent in my attitude and I am not ashamed of it however much you may sneer. Those dons and gentlemen of Oxford were extremely comfortable and likely to be more so – the people who needed Parliament's help were the others and it was to them I pledged myself. I had no guilty conscience about appealing to the labourers for my votes for I knew I should not desert them once elected. All that troubled me was an uneasy feeling that they for their part could not be so confident – wasn't I a famous snob, and didn't I brand myself as something I was not the minute I opened my mouth ? That is the tragedy of the lower classes – they are constantly obliged to trust to the good offices of those who, because they are not one of them, must always be impossible to test. They need one of their own kind who knows their plight to speak for them but that is the very thing they cannot have – no labourer could go to Parliament, illiterate and impoverished, and make the mighty do what they should and it is manifest nonsense to suggest either that he could or should. The labourers, the workers – all their kind – are forced into the pathetic position of having to believe any superior means to help them if he says he does and when it is revealed that he will not it is very often too late – he has put that Judas into power.

If I sound emotional I can only say that electioneering is an emotional business. What, after all, is the candidate appealing to when he makes his impassioned rhetorical speeches ? Certainly not the reason of that mob in front of him – mobs know nothing about reason – half of them are there for the fun and must be catered for or the candidate might as well go home. There he stands, all his arguments neatly marshalled in his head ready to be produced, and they are useless – " What about Sundays then ? " somebody shouts and unless he has something pithy to shout in reply nobody will listen. He can't use his " on the one hands and on the other hands ", he must resort to every trick he can think of to rivet people's attention and therefore his whole address is cheapened and vulgarised. He learns that wit, as coarse as possible, goes down best and so he tries to make everything amusing, even those things which are not, and strains after laughs like any music hall comedian. The only other alternative is to become some kind of monster and compel silence by sheer brute force – by thumping his fist on anything available (a head will do if there be no table) and shouting loud enough to waken the dead, emphasising even the indefinite article as though it contained enough worldly wisdom to inspire the most reluctant. Method is all, I say unto you, and content very little and the parliamentary candidate who does not absorb that piece of information at the beginning will be a disaster on the hustings unless his seat is a safe one.

You may well wonder how I fared if this was the case. Could Titmarsh wheedle and coax ? Could Titmarsh thunder ? Wasn't Titmarsh more inclined to stutter and cough and be altogether feeble and do you fear for his safety ? Well, I admit nature had not equipped me to be a rabble-rouser – ain't got the voice nor the venom – but you would be surprised how I rose

to the occasion. I amazed myself by not shrinking from the platform nor from the kind of performance that must needs be given there and instead I threw myself into the fray and became quite adept at speaking in a sort of shorthand with convincing displays of simple passion every now and again. At least, you know, I am a big man and stand above a crowd and even the most opposed observer would think twice before knocking me down, and then also my lecturing had accustomed me to the sight of large concourses of people and I had no nerves and that was half the battle. I often thought I could not have had a more different audience – where were my silent, neatly dressed, attentive literary types ? Before me I would see such a motley lively crew all talking and jumping about that I could not imagine how I was ever to begin, or once begun to continue without the hush and respect to which I had grown used. But I adapted, and discovered electioneering is a different game and quite enjoyed learning the new rules and playing them to my advantage whenever I could. I was struck throughout these meetings by the readiness of the people to go in any direction – they seemed immensely good-natured and without fixed opinions of any sort and I was surprised at how little genuine resistance I encountered. This perplexed me – was every man in Oxford a drifter ? Had nobody heard of party politics ? Or did nobody take me seriously ? It was hard to decide.

I have gone an awfully long way without telling you the main points of
my manifesto – I expect you will think I had none, but I did, though none
of them was very revolutionary.   My stand was a simple one – I wanted to
see the Constituencies enlarged and the government popularised, I wanted
the Ballot brought in, and I wanted to see the suffrage drastically amended,
though to make it universal seemed to me absurd.   What went down best
was my view on the exclusiveness of the governments we were saddled with –
you should have heard the roar when I was asked why was it that we always
had to send for a Duke or a Lord when we were in difficulties – what was
wrong with a plain Mr. ?   I got many cheers when I proclaimed that it was
simply custom that was responsible for this ridiculous partiality for the
aristocracy and that we had hundreds of talented men in our country who
were prevented from coming through and that I should like to see the way
cleared for them.   You see now why I could only stand as an Independent –
such views would have been impossible for a Whig nominee answerable to
his titled patrons.   There was no doubt that I was not the only one in
England to be sick of this monopoly of power, and I grew quite cunning at
exploiting the hostility it aroused.   My skill at this was not so great as that
of my rivals, however – they were expert at using things I had said and turning them into something quite different and more sinister without actually
falsifying anything.   Take the Sabbath question for example – I said somewhere that I wasn't against opening certain establishments on a Sunday and
that was taken up and blazoned forth as, " Mr. Thackeray says he would
not only open the Crystal Palace, the British Museum, and the National
Gallery but would go further and open the Concert-Rooms and Theatres on
Sundays."   Oh what a fuss!   Oh what an uproar!   I had to spring up at
once and publicly deny that I had said, or meant, anything of the sort.   I
replied saying that though I was indeed in favour of opening Museums and
Galleries and any place where there were beautiful things to look at I had
never thought of the theatres and now that I was obliged to think about it
I was decidedly not in favour.   My sole intention in wanting to alter the
law about Sunday opening was to combat the existing drunkardness which I
believed reached such proportions on that day simply because there was
nothing else for the lower classes to do and that if they were provided with
harmless pursuits it might go some way to solving the problem.   But though
I spoke out at once the damage in a sense had been done and I learned the
painful way that such broadsides have more impact as an attack than when
they are employed as a defence.   I ought to have realised that the Sabbath
question was inflammatory and to have issued my views upon it before my
rivals took it upon themselves to do so.

All this was fun – the speeches and addresses and so forth – but there was
another side to electioneering that I did not enjoy so much and at which I
was bad.   Do you remember how in America I would not stoop to going cap

in hand round the newspaper proprietors in Philadelphia in order to make them favourable to my lectures ?   Well, in Oxford I was forced to swallow my high-minded notions and do precisely that — go round knocking on people's doors I mean and asking them for votes.   It would not have been so bad if it had been a case of requesting five minutes of a gentleman's company in his study to put forward my point of view — perhaps over a glass of wine ? — but instead I had the humiliating experience of either having the door closed rudely and rapidly in my astonished face or of being told by some lout that master was not there but I can ask him to vote for you.   It was mortifying going around smiling and simpering and asking support from a lot of idiots I would much rather tell go jump in the river.   Don't say I didn't have to do it — that you wouldn't — for I tell you it is imperative however much wrong it may reveal about our electoral system.   It was trial by popularity that is what it was, and is, and a very uncertain way of conducting a serious business.   I played it straight all the same — did what I had to and no bribes or attempt to curry favour by calling in influential friends. When I found what I suspected all along — that nobody had heard of me — I thought briefly of asking Dickens to come and speak for me, reckoning that whereas only one or two knew of my reputation there might be as many as three or four who knew of his, but I resisted the temptation.   If I won, it would be on my own, though of course not quite on my own for I had various agents and people helping me and showing me the ropes and would have been lost without them.

My rival at the poll soon ceased to be Lord Monck, to my regret, for I had developed quite an affection for him.   Whenever he met me about the streets of Oxford he would stop and salute me with exquisite courtesy and after a brief chat about everything except the election he would end our discourse with the words, " Goodbye, Mr. Thackeray, and may the best man win."   If I used that phrase to him, as I sometimes did to tease, he would reply with becoming modesty and gravity, " I do hope not, sir." What do you think of that ?   I thought it perfectly splendid and it made me smile and I felt happy that our contest could be conducted in such a civilised fashion by the main contenders at least.   In the atmosphere of roughness I felt all round me it was re-assuring and I admired Lord Monck for it, even going so far as to compose some doggerel for Anny and Minny on the subject:

> My dearest little women so far as I can see
> The Independent Woters is all along with me
> But nevertheless I own it with not a little funk
> The more respectable classes they go with General Monck
> But a fight without a tussle is not worth a pin
> And so St. George for England and may the best man win!

Unhappily, my verse had to be scrapped when Monck was replaced by Cardwell, who was a different kettle of fish. It was Cardwell who had come bottom of the poll in the abortive April election and against him I had little chance. He knew Oxford well and was an experienced electioneer and unlike Monck, who had rather kept himself above campaigning, he was not averse to going out and taking Independent votes away from me. I remained in capital spirits all the same, loving all the excitement and activity and being vastly amused by the sight of my name on placards all over the place. It *is* exciting to be in the thick of all the bustle and to know that you are responsible for the whole city taking on a festive air and forgetting its ordinary everyday business for the duration of the election.

Reader, I lost. Ain't it a shame ? I didn't lose disgracefully, though, for I polled 1005 votes against Cardwell's 1070, which for a first try everyone thought highly respectable. One and all urged me to make myself available immediately for the next chance that came along but I refused to consider such a step – not, mark you, out of any fit of pique or the like but because of the cost. Didn't I tell you it was expensive electioneering ? I did, but didn't even realise myself just what a bank-breaking experience it is. Do you know what that little flutter cost me ? Do you know what I paid for the assuaging of my beastly vanity ? I hardly dare write it down but I must so that you will think twice about it if you are ever tempted to follow in my footsteps – £850! £850, for the privilege of losing. Wasn't that awful ? I don't know what that sum was made up of but I know I checked it pretty carefully and that it was correct. The thought of how many lectures it had taken me to earn that princely sum – of how many weary miles I had travelled or how many pages I had written to make £850 made me groan. So much work and then all gone in a few days, flung in the air so to speak with gay abandon. Was it a wise or useful way to spend my savings ? Did it compare with buying property or laying down a fine cellar or procuring railway shares ? Of course it didn't – it was mere self-indulgence, that is what, and I felt a little ashamed of myself though no one took me to task. It made me query once again the whole parliamentary system when it was demonstrated to me that only the rich can afford to be Independents. I see that this prevents any silly fool from fancying himself as candidate, which is undoubtedly a good thing, but I did not agree that wealth is of itself a qualification and by making the cost of standing so great it seemed to me to be the case.

At any rate, I returned to London not at all depressed but quite invigorated by the battle and though I had no plans to engage once more I did not entirely rule out the possibility. My appetite was whetted and I thought that next time I might win – only let me replace that £850 three times over and who knew what I might attempt ? Well, you must know as well as I that I didn't attempt anything – no Thackeray has entered Parliament that I know of to become the great debater and reformer and I daresay you couldn't care less. I don't suppose Titmarsh would have been much good in the House anyway, do you ? Can't you see him sitting there self-consciously with his brows constantly furrowed as he concentrates his mighty mind on the matter in hand ? Can't you see him trying to catch the Speaker's eye with a tremulous waving hand ? And when he does speak – oh dear, don't

he seem mixed up and don't you feel sorry for him and wish he would sit down ? No, I don't think Parliament lost much by my non-appearance, though I would have taken my role much more seriously than half the gentlemen who loll about those benches doing nothing very much but jeer and yell in a schoolboy way.

There was another loss to be reckoned with after the Oxford election, one not so easily made up, and that was time. After all, I could work for the £850 but no amount of work would replace the month I had lost campaigning. I knew before I began that I could not afford the time, not with lectures promised and – much more dreadful – the Forthcoming Serial hanging over me. I had signed for it to appear in the autumn of 1857 if you remember and August was upon us and the first four chapters not even completed. I knew the name – *The Virginians* – and that was about all. The nightmares I had experienced with *The Newcomes* I soon knew to be pleasant dreams compared to the awful spectres that haunted me while I tried to get *The Virginians* under way – the story simply would not start itself and no amount of trying would bring forth the fluency I longed for. In addition to the creative difficulties, I was hampered by the absence of a good secretary at this crucial stage. If it sounds like a case of a bad workman blaming his tools, I can only say that such things do matter if things are not going well anyway. Don't think I didn't hark back to the good old days when I had sat at my desk night after night scribbling away for dear life with the paper mounting up in reams at my side and never a thought of a secretary in my head – of course I did – writing the thing out yourself is the only decent way to do the job, the only method that gives a man satisfaction and breeds confidence, the only source of excitement in the game, but I could no longer do it. For a long time – since *Esmond* – I had dictated the bulk of my work and I had reached the stage when it was quite impossible for me to contemplate the writing out of a long manuscript by hand. I know that will puzzle you – no mention anywhere of arthritic hands from the old fellow – but it is hard to explain, even to myself. Whoever wrote out what I said did not write any quicker than I did myself – sometimes a good deal slower – but I had found that if I lay on a couch and said aloud the words I wanted to write the strain was somehow much less and I did not grow so exhausted. It took some getting used to of course – the sentences shaped themselves differently and I had to beware of windy parentheses that are tempting to the tongue and not spotted as easily as they are with the eye – but then I read everything over each day and corrected it and I could not see that it harmed my style. The girls, especially Anny, were very good and wrote at my dictation in a most efficient manner, and even helped me by their eagerness and interest and their general desire to know what was going to happen, but when they were in Paris with sick grandmothers or the like I was obliged to employ outsiders and that did not go so well. I tried a secretary in the summer of 1857, a Scotchman, highly recommended, but the trial was a disaster. I can't even remember the fellow's name but I do remember that he seemed deaf to me and that made the whole thing absurd. I would begin, " Anna at this moment entered the room when the Captain observed to the countess – " " What ? " he would shout, stopping the flow of words, " What, I missed that," he would shout again before I had had a chance to resume. " The Captain observed to the Countess," I would repeat and he would laboriously write it and look up and glare at me and I would find that I had completely forgotten what the devil the Captain or anyone else had been about to say so great was my irritation at being interrupted. Now Anny would never have behaved like that – to begin with she listened far more intently than he did and rarely missed any words but also, if she did need to ask me to repeat anything, she would wait until my sentence was complete, knowing I was far more likely to remember the whole sentence than half a clause. She had a natural feeling for my timing that the Scotchman totally lacked and did not seem willing to learn and so he had to go. For a while I laboured on doing the writing myself and hating it – it was much worse dragging my pen to a halt halfway across the page and staring dismally at the blank paper than letting my voice falter in mid air. I was in a furious temper with myself – I hated discovering that I had become so dependent on others and cursed the day I had ever allowed this to happen. It seemed to me that money was at the bottom of this particular misfortune – it tempted me into writing books for which I had no inspiration and then it trapped me into paying other people to help me. Does that sound mixed up ? Well of course it does – and is – I was simply casting about for something to grumble about and seizing upon any old excuse. I ought not to have given up writing things down myself even if it meant giving short measure, and that is that.

Eventually – hello old friend! – eventually, however, I settled down to *The Virginians* and there was a period of calm before the next storm. I held close to port and pulled down the sails and – and I find it hard to move these days without tying myself up in nautical metaphors, for which you must please blame *Dennis Duval*. I was determined not to go under and if there

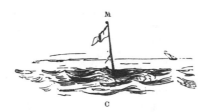

was anything that held me to my task it was my awareness that times were bad and money must be made when it could be. Every man seemed hard pressed with one kind of calamity following another, and I had a steady stream of folk in distress hammering on my door throughout the writing of that serial. They would all come in person, that was the difficulty, and the mere sight of their miserable, pinched, anxious faces would induce in me such a state of nervous agitation that I had the unfortunate habit – unfortunate for my own purse – of pushing money upon them in order to avoid hearing their tales of woe. Is it any wonder that I was considered a soft touch? Is it any wonder that money seemed to slip through my fingers at an alarming rate and that if my income increased so did my expenditure and much quicker? Often, I would look at those poor souls who were driven by want into harrying me and I would ask myself whether I really believed they would do the same for me should the position be reversed. I stared at their features and re-arranged them, banishing the drawn haggard look of penury and replacing it with the complacent beam of prosperity and I thought I detected a hardness in that second face which had been lacking in the first. Still, I paid up, as freely as I could, and thanked God that I was able to do so and shook off that morbid dread we all have of finding ourselves reduced to going cap in hand to a rich friend and begging him to remember our friendship in better days and lend us a few pounds to save the furniture. Worse than that is the vision that terrifies all of us – the vision that haunts our dreams of our women and children gathering their cloaks about them and forsaking pride and dignity and throwing themselves on the mercy of those who have lately been their equals. It is enough to make any man work and save like a demon but we all know that is not always enough – sometimes disaster befalls even the most provident and the most secure fortune can disappear overnight. Peace of mind in our time is property and solid goods and that is why I struggled on with *The Virginians* and grabbed every penny while I could.

It is time to pack myself off, preaching at the top of my voice, to Brighton where I went that summer with my two girls and their convalescent grandmother, little knowing about that next unpleasantness round the corner. I don't know that I could go so far as to remember my exact state of mind at that time, but I do very clearly recall that holiday, not because anything special happened but rather because it did not and yet we were all content. Of all my images of Brighton that must surely be one of the brightest – the girls were delightful and my mother greatly quietened down by her illness so that for a change she was happy to be peaceful and calm and let someone else do the organising. We walked along the promenade and took the sea air every minute we could and read and talked and ate rather well. Roses appeared in all our cheeks, even the old battered ones, and we slept well and rejoiced in each new day with nothing to disturb us except for a certain serial

that would get in the way, but that went better too.   Anny was twenty that year and Minny seventeen and we had reached that blissful stage of being companions on an equal level which was a heartfelt relief.   Little by little Anny had taken into her own capable hands – though she was scatter-brained sometimes – the running of our household and the relief was enormous.   I love families of any kind but grown-up ones are quite the best – none of the strains imposed by small children who while charming are also demanding – only the good parts are left once a certain stage is over and they grow larger and more satisfying every day.   It is quite beyond my comprehension how any man could wilfully forsake the bosom of such a family whatever the temptation and yet all around me there are men who ought to know better who do it all the time.   Take Dickens – I don't think it is unseemly to do so since I can't tell you anything the whole world does not already know – take Dickens, then, and his separation from his wife and family on account of an intrigue with his sister-in-law – can you credit it ?   And yet you must, and so must I, and for one who knows the wife and the sister-in-law and the children it is very hard.   Fancy that poor matron leaving her house after twenty-two years of marriage!   Fancy that man wanting her to do so when he enjoyed the love and company of those wonderful daughters!   There is nothing in the world could separate me from my girls, nothing that could be worth trading in for their affection and daily friendship, nothing I truly believe that could give me half as much pleasure.   If Isabella had only been with us to complete the circle I do believe I could with justice pronounce myself the happiest man in the world.

But I was not, was I ?   I was only happy for a short season at Brighton, watching the sun on the waves with Anny and Minny laughing somewhere in the background and my mother singing and everything that was good centred in 126, Marine Parade.   I thought again about what was meant by it all — by those physical sensations of happiness I mean — and I wondered if a sense of wellbeing is not more to do with health than the actual circumstances surrounding us.   Which comes first — illness because we are feeling depressed, or depression because we are ill ?   Nobody has been able to prove that our body affects our mind or our mind our body but I am sure the two are much more closely connected than anyone realises. It is quite impossible for even the most determined optimist to remain even-tempered and cheerful when he is assailed by genuine illness, and equally difficult for a pessimist not to let the gloom lift a little, if only for a day, when he is feeling full of energy and vitality.   I had known for a long time that the hydraulic complaint with which I am afflicted poisoned my whole system, mental and physical.   I struggled against it — had done for years — but even during good spells I was aware of a sluggishness and difficulty in all my functions that impaired my general health and prevented me from enjoy- ing life to the full.   I think I may have come to terms with these conditions now but I had not then and if I look back to the summer holidays in Brighton with a nostalgia that seems out of proportion it is because August 1857 was the last long remission of illness that I can remember, and do you know what pleases me most about remembering ?   That I knew I was fortunate, that's what — I won't say that I had a foreboding of calamity henceforth because I did not, but I did have a strong sense of the need to grasp and appreciate a happy time while it was given to me.   If my girls wondered sometimes at my strange melancholy in the midst of our jollifica- tions, it was merely wistfulness that they could not last longer, but I had not the heart to speak to them of my thoughts in that dreary Voice of Experience we are always inflicting upon the young — rather, let them be heedless and we old ones can worry for them.

The rest of that year was filled with *The Virginians* and nothing much else. Oh God how I laboured over it!   It took me as much trouble to write as a history of England would have done and I many a time wished that I had chosen to do a straightforward historical survey of the years in which I had set my story rather than a novel.   I found I read nothing at all that was not to do with 1756 — no books, newspapers or magazines.   I was obsessed with the wretched novel and yet no good seemed to come of my devotion and I was not surprised at the cool reception it received — I gave it a pretty cool one myself.   I wasn't afraid to confess I was disappointed, or to acknowledge criticism however violent.   I said to Douglas Jerrold, beside whom I frequently sat at *Punch* dinners, " I hear that you have said *The Virginians* is the worst novel I ever wrote."   " You are wrong," replied that scoundrel,

" I said it is the worst novel anybody ever wrote."   Well, what is the use of
quarelling with a man if you have to meet him every Wednesday for dinner ?
On the other side of the Atlantic, where it appeared simultaneously, it fared
little better, though one or two kind friends wrote and told me they thought
the pictures of Virginian life I painted quite perfect and seemed pleased with
me.   I didn't believe them, though I would like to have done, but instead
I became perfectly convinced that no publisher would ever want me to write
another novel on this showing and I must straight way start reducing our
expenditure.   I think the girls thought I had gone mad – out came the
account books and there I was day after day poring over them and pouncing
on possible economies.   I looked at my outgoings for one typical three-
month period – the first three of 1858 – and I trembled.   You must give
me leave to reproduce that little list to show you why:

Spent in 3 months: –	£792
of which	
last year's bills	250
Horse, plate, bks, gimcracks	100
Mrs. Bakewell & Charles Pearman	25
Charitable disbursements	25
Left for actual money expended	392

Received B & E for Virginians	750
Lectures (25 to agent)	50
Harpers New York	60
Railway Div. (quarterly)	90
Copyrights	140
	1090

Surplus of gross receipts over gross expences	300

That is a pretty sum, ain't it ? It meant I was living at the rate of more than £3,000 a year and making £4,500 and yet we made less show than many people on £2,000 and lived no better so far as I could see than we had done on £1,000. The clue to all this was that we were not good managers, and prone to too many treats, and I knew it must stop. I was determined to get our expenditure down to £2,000 a year and salt away the rest. I announced in a fine old panic that the carriage and one must be sold – we kept a carriage and one and an open carriage and a brougham if you please – and that Jeames must go – Jeames being the footman that dear Chawls, who had had ideas above his station ever since America, now had to have – and that all sorts of other sacrifices must be made. The family agreed and soothed me and they were quite used to it and knew they could go on exactly as before. Papa was always having these fits and going back on them and all they needed to do was have cold mutton scraps for three days running to put him in a good humour and then everything would rapidly return to normal without him even noticing till the next catastrophe on the stock exchange attracted his attention on the financial pages and set him off again.

All the same, I meant it. 1858 was intended to be a Year for Cutting Down but in truth it turned out so dismal none of us had the heart to add to our troubles by doing that at all seriously.

Chapter XXI

AN UGLY QUARREL

THERE will be one man who will speak ill of me when I am dead in a loud, clear voice – perhaps more, but certainly that one – and I expect there will be many who will hearken unto him and my name will be blackened in their eyes. I shan't be there to defend myself, but I am not sorry, for in this case defence would suggest guilt and I feel none. The quarrel I had with this man lies like a large blot on the open book of my life and therefore I cannot forget it and leave others to tell you about it however much I would like to – it must be gone into and explained. There are those who would argue that I shouldn't mention it, that for the sake of peace I should contrive to forget even if I can't forgive, but I don't agree with them – they are the same people who told me at the time that a quiet life is worth anything – any silence, any glossing over of awkward facts, any acceptance of dishonourable treatment – but there have always been for me some things that I will not stand for and which I will always go to great lengths to condemn publicly whatever the cost. One of them is insincerity – I would never let anyone charge me with that and let it pass be they ever so powerful or famous. Another is the imputation of dishonourable motives – I will fight any man with pen or sword who attributes those to me. Lest you imagine that in my dotage I roar away fiercely only because I know I have no teeth left in my head – true, but we will let that pass in the interests of sustaining the metaphor – let me say that even now I would engage in a desperate struggle with anyone who was foolish enough to try me and that they would do so at their peril.

If there is one thing wrong with public life today I believe it to be a lack of regard for the standards that matter. Future generations will look back on this Victorian era – I suppose that is what it will be called though it do sound peculiar – as a time when men said one thing and did another and I shouldn't be surprised if we go down as the most awful lot of hypocrites who ever lived simply because of the reputation our public figures will give us. People today are afraid that they will be laughed at, or attract too much of the wrong sort of attention, if they protest loudly at any calumny against them. Daily we are provided with the disgraceful spectacle of men in public life being held up to contempt or ridicule by what is said about them in the press, but do they object ? Do they issue a broadside thundering against such lies ? Do they run their true colours up the flagpole for every-one to see ? They do not. Instead, they smile rather wearily and say it is of no importance, let the cub reporters have their fun, it is beneath my dignity to correct them. Mr. Grubstreet is therefore given *carte blanche* and publishes what he likes and his readers for the most part take it as gospel truth not being in a position to judge otherwise and who can blame them. It is not good enough and I for one am prepared to stand up and say so. Let nobody think this is an easy position to take up – on the contrary, defending yourself against this kind of slander is painful and difficult and brings down upon your poor head all kinds of unwelcome attentions you would much rather do without. Nobody enters the arena lightly – nothing is carelessly done in those circumstances. When my turn came – when this dreadful quarrel I have referred to began with a libel published against me – I found I conducted a regular Star Chamber of Inquiry before so much as setting pen to paper to begin a counter-attack. Was I acting out of rage ? Was my object revenge ? Was I perfectly in the right ? I turned these and other questions over and over and would not be satisfied until the answer to the first two was a resounding no and to the last question a firm yes. There is, I believe, a large box still in my possession full of rejected drafts of letters so anxious was I to hit the right note, so let no one imagine that I read that offending article during a bout of indigestion and then dashed off a reply without thinking of the consequences.

It is absurd to go any further without giving you the text of the article that caused me such pain and began the quarrel which continues in part to this day and which will result in one man vilifying me even after death, but I find that however eager I am to set it all before you I cannot quite bring myself to copy out the offending words in full. Perhaps when I am gone some other hand can insert the relevant document but I shall not do it. I don't even like to look back to the time when I read the magazine in which it appeared for at once my memory is clouded with a host of depressing recollections I would rather banish. From the beginning it was not a good year – my health was poor, Charles Pearman left my services for a better place in spite of our mutual attachment, and the wretched *Virginians* tormented me day and night. Nothing nice ever seemed to happen, and it was in this atmosphere of gloom and pessimism that I sat down one day and

picked up a little paper called *Town Talk* to read. I turned the few pages in an idle fashion, looking for something to divert me from mournful thoughts, I expect, and among the items it contained I hit upon an unsigned article which to my astonishment began as an apparent pat on the back for me and ended as an almighty thump on the jaw. I don't need to look at it again – every word is unhappily printed on my mind – but I would ask you, asuming that hand I spoke of has indeed attached the evidence for you, to study it most carefully. Do you recognise the technique ? Do you see how I am first praised to take me off my guard and then slammed all the harder for that meagre acknowledgement ? Therein lay the cleverness of the author – he knew that anyone can recognise an out-and-out enemy for what he is and knows how to weigh what he says accordingly, but that when an enemy appears at first as a friend what he has to say will carry twice the conviction. This author called *Vanity Fair* " the most perfect literary dissection of the human heart " and *The Book of Snobs* " perfect in its way ". I think I was meant to blush with pleasure when he referred to my " brilliant sarcasm " and my " most perfect knowledge of the workings of the human heart ". I think this silly flattery was calculated to make me smile and then, when I had read what came after, decide that it would be ungrateful to object. I think it was intended to make anyone who did not know me accept both flattery and abuse as nothing short of the entire truth and if I raged against the latter I raged just as much against the former. You may ask why I did not simply screw the paper up and throw it onto the fire or treat it in some other way as the rubbish it clearly was, and I suppose I might have done that if curiosity had not compelled me to inquire as to the identity of the author. Does that surprise you ? Does it seem irrelevant to you who wrote the piece ? Do you wonder that my interpretation of it should appear

to depend upon the name of my opponent ?   Let me enlighten you: if it
had turned out that a stranger had penned that attack – if someone who did
not know me had invented that malicious nonsense – then I would have been
able to dismiss him in my mind as an ignorant fool and I would have known
that those I cared about could do so too, but when it transpired that the
article had been written by a friend, or someone who passed as a friend, then
an entirely different complexion was put upon the matter.   I sniffed betrayal
and I did not like the smell.   I tasted deceit and I spat it out.   I heard
mockery and shut my ears.   In short, something I cared about was in
jeopardy and I knew I had to act.

The man who wrote that article attacking me – two articles in fact though
I had let the first pass – was a young fellow called Edmund Yates.   Does the
name mean anything to you ?   I thought not – Edmund Yates is and was a
nobody.   He was a journalist of a not very high order but with literary
aspirations – for which I do not in the least despise him – who had been
introduced to me at the Garrick Club.   How the devil he got into the place
I don't know but that is another matter.   At any rate, I met him there and
chatted to him when we were thrown together and was, I thought, in every
way civil though we were not in any way intimate – I hardly saw the man
to tell the truth and had little personal knowledge of him.   I neither liked
nor disliked him but then I could say that of half the Garrick.   The point is,
I had shaken Edmund Yates by the hand, I had allowed Edmund Yates to
share in my private conversations, I had sat down with Edmund Yates at the
dinner table.   Scores of people were aware of this – we had been seen if not
together then as part of a larger crowd and in the widest sense of the word
we would therefore be judged as " friends ".   Do you see now why the
authorship of that article mattered ?   Edmund Yates had abused his position
as a gentleman and as a member of a private club to secure information which
he blazoned forth to the world with every appearance of authority.   Men
would say that Edmund Yates was a friend of Thackeray's – seen 'em
together often – and that therefore his word was law.   It seemed to me that
I was honour bound to take up the cudgels to protect not just myself but my
club – it was not only I, as a private individual who was wronged, but I, as a
member of an exclusive club, who had been insulted.   I could not fight one
case without fighting the other and the more I thought about it the more
convinced I became that a principle dear to me and to many others was in
danger.   In defending the right to privacy I might end up looking a pompous
ass but I came to believe that if I did not I would be a much worse thing –
a coward of the first order.   Where, after all, would the Edmund Yateses of
this world stop if they were allowed to dash down any old lies in order to raise
a few cheap laughs ?   How else, other than by direct confrontation, could
they be made to realise that some things had better be held sacred ?   No
amount of fawning comment upon my books would make me stand for

mendacious verdicts upon my character and the sooner Edmund Yates
learned there were some gentlemen left in England the better.

If, at this point, you are looking for a facetious remark or two to leaven
the dead weight of my anger, you will look in vain. I think I can safely
say I have never taken anything more seriously in my life and that even if
Yates had had the decency to present me with an abject apology I should
have remained solemn about it all and would have been unable ever to

look him in the face again with any degree of pleasure. I gave him the
chance, of course, to retract what he had said but none was forthcoming –
quite the contrary for in replying to my letter he added further insults. I
admit that my letter to him was couched in strong terms – I hope any man
would not feel guilty about expressing himself strongly in these circumstances
– the case admitted no other approach – but I said nothing to call forth the
unpleasant accusations then hurled at me. I simply told Yates that, as I
understood his phrases, he was imputing insincerity and dishonourable
motives to me and that, as he was a man known to me, I was obliged to take
notice of his statements. I pointed out to him that he had abused his
membership of a club I had belonged to before he was born, and I ended

by telling him to refrain from printing comments on my private conversations, from discussing my business affairs about which he knew nothing, and asked him finally to regard any questions of truth as quite outside his province. I suppose that last remark was fairly outrageous – it wasn't turning the other cheek, was it ? I suppose I would have done better to be saintly and make my rebuke dignified – I suppose I was in a way lowering myself to the bounder's own level by coming out with that kind of offensive judgement – but I could not help myself. Yates was furious and announced that since I had labelled him a scoundrel and a liar I had made it impossible to discuss the article in question or to apologise and that he now had nothing more to say. I was sick with rage at his impudence – though I heard later that Yates had in fact been restrained from sending me a violent and flippant reply I cannot imagine anything more wounding than the one which found its way onto my desk.

Well, there was no going back. I thought about nothing else but the wretched Yates affair. What chiefly preoccupied me was the thought of how I should have behaved if I had been in his shoes – indeed, how I *had* behaved when I was in a similar position. When I discovered in my young days that I had wronged a man as Yates had wronged me, what do you think I did ? Why, apologised profusely and begged his pardon humbly and all before he was driven to demand either of me. I don't think I have ever been guilty of attacking a man by name on the delicate subject of his character but I have on several occasions given offence by caricaturing certain individuals in my novels, and the minute I was told of the distress I had unwittingly caused them I instantly explained I had not intended to hurt or even identify them and apologised warmly. I could give you countless examples of my contrition and show you drafts of letters I have sent that are slavish in their abjectness. A man's work I have always considered fair play – if he sets himself up as a writer and says his say then he must not be surprised if other people say theirs – he began it, after all, and must expect a pot-shot or two. I have never complained about any verdict, however unjustified or wrong in my opinion, and God knows I have had vile reviews enough in my time and been the subject of many a burlesque. Yates could with impunity have said what he liked about anything I had written, but it was quite different to talk about me as a person. I don't think I could rest happily when my time comes if I thought you were unable to see the distinction. I wanted Yates to see it and to admit his error in confusing the two things – a man's character and his work – and to own up and say he was sorry like a gentleman. I did not require him to grovel at my feet nor to lick my boots or in any other way debase himself. All I looked for was a simple line or two: " Dear Thackeray – I am sorry to hear I offended you and regret very much that any careless words of mine should have been interpreted by you as intending to wound. I apologise unreservedly. Can

we shake hands upon it ? " Something along those lines would have done. Instead, I was slapped in the face.

You may question my wisdom in doing what I then did – I have asked myself a hundred times since if in that at least I was not perhaps presumptuous. Since I could get no satisfaction from Yates, I sent my letter and his reply, together with copies of the offending article to the Committee of the Garrick Club and asked them to adjudicate between us. Was it just, or merely cunning of me, to ask if the practice of publishing such articles was not fatal to the comfort of the Club ? Was I trying to find other champions to defend me because I was beaten on my own ? Don't think I didn't put these suggestions to myself – I did, and I considered them most carefully and when I brought in the Committee it was out of a deeply held belief that it could not help but be involved. I know my course of action took everyone by surprise, Yates most of all. I am told he was shocked and horrified – I am told he thought I had gone quite mad – I am told he was shaken to the core by my obduracy. It may be wrong, but I know I derived some small shred of comfort at the time from hearing that he was experiencing the kind of turmoil I had gone through and that he was as devastated by my counter-attack as I had been by his original one. I, on the contrary, felt easier once I had handed the matter over to the Committee – I felt that any lingering suspicions I had about my sanity in this affair would be put to the test, and that if I was behaving in an unreasonable fashion there was now a body of sound men who would be obliged to tell me so. Though I did not relish the thought of what must follow, I think I had my first night's sleep since the

whole business began when I received a letter from the secretary of the
Garrick Committee to say that they were calling a Special Meeting to
consider my allegations.   I am willing to bet that Yates, on that same night,
never closed his eyes.   Whose conscience would you therefore say was the
more troubled ?

Hold hard – whoa there old man! – this running away with harsh, bitter
reflections will not do.   I am distressed that you will be bound to think I
was uncommonly satisfied with the torment I imagined Yates to have
endured, as though my principal aim was to make him suffer, when nothing
could have been further from the truth.   I took no pleasure in contemplating
his ruination.   I did not like to think about him at all, though his features
haunted me night and day and I carried on interminable dialogues with him
in my head – his eyes, enormous and horrible in my dreams, obsessed me and
so did his voice, rasping and malicious.   I struggled to view objectively
something entirely subjective and to intellectualise something overwhelm-
ingly emotional.   I tried above all else not to think about Yates as I had
known him for that upset me most of all – I did not like to think I had been
duped, you see, even to the extent of the week before all this began writing
a testimonial for him.   There were those who said I could not possibly
imagine what I was doing to Yates – I, the great literary lion remorselessly
crushing the young penny-a-liner with a family to feed – but I tell you no
one adequately imagined what he was doing to me.   I was ill enough as it
was but his obstinacy on top of his original cruelty made me twice as ill and
his hold over me because of what he had done and was doing amounted to a
tyranny from which there was no escape.   Night after night I lay awake
examining my own conduct – had I been overbearing when I should have
been submissive, grasping when I should have been humble ?   There was
no end to my anxiety – I was miserable from start to finish and hardly
smiled for weeks on end.   I could not go anywhere without being assailed
from all sides by opinions for and against me, and I preferred to lurk at
home where the support of my family was the only thing that gladdened my
heart.

It was a horrible summer, that summer of 1858.   There I was, struggling
to continue to bring out *The Virginians*, trying to overcome recurring attacks
of spasms and fever, bothered endlessly by people wanting help or money or
both, and in the air all the time hung the Yates affair.   I wanted above all
else to wipe it out of my mind and yet I could not leave the subject alone –
unless I was gently stopped I talked of only that.   " Don't tell me what is
happening," I would say, " I don't want to hear " – and yet I wanted to hear
nothing else.   At the end of June the Committee unanimously resolved that
my complaints were well founded and required Yates to apologise, to them
as well as to me, or retire.   I own to feelings of vast relief – a committee of
impartial men could not all be wrong and I felt justified in my actions.   The

matter .would now be quickly settled and forgotten and perhaps the sun would re-appear. Unhappily, Yates, with alarming ferocity, refused either to apologise or to retire. I was not unduly surprised by the former decision, which was entirely in character, but the refusal to withdraw from the club dumbfounded me and put quite a different complexion on the miserable case. How could Yates refuse to retire if the Committee told him he must ? I did not rightly understand what he was about and only hoped that he did. A General Meeting was called, which met in July, when by a vote of seventy to forty-six the Committee's decision was upheld and the handling of the matter referred back to them. At this point, before I heard Yates did not intend to rest there either, I went off to Switzerland convinced I could now forget Yates had ever existed. I had been vindicated and whatever Yates chose to do it was no longer any concern of mine. Absolutely nothing had been gained – my moral victory gave me no pleasure – but on the other hand, though my health had suffered dreadfully, nothing had been lost either. Men could still meet and talk in their clubs with other men without losing their precious sense of privacy and that was something.

We are there again, back in that bottomless pit of despondency which we have already visited once or twice before. Do you remember what it looked like from that first time I described it ? Those black walls without a glimmer of light anywhere, that leaden atmosphere which made breathing difficult, that confined space that rendered all movement impossible so that there was nothing I could do but crouch down and fumble around with my hands until I found a rope upon which I could pull with all my strength in the hope that bit by bit I could haul myself clear. Every now and again when I am in that pit somebody throws something down on top of me until

I am all but smothered and cry out against the injustice of it all, but I know before a sound leaves my throat that nobody will hear me and that I must not look for outside help.   Instead, I must conserve my energies and bide my time.   It is a philosophy that suits a young man better than an old – when I left for Switzerland I was beat and unwell and all I wished to do was stay in that pit forever.   Nor did I have long to wait before more calamity struck – down came a boulder on top of my weary shoulders in the shape of a domestic disaster – my mother fell and broke her hip and once again I was engulfed by a whole heap of necessary arrangements.   I found myself sitting day after day wondering in a near blasphemous fashion whether there was any point in life at all.   Why not go to the top of a rock and jump over and end our troubleoubleoubles in the midst of the sad sea waves' bubbleub-blubbles ?   Everything seemed a struggle, even small things.   All I could positively find to look forward to was the occasional meal and bottle of wine – oh how prosaic.   I came to believe for a while that pleasure consisted of such shallow transitory things and that there was nothing deeper to remind me I have a soul   What *is* pleasure, I asked myself, and after a good deal of staring dully out of the window came up with the unexciting answer that it is nothing but the fruition of some sort of desire.   But what did I desire ?   Nothing but negative things – an end to worry, peace and quiet, that kind of wish.   There was nothing specific I wanted any more. What was there in

life I had not tried ? I had eaten the best meals, drunk the best wine, laid my poor heart at the feet of two of the best women, had two of the best children, written one of the best books, travelled in the best countries, enjoyed the fellowship of the best friends – I declare I had done and seen it all and had no desire to do it all again. I wanted only the unattainable and I did not even want that very much any longer. I was a dull dog, getting daily duller and likely to expire of dreariness any minute unless something happened quickly to lift my jaded spirits. But Life does not work out like that – haven't you seen in this chronicle how the bad patches have to be worked through ? The head must be forced down, the brows contracted, the lips set in a hard firm line, and after pushing and shoving and straining and pulling we are likely to get a hold with our feet on the sides of the pit and find the rope we always knew was hanging there just out of reach and lift ourselves clear.

It took a long time to happen. I returned to England to find Yates was proposing to sue both the Committee and myself – he had taken counsel's opinion and was determined to stir up a hornet's nest all over again. My heart, which was pretty low anyway, sank like a stone to the very depths of my being. Was I never to be rid of that man ? Would I really have to go through the ordeal of supporting my views again ? I did not know how I could stand it and wondered what I had done to deserve such an ordeal. I received, at the end of November, a letter from Dickens written on Yates' behalf asking me to agree to mediation in this stormy affair, and that upset me deeply. You may ask why such a reasonable sounding request should upset me, but then I have not told you of Dickens' part in all this as yet. From the first, it had seemed obvious to me and to those others who knew anything of Yates, that he was incapable of sustaining the position he had adopted without support from someone else. That someone else proved to be Charles Dickens. Now, I do not know the extent of Dickens' involvement at the beginning, but I do know that by the time the first letters had been exchanged he was deeply implicated. Yates, who had long been a follower of his, turned to him at every step. He helped Yates write all his communications and backed him up in everything he did and there is no doubt in my mind or anyone else's that Dickens was a prime mover in the whole affair. I gather he thought I had in the first instance been over-violent in my reaction, then rude in my demand for an apology, and finally that I had made myself totally absurd by handing the matter over to the Committee of the Garrick Club, thereby transforming a silly squabble into a major drama. Well, he is entitled to an opinion, but all I can say is that I do not like the way in which he conducted himself throughout this sorry business.

Consider what he could have done instead of what he did – what was there to prevent him coming round to see me when first Yates came to him and talking to me, man-to-man, about what should be done ?　I would have been delighted to see him — would have listened to his point of view — put my own — and I shouldn't wonder if the whole thing might not have been settled over a bottle of wine.　He behaved like an enemy and I was bitterly hurt, and because of the lead he gave all literary London split into two camps when

it was the good of all I had at my heart.　His letter was a trick — whatever I replied I knew I should be in the wrong.　I could not agree to forget the whole quarrel and accept Dickens' mediation when I had asked the Garrick Committee to adjudicate—how could I forsake those who stood by me?　No, however much I wanted to end it, that was not the way.　On the other hand, if I turned Dickens' offer down flat I would look as if I did not want

peace when I most surely did and in refusing I would so anger the other side
that their determination to continue would be strengthened. I came firmly
to the opinion that I must hold to the verdict of the Committee. What,
after all, did Dickens' friendship mean to me ? What was his offer worth ?
Not much when I considered the pain and disappointment his alliance with
Yates had caused me. When I looked back on the history of our relationship
I saw that I was a fool to have imagined any real friendship had been there –
I could see only wariness and suspicion and a lack of generosity and little
true warmth. I resolved not to delude myself any longer – Dickens was
not my friend and I owed nothing to him and must not delude myself.
However much I loathed the idea of appearing to spurn the outstretched
hand I must reject his offer even at the cost of besmirching our public
image. I don't know that Dickens cares much for public images but I do –
I do not like to think that all London watched us fight like spoiled children
and that all writers would be thought less of because of us. I wrote to
Dickens saying that the affair had been for some time out of my hands
as he knew perfectly well and that having submitted my case to the
Garrick Committee I could not now presume to speak for them but that I
would write to them saying I would welcome any peaceful honourable
solution.

The affair roared on for weeks afterwards with no signs of stopping. I
began to get unpleasant letters taking Yates' side, not to mention articles in
the press fulminating against me. My head was full of thoughts about how
I would stand up to cross-questioning in the Witness Box when it came to
that, as it looked as if it would – oh the horror of it! Please, your honour,
it was not my fault and I really don't know why you have me here at all –
silence – take him away – twenty years' imprisonment for daring to defend
his character. It would be ghastly and what a foolish figure I would cut and
how weak my voice would sound and how dashing and vigorous Yates
would appear and really I had better just let them chop off my head and be
done with it. Then think of the expense! Oh Lor, it made me faint – have
you ever known anyone step into a court of law and not come out ruined
however innocent they are proved to be ? I might be as pure as the Arch-
angel Gabriel and still find myself damned. I reasoned that the Garrick
Club would be the protagonists and that therefore I did not need to worry,
but all the same I had a nagging fear at the back of my mind as to what
might happen – I might somehow find myself at the eleventh hour alone in
that dock and responsible for all the prodigious legal expenses. What price
honour then ? In the event, Yates abandoned his suit at the last minute,
finding that if he sued the Garrick Committee he must sue the trustees and
that this would involve an action in Chancery which, thank God, was beyond
his means. I don't think he ever forgave the Garrick Club for presenting
him with this fact about the trustees and robbing him of his case, but I for

one, and not through self-interest, think they may have done him a good turn by so abruptly halting his desire for vindication. All that was left to him was the publication of a pamphlet setting forward his case which I don't think many people bothered to read any more than they would have read one by me if I had been misguided enough to publish one for they were heartily sick of the whole business. Yates, to all but a few cronies, vanished into the oblivion from which he had briefly emerged, and I sighed heavily and felt very sad and wished I had never heard his name.

I wonder if he knows how often I think of him still ? I knew at the time – though many thought I did not – how heavy he must be finding the hand I had figuratively laid upon him and I was sorry for the suffering he had brought on himself and sorrier still for the hardship his family had to endure when his action was no fault of theirs. After all, what was he ? A penny-a-liner, and hadn't I been one once ? I knew exactly how he had written that piece about me – I could imagine him sitting at his desk where his job was to supply short copy, with the master printer at his elbow impatiently urging him on. It plays the devil with a man's nerves – it makes him temporarily feverish – it makes the pencil slip in his hands as he struggles to be witty and informative and above all quick. And as for the domestic situation – wasn't I very well acquainted indeed with that ? Didn't I know what it was to be only twenty-seven with a wife and three children and all existing on a Post Office salary apart from the vital extras these journalistic jobs brought in ? I did not enjoy thinking of the consequences for that little family – how they must hate me, how I must appear an ogre to them, how my name must become synonymous with the devil! I would not for the world wilfully hound any man but they were not to know that – it must appear to them that I existed merely to torture and torment them. I longed for Yates to withdraw for their sake – I longed all the time for Dickens, powerful Mr. Dickens, to take him by the hand and bring him round to Onslow Square and make us have it out – why couldn't he have done that ? Have I ever barred my door to any man ? I cannot accept that any words of mine had made such an action impossible. Dickens' attitude throughout the whole business remains incomprehensible – why send a young man headlong down the path to ruin ? Why push him into challenging the verdict of a whole Committee ? Why encourage him to believe he is championing a splendid cause instead of perpetuating a deplorable quarrel ? I believe it was Dickens who dictated Yates' letters and Dickens who was behind his every action and the significance of Dickens' role in this sordid affair is really too sinister to dwell upon – but at the time dwell upon it I did – laid low by illness there was nothing to distract me except pain and that is more of a running accompaniment than a distraction.

I ought, by this time, to be able to look at the Yates affair more coolly and I ought to be able to stand aside and assess the actions of the major

participants objectively, but I find I cannot – throughout the writing of this chapter I have been in the most infernal temper and I know I feel as passionately about the original crime today as I did then. The tragedy for me is not the agony all the subsequent trouble caused me, but the bitterness of realising that Yates never properly understood the basis of my complaint – he was incapable of appreciating what his sin was and therefore everything I said or did was in one sense in vain. But Dickens knew – he knew exactly what hurt me and in my opinion he worked on that shamefully. I have often wondered if he was influenced by his own troubles at the time – did his separation from Mrs. Dickens and the fact that I sided with her and even visited her to express my sympathy – did that anger him and make him look for a chance to injure me ?   Or do I judge him too harshly – was he merely implicated by Yates when he had no wish to be and did he perhaps give other advice which I don't know about because it was ignored ?   Yates is an impetuous fellow – it is perfectly possible that he misinterpreted whatever Dickens had to say, and then again Dickens may have said something he later regretted when it was too late.   After all, I have experience of that myself – my conscience is far from clear – didn't I become unwittingly involved in Dickens' personal problems and may he not with justice have inferred I intended him harm ?   I once volunteered the information in a general discussion that it was an actress, not his sister-in-law, that Dickens had fallen for – I only said it to prevent everybody believing the worse of the two bits of gossip but I should have minded my own business.   Then also I may have let too many people know how Dickens' love life turned my stomach and he may have hated me for being self-righteous and smug.   All this could be quite simply settled of course – I could ask Dickens what happened and why he did what he did – but I shan't.   Some wounds are best left unopened and it would do no good at all to re-examine them.   One thing is plain – Dickens and I were never intended to be friends.   Too many things, too many people conspired to keep us apart, and I for one regret it. We ought to have been friends, don't you think ?

A horrid time, for everyone, and me feeling sick most of the year.   My doctor was Thompson – a good honest name, a good honest man, though by selecting the adjectives " good " and " honest " I feel I somehow imply he was not clever.   Well, he was, especially in the treatment of my wretched condition – in fact, nothing I have said about doctors applies to Thompson, who was quite above the ordinary run of medical men.   He was interested not only in the practice of medicine but in the theory which lay behind it, and I found his book *Pathology and the Treatment of the Stricture of the Uretha* which he published in 1854 most helpful and illuminating in under-standing my problem.   I do believe that a doctor like Thompson could persuade me to submit to the knife but for some reason he does not try to push me, only explains the situation clearly and recommends the operation and leaves me to make my own decision.   Naturally, I admire his attitude but all the same there is a part of me, and not a small part either, which would like to be forced into surgery – or I think I would – something along the lines of " There is no doubt about it, Mr. Thackeray – I will not tolerate a refusal – the arrangements are all made and I positively order you to agree to this simple nick of the knife which will instantly restore you to your former health and strength – come along – this minute – I beseech you as your doctor and friend " – and so on.   Poor Thompson.   He never knew what I wanted of him and would have been astonished if I had enlightened him.   As it was, I went to his house for a few days – used it as a hospital you might say – and had my waterworks tinkered with and the cisterns and

pipes put in good order once more and that was all. I don't think the repairs
will hold much longer but who can tell ?

I was thankful when this job was done and the Yates affair fizzled out,
leaving only a bad taste in my mouth. I persuaded myself I almost liked the
man for the determination of his animosity, and as for Dickens, perhaps he
couldn't help hating me any more than he could help not being a – you know
what, I daresay. My head cleared and some energy came back and at last I
could get on with the confounded *Virginians*. God knows, that novel had

been doomed from the start – so extreme was my agitation due to one cause
or another during the writing of it that the entire construction of the story
was changed several times and I was frequently as a consequence out of my
depth to an extent it is painful to confess. It was meant, you know, to be
a continuation, though not a sequel, of *Henry Esmond*, being the story of the
further adventures of Esmond's grandsons, the Warrington twins, and
continuing the chronicle of the House of Castlewood. The background
for much of the novel was meant to be America, and in particular the
American revolution with a twin on either side. The canvas, as you will
appreciate, was therefore wide – too wide – before very long I was absolutely
lost in it and struggled madly to tighten and restrict the sprawling narrative.

The twin brothers, who I wished to portray as identical in appearance but totally unalike in temperament and ability, gave me nothing but trouble, and as for the women — well, I don't know why anyone ever thought I could write about women.   Don't read that novel — it is the worst I ever wrote — and I am not proud of it.   It came to an end, that is the best that can be said of it.   I won't make the same old excuses which I seem constantly to have made — that I was ill, that I was rushed, that I was distracted — but instead I will make you a promise that this novel I am working on now, *Dennis Duval*, will not leave my hands until it is as I wish it to be.   I would, if I could, call in all the pieces of work which I have been dissatisfied with and try again to get them right, or else I would burn them, but that is impossible.   I pay the penalty, not you — it is punishment enough to know that posterity is bound to judge me more harshly than my contemporaries and that only — God willing — *Vanity Fair* and perhaps *Esmond* will survive.

Do you know, there is a jolly chapter coming just round the corner ? Ain't that a surprise ?   It was a surprise to me and for once I would have been glad to look ahead and see what was in store for me.

Chapter XXII

---◆---

MEET AN EDITOR OF
THE *CORNHILL MAGAZINE*

I CAME to the conclusion long ago that I was never meant to be serene nor was my life ever intended to be calm and unhurried, and on the whole I think I prefer the hectic pace that has been my lot. Jane Brookfield used to chide me with living too fast and swore that I would wear myself out acting two or three different characters at once. In those days when she cared, she was always begging me to " lower the steam " and for a while I tried, but it didn't work. I suppose there may yet come a day when nothing is happening and I am not involved in any kind of project and will not for the life of me be able to think of anything that needs doing, but I doubt it. I seem to bring upon myself a host of duties, some enjoyable, some not, which crowd my days and create an illusion of activity. I don't ever want to have days stretching ahead week after week full of nothing. Every time in the last ten years when it has looked as though a nice vacant stretch was looming ahead I appear to have taken fright and rushed headlong into battle again. It must mean something, don't you think ? I don't like to be bored, I know that much – I like new schemes, not day-to-day sameness, not that awful grey monotony called security. I can't sit and write novels or anything else in a vacuum. Is that bad ? Should I have tried to tame my wild nature and discipline myself into regular habits ? Ought I to have deliberately cut myself off from the kind of panic and confusion that attracts me, and if I had, would I have written better books or been a better man ? Perhaps genius feeds upon itself and must have isolation to breed, but I am not a genius – I am a lesser mortal, a mere humble journeyman, and as such I need more substantial fare. I hope I came to terms with that realisation before I was forty, and acted upon it. Nothing, in my opinion, is quite so pathetic as an old man who right up to his grave resists the demands of his own nature and strives to change his personality into something it is not. We can change our aims and ambitions, we can curb our desires, we can subdue our tempers and try hard to become better Christians but we cannot change our temperament and it is absurd to try.

Does all that sound like some lofty excuse for rushing around like a mad fool ? At any rate, whatever you think, try me with something different and see how I jump, even at my present great age. In 1859, when George Smith of Smith, Elder & Company — the publisher I have mentioned more than once and always I hope in the most flattering terms — when he came to me and suggested that I might care to edit a new literary sort of magazine can you imagine my answer ? Do you think I frowned and said he could have no idea how busy I was ? Do you think I passed a weary hand over my brow and said he didn't understand how tired I was, how much I needed a rest ? Do you think I looked anxious and pointed out I had hardly any experience of editing and might not be able to do the job ? Of course you know I did none of those things, but you don't know all the same quite how extreme was my delight. It may have been a little unseemly in a man of my years but I could not refrain from exhibiting the most tremendous enthusiasm — I could have jumped over the moon for joy and had to make do with a chair instead which I am glad to say I cleared safely. What a departure! What a diversion! To the devil with novels and lectures! I seized the opportunity to try my hand at something different with the alacrity of a man half my years, but then the minute I had considered Smith's offer I immediately *felt* half my age. Enthusiasm is a marvellous tonic — better than love sometimes — it has the power to clear the eye and quicken the step and brighten the whole outlook. I daresay there is some dull medical explanation for all this but I don't want to know it — I will settle for the effects and not bother with the reasons which I won't understand anyway. I am quite content to accept that enthusiasm is a kind of magic and I only wish that there was more of it about to rejuvenate all of us.

It was not sensible of me to respond like that, of course, but then what is that attracts a man ? It was not sensible to do most of the things I find I regret least — not sensible to marry so young, not sensible to travel with young children, not sensible to try to write the novel I wrote that made me, not sensible to go to America, not sensible to have loved Jane Brookfield — oh there is no end to the things I have done that have not been sensible and I am glad of it. Life is a gamble and thank God I have always been a gambling kind of man. I saw, in 1859, that editorship was the challenge I needed — it would give me another string to my bow when all the rest were out of tune with so much playing. Why be afraid of the responsibility ? If others thought I could do it and had done me the compliment of asking why shouldn't I share their faith ? It seemed to me that a man nearing fifty — a man of half a century — ought to change his role in any case. Was it not

PRICE ONE SHILLING

No. 1.

JANUARY.

THE

CORNHILL

MAGAZINE

1860

LONDON:
SMITH, ELDER AND CO., 65, CORNHILL.

perhaps time for me to retire from attempting to hog the front of the stage and instead concentrate on bringing other people's talents to the public notice ?   Knowing as I did so much about literary tastes was I not perfectly situated to provide readers with what they wanted ?   I saw myself as an avuncular figure, kindly but sternly directing the efforts of my young staff and the image pleased me.   I had the conceit to think I would make a good editor, seeing none of the pitfalls at that point.   I flattered myself that I was a connoisseur of literature and saw myself selecting gem after gem for my magazine while somewhere in the wings everyone applauded.   The thought of effacing myself appealed to me strongly – oh my goodness how I should enjoy being modest and putting other people's pieces in instead of my own – I wouldn't even want my name to appear anywhere except on the cover unless the proprietor insisted.   What joy to accept or reject, to endorse or to criticise other people's work instead of slaving away on my own and waiting for the verdict.   Editorship would satisfy my desire to influence rather than to lead – I had no doubt that editing a family magazine would be a worthy task and I had strong ideas as to what was needed.   People were crying out for a well-written magazine that could be read by fathers, mothers, children and servants and all without a blush.   Who had not grown tired of the limp anecdotes that passed as stories, the doggerel that masqueraded as verse, the banal repetition of old ideas used as a cloak to cover the lack of originality ?   Every family was obliged to operate a form of censorship which

only irritated – this magazine was not suitable for the ladies on account of occasional lewdness aping wit, this one was unfit for children containing as it did quite unnecessary descriptions of brutal events, and that one could not be left lying around for the servants to pick up on account of the subversive politics in which it tiresomely indulged. I had heard very often heads of households wishing for a wholesome magazine fit for everyone but not dreary or pious – oh how they would buy it, they said. Now it may not have been a particularly noble aspiration compared to wanting to abolish slavery – wouldn't you have adored me, ladies ? – or climb Mont Blanc – your hero, gentlemen – but the desire to edit an excellent, stimulating, enjoyable family magazine became my burning ambition. The thwarted journalist had been part of me ever since the failure of the *National Standard* when I had dreamed of being at the head of just such a paper. You may say it was a small ambition to be inspired by, but why despise it for that reason ? I don't think I had things out of perspective – I didn't see myself as a kind of Saviour or anything so silly – but I recognised a mission that needed accomplishing which I could accomplish and it seemed right to try to do so. Would you rather I had strained after more worthy but less realisable goals ? Then I am not your man, though don't think I have not tried to do that too, for I have and you know I have, but I am old now and must re-adjust my sights and can't lumber myself with quite impossible tasks that I have neither the time nor the energy to fulfil.

There was one task that absolutely had to be completed before I could even think about editorship and that was bringing *The Virginians* to an end. I can only say that the ending proved the easiest part, spurred on as I was by thoughts of my magazine. You will note the personal pronoun and perhaps think it rather odd that I should have adopted such an openly possessive air about something that by its very nature was bound to be a collective venture, but it all seemed very personal to me and made me quite solemn. The new magazine would indeed by " my " magazine, there was no doubt about that, for I had no intention of being one of those absentee editors who do everything from home and leave half of that to other folk. Every detail of my magazine I saw as my concern – the making of the cover, the choice of material, the setting of the print, the selling of the copies – everything was my responsibility even if it were not properly the province of the editor. I didn't see how I could call it my magazine otherwise any more than a woman can call her children her children unless she has wiped their tears as well as watched their smiles. In my opinion, a magazine is only as good as its weakest department and I saw it as my job to find that out and make it strong. I knew I should only make work for myself but I wasn't afraid of that, nor of anyone labelling me as a busybody determined to have a finger in every pie – that was my ambition. I wanted to be a working editor with ink on his fingers and everyone's business his from the most insignificant copy boy upwards.   Don't make the mistake of thinking this lowly creature does not matter – the copy boy I mean – you have only to visit a newspaper office to learn that beautifully written articles are of no use at all if you have not the right man there to sub and set and illustrate them and see them into print, and once they are in print nobody will have the chance to read them unless the pages are cut and numbered and bound and wrapped into bundles and distributed and sold, and should there be but one slip in the whole complicated chain then your beautiful articles might as well never have been written.   My main function would be to commission material, but my other was to smooth the path of everyone engaged in the actual production of the magazine and was no less important for being less exciting.

My first concern was to find a title for the magazine.   Does that surprise you ?   Does it sound a case of putting the cart before the horse ?   Does it seem too trivial to be top of an editor's list ?   Well, it ain't – a title is very important right from the start for a new publication which you want to be talked about.   I spent many hours concentrating hard on what I could call my magazine and seeking for something that would reflect the image I had of it.   *The Thames on Fire* was suggested to me but though I thought it a splendid selling title which would excite curiosity, I felt it implied those flashy literary fireworks which we were not aiming at in the least.   My magazine was to be a steady, family affair, not a man-about-town sort of thing, though I did not want to exclude that exotic fellow.   I wanted a title that was cheerful and simple but staid, something that sounded attractive not alarming, something not too precise so that we could develop as we liked. I finally settled on the *Cornhill Magazine*, because our offices being at 65, Cornhill I had the name in my head and liked it – " Cornhill ", I thought, had overtones of abundance and ripeness, and though it was not clever and would make no one stop in their tracks, it was easy and jolly and suggested what I wanted.   You can't go on forever thinking of titles – something has to be got hold of fairly soon to give to people – and the longer you go on thinking the harder it becomes to make any combination of words appear striking.   An unnamed magazine is like an unnamed child – there is always the fear that it will die before it gets one so christen fast I always think. Once we had the title, we could work on the cover – now even the in-experienced among you will appreciate how vital is the cover of a new magazine.   Later, when you are successful, you may have a plain buff cover and discreet type, but at the beginning the cover is a selling point and must be approached with respect and trepidation.   It must be colourful but not vulgar, bold but not brazen, cheerful but not gaudy, simple but not cheap, attractive visually but not so that the serious reader will think it is all art and pass it over as lightweight.   Not an easy matter, a cover.   I thought at first of having a stab at it myself but the job required such a lot of time and skill that I saw I could not do it and get on with everything else that must be done. An editor must delegate and place complete trust in whoever he chooses. Accordingly, knowing that there were likely to be scores of young artists able and willing to slave over such a project, and wanting very much to branch out and not restrict myself to famous names, I asked my friend Mr. Cole of the South Kensington School of Art to suggest an artist who might be suitable and he introduced me to a Mr. Godfrey Sykes, who forthwith produced just the kind of design I had in mind. I knew it would strike the popular taste and give us a good send off and I was delighted.

Title, cover – good heavens, when is the man going to get to something important ? The hub of the matter was indeed the contents of my magazine – don't worry if I constantly fluctuate between " my " and " our ", it will settle down into " the " magazine soon – and I sat down and thought long and hard about what sort of writing I wanted. It seemed important to have a carefully worked out plan for each monthly issue so that the balance would

always be right, and that balance I wished to be between fiction and fact, between entertaining and informing, between amusing and stimulating to deeper thought. Haphazard commissioning of everyone I knew would not therefore provide what I wanted. My contributors must have explained to them the purpose of the magazine – being to interest a large number of readers of all ages and classes by opening to them the experience and wisdom of others. Does that sound too high-minded ? Well, I suppose I *was* high-minded about it. Fiction is all very well – I naturally support fiction – but at that time I also believed readers should be introduced besides to as much reality as possible, the kind of reality that was normally out of reach. I envisaged contributors who knew about unusual things to impart their knowledge to those not so privileged. I don't mean that I wanted the magazine filled with pompous academic treatises on obscure subjects, but that I wanted easy, pleasant discourses on matters of general interest but perhaps those not normally written about. Thus I wished to recruit not only literary men but the Engineer and the Foxhunter and the Geologist and so on and get them to open up doors which would otherwise remain firmly closed to the majority of the population. I wanted a doctor, for example, to describe the cutting off of a leg as a surgical operation but to do it so that a ship's captain at sea, who had no medical man on board nor any medical training himself, would be able to do it himself successfully from reading about it in my magazine. That may not be a good example of what I mean – I agree it sounds much too bloodthirsty – but if you extract the principle and apply it to all the other professions then you will see what I meant. Every month I wanted at least one informative article of this nature besides a poem, a serial, perhaps a story and an essay and a piece of critical literary appreciation on a topic of current interest. The tone throughout was to be informal and good humoured but at all times proper and the language must be always easily understood but not slipshod – correct English if you please. If nothing else I saw us maintaining the highest standards of written English and adhering to the best manners.

High ideals, you see – nothing ill-considered. All that was left with title, cover and plan of contents mapped out was to put them into practice. It was obvious to me that the way to get the material I wanted was to approach the people I knew to be capable of producing it and asking them to do so. I knew that somewhere in England were scores of totally unknown writers who would have just the thing but I could not begin with them – they would come to me once we were launched and what an exciting prospect it was. I longed for the stage – oh foolish man! – when I would be inundated with manuscripts from unrecognised geniuses and be able to elevate them to the position they deserved and to employ their talents to make my magazine great, but until that day it was out with the pen and paper and pretty compliments as I beseeched my more famous friends to contribute. It was not the enjoyable task you might suppose but rather a delicate one requiring an exhausting amount of tact. Consider my position – there I was, soliciting help for a totally unknown magazine and yet not wanting to commit myself to using the contributions I was begging for. The possibility of profound embarrassment on both sides was never out of my mind – suppose I asked the great T– for a poem and he sent me one and I didn't like it or think it suitable, what would I be obliged to do? Why, send it back, however famous the name, and then what a how-d-ye-do! It would be quite enough to make me the most unpopular man in town and I knew I must step carefully and be ever so humble. I wrote to Browning, Carlyle, Hood, Landseer, Longfellow, Tennyson and Trollope and to many lesser mortals asking them if they could find it in the goodness of their hearts to contribute but knowing that time would have more to do with whether they did or not

than kindness. They all replied revealing a gratifying readiness to help me make my magazine as good as I wished it to be and I was touched by their enthusiasm and encouraged by their support. Those who had something suitable to hand sent it with their good wishes and those who did not promised that they would immediately set to and produce something fitting. Wasn't that noble of them? I knew of course that leaning on famous friends would not get me very far and had no intention of operating on that level alone, but the launching needed the famous. A poem by Tennyson would boost my circulation in a way that a poem from some unknown genius would not and I would have been silly to ignore that fact. I would also have been silly to ignore everyone's expectations that the *Cornhill Magazine* would carry something by the Editor and though I tried hard to protest that it was not necessary I knew I must write a serial for it to get it going. There was nothing that appealed to me less but my contribution in that form was considered essential by everyone else so I complied and produced with the usual struggle *Lovell the Widower*. Besides that, I occasionally wrote an essay on anything that took my fancy and since these were odd pieces that did not fit into any scheme I called them " Roundabout Papers ". They turned out to be a pleasure to write and were remarkably successful, seeming to hit the right note with everyone who read them, to my great surprise.

I grew horribly nervous as the day came near for the publication of our first number – it was worse than waiting for a novel to come out by far when so much more depended on it. You may easily imagine how I had arranged and re-arranged that first issue until I lost all critical sense and couldn't see that anything in it was either bad or good, but I placed a great deal of faith even in that nervous state on a serial we began with by Anthony Trollope – I am sure I will not need to tell you who he is for in whatever century you read this he will be remembered if there is any literature left at all. It was called *Framley Parsonage* and I thought it capital, combining as it did an excellent style with shrewd observation and blending the whole into an absorbing but domestic narrative. Then there was an interesting piece on " The Chinese and the Outer Barbarians " which told me for one a great many things I had not known and would never have thought to find out, and my own *Lovell the Widower*, about which the less said the better, and then the beginning of what I hoped would be an instructive series on studies in animal life with some detailed explanatory diagrams and drawings. Besides this there was an appreciation of Leigh Hunt, who had just died, for though there had been obituaries enough I thought a magazine like ours ought to have room for something more and then a splendid article about the search for Sir John Franklin by a member of the expedition that had tried to find him – now that was a real adventure story calculated to satisfy the most demanding reader of fiction and yet it was all true and a fine bit of reporting. I think I was prouder of that item than any other for it represented exactly what I was after. We had a drawing of the departure of the exploring parties from Port Kennedy – the children would like that, I knew, with the ice floes and huskies so clearly visible and the brave ship flying its flags in the background – and a map to scale upon which the whole thrilling episode could be followed. Finally, a poem suitably entitled " The First Morning of 1860 " and a " Roundabout " paper by me containing I hoped some amusing reminiscences completed the number. The package was ready and I could do nothing but deliver it with many misgivings as to how it should be received. Would people be bored by the biology and say they knew all about Sir John Franklin? Would they sneer at the poem and ignore the Chinese politics as nothing to do with them? There was no knowing until the magazine was on the stands. We had worked hard and our consciences were clear — four months of reading and sifting and trying to choose — but would that be enough? Nobody knew.

We finally went to press on December 15th, by which time I was faint with anxiety. In our day — I say this not knowing if conditions have changed — a magazine could fold overnight without any second chance. George Smith knew this and was prepared for initial failure but he had not the means to keep producing for any length of time a magazine that was clearly a failure. Even if the first issue did not sell out we would need good

omens to encourage us to bring out the second and if they were not forth-coming — if our magazine was savaged by the critics as well as left on the stands — nobody would know what to do. The suspense while we waited to see what would happen was so intense that I could not bear it and took myself off without delay to Paris, where I awaited my fate. I felt as if I were in the dock expecting judgement any minute from the judge sitting in front of me – would he put on the black cap or would he dismiss the case ? It would be one extreme or another I was sure for I knew he was a most capricious judge, not at all consistent, given to compassion when the victim least expected it and viciousness when the accused least deserved it. There was no way of telling which verdict would be brought in, except that curiosity might swing it in my favour – people will try anything new once if only to reject it. I was staying at an hotel in the rue de la Paix working myself into a terrible state of nerves when news was brought to me of the first sale and I remember thinking as I opened the telegram – or was it a letter – I really do forget even though the moment itself is imprinted on my mind forever – at any rate, I remember a great feeling of depression and a conviction that we had failed and when I read the news I was so astounded I could not at first take it in. Do you know what the first number of the *Cornhill* sold ? Has it gone down in history ? Nobody could have predicted such a colossal, stupendous, overwhelming success for we sold ONE HUNDRED AND TEN THOUSAND COPIES! Do you blame me for jumping with joy and letting out a great shout of exultation ? My friend Fields came to call on me just after I had absorbed the news and I remember embracing him in my excitement with a fervour that must have alarmed him and then seizing him by the arm and propelling him through the doors and into the street so that I could walk off some of that boundless energy which success brings. We ate a wonderful meal at a wonderful restaurant and then walked round and round the court of the Palais Royal looking at all the jewels and gold – I felt like a prince who has just come into his kingdom and cannot get over the treasure he finds there. Never before and never since has that kind of instant success come to me and I was wild with delight. Perhaps I should not have displayed my excitement so openly, but I am not the kind of man to mumble modestly and say it is of no importance, I haven't done anything, no fuss please – I have not the temperament to wait cautiously for the second or even the third success before celebrating the first – I have not the personality that keeps things quiet and makes a secret of news – good heavens, it was stupendous and I wanted the world to know. I thought every group of people I saw was talking about the famous new magazine just out in London not to mention the even more famous Editor – it is I, sir, I, I am the Editor – here is my back, thump it as hard as you like and I shan't care. How I cursed leaving London – oh how I wished I had been there in the thick of my own triumph instead of lying awake counting up subscribers like so many sheep. I can't help smiling when I think of that blissful time and I don't berate myself at all for enjoying it so much. It pleases me to recall the thrill I experienced when I heard the news and I am proud not ashamed of my extravagant reaction – how awful it would be to look back and find I had not relished the largest

and most unexpected single gift Dame Fortune ever bestowed upon me. Call it blatant egotism if you like – I don't care.

I returned to London with all haste quite expecting to find the crowds lining the streets but perfectly satisfied to find instead an abundance of verbal bouquets from friends and enemies alike. Nobody held back – on all sides people said that the first issue was almost too good for the public since it contained such excellent material that the standard could not possibly be maintained. Do you know, Macaulay's brother wrote to me and told me that my story in the *Cornhill* was the last thing that great man read before he died and that he pronounced it excellent ? That kind of compliment made me feel very humble and determined to keep the standard up. I was urged to hurry along with the next number to prove that it could be done and we set to with a will forthwith. The third and fourth issues followed suit and before we had quite realised it we were established and steadied down to a circulation of around eighty thousand sales per month, which was far more than we had ever dared to hope. I may say there was never any scratching around for material but rather the opposite – as each number seemed to delight people more than its predecessor we were inundated with copy, and there I must say my troubles began. As Editor, I had sworn that I would personally read every manuscript submitted, but by number five that was an impossible task to set myself. If it had been a simple matter of skimming through everything and saying yea or nay then I might have managed, but it was not – often I would be sent an excellent piece which only needed correcting to be exactly what we wanted, but then I had to suggest what ought to be done and there was an hour gone. Without meaning to I found myself engaged in a lengthy correspondence with contributors for which I simply did not have time. Quite apart from dealing with manuscripts, there were the letters – the sheer volume of them drowned me. I was snowed under with paper. It became a nightmare trying to sort out who had sent what and keeping track of articles and stories. Then I had my own work to do, my own writing to get on with – it was all too much for one man but oh how I tried for I loved the battle.

It was very like a battle, that happy period of my life. My antagonist I saw as Public Taste and I did not like the look of him at all. Public Taste is a devil of an opponent for an editor – one minute he is plainly before you and you think you see him clearly and the next minute he has disappeared altogether only to turn up in another suit of clothes at the most inconvenient moment. If you pay no attention to Public Taste then you are lost but if you pay too much attention the outcome might be just as fatal and you will have compromised your ideals besides. I had set my magazine the highest standards of morality and that led me into all kinds of pitched battles over Public Taste. Were certain subjects suitable or not ? Would Public Taste stand for them ? If it would, ought it to be asked to ? Was our duty to conform or reform or mind our own business and let contributors decide what was best for us ? I pride myself on taking a strong line here – I decided it *was* my duty to uphold the virtues I valued even if it did give me the appearance of being over-squeamish. It was better to be cautious, I reasoned, and err on the side of the prudish than risk offending one innocent soul by keeping up with the broadminded. This led me into several difficult exchanges with the most unexpected people.

Would you have thought that Anthony Trollope, that same Trollope I have just openly admired, would cause me a moment's unease in this respect ?

Well, he did, and I will tell you how. He offered to me a story called
Mrs. General Tallboys which I felt bound to reject on the grounds that it
was not suitable because it dealt with a woman not as pure as she should be
who had illegitimate children.   I hesitated a long time before making my
decision – read the story a dozen times – culled over what I had read in
contemporary fiction – sounded out several ladies of my acquaintance who
were pillars of respectability – but in the end I felt I had no alternative but

to turn down what was otherwise a fine piece of writing. It seemed to me that if the subject matter was so plainly offensive then it did not matter how admirable or subtle the treatment of the theme was – it remained offensive for a family magazine to use it and there could be no further argument. I was rather nervous about how Trollope would take the news but I need not have feared his wrath – he accepted my opinion without offence, though he put up a spirited defence of his position and even accused me in passing of having dealt with the very same subjects myself, if heavily veiled. He maintained he could not think of any pure English novelist, not even Dickens who is accepted by every family, and even challenged me to defend my opinion. I didn't take up the challenge, though perhaps it would have made an interesting debate in the magazine, but I went on thinking about the subject for a long time. It occurred to me with something of a shock that in seeking to uphold public morality I was merely prolonging an unhealthy situation and that this was wrong. Ought writers to write about even the most intimate and sordid things ? Ought readers to read them ? Was all censorship hypocrisy ? I remain undecided on these questions as a private individual but as an editor I felt on firmer ground – the minds of too many women and children were in my hands and until it was proved otherwise I could only conclude that I would harm them by treating subjects not acceptable in the best homes.

You will notice how extremely seriously I took my calling and with what fierce pride I regarded the success of my magazine, but in some quarters I was given credit for neither. The world being the envious place it is, I was from the beginning not without my detractors, though everyone who mattered did not stint their praise. The most underhand of attacks came from across the Atlantic, strangely enough. You had hoped, I daresay, as I had hoped myself, to have done with Edmund Yates but I am afraid I am obliged to return to this man, though with the greatest reluctance. You will remark that I do not preface " man " with " gentle " but there was never anything of the gentleman about Yates, which was always my point, and therefore I do not see why I should extend that courtesy title to him. In the *New York Times* of 26th May there appeared a column entitled *Echoes from the London Clubs* in which Yates sneered at my magazine. Though he could not, even for malicious purposes, deny that it was an outstanding success, he maintained that the sales were falling dramatically with each number, and then went on to suggest that I spent the proceeds on enormous dinner parties where I embarrassed my less literary guests by making fun of their lack of knowledge. This slander was taken up and repeated by the *Saturday Review* over here on the pretext of discussing the low moral standards of American journalism. Once more I was doomed to lying awake on Yates' account, wondering what I ought to do. The same questions rattled around in my head and the same answers popped up.

Ignore him ? Certainly not. Counter-attack ? Counter-productive. Sue him ? Out of proportion and impossible anyway. Demand an apology ? Waste of time. Something had to be done – I was in no doubt on that score – but what ? In squashing this kind of vindictive story I had to beware I did not do more damage in the process – there is more of an art in putting an end to gossip than starting it. In the end, after much thought, I chose what I hoped was the dignified approach and wrote an article entitled " On Screens in Dining-Rooms " which dealt effectively with the way in which Yates had obtained his story and how he had mangled it accordingly. My article needs to be read in conjunction with Yates' or nothing makes sense but whether you choose to do that is your business. I did not feel my solution was wholly satisfactory but it was infinitely preferable to the long drawn out Garrick affair.

As an editor there was no doubt in my mind that I would have to learn to take that kind of thing – it is all part of the job and it is no good setting yourself up for all to shy at and then ducking to avoid the blows. If a man does not have the stomach for that sort of scrapping then he should stay at home and not attract attention. I think, on reflection, that I accepted the Yates attack as all part of my job and stood it better for the realisation, but I was far more hurt by another lie which I considered hit below the belt and was not at all in the line of duty. The Yates thing that time was a lot of confounded nonsense, but when it was put about that the editor of the *Cornhill Magazine* published his daughter's work simply because she was his daughter then it was going too far. In the *Cornhill* for May 1860 I published a story called " The Little Scholars " which Anny had written and submitted in the usual way. I hope you will read it yourself and agree with me that it is charming and fresh and quite worthy of a place in that issue. The fact that Anny was my daughter did not seem to have anything to do with whether I should publish her story or not – would it be any better to refuse to publish it because of the relationship between us than to publish it for that reason ? Of course not – her work must stand or fall on its own merits. The girl could write, and write well, and I did not see why she should either be denied publication or be granted it by some other editor who would reap the benefit of her talent. But my enemies thought other-wise and held it against me and bided their time. When Anny two years later – last year in fact – brought out her first novel *The Story of Elizabeth* they set out to get at me through her and we all suffered dreadfully. I don't know if I can bear to go over all that when I get to it – perhaps this is a better place to say I never read my poor girl's novel for fear of seeing her heart exposed and not being able to stand it but friends told me that it was good and that the attack mounted against it was nothing but spite directed at me. I find it hard to forgive such an approach – to wound someone by wounding another I mean. I can take any amount of firing away at any-

thing I have written, but not that, not that.   You won't see me flinching
from lashing criticism myself – isn't there always something to be learned
from it ? – but I winced at the barbs meant for Anny.   Once, in the middle
of *Philip*, the next serial I wrote for the *Cornhill*, I received an anonymous
letter that upbraided me for the shoddiness of my work and I did not mind
a bit.   The letter said that my writing showed great degeneration recently
and that if I could not stop the process I ought to pack up and not try.   Oh
my dear fellow did you think I did not know that what you said was true ?
Did you really imagine I had to be told ?   Do you seriously believe that a
writer " degenerates " as you put it without smelling the rot and tasting the
decay and seeing the visible signs of his failing powers ?   I tell you the writer
knows what is happening before anyone else and is terrified and can do
nothing about it.   Yates and Co. could have said anything they liked on this
subject and I would have bowed my head and taken the whipping and bled
silently, but when they took the work of my little daughter and mauled it in
front of me they did something quite different which one day they will
answer for.

That little squib has put me off course, but then I was about to go in any
case.   Leave me at the end of this busy chapter up to my eyes in work, half
mad with the pressures of it, and see if I shan't tidy everything up and slow
the pace in the next.

Chapter XXIII

---◆---

NO. 2, PALACE GREEN:
AN AUTHOR'S FOLLY

GAVE up the editorship of my beloved magazine in March 1862 after long heart-searching. I still have the yellow slip which was inserted into that month's edition telling the readers of my decision and as I look at the words upon it, it seems to me, a year later, that I only told half the truth. It was all very well to jest about the hours of madness spent searching for Louisa's lost lines to her dead piping bullfinch, and no doubt that adequately conveyed to some why the cares of editorship had become too much, but I think now that it would have been more honest to strike a deeper note and at the risk of appearing pompous to have taken my readers into my confidence and told them what was really amiss. The fact was, I felt that everything was slipping away between my fingers – not just the control of the magazine but my own writing and indeed my own life. Every day I had the unpleasant sensation of falling through time without ever being able to stop – my head swam with all that I had to do and I was permanently giddy with confusion. How swift the transition from excitement to panic had been! How soon I had stopped rejoicing at all the activity! There were days when I was terrified – yes, positively afraid – of the work in front of me, days when I was no longer sure of who I was or where I lived, days when I fought through a fog of decisions to find a resting place. In a man of over fifty, a man of poor health, it would not do. It had to stop. No matter how deep my commitment – and I, at least, felt it to be deep – I knew that I had to extricate myself, however much it hurt my pride and whatever my enemies would make of it. It was not simply that I was tired or overwhelmed and only needed a break to be restored as at other times, nor that I was taking too much upon myself unnecessarily and might be put right by the appointment of an assistant – it went deeper than that. I felt utterly weak and cast down and vague, and these dreadful feelings were not helped by repeated attacks of my old illness which came upon me with great suddenness.   There appeared to be no more tinkering that Thompson or anyone else could do and it simply had to be endured as cheerfully as possible.   I thought that if I gave up the magazine and conserved my energies I might manage rather better.

It was not too sad, the going from the magazine I mean.   I had, after all, achieved my ambition by not only launching the ship but keeping it afloat and sailing at a spanking rate which showed no signs of slackening.   My imprint was on the *Cornhill Magazine* for all to see and when I looked back on the twenty-odd issues I had edited I could not but congratulate myself on the high standard and above all on the variation contained within them. It would be unfair to select any one contribution as better or more valuable than another, but if I tell you that we had poems by Elizabeth Barrett Browning and Matthew Arnold and articles by eminent philosophers and scientists whose names will mean nothing to you for they are famous only within their own field, then you will see that the claim to have instructed and entertained was not an idle boast.   Our magazine lasted the whole month through – it needed careful reading and I do believe it received it. Rivals said we went above people's heads with our essays on the electric telegraph or physiology, they said no one could understand our table on Injurious Substances Detected in Adulterated Articles of Consumption, they swore our attack on London's defences was quite incomprehensible to the common reader but I say they were all wrong and our sales figures bore me out.   Nobody should write down to people – I am convinced that providing the style is clear and simple the content can be as rarefied as you like and that far from rejecting something unusual or specialised as too difficult the average reader will be intrigued enough to give it a try and then he will be amazed and delighted with his own progress.   And as for children – good heavens, children can take anything – their powers are elastic, stretching as far as you pull them.

You will see how gratified I was by the success of the *Cornhill* and appreciate how hard it was for me to accept that one phase at least of my involvement with it was over, but when I tell you that I had a new plaything in my hands you will understand better why leaving the Editor's chair was not too dreadful.   What, you cry, is the man insane ?   Do you mean to tell me that having reduced me to tears – see, my handkerchief is still wet, I do declare – over the state of his health and his poor white head whirling and all that pathetic business – do you mean to tell me he actually has the temerity to take on something else ?   Oh, I have lost my patience entirely and I don't want to know any more.   Madam, I shall have to get round you – I shall have to wheedle and coax you into a better humour for I do very much wish you to enjoy my new toy as heartily as I do, and I know you will regret turning your face to the wall in exasperation. Truly, I have not done anything so wrong – I promise I did not leave the *Cornhill* only to become Prime Minister, that I did not relinquish one sort of power to seize another which would exhaust me as completely and justify your indignation at my folly. No, it is nothing like that – I simply bought myself a new house and devoted myself to making it one of the most beautiful in London. There, have you relented ? Will you come with me and look at it and share my pleasure ?

I lie only in one detail – there was nothing simple about the purchase of this house where I am now sitting writing to you. I bought the existing house at this address – No. 2, Palace Green, Kensington – in May 1860 as soon as I saw which way the wind was blowing with the *Cornhill*, intending to restore it to its original splendour, but this proving impossible I was obliged to knock it down and build an entirely new mansion on the site. This of necessity involved me in precisely the kind of aggravation I had wished to avoid – hours and hours of consultation with the architect, endless discussions with builders, hundreds and thousands of decisions to be taken every day. Far from the business being simple it was incredibly complicated with no shortcuts available that I could find. I could not afford to ignore a single pencilled line on the drawings submitted to me or I knew I would find in due course a brick wall exactly where there should have been an open space and so forth. Naturally, with this kind of personal supervision being imperative, progress was slow, but then there was a great deal at stake – hadn't I set my heart on a house of great elegance, of dignity, of beauty and was I going to spoil the construction of this dream by leaving it to others ? No, I was not. For years my soul had been cramped in Young St. and Brompton and I had no intention of not indulging myself at last. That is precisely what the building of this house amounted to of course – self-indulgence on a massive scale.   I need hardly tell you the expense was prodigious.   When I embarked on the venture I fancied £4,000 would be sufficient to do what I intended, but before I was done I had spent twice that.   Very well, more than twice that but never mind how much more. I don't regret the money – best way to spend it – property is an investment like no other – the best investment a man can make for houses don't fluctuate like stocks and shares and they are always there.   If, upon the sight of some particularly large bill for bricks or the like, I experienced a moment of horror

at what I was doing with my money, I quickly reassured myself and re-covered my nerve by remembering how quickly London was growing and how much more valuable homes in the best places would become.   If I were to die tomorrow, as well I might, my daughters could already make a profit on this plaything of mine, and if I don't die for another ten years then I am confident that they could make ten times that profit.

The house took two years to build.   We did not inhabit it until March 1862 when I left the *Cornhill* and even then there were things to complete. If it is still standing when you read this – and it gives me a most perkuliar feeling to think it might not be – then go and look at it if you possibly can. You won't regret it.   An old uncle of mine who never made a joke in his life before came to look it over when it was done and with the most awful smirk suggested that I should call it Vanity Fair House on account of the lavishness exhibited therein.   Well, why not ?   I ain't ashamed of it – certainly this house is a showpiece – certainly no expense has been spared to make it perfect – why should I try to hide that ?   To be sure people might get the wrong idea from Uncle Carmichael's description and think the money to build the house had come from the writing of *Vanity Fair* which, as you know, would be wrong, but then as it did all come from the inkstand in one way or another I don't see it would matter.   I have earned my money and I have spent it – does that seem remarkable ?   I am no St. Francis of Assisi content to wear sackcloth and live on scraps and give all I have to the poor – however wrong and sinful it may be, and I am prepared to accept it is both, I love beautiful houses and furniture and I won't pretend I don't.

I don't think it is pitching it too high to say that equipping a fine house down to the last teaspoon is almost as creative as writing a novel or painting a picture, or at least it is for me.   You will only laugh at me if I go into detail about Axminster carpets and Brussels lace and figured tapestry curtains but if somebody still has it I pray you to go and look at my Louis XV walnut writing-table – say I said you could – and see if it does not warm your heart as it did mine.   Play a tune on the Broadwood Grand Piano and run your eye along the china – Crown Derby, Spode, Dresden, Minton – they are all there – and afterwards sit yourself in any one of the comfortable easy chairs and sip some of the Croft's Port or the White's and I defy you not to share my enthusiasm for elegant living.

My pleasures are few and No. 2, Palace Green I declare to be the principal one.   I haven't spent money on tawdry or vulgar or distasteful objects bought simply to impress – nothing has gone into this house which is not perfect of its kind and I consider that a fine achievement whatever you may think. I show people over the house and lecture them upon every item in it and I daresay they think I have become quite above myself but I don't care because I know that I have not.   Fine houses and fine furniture don't mean much – when the day is done they won't get you very far, don't think I don't know that simple truth – but meanwhile I can relish living in this mansion and suffer no qualms of conscience.   It is the perfect place in which to write that history of Queen Anne I keep bothering you with – all very well to rush off to inns at Richmond or Greenwich to get on with my novels, though in truth I have not done that for a while, but public places won't do for writing the kind of measured book I have in mind.   I shall sit in this study over-looking the old palace and the green and those magnificent elms and the view and the atmosphere will give me the right kind of feeling for that period a century and more ago.   I haven't begun yet, but every time I come into this room I know that it is waiting for me and none the worse for that delay. I don't rush pell-mell any longer – one thing at a time, say I. About time, says you. And neither of us is fooled but it is convenient to pretend sometimes, ain't it?

Leaving the editorship of the *Cornhill* hardly brought me those long empty days I had envisaged but it made this last year a good deal easier than it might have been. I stopped feeling persecuted and was overtaken by a kind of gentle melancholy which sounds dismal but which was almost enjoyable. There was a sense of relief and of acceptance that is still with me where before, during six months at least, there was a wildness in me that I did not understand. People speak, rather too grandly in my opinion, of the sick " coming to terms " with their disease, by which comfortable phrase I suppose they mean they stop complaining, but I think the silence comes from the certainty that life can be enjoyed all the same rather than from any acceptance of disease itself. The sick man who is in constant pain and knows that only death or a miracle will ever relieve him of it learns to transcend that pain and cherish all that is good which is still available to him. He may still rage internally night and day against the tyranny of suffering but gradually there creeps upon him the discovery that with the development of a little cunning he can grab a little happiness all the same. I have often been confined to my couch this last year and likely to go under with attacks of excruciating spasms, but every one of those horrible days there has been something to redeem them – the sight of a pretty face hovering over me, a piece of music floating up from below, the sun coming through the windows, a laugh, a friendly hand that grasped mine – something to make me glad I had lived that day in spite of the pain. What I should do if a black day arrived when there was nothing – not one little thing – to shine among the murkiness of physical suffering I don't know and believe me I have had plenty of time to think. Thank God it has not yet arrived and that I am surrounded by loving family and friends who with luck will see that it never does.

It makes a man awfully solemn to face his own mortality, to look it in the face and acknowledge it is so. I cannot, for all the practice I have had, do this with any degree of conviction however real I know my own death to be one day. I don't know if anyone ever does regard their going with equanimity – does it become a habit as we grow older, or do even centenarians die surprised that at last they have been cut down? I used to think – only let my girls grow to an age to fend for themselves, only let me be spared to see that they are well provided for, and then I shall be content to go, but though I have proclaimed my readiness many times of late, that happy stage having been reached, I do not truthfully find the process of taking my leave as easy as it sounds. The manner of my going bothers me unduly – will it be sudden? Shall I collapse with one agonising pain while going about my

business ? Will I go – ah blessed thought – in my sleep ? Or shall I linger,
gasping for breath, leaving the shore most cruelly inch by inch, my loved
ones visibly distressed in front of me ? It is no good speculating, but we do
speculate and it can't be helped – or perhaps the sudden deaths only come to
those who do not. Did my stepfather speculate ? I don't know – we talked
about many things near to our hearts but never that. His death in September
1861 was a shock, ridiculous though it may sound to express shock at the
death of someone over seventy. Death always comes as a shock – there is
no guarding against that. When I go, I daresay a large number of people
will profess to be " shocked " as though they had never heard of anyone
dying before, and yet I have been ill for more years than I care to remember
and my name long written on the list for departure as they know perfectly
well. I will not be shocked. I declare I shall die quite unsurprised if I have
time to think about it at all, though I hope at the end to have as little warning
as my stepfather, who had but a few hours' illness before he was taken. What
a blessing a death like that is! Don't we all want to escape the hand-holding
and last words and agonised looks of those we are leaving in this harsh world ?
Aren't we all worried that we will not bear up under the strain and will set
off on that long journey with the sound of our own cries of anguish ringing
uncomfortably in our ears ? My stepfather was perfectly well and cheerful

the night before he was sent for – none of us believed what ailed him was anything but the usual aches and pains – and how kind it was for my mother to have that happy last memory of him.

I think I must have been preparing for my own end for longer than I think in a practical sense, though I begin now to feel so uncommonly well that I am rather shamefaced about such an admission. Not only did I move into what I wanted to be my final home, in a great hurry to achieve my ambition to live in state as it were, but I had also moved my mother near at hand. I don't know what gave me the courage to insist at last that she and my

stepfather should stop trying to live by themselves in Paris, which made us all suffer, and move permanently to London, but I did and they set up house in Brompton Crescent close by us in 1860. Don't say I was hard on the poor old folk – it was absurd for us to try to look after ailing parents at that distance – I don't know why I hadn't put my foot down years before and saved myself a small fortune in travelling expenses and a head of hair in worry. When I am old – you see what I mean about not really facing up to my own mortality ? – I hope Anny and Minny will find me a good deal more tractable than I have found my parents.

It is a far more difficult business looking after old people than it is caring for children – they are equally helpless when they become afflicted by failing powers but they cannot simply be picked up and carried off – they talk and argue and blackmail without meaning to and must be treated with respect and the whole thing is an insurmountable ordeal. It was while I was plagued by editorship that I finally decided I had had enough – I had no intention of losing my girls when I needed them most to sit by sickbeds in Paris. They could sit in Brompton and be home for tea. In my opinion I ought to have done this ten years before. The benefits on both sides were incalculable – I was able to visit my mother every day for half an hour and be jolly instead of three times a year for two weeks when I quickly became rather surly, and she was able to share Anny and Minny's life in a wholly delightful way, and yet that good lady was grumbling and wanting to be off within the year. I could not believe she could be so perverse and yet, if my stepfather had not died, I do believe the pair of them would have given us the slip and gone back to Paris. Absurd as it may sound, she may yet do it on her own and start up the same old wearisome shuttle service again. I confess I do not understand my mother – here is her son, far from well, needing her care in so far as she is able to give it, and here are her loving granddaughters at her beck and call and there she is threatening to go back to live in Paris. In heaven's name why? It is no good me trying to put myself in her position for I can't. I can only suppose that after fifty years of living with another human being, losing him felt like losing a limb and she wishes to return to their old haunts in the hopes of finding it. Perhaps – though it makes me sad to think this – perhaps my mother would find more consolation among the people in the circle to which she and my stepfather had belonged than she does with her own relatives. I must let her do what she likes, but I hope and pray that she realises her true place is here and that I want and need her to be about when my time comes. I can't tell her that – how can an old mother face the prospect of her son going first? – but I hope she knows.

There isn't much incident in this last year or so, but then I have almost brought myself up to date and you must expect my narrative to disintegrate slightly under the pressure of events as they happen. You cannot fail to observe that I have become quite the domestic character of late, hardly stirring from my own fireside, quite content it must seem to play whist of an evening and ruminate gently. Do you mourn the passing of the swash-buckling Titmarsh, his bags always packed in those days when he was used to dashing here, there and everywhere taking you with him? Is it over, that part, is my wanderlust satiated? Sometimes I think on grey November days like this day that I would like to make one more journey, a pilgrimage to the land of my birth. I would like to take my girls and wend my way ever so slowly through Europe and along the Mediterranean and over Egypt until eventually we came to India and then we would follow the Ganges to its source and have all sorts of adventures. Never mind if it took years — we shouldn't care, and oh what fun to see if anything at all called to me over the half century since I had last been there — what bliss to find the warmth and colour of that other continent unlocked tenderest memories. But I don't

suppose I will make that journey and I don't care too much — I can make it in my imagination and that is a very comfortable way to travel. As we get older we are content to discard many ambitions once held sacred and it hardly hurts at all — we notice only the lightening of the load and a strange peace afterwards. It is not nearly so dreadful as I once feared it might be to be limited by my powers and those failing all the time — except, I confess, I could not bear my brain to go, but then if it did I don't suppose I should know anything about it. The truth is, if you *can't* do something you very often discover you don't want to any more and that is a marvellous consolation.

I feel a little uneasy about that last statement — sounds good, but is it true ? How can I test it ? What can I no longer do that I have decided I do not want to do ? I suppose engraving is a case in point and will do nicely as an example. I have always enjoyed doing my own engravings but when it came to doing them for *Philip* in the *Cornhill* I experienced great difficulty drawing straight on to wood and made an awful mess. I didn't know whether it was my hands — not nearly so steady — or my eyes — dim even with spectacles — that let me down but at any rate I had to admit defeat and I didn't like it. I can't say I then decided all of a sudden that engraving was something I no longer wanted to do, but I know that within a very short time I was quite happy to hand it over to someone else and surely that is significant ? I don't much care for old folk who won't let go and make way for younger ones, especially younger ones with more talent than they ever had themselves. I have never felt so relieved and happy in my life as when Frederick Walker took over the job I was making such a hash of — there I had been, getting into the most foul of tempers as I sketched what I wanted onto paper and then had it sketched by someone else onto wood and oh dear what was lost in that clumsy transition! And into my life came Walker, who instantly did the whole thing just as I wanted. Good, I thought, good — and goodbye engraving. Why grieve for my lost ability when Frederick Walker could translate for me so well ? Why make myself miserable trying to do what I no longer could, or sulk because my talents had left me ? I think this proves my argument, but don't carry it too far — you might be tempted to assume that because I have not for some while been able to write the novels I want to write that I should therefore get someone else to write them for me and cry hurrah because I need no longer bother myself — but I do not feel at all like surrendering — writing is quite different. I have had the lull I wanted — the pressures upon me to write books for money are lifted — and thank God I have for it has given me time to examine my vocation, if that is what it is, and to be quite certain that writing is more than a way of earning my living. I can't hide any longer under that particular bush — I want to write, I must write, and the only difficulty is what to write and how to write it.

I have tried very hard, for my own benefit as well as yours, to see where this urge begins and I think, for my part, that it begins with curiosity about people. That sounds awfully vulgar, but I can't help it if the truth isn't edifying. With novels I can put into them all the speculation I have indulged in while watching the world go by and satiate entirely that consuming desire to know everything about everyone. I can't even walk out in the street without meeting some character that stirs my imagination, and once stirred the brew must be drunk. It isn't enough simply to look and listen and inwardly exclaim — I must work it all out on paper and push my ideas into shape before I can let them go. That man in the street was only the merest glimmer of an idea — he made me twitch and that is all — but sometimes, at a party perhaps, I will see a face across a room and be quite startled by what it means to me. Oh, I will say to whoever I am with, oh keep away from that man over there, he is going to come to no good, he will taint everyone he touches, and my companion thinks I am talking gibberish and hides a smile, but then six months later at another function he is quite likely to rush up to me and seize me by the arm and tell me how that man I had warned him about had just run off with the firm's gold, or had knifed a man in anger, or cheated at cards in a spectacular way and then it is a case of how did you know, how could you tell that someone respectable all his life would break out like this ? All I can say is that it is all based on the

look of a man – not his exact features or even the arrangement of them, but more the expression and the soul that shines through both beauty and ugliness. I can sense evil quicker than a cat smells fish and the odour is about the same. Good is more evasive – good people mostly lack confidence and are in general nervous and that can confuse a soothsayer. It is a sad fact, but I don't find goodness inspires me to quite the same flights of fancy as evil or at least contrariness. I have tried often enough, but goodness is a mite tame and slows the pen and is difficult to handle and I don't myself want to know so much what happens and then I end up sermonising and nobody has any fun and that is what I dearly want – to have fun, by which I mean I would like to write not just about people who have intrigued me but a story that is compelling in its own right. That is the second part of writing you see – I don't just want to get rid of my curiosity about people but also to connect up all kinds of strange threads that run through our lives and make them into a fabric that readers will enjoy looking at. It is that weaving in and out of threads that I find hard and has persuaded me in the past that I do not like writing at all. My cousin Mary, that spiteful lady I have introduced you to once or twice, is fond of congratulating me on my " luck " in writing, by which she means the money I have made, but if she could appreciate even a tenth of the effort which goes into the making of a book she would not talk so lightly of " luck ". I don't see much " luck " or inspiration about it myself. It is all hard work and not at all to be envied. Take my current *magnum opus* – take *Dennis Duval* – do you suppose Mary will rate the hours I have put in grasping the difference between a marling-spike and a binnacle, or the days learning how to describe keelhauling a bowsprit, or the weeks of endless correspondence with every naval man of my acquaintance ? Of course she will not – if *Dennis Duval* is a success, as I pray God it will be, then she will talk once more of my " luck ", convince me that I only think I lie awake at night reciting nautical mumbo-jumbo, I only invent the frequent visits to Rye and the note taking and the endless walking about to get the right atmosphere. And if *Dennis Duval* fails ? If once more my aspirations are pitched too high and I end up with another dreary tale ? Will that be bad luck ? Ah no – that will be lack of talent.

I hope I have convinced you, for I shall never convince Mary, that writing may start with idle speculation but that there is nothing idle in the ensuing struggle to make something of it. I swear I have slaved over all my books even if you think them careless. I won't pretend that I just tossed them off and that if I had tried I could of course have done much better. I *always* tried and I must tell you that even if it makes me look stupid and a fool. That trying – that mighty endeavour to excel at my craft – is essential to my well being. If I did not feel compelled to make that effort I would lie all day on a couch and mope and be a curse to everyone. Don't you think I am lucky to have had time to discover that important truth ? Do you see how, if I had been struck down in the midst of violent activity some years ago, at a time when I firmly believed that all I wanted was an end to scribbling and some peace and quiet to enjoy myself, then I should have died without knowing how much writing mattered ? You may think that is hardly important but for my part I think that it is. There is nothing more upsetting than the death of someone who was experiencing a difficult time, nothing more heartrending than knowing they never had the opportunity to come out of the storm and sail calm seas and enjoy some measure of serenity. I had far rather death came in the middle of great happiness so that we could imagine the soul winging at once to its eternal resting place instead of wandering tormented, wailing and sobbing until earthly misery was forgotten.

Last Christmas Day I remember sitting at this desk struggling to write one of the saddest letters in my life on just such a subject. Sally Baxter, that same Sally Baxter who dropped from my view so long ago, died of consumption in the Civil War and I had to write to the dear old Brown House and offer my poor condolences. Her death was a shocking thing – I declare myself more shocked by it than by any other, even that of my own child. It was not Sally's youth – she was not so very young after all – nor the circumstances of her death that made the event so tragic, though they were awful enough, but the knowledge that for a long time that young woman had been so unhappy and troubled and that her last days had been such bitter ones. I would rather she had died as I first knew her, smiling and pert, a beautiful young girl of eighteen, happy and confident of her good fortune, looking forward to a glittering future as well she might, than a miserable matron old before her time, worn out from the danger her husband was in on the one hand and the grief that the separation from her loved ones caused her. The Baxters, you see, were in the north and Sally in the south and so they were not allowed to fraternise and that quite did for our girl. Do you know, when she was actually dying the soldiers would not let her sister Lucy – harmless, gentle Lucy – through the lines to comfort Sally and take care of her children ? What kind of a war is it when such callousness reigns ? What can an army like that be fighting for ? The sweat breaks out on my brow at the thought and I won't even beg your pardon for saying so. It is too awful to think about and yet I do think about it, often, and curse the day I was born with the imagination to live in Sally's life for her those last few weeks. It amounts to a kind of self-inflicted torture, and I find I must bring the shutters down with a crash or I would go quite mad myself. Better to turn my thoughts instead to those left behind – those poor parents and brothers and sisters – and concentrate on cheering and distracting them. But you see why I thought of Sally then – why I am glad to have escaped her fate and to have lived to view my life calmly and dispassionately without a trace of regret. Nobody that I know of has ever pointed that out as one of the advantages of old age but I count it as one of the greatest. As we grow older it cannot escape our notice that daughters die every day and parents grieve and other daughters are born and parents rejoice and everything goes on just the same which ought to be a source of comfort to us all, that endless procession of deaths and survivals and tears and laughter, so that our own end seems but a tiny part of an immense design and nothing to make a fuss about.

I wonder if my girls know why I took them last spring to the birthplace of the Thackerays in Yorkshire ? I suppose it seemed just a jaunt – and how they love jaunts – no different from any other of Papa's sudden whims, or did they sense there was more to it than that ? I don't know, I didn't ask them and don't want to now for it makes me feel too solemn. That excursion, which I had planned for years but never executed, was not for pleasure exactly though it was pleasurable, but was more in the nature of a pilgrimage and I made it when I did in the company I did because of a sudden feeling that with my end so near I wanted to go back to where it had all begun – I wanted to go to the seat of my ancestors and walk over their remains and see if I couldn't fit myself into a grand scheme of things somewhere. Hampsthwaite, near Harrogate, was the native town of the

Thackerays and here we all went expecting I don't know what. I would be surprised if you knew the place or had even heard of it – it is an extremely small town with nothing remarkable about it. We found the church-yard where our grandparents and uncles and aunts and cousins were buried and

sat for a long time among the tombstones thinking about them. In front of the place where we chose to sit was a large grey stone with the name WILLIAM MAKEPEACE THACKERAY on it in black letters and I pointed this out to my daughters and asked them if it did not make them feel strange to look at it ? I hope I didn't labour the point – I don't think I did for their reaction was quite unalarming. I myself was greatly moved – I could not tear my eyes away from that stone and yet there was nothing horrible in the fascination it held for me – rather, it was re-assuring as I had hoped it would be and even gave me a strange pleasure, a sensation I cannot possibly hope to explain to you as I don't understand it myself. That William Makepeace Thackeray had died long ago, and the world had gone on, and the sun was now shining on his grave – at least, I think it was – and another William was sitting looking at it with his children and soon he would be under the soil and why cry about it ? Dust to dust and ashes to ashes – nothing at all wrong with those fine words – excellent idea. I wasn't in the least depressed but on the contrary enormously cheered to find myself part of this eternal circle, just as I had wanted. We walked a little more round the gravestones and compared the names and wondered about some of them and if my girls clung a little tightly to my arms I only squeezed their hands in return and smiled and thought aloud what would be for tea. Young people can't believe anyone will ever be ready to die – they can't entertain the notion at all even if they are all the time surrounded by it – it terrifies them and I think it wrong to rob them of their fantasy that *they* will be the first to live forever.   Quite right, I always say, and so you shall, for I think comfort ought to be the order of the day – they will be brought soon enough into a state of readiness and I would spare them the turmoil that precedes it for as long as possible.

Don't cough so and point out that I have been rambling for quite most of this chapter for I am well aware of that and have my excuses ready – reader, I am there, I am into the harbour and all but ready to tie up.   All that remains is that I leave the vessel shipshape and bring the log-book up to date and do you know I am very glad I made this journey ?   I began so mournfully, convinced that a look at my life would only prove what a waste it had been, and instead I find I am positively rejuvenated by the experience.   It has cured me of bewailing my waste of time and shewn me no time is ever wasted.   There isn't any need for me to cower before my Maker – I can go to Him quite humbly and hand in my accounts and know that whatever the bookkeeping is like the final audit is honest.   In the next chapter I shall stand on deck and salute and oh what a fine closing ceremony we shall have.

Chapter XXIV

———◆———

AN ABRUPT CONCLUSION
WHICH MAY BE CONTINUED

T is time for me to pause and read this bundle of egotism though I don't relish the prospect – are other people's thoughts on themselves as restless and indefatigable as mine ? – and make one or two corrections and then to put all this into a large envelope and bury it underneath some dull papers in the bottom drawer of my cabinet over there. How quickly I seem to have travelled over fifty years and how little wisdom I seem to have extracted from them! At thirty I am sure I could have filled three volumes with my doings and sayings – ain't you lucky I didn't set about it then ? I must surely have left out a great deal and done at length those things not worth mentioning and glossed over those things of vital importance. I don't suppose I have got the chronology right and oh how bad it will look if I have not ! Arguments will begin all over the place as to whether a man can make a mistake in his own life – if Mr. Thackeray says he travelled to New Orleans by train in 1856 how dare you protest the railroad was not built until 1857 ? Well, I am sure I have not gone so far as to get that kind of fact wrong but don't be surprised if other things don't tally. I ought to make sure everything I have said is right, but that is dreary work and someone else can do it for in this case I don't think it matters. We would all rather write new things – we all dread reading what we have just so hopefully written and wish that we did not need to, wish we were one of those geniuses who could write what they wanted straight out and get it perfect first time. I know I hate the shock of discovering, as I many times have had to, how unfulfilled my expectations are, and then the agony of trying to revise the old work and make it better! That kind of thing is enough to put a man off writing for life.

This afternoon I went to a service at the Temple Church with Anny and

Minny and our friend Lady Colville. I went in feeling rather low, wondering it must be confessed whether I had made a mistake in embarking upon *Dennis Duval*, whether I was up to it or whether it might not be the better part of valour to cry *finis* and rest upon the few poor laurels I had. I don't need to tell you once again how I had made the discovery that without writing I was nothing, but all the same I thought that perhaps I ought to face up to the inevitable and admit that however much I wanted to write a good yarn again before I died I was incapable of it. These gloomy thoughts sat heavily upon me throughout the service — oh may you never know the despair of feeling your powers are at an end! — but then as the anthem was sung a strange feeling of exultation began to creep over me and I found myself joining in and singing with the best of them and not minding a bit that my voice was croaky. The anthem was " Rejoice and again I say unto you rejoice " — simple words, but a command I could not resist for all that.

Those words had to be obeyed, and obeyed gladly, and I found the same
re-assurance in them as I do in those lines of Goldsmith:

> Like as a hare whom hounds and horn pursue
> Pants to the place from whence at first it flew
> I still had hopes my long vexations past
> Here to return – and die at home at last.

There is, for me, peace and happiness in both anthem and poem and I
suddenly saw how foolish I was to be fretting away about *Dennis Duval* and
how I ought instead to have faith in a divine purpose I could know nothing
about. Go home and write, I told myself, write your story and stop worrying about the outcome – write because that is what you want to do and there
is no reason at all why you should not.

We did not come straight home, but went to the Merivales for tea and
have only just returned now after a very merry hour or two. Anny said to
me as we drove through the streets that it seemed as if we were always on
holiday now and though I immediately produced a page or two of *Dennis
Duval* from my pocket and waved them sternly in front of her as evidence
that some of us worked all the time, I was more glad than I could say. Life
should be a holiday – too much of mine has been uphill work of one kind or
another and not nearly enough dancing in the streets. I ought to have
played more and sat in the sun with my girls on either side instead of all this
ridiculous striving after goals I had set myself and which were not always the
right ones. All my daughters have is me – I wish sometimes, in that
perverse way we fathers have, that they were not quite so devoted – I
simply cannot bear to think of their distress when I am gone. Perhaps I
ought to have kept more aloof – perhaps I ought to have discouraged the
development of that close harmony there is between us and then they would
not have to pay the price that will be exacted when it is broken. We three
are so close, we agree with each other so well, that when one is away the
other so determinedly. I am not the only one to realise this – lately, I think
autumn and do you know before she was half way through the visit I had to
write and ask for her to be sent home because neither Anny nor I could do
without her. Now, is that not a dangerous state of affairs? What we need
is not an end to this closeness but a natural enlargement of it – we need
husbands for those girls and children and then we would not cling to each
other so determinedly. I am not the only one to realise this –lately, I think
both girls have begun to bewail their virgin state – their conversation is full
of references to perfectly hideous friends who have had their hand asked for
at least three times and are considering upon whom to bestow it. I cannot
help but smile when I hear their aggrieved tones and see Min toss her pretty
little head, but all the same I feel anxious myself for there is no denying that

at their age the girls' mother was married and had children and both their grandmothers likewise.   I don't believe they will not marry, but I worry that I have inadvertently spoiled their chances by hugging them close to me and not allowing that freedom of circulation which every good mother makes sure takes place.   I know I am not a bit like Miss Austen's Mrs. Bennett — I don't in the least want my girls off my hands — but neither do I want to tie them to my apron strings, or whatever the male equivalent is.   I know it would make me feel a lot easier about taking my leave if only two likely Tompkins would come along and join us and leave me in no doubt that my girls will have someone else to lean on.   I don't worry so much about Anny as about little Min — but then I tell myself she will always have her big sister.   When I look at Anny's untroubled brow as she sews or reads, or see her calm smile when she looks up, I think good God what serenity is in that soul, and I am comforted.   I cannot believe that anything awful will ever happen to Anny — she won't let it.   She will turn every misfortune into a blessing as Midas turned everything into gold.   Yesterday burglars entered our house and stole all poor Anny's pretty trinkets — every bauble I had given her since she was fifteen — but do you think she cried or raged or went into hysterics ?   No, she did not.   She simply looked puzzled and wondered why it should have happened and then she closed the empty boxes and we heard no more about it.   Whatever pain the robbery caused Anny was concealed from me so that I might be spared distress myself.   Oh will Tompkins appreciate what he has got when he gets it, do you think ?

A new fear comes to me as I sit here, tidying up this narrative.   Do you suppose I have doubly endangered my girls' chances of good marriages by securing for them that £10,000 apiece I never stopped telling you about ?   Fortune-hunters, you see — people after my little Infantas for their worldly goods.   Somehow that seems even worse than having shut them up for so much of the time — to have made them rich enough to be sought after for their money and nothing else I mean.   How horrible, how awful, what a wicked turn of fate, for there is nothing I have railed against more consistently than that end of the marriage-market.   Do people talk of the Misses Thackeray dripping with jewels and worth a mint — get yourself an invite to one of the old boy's dinners and see if you can't grab one for yourself.   All my free and careless talk these years past of wanting to make Anny and Minny secure for life can only have helped the rumours and I wish now I had kept my mouth shut.   Well, it can't be helped — I can only trust in the characters of my heiresses and hope they will see through worthless suitors.   I shan't try to guard against them making a bad choice — no hedging my will about with conditions or anything so absurd.   If they fall in love with that tubercular curate they teased me about once then good luck to them — I shan't mind a bit if my money supports his reverence and gives him a warm house to help ease his cough.   Don't believe any of the gossips who maintain Thackeray was after a lord for each of his daughters and was too snobbish to let ordinary gentlemen near them – rubbish – how could a man who wrote *Vanity Fair* want a lord for his daughters ? – how could a man who wrote *Pendennis* despise an ordinary gentleman ? I should

be delighted if Anny or Minny were so fortunate as to fall in love with someone so estimable as an ordinary gentleman, for being a gentleman he would not ask for their hand unless he could support them like a lady. Does that sound too clever for your taste ? Does it seem to rule out a whirlwind romance with a penniless artist ? You know my feelings on that, but I fancy they may be changing and that with the right artist I might surprise both him and you. I would never do anything so selfish or foolish as to risk a rift between my girls and myself by positively banning any course of action

– nothing could be worth that.   There is always the point that worrying about what Papa would think would steer my girls towards the " right " but the wrong man and I couldn't sleep easy if I thought that.   Anny and Minny must know that their happiness is my sole concern.

Not so long ago I saw advertised in a newspaper a place in Sussex that I fancied buying and it immediately set me off on that train of thought which led to the above.   I was not sure, you see, that I had quite done with spending and wondered if that niche in the country I had long craved might not be a good idea.   This house I read about was near Chichester, which I would like, not too big with a decent walled garden and the right price at £750 freehold.   I am convinced that there will shortly come a time when those sort of properties will no longer be available and then won't I kick myself for missing a bargain ?   At any rate, I thought about it and made some preliminary inquiries and grew quite excited about the prospect of a country seat and owning a field or two of English soil before I died.   What more basic ambition in an Englishman ?   I had always liked Devonshire as a child but it is a devil of a way from town and I like town too – Sussex would be about right.   Then all of a sudden I thought of Anny and Minny and saw how ridiculous I was being.   What on earth would they do stuck in the country with their old and ailing Papa ?   It would turn them into disgruntled prisoners before my very eyes.   I saw how their future was so closely bound up with mine and how I must have a care that in satisfying any more whims I did not unwittingly ruin their lives.   Nor was that the only way round to look at it – suppose they did marry, what on earth would I do encumbered with not one but two houses and nobody to share either ?   I tell you the follies of old age are far, far worse than those of youth.

My pre-occupations as I write this sorting out chapter, which will be the last for the time being, are clearly those of work and children.   Is that so very different from any other man's ?   I don't think so – most men remain pre-occupied with their work right to the end, that is if they like it and haven't been forced into a career they never wanted.   It sounds common-place to say a man died thinking about the work he was going to do the next day but I think it rather fine and hope to go that way myself.   Better by far to be obsessed by work than by power or money or lust.   And as for children – why, who that has been blessed can ever stop suffering on their behalf ?   It is built into the overpowering love we feel for them and is all part of the natural order of things.   It would be an odd father indeed who did not agonise over the fate of his children when faced with the prospect of leaving them and when they have no mother or brother the agony is all the greater.   I can't tell you what happened to Anny or Minny – you will know that before I do – and that gives me a strange feeling of release, as though because I cannot know their fate that makes me not responsible for it.   This happens in old age – the gradual shortening of the horizon instead of inducing panic

brings instead a kind of calm – I will not be there when it happens *ergo* I am free – or something like that.

There are other people I can tell you about though – people, real people, who have crowded the pages of this story and then disappeared. Ain't it maddening when that happens and nowhere can you find out whether Lucy married or Charles turned out a spendthrift and all the other trivial details which aren't trivial at all if you are interested in the people concerned ? I am resolved it will not happen to you, dear reader, but I own to some confusion over which ends you will want tied up and which you would much rather have left hanging in the air. Now if I were you I think I should be much more intrigued as to what happened to J– B– than to my cousin Mary, but then for all I know you may have found every word I wrote about Mrs. Brookfield insufferably tedious and every line about Mary quite riveting. I cannot guess, and therefore I will try to cover as many of the *dramatis personae* as possible and beg your pardon if I miss out some I had not even known I had included. My mother is hale and hearty and still threatening to go back to Paris for good and still loved and spoiled by all of us. She doesn't command my total respect or have that absolute power over me that once she did but I love her all the same and count myself fortunate to have had such an energetic, life-loving lady for a mother. Where would I have been at so many stages in my life without her support and how dare I complain, as I know I have done, about her absurd ideas on certain subjects ? All along she has championed me and boosted my ego and above all, been there. I must be stern with myself and not embark on any maudlin reflections which I should regret, but though I shall adhere strictly to the facts with the rest of my cast, I cannot forbear to regret that I have not been the son I should have been and to have wished that it had been otherwise. There – and now onwards. Isabella is still with the Bakewells, still youthful in appearance, still playing her piano and laughing a good deal and being in general childlike. I haven't been to see her so regularly lately – should I have ? It became too sad and when I was sad anyway it was altogether too much. In her way, Isabella is happy, but she is lost to me and the world and I don't think either of us ought to bewail her seclusion. My stepfather is of course dead. My cousin Mary is still sowing dissension whenever she gets the chance and has grown into a fat and complacent matron wielding dreadful power within her limited domain. My grandmothers are dead, but all my uncles and aunts and cousins flourish and seem to produce at an alarming rate. I have a couple of nephews I am fond of and take to the play now and again but I could not claim to be close to any of the family – it needs a wife

to keep that sort of thing going. They visit me when I remember and I do the same and everyone is quite happy with the arrangement. That brings us to friends. The Brookfields are, I believe, in good health and have a fine family of two sons and a daughter. I see them sometimes and feel nothing except a certain depression. Jane has lost none of her looks or charms but something has gone from her spirit and the difference is noticeable to one person at least. William is more gaunt and gloomy – no trace of my dashing Cambridge friend but we can share a bottle of claret equably and even clap each other on the shoulder affectionately. I don't see Fitzgerald but I think he is happy up there in Cumberland. Here in London there are enough staunch friends to help Anny and Minny when the time comes – Kate Perry and her sister and the Carlyles and George Smith and the Proctors and the Sartorises – oh there will be no end of support. Have I left out anyone? Only Mrs. Shawe, I think, that dragonian mother-in-law and I am quite hurt you insist on having her mentioned – all I can tell you is that she is still alive and odious and living in Cork and making her daughter's life hell. I don't want my daughters to have anything to do with her either before or after my death.

Does that sound as if I rejoiced in bearing grudges to the end of my days? Well, I don't, and to prove to you that I do not I will tell you that I shook hands with Dickens not so long ago and made it up and that was a far harder thing to do than crawl to Mrs. Shawe or cousin Mary, which I shall never do. I was standing in the Athenaeum Hall one day chatting to Theodore Martin when I saw Dickens coming out of the Reading Room and suddenly I couldn't bear the cold way we were always passing each other and curtly bowing and I thought it shouldn't be allowed to continue no matter what the quarrel and so I rushed after him and caught him at the foot of the stairs and shook his hand and said a few words and he replied in kind and it was done. Will people say I climbed down? Then let them be so foolish – all I know is that I immediately felt a lot better and know I was right to do what I did and that I only wish I had done it sooner. We ought to be friends, Dickens and I, situated as we are – perhaps we would have been if it had been allowed and oh how I would have valued it. At any rate, we are reconciled and shan't die enemies and that is better than nothing.

I have been bedevilled all my writing life by trying to get my copy to the right length and I recognise now that I am struggling to make something of this chapter in just the way I tried so often to stretch a mere nothing to half a book on too many occasions, and I know perfectly well why this has suddenly happened after the ease and pleasure with which the rest has been written – I am finished, I am here, arrived, up to date, and instead of writing the final words with a frail hand as I lie back gasping on my pillows I have not felt so well for years. It is absurd to be trying to write a " final " chapter when I know there would be nothing final about it and I ought to stop straight away and not be afraid to leave this story undone. Perhaps if we all started to write our farewells when we reckoned we were about to die then none of us ever would — perhaps anyone with enough energy and conceit to undertake writing their own life ought to know that they cannot possibly be anywhere near dying. Do you suspect you have been made to read all this under false pretences ? Then I am sorry. I promise I shall take this out when I am really dying — it can go in a drawer in my bedroom to be near at hand and as I lie there positively knowing my last hour has come I shall point to it with a shaking hand and have Anny bring it here and dictate to her the real final chapter so that you will not be cheated, and then you can have an entertaining time comparing what I wrote when I thought I was dying with what I wrote when I was really dying and won't that be curious ? Shall I turn solemn and preach do you think, or will facetiousness take hold at that awesome time and shock you ? I dunno. Either way, I shall know nothing about it. Whatever happens, I will have beaten those dreary scholars with their three volume appraisals for *you* will prefer to read my account and not theirs' won't you ? I suppose there have been times when you would dearly like to have known the other side of things, times when although you know I am honest I may all the same have appeared too heated to be objective, and I suppose those stern official biographers may be better able to put you right, but only think what you would lose in the process and ask yourself if it is worth it. Do you really want to be overwhelmed by everyone's point of view ? Do you really want to hear from Yates and Dickens and every member of the Garrick Club so that you can better evaluate my part in that affair ? Do you want Jane and William Brookfield's testimonies taken under oath to make sense of that drama ? Do you want doctors' certificates for Isabella, and the Captain's log-book on my American crossings, and every review of every book ? Surely not — surely you only want to satisfy your curiosity about me and be entertained and I hope I have done that. If you can find something in this book that makes you laugh and something that makes you cry and something that amazes you and something cheerful and something to ponder over and a great deal that is mildly instructive which you did not know before then I shall not have written in vain. Other men's lives ought merely to be pointers for the rest of us — all I wish you to do is take what is useful and throw the rest overboard. Don't concern yourself with learning about me — I ain't worth it so there and there are at least a hundred other ways that you might better occupy your time. I want you to read this as I read things — as I grow older I become more and more of a magpie, picking and choosing paragraphs as I go along, attracted by all kinds of images that spring up from the page and hardly doing any author the compliment of beginning at his beginning and working steadily through the middle to the end. I want you to pick and choose what you like from this — let the pages fall open and read a little to send you to sleep, and then prop them against the teapot at breakfast and read some more, and afterwards push them into your overcoat pocket when you go to work and read what takes your fancy in dull moments. My life ran an uneven course and I don't see why it should not be read as it was lived – erratically.

It occurs to me before I stop meandering in this compulsive way that these fifty years I have tried to tell you about may only be Part One, and that when I am eighty with who knows what triumphs behind me I shall laugh to think that I was once going to present this volume to you as all there was. Won't it be a joke, when *Dennis Duval* turns out to be the first in a long line of best-sellers, to read how I thought I was finished ? Won't you mock me for worrying about the girls marrying when I can hardly hear myself think for the yells of scores of grandchildren ? Who knows ? Who indeed – that is why Life is so attractive and Death so fiendishly clever, and that is why I shall put down my pen in a minute feeling immensely cheerful and go down looking pleased with myself to talk to my daughters. And please note, I will have stopped in the middle of a chapter without being in the least ashamed. Cockadoodledoo!

AUTHOR'S NOTE

Thackeray forbade his daughters to authorise any biography. There was nothing he hated more than the weighty panegyrics which were very much in vogue at the time. His wishes weighed heavily with me as I became more intimate with him and I found myself in total agreement. But if not a biography, what ? Nothing ? That seemed too literal a translation of his instructions. Turning to his opinion of autobiography as an alternative, I found that in his lecture on Steele, in which he condemned it, he had this to say :

> " Out of the fictitious book I get the expression of the life of the time ; of the manners, of the movement, the dress, the pleasure, the laughter, the ridicules of society — the old times live again, and I travel in the old country of England. Can the heaviest historian do more for me ? "

The longer I pondered this opinion and the more I set it in the context of Thackeray's own life, the more convinced I became that he had un-wittingly pointed the way to an unusual method of portraying himself. Would it not be possible, I reasoned, to allow Thackeray to write his own life using the very full published private papers together with the rich manu-script sources ? It would not be neccssary to fictionalise anything because everything was there — and if it was not, it need not be used. This would preserve that freshness and easiness which Thackeray so admired without plunging into the judgements and detail he so abhorred.

The objections to this approach were obvious. No book written solely from Thackeray's point of view could be unprejudiced. This, more than anything, was the decisive factor. I wanted to be prejudiced. I can pinpoint exactly the moment when I realised I had no desire whatsoever to know how far Thackeray was telling the truth about himself. It was while reading some letters which passed between Jane and William Brookfield. In these letters it became clear to me that, contrary to Thackeray's representation, Jane and William Brookfield loved each other. Furthermore, it was clear they slightly mocked Thackeray. I found this discovery unbearable and suddenly decided that I would read no more of " the other side ", not only in the Brookfield affair but in all the other aspects of Thackeray's life. I wanted to tell his story as it seemed to him and, in doing so, re-create the man and his life so completely that my own influence would be non-existent.

Immediately, there was a problem. Would I paraphrase Thackeray's own writings? Decidedly not – and yet I knew it would be quite impossible not to use his actual words when they sprang unbidden to my pen. Should I therefor erase them, or acknowledge them? I have done neither. To anyone who knows their Thackeray, the phrases will leap out of the page. To those who do not, it is my fond hope they will be indistinguishable. I see nothing immoral in this method – if I use an actual phrase of Thackeray's it is because I know it so well it has been impossible not to use it. It is the fault of memory, not deliberate plagiarism.

This book rests on Thackeray's own private papers with additional material from the published recollections of his daughter, Anny Thackeray. I have read no other life of Thackeray except Gordon Ray's, which I consulted briefly and rejected as quickly when I realised it was telling me a great deal I did not wish to know just as surely as the Brookfield correspondence. It is of course impertinent of me to presume I can write in the style of Thackeray, though to those purists who shudder with horror and anger I would point out that the style of Thackeray the letter- and diary-writer is quite other than that of Thackeray the novelist and essayist. Thackeray wrote beautiful English in his books but was a different fellow – as most of us are – in his notes and letters, which were colloquial and relaxed and often racy to the point of being ungrammatical.

I believe Thackeray would have been amused by my impertinence. He loathed stuffiness (though he could be stuffy himself), and he liked irreverence. It might have made a better book to have approached Thackeray's life from every angle, but it would not have been such fun and to all those who may say this is neither one thing nor the other – neither fiction nor fact – I would say with Thackeray that it is through fiction we get our fact and that there is precious little fact that, when closely examined, *is* indisputably fact.

I would like, finally, to stress that in no way have I invented anything. If Thackeray says in my book that he admired some dressing-gowns in Paris then he will have said somewhere in his letters or diaries that he did. If he has a picnic at Watford, then it is because he has mentioned one. It may strike you as unlikely, but the research involved in this kind of book is considerably more taxing than in a straightforward biography where one is not striving for atmosphere quite so hard. It would have been a great relief also to have allowed my imagination some licence, particularly over Jane Brookfield. It seemed to me, when I sat in the Rosenbach Foundation building in Philadelphia reading Thackeray's love letters – until now only available in a radically different transcript – that there had been physical lovemaking between them. There is one letter in particular in which Thackeray reminisces about Jane calling to him in the night at Clevedon, and how he went to her. But his words were not quite conclusive enough, and therefore I had to reject the interpretation I felt right – and reject also mentioning it, as I could have done in a balanced biography.

It remains simply to say that I have never enjoyed writing anything as much as I have enjoyed writing this. If I have made Thackeray live then I consider his wishes complied with, and say down with all those heavy historians we both despise.

London, 1978

The History of Henry Esmond

The actors in the old Tragedies as we read, piped their iambics to
a tune, speaking from under a mask ^and a great head dress^ and wearing stilts. 'Twas
thought the dignity of the Tragic Muse required these appurtenances
and that she was not to move except to a measure and cadence; So
Queen Medea slew her children to a slow music: and King Agamemnon
was perished in a dying fall: (to use Mr. Dryden's words) the chorus
^in a set attitude;^
standing by, and rhythmically and decorously bewailing the fates of
those great crowned persons. The Muse of History hath encumbered her
self with Ceremony as well as her Sister of the Theatre. She too wears
a Mask and the Cothurn and speaks to measure. She too, in our age
uses herself with the affairs only of Kings: waiting on them, obseq
ious and stately as if she were but a Mistress of Court Ceremonies
and had nothing to do with the registering of the affairs of the common
^French^
ople. I have seen in his very old age and decrepitude the old King
ewis XIV – the type and model of King-dom, who never moved but
measure, who lived and died according to the laws of his court-etiquette
siting in enacting through life the part of Hero; and divested of
^wrinkled^
try, this was but a little old man;